D1104875

The Spatial Economy

Cities, Regions, and
International Trade

Masahisa Fujita,
Paul Krugman,
Anthony J. Venables

The MIT Press
Cambridge, Massachusetts
London, England

First MIT Press paperback edition, 2001

© 1999 Massachusetts Institute of Technology
This book was set in Palatino by Achorn Graphic Services, Inc.

Printed and bound in the United States of America.

Library of Congress Cataloging-in-Publication Data

Fujita, Masahisa.
    The spatial economy : cities, regions, and international trade / M. Fujita,
P. Krugman, A.J. Venables.
        p. cm.
    Includes bibliographical references and index.
    ISBN 0-262-06204-6 (hc. : alk. paper), 0-262-56147-6 (pb)
    1. Economic geography. 2. Space in economics. 3. Urban economics.
4. Regional economics. 5. International trade. I. Krugman, Paul R.
II. Venables, Anthony. III. Title.
HF1025.F973   1999
330.9—dc21   99-10744
                                                                       CIP

Contents

Preface

Mainstream economics has traditionally paid remarkably little attention to the location of economic activity—to the choices firms and households make about where to produce and consume, and about how these choices interact. The most recent edition of Mark Blaug's *Economic Theory in Retrospect* (1997) speaks of a "curious disdain of location theory on the part of mainstream economics," and asserts that "this neglect largely continues to this day."

But these remarks are, it turns out, a bit out of date. Since about 1990 there has been a renaissance—or perhaps simply a naissance, because the field has always been neglected—of theoretical and empirical work on the spatial aspects of the economy. Relying on new theoretical tools, this "new economic geography" has quickly emerged as one of the most exciting areas of contemporary economics.

Experience shows that a few years into such a new movement, it is often helpful if someone provides a synthesis—typically a book that shows how many seemingly disparate models can be viewed as variations on a few main themes, that develops a common "grammar" for discussing a range of issues. Such books as Helpman and Krugman 1985, on imperfect competition and international trade, or Grossman and Helpman 1991, on endogenous growth, helped give shape and direction to the new fields they surveyed. We believe that the time has come for a similar effort on the theory of economic geography. This book shows, in particular, how a common approach—one that emphasizes the three-way interaction among increasing returns, transportation costs, and the movement of productive factors—can be applied to a wide variety of issues in regional, urban, and international economics.

Not everyone will want or need to read all of the book. Here is a brief guide to its contents. Part I is essentially background material: a review of the motivations for doing this kind of economic theory, and of some themes in earlier work that bear directly on our approach. The base-multiplier model of chapter 3 and the discussion of bifurcations in that chapter's appendix will probably prove useful as warm-up exercises for subsequent discussions. Part II then develops the basic approach, applying it to "regional" models, by which we mean models in which some factors of production are free to move among locations. Even for those whose principal interest is in either urban or international economics, chapters 4 and 5 are essential reading: The former sets out the market structure we use throughout the book; the latter, in the course of developing a basic core-periphery model, also develops a number of concepts and algebraic results that recur repeatedly. Chapters 6 and 7 are more optional (although each introduces concepts that are used in part IV; in particular, chapter 6 is a prerequisite for the similar discussion in chapter 17).

With these preliminaries under his or her belt, the reader has more options. The order of parts III and IV is arbitrary: You can proceed from regional directly to international economics rather than via urban economics, if you like. Within part III, the heuristic introduction in chapter 8 provides a road map to the material; from then on the development is sequential, except for the empirically motivated digression in chapter 12. In part IV, chapter 14 is essential background for the remaining chapters, but thereafter they can be taken on a stand-alone basis.

Some of this book is based on earlier publications by the authors, in some cases in collaboration with others. We would like to give particular mention to Tomoya Mori's role as a coauthor of the original papers on which much of chapters 10, 11, and 13 is based; to Diego Puga's role as coauthor of the basis paper for chapter 15; and to Raul Livas-Elizondo's corresponding role vis-à-vis chapter 18.

The book also benefited immensely from comments from many people. Portions of the manuscript have been used as the basis of courses at both the Massachusetts Institute of Technology and the London School of Economics, and students in these courses provided important input. Among those who have read draft versions of the manuscript and provided valuable suggestions are Jacques Thisse at the Center for Operations Research and Econometrics (CORE), J. Vernon Henderson at Brown University, Yannis Ioannides at Tufts University, Gianmarco Ottaviano at the University of Bologna, Martin Wagner at the Vienna

University of Technology, and Hiroyuki Koide at Nagoya Economics University.

Thanks also go to Hiroyuki Koide and Tomoya Mori for their excellent work in editing parts of this book and, for research support, to the U.K. Economic and Social Research Council–funded Centre for Economic Performance at the London School of Economics and to the British Taiwan Cultural Institute.

1 Introduction

1.1 The Rediscovery of Geography

Around the corner from the English National Opera lies St. Martin's Court, a short street occupied mainly by sellers of secondhand books and prints. It is a reasonable location for such shops, but there are no doubt other locations that would serve as well. Why, then, have the shops' owners chosen to be there? To be near each other. No doubt there is some interesting story about how that cluster of book and print shops originally became established, but what sustains it now is a sort of circular logic: Potential customers come to St. Martin's Court because they expect to find a range of shops to browse in, and shops locate there because they know they will have access to a large pool of potential customers.

The phenomenon that St. Martin's Court illustrates in microcosm pervades every economy. Agglomeration—the clustering of economic activity, created and sustained by some sort of circular logic—occurs at many levels, from the local shopping districts that serve surrounding residential areas within cities to specialized economic regions like Silicon Valley (or the City of London) that serve the world market as a whole. The distribution of population and activity across the landscape is radically uneven; in advanced countries the majority of the population lives in large metropolitan areas, and these metropolises are themselves clustered into regions like the Boston-Washington corridor. Yet although agglomeration is clearly a powerful force, it is not all-powerful: London is big, but most Britons live elsewhere, in a system of cities with widely varying sizes and roles.

It should not, in other words, be hard to convince economists that economic geography—the study of where economic activity takes place and why—is both an interesting and an important subject. Yet until a few years ago it was a subject mainstream economics largely neglected. Even now, introductory textbooks seem to describe a curiously disembodied economy, without cities or regions. (Most such texts, indeed, make literally no mention at all of such questions as the reasons for urbanization or the role of location in economic decisions). In the last few years, however, research on economic geography—that is, on where economic activity occurs and why—has increased dramatically. Real-world concerns have, to some extent, driven this surge of interest: The field has been given a big boost in particular by plans to unify the European market and the attempt to understand how this deeper integration will work by comparing international economics within Europe with interregional economics within the United States. But economic geography has always been important; if the economics profession has notably neglected it, this is not because economists have been uninterested in the subject, but because they have regarded it as intractable. Their new willingness to work on economic geography comes from their sense that new tools—in particular, modeling tricks that have been developed to analyze industrial organization, international trade, and economic growth—have removed crucial technical barriers and transformed a once inhospitable field into fertile ground for theorists.

The basic problem with doing theoretical work in economic geography has always been that any sensible story about regional and urban development hinges crucially on the role of increasing returns. Suppose that we really lived in the constant-returns world that much economic theory still assumes. Then it would be hard to understand why the economy is not characterized by "backyard capitalism," in which each household or small group produces most items for itself. There would, admittedly, be some unevenness in population density and some trade among locations because of the variation in the natural environment: Land differs in fertility, and differences in soil, climate, and resources mean that no one locality would produce all goods even under constant returns. Nonetheless, the dramatic spatial unevenness of the real economy—the disparities between densely populated manufacturing belts and thinly populated farm belts, between congested cities and desolate rural areas; the spectacular concentration of particular industries in Silicon Valleys and Hollywoods—is surely the result not of inherent differences among locations but of some set of cumulative processes, necessarily involving some form of increasing returns, whereby geographic concentration can be self-reinforcing.

Unfortunately, increasing returns have always posed difficulties for economic theorists. Except under very special circumstances they lead to a breakdown of perfect competition; even if this problem can somehow be finessed, they pose problems for the existence and uniqueness of equilibria. For the theorist determined to make some headway in understanding the location of economic activity, these difficulties have not been insurmountable. For example, one can, like much of urban economics, simply take the existence of cities (or central business districts within cities) as a given and trace out the consequences for land rents and land use; this is the basis of the famous von Thünen model, which has given rise to a rich and productive literature. Or one can, like urban systems theorists (above all Henderson (1974, 1980, 1988)), represent increasing returns in a somewhat black-box way as localized production externalities; this approach sidesteps some important questions but opens the door to a powerfully insightful analysis of others. Still, until a few years ago these efforts remained peripheral to the main body of economic theory.

In the last few years, however, a "new economic geography" has emerged, the fourth wave of the increasing-returns revolution in economics. The revolution began in the 1970s in the field of industrial organization, when theorists began for the first time to develop tractable models of competition in the presence of increasing returns; in particular, Dixit and Stiglitz (1977) developed a formalization of Chamberlin's concept of monopolistic competition that, though admittedly a very special case, has turned into the workhorse of theoretical modeling in a number of fields. Beginning at the end of the 1970s, a number of theorists applied the analytical tools of the new industrial organization theory to international trade; a few years later the same tools were applied to technological change and economic growth. In each case it was, of course, necessary to do much more than mechanically apply the Dixit-Stiglitz model to the subject at hand: New concepts needed to be developed, and at first seemingly inconsistent models and approaches proliferated, in which each author appeared to be inventing his or her own private language and notation. In time, however, it became clear in each case that a core set of useful insights had emerged; indeed, in retrospect it is remarkable how tightly integrated, how classical in feel, both the "new trade" and "new growth" theory have turned out to be.

Our sense is that the state of the "new economic geography" is currently similar to that of the new trade theory circa 1984, or the new growth theory circa 1990. That is, an exuberant and initially exhilarating growth of theory has reached the point at which it has become difficult to see the forest for the trees; and yet there is, if one looks for it, a strong element of commonality among many if not all of the analyses. The integration of new trade and new growth theory was, we believe, powerfully aided by the appearance of judiciously timed monographs that endeavored to synthesize each field into a coherent whole: Helpman and Krugman's *Market Structure and Foreign Trade* (1985) and Grossman and Helpman's *Innovation and Growth in the World Economy* (1991). This book is, of course, an effort to do the same with the new economic geography.

In the remainder of this chapter, we describe what we regard as the unifying themes, methods, and questions of this new field and set out the plan of the book.

1.2   Linkages and Circular Causation

We would argue that the defining issue of economic geography is the need to explain concentrations of population and of economic activity: the distinction between manufacturing belt and farm belt, the existence of cities, the role of industry clusters. Broadly speaking, all these concentrations form and survive because of some form of agglomeration economies, in which spatial concentration itself creates the favorable economic environment that supports further or continued concentration. And for some purposes, as in the urban systems literature described in chapter 2, it may be enough simply to posit the existence of such agglomeration economies. But the main thrust of the new geography literature has been to get inside that particular black box and derive the self-reinforcing character of spatial concentration from more fundamental considerations. The point is not just that positing agglomeration economies seems a bit like assuming one's conclusion; as a sarcastic physicist remarked after hearing one presentation on increasing returns, "So you're telling us that agglomerations form because of agglomeration economies." The larger point is that by modeling the sources of increasing returns to spatial concentration, we can learn something about how and when these returns may change, and then explore how the economy's behavior changes with them.

How should the returns to spatial concentration be modeled? More than a century ago Alfred Marshall suggested a threefold classification (1920, p. 271). In modern terminology, he argued that industrial districts arise because of knowledge spillovers ("the mysteries of the trade become no mysteries; but are as it were in the air"), the advantages of thick markets for specialized skills, and the backward and forward linkages associated with large local markets. Although all three of Marshall's forces are clearly operating in the real world, the new geography models have generally downplayed the first two, essentially because they remain hard to model in any explicit way. Instead, they have focused on the role of linkages.

The linkage story is easy to tell if one is willing to be a bit vague about the details. Producers, so the story goes, want to choose locations that have good access to large markets and to supplies of goods that they or their workers require. However, a place that for whatever reason already has a concentration of producers tends to offer a large market (because of the demand the producers and their workers generate) and a good supply of inputs and consumer goods (made by the producers already there). These two advantages correspond precisely to the backward linkages and forward linkages of development theory. Because of these linkages, a spatial concentration of production, once established, may tend to persist, and a small difference in the initial economic size of two otherwise equivalent locations may grow over time.

Discussions of linkage-based spatial concentration that embody more or less this story have been familiar to regional scientists for many years. In chapter 3, we describe in particular two such stories: the dynamic extension of the base-multiplier approach largely identified with Pred (1966) and the widely used concept of market potential associated with such authors as Harris (1954). And provided that one is prepared to be strategically sloppy about details, it is possible to jump straight from such stories into heuristic models that are quite useful both for quick and dirty discussions of real-world issues and as guides to the results of more careful modeling. Such loose-jointed modeling is, we believe, underappreciated in economics; we try to give it its due.

Nonetheless, traditional discussions of linkages and economic geography do not address certain questions that nevertheless become crucial once one tries to get beyond the simplest stories. Most important of these is the nature of competition. Linkage stories work only if there are increasing returns to production at the level of the individual firm; otherwise, the firm would not concentrate production where the market is largest, but rather establish a separate facility to serve each market. But if there are increasing returns, competition must be imperfect;

how do firms compete and set prices? Models like the base-multiplier story are also sloppy about budget constraints: It is unclear where all the money comes from or where it goes. And in any story in which transportation costs play a crucial role—as they must in linkage stories about location, because otherwise why does location matter?—one must worry about how the resources used in transportation fit into the picture.

The key enabling technology for the new economic geography has been the development of a basic approach that deals in a consistent, if more than a bit artificial, way with these problems, together with an angle of approach that allows theorists to cut through what might at first sight seem to be intractably complex problems of analysis.

1.3 Modeling Tricks: Dixit-Stiglitz, Icebergs, Evolution, and the Computer

We believe that economists' historical unwillingness to address issues of economic geography was mainly due to the sense that these issues were technically intractable. As a result, we are only mildly apologetic about the fact that our analysis depends crucially on what might perhaps best be called modeling tricks: assumptions that reflect not so much a realistic view of how the world works as a judgment about what will make the analysis of geographic issues manageable without doing too much damage to the relevance of that analysis.

The first and biggest trick of our analysis is something we have in common with the new trade and new growth literature: a heavy dependence on the Dixit-Stiglitz model of monopolistic competition. To someone unfamiliar with the exigencies of economic modeling, the popularity of the Dixit-Stiglitz model might seem baffling. The model not only assumes that many goods, though constituting distinct products from the point of view of consumers, enter perfectly symmetrically into demand; it also assumes that the individual utility function takes a particular and fairly unlikely form. Yet the Dixit-Stiglitz model has been the basis of a huge body of economic theory in international trade, economic growth, and now economic geography. Although we step away from that model on occasion, especially in our more heuristic discussions, Dixit-Stiglitz assumptions pervade this book.

We are aware that this lends the analysis a certain air of unreality, that this book sometimes looks as if it should be entitled *Games You Can Play with CES Functions*. Nonetheless, we regard the advantages of the Dixit-Stiglitz model as overwhelming for our purposes. Essentially, it offers a way to respect the effects of increasing returns at the level of the firm without getting bogged down in them. By assuming that those sectors of the economy subject to increasing returns also satisfy the peculiar assumptions of the Dixit-Stiglitz model, we can ensure that we have represented market structure in an internally consistent way without repeatedly going through a taxonomy of oligopoly models. Dixit-Stiglitz also happens to lend itself naturally to general equilibrium analysis, in which there are no loose ends about where money comes from and where it goes. Above all, because Dixit-Stiglitz-type markets have a large number of firms, usually represented as a continuum, we can reconcile two seemingly incompatible goals: respecting the integer nature of individual choices under increasing returns (each good is typically produced in only one location) while representing the aggregate of such choices with continuous variables (such as the share of production carried out in a particular location). In short, Dixit-Stiglitz lets us have our cake in discrete lumps while doing calculus on it, too.

Even with Dixit-Stiglitz, modeling a multilocation economy requires some further funny but useful assumptions distinctive to the new economic geography (as opposed to the "new trade" or "new growth" literatures). One key simplification is the assumption that transportation costs take Samuelson's "iceberg" form: Rather than modeling a separate transportation sector, we suppose that a fraction of a good shipped simply melts away or evaporates in transit. There turns out to be a tremendous synergy between the assumption of iceberg transport costs and the Dixit-Stiglitz model, in the sense that combining them causes many potentially nasty technical complications simply to, well, melt away.

A bigger departure from the new trade and new growth literature comes in our repeated use of a sort of evolutionary dynamics to make sense of what are mainly static models. It is very hard to talk about economic geography without using a language that suggests dynamic stories. When one speaks of a *cumulative process* by which spatial concentration reinforces itself, one has a definite image of a snowballing urban or regional concentration, developing over time. Yet to insist that models of economic geography explicitly model firms and households as making intertemporal decisions based on rational expectations would greatly complicate an already difficult subject. It is very tempting to take a shortcut: to write down static models, then impose ad hoc dynamics on those models by, say, assuming that workers migrate only gradually to locations that offer higher real wage rates, and to use this ad hoc assumption to categorize some equilibria as stable, others as unstable. We have systematically given in to this temptation. This may require some further discussion. Ad hoc dynamics have been very much out of fashion in economics for the past twenty-five years; dynamics are supposed to emerge from rational, maximizing decisions by individual agents. Yet what is one to do when a model predicts the existence of multiple equilibria, as geography models usually do? Game theorists have wrestled with this question, suggesting a variety of ways to "refine" the set of equilibria. In recent years, they have increasingly come to accept the idea that it is at least useful to try to assess the stability of equilibria by imagining a process in which strategies become more or less prevalent over time based on how well they perform, in the same way that strategies organisms follow evolve under the pressure of natural selection. The funny thing is that modern "evolutionary game theory" often looks quite a lot like old-fashioned ad hoc dynamics. And indeed, the basic dynamic approach taken in our first model (see chapter 5) turns out to be identical to the "replicator dynamics" now considered respectable among economic game theorists. (Game theorists in biology, of course, regard the assumption that strategies evolve myopically as a principle rather than a dubious shortcut.) In short, we believe that we are right to give in to the temptation to sort out equilibria using simple, evolutionary dynamic stories, even though the models do not ground these dynamics in any explicit decision making over time.

Finally, even with all the special assumptions we have described, models of economic geography can easily seem too complicated for paper-and-pencil analysis. Yet if one is prepared to assign particular numbers to the parameters, the computer can often solve them easily. A hallmark of the new economic geography, as compared with the new trade and new growth literatures, has been its willingness to turn where necessary to computer-assisted thinking: to use high-tech numerical examples to guide and supplement analytical results.

That said, in the course of working on this book we have found that one can often learn more from pencil and paper than one might at first have thought. It often turns out that it is extremely useful to start analyzing a model by looking at numerical examples and simulations, but that these numerical results then suggest the form of a solution that can be derived in large part analytically. We are unabashed about the use of the computer as an analytical tool, but this book has turned out to have a more analytical underpinning, and to be less reliant on purely numerical results, than we expected.

1.4 Two Useful Questions

One might ask many questions about economic geography, and we touch on a number of issues over the course of this book. We are, however, able to stress the commonalities among a number of different models by subjecting each model to one or both of two related but not quite identical questions:

- *When is a spatial concentration of economic activity sustainable?* Under what conditions are the advantages created by such a concentration, should it somehow come into existence, sufficient to maintain it?

- *When is a symmetric equilibrium, without spatial concentration, unstable?* Under what conditions do small differences among locations snowball into larger differences over time, so that the symmetry between identical locations spontaneously breaks?

Or to put it differently, the first question asks whether the economy can support something other than backyard capitalism, whether backyard capitalism is a necessary outcome; the second, whether backyard capitalism automatically unravels, whether it is a possible outcome.

The answers to both of these questions hinge on the balance between *centripetal* forces, forces that tend to promote spatial concentration of economic activity, and *centrifugal* forces that oppose such concentration. They are not quite the same question, however, essentially because the first asks whether a situation is an equilibrium, the second whether an equilibrium is stable. Take, for example, the case of the two-region model analyzed in chapter 5. The first question asks whether, if we simply posit that all manufacturing is concentrated in one region, a worker who defects to the other region finds that doing so improves his real wage; if it does, the concentration of manufacturing is not an equilibrium. The second question asks whether, starting from an equilibrium in which manufacturing is equally divided between the two regions, a movement of a small number of workers from one region to the other raises or lowers the relative wage in the destination region; if it raises it, the symmetric initial situation is unstable against small perturbations.

In the course of writing this book, we have discovered two important (and surprising, at least to us) things about these two questions. First, although the global behavior of new economic geography models is usually analytically intractable and must be explored via the computer, the answers to the two questions can usually be reduced to closed-form expressions. That is, we can derive explicit formulas for the "sustain point" at which an economy with agglomeration becomes possible and the "break point" at which an economy without agglomeration becomes unstable. (Doing so typically involves guessing at the equilibrium, then confirming that guess, for the sustain point; it involves linearizing the model around the symmetric equilibrium and solving it in the case of the break point.) These expressions reveal clearly the role of backward and forward linkages in creating and sustaining spatial concentration.

Second, across a variety of models that seem quite different on the surface, a suitable redefinition of variables leads to the same expressions for break point and sustain point. (This is particularly gratifying in the case of the break point, because the equations are possible but extremely annoying to solve; it is a great relief to find that this need be done only once). In this sense we can claim to have developed a theory of spatial concentration broader than any particular model, one that helps us to see a number of different models as particular cases of a more general approach.

It is not always useful to ask both questions. Some models have no sustain point: Although symmetry does break, the result is not a full concentration of activity in one location. In the urban models of part III, on the other hand, the economic logic makes the question of symmetry breaking uninteresting; as we will see, it makes much more sense to posit the initial existence of one or more cities, then evolve new cities by changing the economy until that initial spatial pattern becomes unsustainable. Still, because it is always useful to ask at least one of the questions and often useful to ask both, we regard the two questions as one of the book's unifying themes.

1.5   Plan of the Book

The remainder of this book is in four parts. Part I is a selective and analytical literature review. We are mainly concerned with the long tradition of analysis in economic geography, a tradition that the mainstream of economic theory may have neglected but that nonetheless engaged in a process of cumulative development. We make a somewhat artificial distinction between two parts of that tradition. What we call "urban economics," surveyed in chapter 2, consists mainly of the von Thünen model, the attempt to explain cities by invoking black-box agglomeration economies, and the use of those concepts in combination in an urban systems theory different from but complementary to much of what we try to do in this book. What we call "regional science" (as a catchall for an eclectic mix of approaches at best loosely modeled) is closer in spirit to the general approach of this book, trying to derive spatial concentration from the interactions among economies of scale, transportation costs, and factor mobility; in chapter 3 we focus on central-place theory, the dynamic base-multiplier model, and the concept of market potential.

Part II introduces our basic approach in the context of "regional" models: models in which a primary sector, "agriculture," is immobile across locations, but "manufacturing," a sector subject to increasing returns, can move between regions. Chapter 4 introduces the necessary technical tools in the form of the Dixit-Stiglitz model. Chapter 5 then applies these tools to a minimal model that shows how a two-region economy can become differentiated between an industrialized core and an agricultural periphery; the chapter offers a first, and relatively simple, illustration of how numerical methods can be combined with analysis of the break and sustain points to understand the economy's dynamics. Chapter 6 applies the same basic approach to multiregion economies, especially to what we call the "racetrack economy," a stylized economy with a large number of locations arrayed around the circumference of a circle. We are able to get surprisingly clear results about this multiregion economy using an approach Alan Turing (1952) originally suggested for the analysis of morphogenesis in biology; equally surprisingly, the Turing analysis turns out to hinge on the same analysis of symmetry breaking that we applied in the two-region case. Finally, both chapter 5 and chapter 6 rely on a very unrealistic simplifying assumption: that agricultural goods can be transported costlessly. This makes a difference; chapter 7 explores the consequences of costly agricultural transport.

Part III turns to a seemingly very different subject: the location of cities in a world in which everything, including agriculture, is mobile. Chapter 8 introduces the subject with a heuristic approach, in the spirit of the regional science discussion in chapter 3, that helps provide a guide to the more formal results. Chapter 9 develops a model that combines a von Thünen–style approach to land rent with a linkage explanation of manufacturing concentration, showing how a spatial pattern in which an agricultural hinterland surrounds a single city can be self-sustaining as long as the population is not too large. If the population does become too large, it will be in the interest of a small group of workers to move to some other location; so by using the criterion of sustainability, it is possible to develop a model of the emergence of new cities and hence of a multicity structure, a task carried out in chapter 10. If one then supposes that there are actually several manufacturing industries, with different costs of transportation and/or economies of scale, the process of city formation can yield a hierarchy of cities of different types and sizes, as shown in chapter 11. Chapter 12 takes a break from the main line of argument to discuss the striking and puzzling empirical regularities that characterize actual urban hierarchies. Chapter 13 then returns to the main line of argument to show how variations in the natural landscape, such as ports and rivers, can influence urban location.

Part IV of the book, finally, turns to the analysis of international trade, defined in this case as models in which labor is immobile among locations. Here, however, we assume that manufacturing firms use each others' outputs as intermediate inputs. Chapter 14 shows that this setup yields backward and forward linkages that can produce symmetry breaking in exactly the same way that the movement of labor does in the core-periphery model; in this case, however, the breaking and restoration of symmetry drives international inequalities in wages. That model suggests that the secular decline in transport costs can explain both the initial division of the world into industrial and nonindustrial regions and the more recent spread of manufacturing to newly industrializing economies. Chapter 15 offers an alternative explanation of that spread, focusing instead on the effects of market growth. Chapter 16 turns to the sources of international specialization within the manufacturing sector and shows how industrial clusters can form and dissolve. Chapter 17, paralleling chapter 6, analyzes international trade without countries, that is, the emergence of regions of specialization in a borderless world with continuous space. Finally, chapter 18 examines a possible interaction between international trade and the process of urbanization within nations. Chapter 19 points to the way ahead.

In all of this, we find remarkable and gratifying the extent to which we can use the same basic modeling architecture to address so many issues in seemingly disparate fields. But then our point is precisely that these fields are not that disparate after all: Be it urban economics, location theory, or international trade, it's all about where economic activity takes place—and why.

I Some Intellectual Background

2   Antecedents I: Urban Economics

Whereas the economics profession has notably neglected economic geography in general, one branch of the field by necessity has always been forced to take spatial concerns into account: urban economics. And indeed urban economics, although often regarded as peripheral to the profession's central concerns, has a long and deep intellectual tradition. It would be beyond the scope of this book to offer anything like a comprehensive survey of that tradition. In this chapter we restrict ourselves to a brief summary of several strands in urban economics on which our own analysis draws: the von Thünen model of land use, which plays a central role in urban theory to this day and also plays a key role in part III of this book; the general notion of external economies as the explanation of urban concentrations; and the seminal work of J. V. Henderson and his followers on models of urban systems, which provides an alternative and complementary take on some of the issues this book raises.

2.1 The von Thünen Model

How do economists routinely deal with the question of how the economy organizes its use of space? The short answer is that mostly they do not deal with the question at all. But when they do, they generally turn to a class of models pioneered in the early nineteenth century by von Thünen (1826).

Von Thünen envisaged an isolated town supplied by farmers in the surrounding countryside. He supposed that crops differ in both their yield per acre and their transportation costs and allowed for the possibility that each crop could be produced with different intensities of cultivation. And he asked two questions that might seem very different: How should the land around the town be allocated to minimize the combined costs of producing and transporting a given supply of food to the town? How will the land actually be allocated if there is an unplanned competition among farmers and landowners, with each individual acting in his perceived self-interest? Von Thünen showed that competition among the farmers will lead to a gradient of land rents that declines from a maximum at the town to zero at the outermost limit of cultivation. Each farmer will be faced with a trade-off between land rents and transportation costs; because transportation costs and yields differ among crops, a pattern of concentric rings of production will result. In equilibrium, the land-rent gradient must be such as to induce farmers to grow just enough of each crop to meet the demand, and it turns out that this condition together with the condition that rents be zero for the outermost farmer suffices to fully determine the outcome.

Figure 2.1 illustrates schematically the typical outcome of a von Thünen model. The upper part of the figure shows the equilibrium "bid-

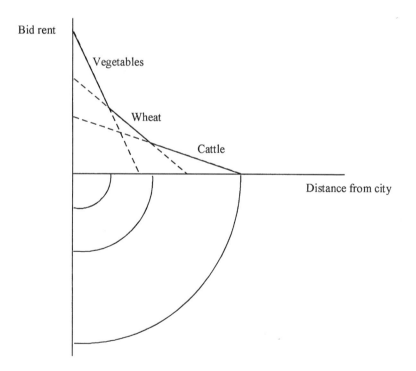

Figure 2.1
Bid-rent curves and land use

rent" curves, the rent that farmers would be willing to pay at any given distance from the town, for three crops. The heavy line, the envelope of the bid-rent curves, defines the rent gradient. Along each of the three segments of that line, growers of one of the crops are willing to pay more for land than the others. Thus one gets concentric rings of cultivation, with the bottom half of the figure showing a quarter section of the layout.

Von Thünen's model may now seem quite simple and obvious, but it is actually an ingenious and quite deep analysis. In particular, it is a striking example of the power of economic modeling to generate unexpected insights. After all, the problem of which crops to grow where is not that easy: By allocating an acre of land near the city to some one crop, you indirectly affect the costs of delivering all other crops, because you force them to be grown further away. Except in the case where there is no possibility of varying the land intensity of cultivation, it is by no means trivial to determine either what should be done or what will happen in an unplanned market. Yet von Thünen analysis shows us that there is a clear answer to what will happen: the spontaneous emergence of a concentric ring pattern. Indeed, the concentric rings will emerge even if no farmer knows what anyone else is growing, so that nobody is aware that the rings are there. Moreover, that analysis tells us something that economics has trained us to expect but that remains startling (and implausible) to most noneconomists: this unplanned outcome is efficient, is indeed the same as the optimal plan. More specifically, unplanned competition will allocate crops to land in a way that minimizes the total combined cost of producing and transporting the crops—not including the land rent. This is surely as nice an example of the "invisible hand" as you could want. Each farmer is trying to maximize his income and is therefore very much concerned with land rents, yet the collective behavior of farmers minimizes a function in which land rents do not appear.

The von Thünen model had an important rebirth in the 1960s, when Alonso (1964) reinterpreted that model by substituting commuters for farmers and a central business district for the isolated town. This "monocentric city model" again yielded concentric rings of land use, and it remains to this day the basis for an extensive theoretical and empirical literature.[1]

Yet von Thünen–type models have an important limitation: Although they give a beautifully clear explanation of land use surrounding a town (or land use within a metropolitan area surrounding a central business district), they simply assume the existence of the town or business district itself. That does not make for a bad model, but it does make for a limited one. If your question is not simply how land use is determined given a preexisting town, but rather how land use is determined when the location of the town or towns—indeed, their number and size—is itself endogenous, the von Thünen model offers no help. Urban economists have, of course, been aware of this limitation; thus in practice they have always supplemented the von Thünen model with at least a sketchy theory of agglomeration based on external economies.

2.2 Explaining Cities: External Economies

The concept of external economies was introduced by Alfred Marshall, who illustrated that concept by discussing the advantages of producing in an "industrial district," such as the Sheffield cutlery district. From its beginnings, in other words, the concept of external economies has been closely allied with the reality of spatial concentration, and external economies have been given a central role in urban theory at least since the work of Hoover (1948).

As we pointed out in chapter 1, Marshall's discussion identified three reasons why a producer might find it advantageous to locate near other producers in the same industry. First, a geographically concentrated industry could support specialized local providers of inputs. Second, a concentration of firms employing workers of the same type would offer labor market pooling: Workers would be less likely to remain unemployed if their current employer did badly, and firms would be more likely to find available labor if they did well. Finally, geographic proximity would facilitate the spread of information.

Marshall's trinity of external economies has proved notoriously hard to model in any formal way. In effect, the approach taken in this book amounts to a formalization of something like his first source of external benefits: market size / market access effects, when producers are subject both to transport costs and to increasing returns. We make no effort to formalize the rest of his story. However, Marshall's argument convinced urban economists that they did, in at least a rough sense, understand why cities and central business districts exist. And by putting external economies into their models, albeit in a sort of black-box manner that left the nature (and, a crucial defect for our purposes, the geographical reach) of those external economies unspecified, they were able to come up with a useful and insightful analysis that views the whole economy as a system of cities.

2.3 Urban Systems

A generation ago Henderson (1974) introduced a model of the economy as an urban system—that is, as a collection of cities—that remains the workhorse approach for research into the actual distribution of sizes and types of urban areas (see in particular his own later work (1980, 1988)).

The basic idea of Henderson's analysis is extremely simple: As authors such as Mills (1967) have emphasized, there is a tension between external economies associated with geographic concentration of industry within a city, on one side, and diseconomies such as commuting costs associated with large cities, on the other. The net effect of this tension is that the relationship between the size of a city and the utility of a representative resident is an inverted U, like the one shown in figure 2.2.

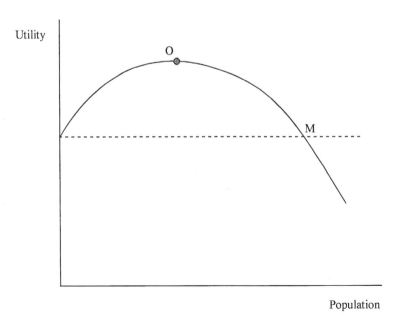

Figure 2.2
City size and utility

It might seem obvious that if this is the trade-off between city size and welfare, all cities will be of the optimum size, as indicated by point O. This is in fact Henderson's assertion; but it is, as he recognizes, not quite that easy. The way he argues that cities will in fact tend to be of optimal size and the way he alters the model to get multiple sizes of cities are what makes his work distinctive.

Suppose for a moment that there were too few cities—and thus that the typical city were too large, that is, it lay somewhere along the arc OM.[2] Then it is straightforward to see that no individual resident would have any incentive to move to a new location: Any existing city would still yield a higher level of welfare than moving in isolation to a new location. This seems to imply the possibility both of substantially excessive city sizes and of multiple equilibria in the size distribution as well as location of cities. Henderson argues, however, that reality is simplified through the forward-looking behavior of large agents: Any situation with too few cities would offer a profit opportunity. Anyone who could organize a "city corporation" that moves a number of people to a new city of optimal size would be able to profit (perhaps through land prices). It turns out that developers of often startling size play a significant role in urban growth in the United States. So Henderson argues that the actual city sizes are, to a first approximation, optimal.

But then why are cities of such different sizes? Here Henderson's argument runs as follows: External economies tend to be specific to particular industries, but diseconomies tend to depend on the overall size of a city, whatever it produces. This asymmetry has two consequences. First, because there are diseconomies to city size, it makes no sense to put industries without mutual spillovers in the same city: If steel production and publishing generate few mutual external economies, steel mills and publishing houses should be in different cities, where they do not generate congestion and high land rents for each other. So each city should be specialized (at least in its "export" industries) in one or a few industries that create external economies. Second, the extent of these external economies may vary greatly across industries: A textile city may have little reason to include more than a handful of mills, whereas a banking center might do best if it contains practically all of a nation's financial business. So the optimal size of city will depend on its role.

The last step in Henderson's analysis is to argue that relative prices will adjust so that the welfare of representative residents in cities of

Utility

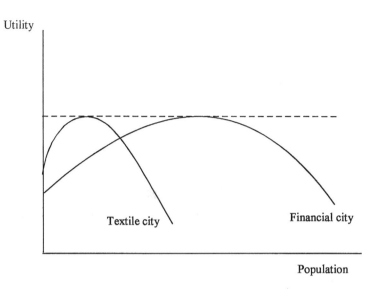

Population

Figure 2.3
City specialization

whatever type is the same. The end picture will look like figure 2.3: Each type of city will have an optimum size; at the optimum size, each will yield the same utility, but that size will vary depending on the type of city.

It is a beautifully clear analysis. It does, however, have two some-what disturbing aspects.

One difficulty with Henderson-type models is the way that they rely on the hypothetical city corporation to tie down the actual numbers and sizes of cities. Henderson is surely right that developers often do internalize agglomeration externalities. The formation of "edge cities" (a term introduced by Joel Garreau (1991) to describe the vast suburban shopping mall and office complexes that nowadays rival or even dwarf American downtowns) is sometimes spontaneous but often reflects de-liberate large-scale planning by huge real estate operations. How-ever, when we come to the economy's really big spatial aspects—the emergence and growth of whole metropolitan areas, regions, or even nations—one would like a story that places more emphasis on out-of-control invisible-hand processes.

The other slightly frustrating limitation of Henderson-type mod-els is that although they deal with an essentially spatial issue, they are themselves aspatial. In general they do not even model cities' internal structure, although that can be dealt with by assuming that the externality-yielding activities must all be concentrated in a central business district. And they certainly have nothing to say about where cities themselves are located, relative to each other or to anything else. For many purposes this may not be an important question, but if our intention is to bring space back into economics, explaining where cities are and why becomes a central concern.

2.4 Multiple Subcenters

Our mention of edge cities brings up an issue that has often proved awkward for urban economists but has also been the subject of some interesting economic research. As suggested above, the main spatial tradition in urban economics has derived from von Thünen; the classic monocentric city model represents a more or less direct substitution of urban commuters for von Thünen's farmers, with the central business district substituting for von Thünen's isolated town. And urban economists have justified the central place, town, or business district by an appeal to some kind of external economies.

Unfortunately, modern metropolitan areas are not monocentric and have become steadily less so. Even those cities that still have a vital, traditional downtown typically have a number of subcenters that rival that downtown in terms of employment; in this sense they are more like countries with a number of large, competing cities than like von Thünen's isolated state. This means, in turn, that an attempt to model a modern metropolitan area, even taking the existence of that area as a given, requires some way of thinking about how the location of employment within that area is determined.

To do this, one must get at least slightly inside the external economy black box to ask how far external economies reach. That is, it will no longer do to assume that they apply equally to all producers within a central business district and not at all to producers outside that district.

An example of an attempt to open up the black box a little bit is Fujita and Ogawa (1982), which assumes external economies between producers that decline with distance. These external economies provide a "centripetal" force that pulls employment into concentrated business districts. On the other side, they maintain a structure of workers who require living space and thus must commute to these business districts, which means that given any particular distribution of employment there will be a von Thünen–type trade-off between commuting costs and land rent; this in turn creates a "centrifugal" force, because businesses that locate in low-rent locations well away from existing concentrations can attract workers at lower wages. Fujita and Ogawa found that this type of model can support polycentric urban structures that look more like modern metropolitan areas than the monocentric model. They also found that the attempt to characterize the possible equilibria even of a simple model of this kind can rapidly become a daunting task; as we will see repeatedly in this book, it is crucial in spatial analysis to have some way to narrow down the set of equilibria one considers. (Our usual answer will be a "hypothetical history," a story about how the economy evolves over time that allows us to visit only a limited subset of the large, perhaps infinite possibilities.)

2.5   Uses and Limits of Traditional Urban Economics

We have surveyed only very briefly a substantial and valuable field. Traditional urban economics has provided valuable insights into land use within and around cities and the reasons why cities exist as well as a convincing view of the economy as an urban system. We do not expect the approach taken in this book to supplant or even to compete with the urban economics tradition: Rather, we hope that the two approaches will prove complementary.

That said, traditional urban economics has some obvious limits. To the extent that it does provide a theory of the spatial economy, it is a theory of why and how activity spreads out—of centrifugal forces— without any comparable attention to centripetal forces. (One might say that urban economists have been a bit like geologists before plate tectonics: deeply sophisticated about the forces that tear mountains down, but lacking any real model of why they rise in the first place.) Although urban economists have some plausible stories about agglomeration, these are an ad hoc add-on to their models. Above all, because the stories about agglomeration lack a spatial dimension—because they do not explain how such effects might fall off with distance—traditional urban economics lacks the kind of distance-related tension between centripetal and centrifugal forces that, as we will see, is at the heart of our attempt to develop a theory of spatial economics.

There is, however, a quite different intellectual tradition that has tried to understand that tension. We turn to that tradition in the next chapter.

Notes

1. Much of that literature is concerned with determining the rent curve and the pattern of land use when labor and capital may be substituted for land in the production of housing and other services. There have also been extensive investigations of the implications of congestion, of the use of land for roads, and other issues. A detailed examination of these issues may be found in Fujita 1989. We concentrate here only on the literature directly relevant to the line of inquiry in this book.

2. It is straightforward to see that a situation in which there are too many cities, and thus where the typical city is too small, is unstable: Some of the cities will simply collapse.

3   Antecedents II: Regional Science

It may seem peculiar that we offer two chapters on antecedents, one on urban economics and one on regional science. Aren't these the same subject? In practice, however, modeling in economic geography has progressed along two largely independent tracks.[1] On one side, urban economics as surveyed in chapter 2 has evolved as a part of mainstream economics; it has the great virtue of being characterized by meticulous and clear-minded modeling but has tended to neglect certain issues, above all the question of where cities form and their spatial relationship to each other. On the other side, another tradition has at least partly addressed the questions that urban economics has slighted. This tradition is largely German in origin but was made available to the English-speaking world through the seminal writings of Walter Isard (1956), who made it the basis of a new field he called "regional science."

Both this older German tradition and modern regional science have a characteristic looseness in reasoning: Not only is the analysis usually vague about market structure, it is often blurry about budget constraints and sometimes seems to confuse planning solutions with market outcomes. These weaknesses have played a significant role in keeping the contributions of regional science in particular from being widely accepted or even known among economists. Yet regional science offers valuable insights that survive the translation to more rigorous models. Indeed, once tightly specified models have confirmed some of these insights, one can see that looser, deliberately sloppy models often have their place: they can serve as back-of-the-envelope "models of the models," helping us develop intuition without the algebraic complexity that easily emerges when one tries to dot all *i*s and cross all *t*s.

In this chapter we selectively survey several ideas from location theory and regional science that bear directly on the questions addressed in this book: the famous but problematic "central-place theory" developed to explain the pattern of city sizes and locations, the crude but useful tool of "base-multiplier" analysis of regional growth, and the ad hoc but also useful idea of "market potential" analysis.

3.1   Central-Place Theory

Economics as we know it is largely, though not entirely, an Anglo-Saxon tradition. Location theory, however, was long a German tradition, containing at least three streams. One stream followed from the von Thünen analysis of land rent and land use, discussed in chapter 2. A second stream, associated with Alfred Weber and his followers, focused on the issue of optimal plant location; that literature plays no role in our discussion. But a third tradition at first sight seems to offer an answer to the question of how economies of scale and transport costs interact to produce a spatial economy: the central-place theory of Christaller (1933) and Lösch (1940).

The basic ideas of central-place theory seem powerfully intuitive. Imagine a featureless plain, inhabited by an evenly spread population of farmers. Imagine also that some activities that serve the farmers cannot be evenly spread because they are subject to economies of scale: manufacturing, administration, and so on. Then it seems obvious that the trade-off between scale economies and transportation costs will lead to the emergence of a lattice of "central places," each serving the surrounding farmers.

Less obvious, but still intuitively persuasive once presented, are the refinements introduced by Christaller and Lösch. Christaller argued, and produced evidence in support, that central places form a hierarchy: There are a large number of market towns, every group of market towns is focused on a larger administrative center (which is also a market town), and so on. Lösch pointed out that if a lattice is going to minimize transportation costs for a given density of central places, the market areas must be hexagonal. Thus every textbook on location theory contains a picture of an idealized central-place system in which a hierarchy of central places occupies a set of nested hexagons.

The original story in central-place theory applied to towns serving a rural market. But a similar story can obviously be applied to business districts within a metropolitan area. Small neighborhood shopping districts are scattered across the basins that surround larger districts with more specialized stores, all eventually centering on the downtown, with its great department stores and high-end boutiques. Indeed, the hierarchical image is so natural that it is hard to avoid describing things that way.

Unfortunately, as soon as one begins to think hard about central-place theory one realizes that it does not quite hang together as an economic model. In economic modeling we try to show how a phenomenon emerges (there's one of those words again) from the interaction of decisions by individual families or firms; the most satisfying models are those in which the emergent behavior is most surprising given the players' "micromotives." What is therefore deeply disappointing about central place theory is that it gives no account along these lines. Lösch showed that a hexagonal lattice is efficient; he did not describe a decentralized process from which it might emerge. Christaller suggested the plausibility of a hierarchical structure; he gave no account of how individual actions would produce such a hierarchy (or even sustain one once it had been somehow created).

What, then, is central-place theory? It is not a causal model. It is probably best to think of it as a classification scheme, a way of organizing our perceptions and our data. It is at best a description, rather than an explanation, of the economy's spatial structure.

3.2   Base-Multiplier Analysis

When one looks at the economy of a city or region, it is fairly natural to think of that region's economic activities as being divided into two types. First, there are those activities that satisfy demands from outside the region: the region's "export base"; second are the activities that mainly supply goods and services to local residents. Thus the economy of metropolitan Los Angeles consists on one side of film studios, arms manufacturers, and so on who produce for the U.S. or world market, on the other side of restaurants, supermarkets, dentists, and so on who sell only locally.

The main idea of what has come to be known as base-multiplier analysis is that the export activities are, in effect, a region's economic raison d'etre—its "economic base"—whereas the other, "nonbase" activities are derived from that base and grow or shrink depending on the base's performance. For example, the Center for Continuing Study of the California Economy estimates that California's export sector employs only about 25 percent of the state's labor force; nonetheless, when the center analyzed the severe California recession of 1990–93, it focused its

attention on the reasons why employment in California's export industries had shrunk (mainly defense cutbacks following the end of the
Cold War and a slump in the world aircraft industry), treating the decline in the rest of the state's economy as a derived result.

Base-multiplier analysis is often given a specific linear formulation
that gives it a textbook Keynesian feel. Suppose we let X be the income
generated in a region's export sector and treat that income as exogenous. And suppose that a constant fraction a of income is spent locally
on nonbase products. Then the direct earnings X from exports will lead
to a second round of earnings aX as some of the money is spent locally,
which will in turn generate a third round a^2X as this income in turn
is spent, and so on. Taking all the multiplier effects into account, we
find that regional income Y is determined by

$$Y = \frac{1}{1-a} X. \tag{3.1}$$

So far this looks like a useful approximation for short- or medium-
term forecasting but an approach with little bearing on the kinds of
questions we want to ask in this book. However, the base-multiplier
approach becomes much more interesting if we adopt a view largely
associated with the influential book by Pred (1966): that the share of
income spent locally is not a constant but rather depends on the size
of the local market.

What Pred and others suggested was that as the size of the regional
economy grows, it becomes profitable to produce a wider range of
goods and services locally, because the market becomes large enough
to support an efficient scale plant. (Pred also suggested a number of
other reasons why growth of the regional economy might encourage
increased production, but let us focus only on this reason for the moment.) Pred then argued that this relationship could set in motion a
cumulative process of regional growth: As the regional economy expands, a rises, which means a larger multiplier and thus a further rise
in Y, and so on.

Rather oddly, neither Pred nor any of the many geographers and
regional scientists who have cited his work seem to have been inclined
to formalize this extension of the base-multiplier model. A simple algebraic representation of the basic idea turns out, however, to reveal
some unexpected subtleties in even so simple a story.

Consider, then, the following simple extension of the base-multiplier
model: We suppose that a is an increasing function of the previous

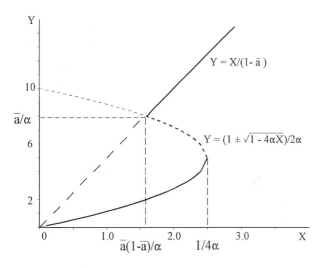

Figure 3.1
Equilibria in the base-multiplier model

period's Y. (We introduce this lag to give the model some rudimentary dynamics.) In particular, let us suppose that a_t is proportional to Y_{t-1} up to some maximum value, $\bar{a}$:

$$a_t = \min[\alpha Y_{t-1}, \bar{a}]. \tag{3.2}$$

The interesting case turns out to be when $\bar{a} > 0.5$, so let us assume that to be true. In that case, the equilibrium relationship between X and Y turns out to look like figure 3.1, where bold solid lines represent stable equilibria and the bold broken line represents an unstable equilibrium. (The figure is calculated for $\alpha = 0.1$, $\bar{a} = 0.8$.) To derive this figure, we make two provisional analyses, then modify them.

First, ignore for a moment the upper limit on a. Then the equilibrium relationship between X and Y would be determined by

$$Y = \frac{X}{1 - \alpha Y}, \tag{3.3}$$

with the equilibrium values

$$Y = \frac{1 \pm \sqrt{1 - 4\alpha X}}{2\alpha}. \tag{3.4}$$

This equation defines "high" and "low" equilibria for Y up to $X = 1/4\alpha$. However, the high equilibrium is not relevant if it implies an a

greater than $\bar{a}$. And if we use the dynamics given in (3.2), then the high equilibrium is also unstable, because an increase in Y_{t-1} brings a greater than proportional increase in Y_t.

Second, ignore for a moment the dependence of a on Y. As long as a takes on its maximum value, we have

$$Y = \frac{X}{1 - \bar{a}}. \tag{3.5}$$

Notice that the high value of Y from (3.4) is relevant only if it is less than the value of Y implied by (3.5). However, (3.5) itself describes an equilibrium only if $\alpha Y > \bar{a}$, which is true only for

$$X > \frac{\bar{a}(1 - \bar{a})}{\alpha}. \tag{3.6}$$

We now have all the pieces. For $X < \bar{a}(1 - \bar{a})/\alpha$, there is a unique equilibrium:

$$Y = \frac{1 - \sqrt{1 - 4\alpha X}}{2\alpha}. \tag{3.7}$$

For $\bar{a}(1 - \bar{a})/\alpha < X < 1/4\alpha$, Y has three equilibrium values: a stable equilibrium corresponding to (3.7), another higher stable equilibrium corresponding to (3.5), and between them an unstable equilibrium corresponding to the other solution to (3.4). Finally, for $X > 1/4\alpha$, (3.5) determines the unique solution.

To understand the economic significance of this picture, let us consider two imaginary economic histories: one in which the size of the export base gradually increases from a very low level, another in which it gradually declines from a very high level. In the first case, we can imagine ourselves moving gradually up the lower solid line in figure 3.1. As export income rises, total regional income also rises and does so more than proportionately as the share of income spent locally increases. When X exceeds $1/4\alpha$, however, the process undergoes a qualitative change: Now Pred's cumulative process sets in, in which rising regional income leads to a higher multiplier that raises regional income even more. In the case illustrated in figure 3.1, an increase in X from slightly less than to slightly more than 2.5 causes Y to rise from 5 to 12.5.

Conversely, suppose that X gradually declines. Then regional income first declines proportionately as we slide down the upper solid line. When X falls below $\bar{a}(1 - \bar{a})/\alpha$, however, a cumulative process of decline sets in, in which falling regional income leads to a falling multiplier. In the figure, a drop in X from slightly more to slightly less than 1.6 leads to a drop in Y from 8 to 2.

This extended base-multiplier model is unsatisfactory in a number of ways. In terms of modeling strategy, it suffers from a severe case of ad hockery: The nature of competition, in particular, is completely unclear. In terms of real-world relevance, the model also has some severe defects. In particular:

• As an empirical matter, the influence of market size on the local share of spending, although real, seems unlikely to be large enough to generate the kind of interesting dynamics shown in figure 3.1. The problem is not that large regions have too low a local spending share: As pointed out above, California's nonbase employment appears to be about 75 percent of the total. Rather, it is that even quite small local economies appear to have a surprisingly high local spending share: Henderson (1980) suggested, using the examples of one-industry towns, that even in small cities nonbase employment is more than half the total. To rescue the idea of cumulative growth, one must suppose that a large regional economy offers other sorts of benefits, for example, forward linkages from the supply of intermediate inputs. Indeed Pred emphasized such additional linkages, but they do spoil the simplicity of the basic story.

• Associated with this difficulty is the clearly unsatisfactory device of treating the size of the export base X as exogenous. Many of the most celebrated examples of cumulative agglomeration processes, such as the rise of Silicon Valley, arose not from import substitution but from the self-reinforcing growth of the export sector.

• Finally, the whole base-multiplier distinction runs into substantial difficulties when one tries to apply it not to a region in isolation but to the economy as a whole. For the world as a whole, all goods are sold "locally," and all income is also spent locally; that is, equation (3.1) becomes $0/0$, which is not a very helpful result.

For all these reasons, it is essential to go beyond the base-multiplier approach to the more fully consistent models developed in the rest of this book. Nonetheless, this model does give us four insights that are useful throughout the book:

1. The interaction between economies of scale and endogenous market size can lead to a cumulative process of agglomeration.

2. It is important to study not only static equilibria but also, at least in a rudimentary way, dynamics, because dynamics play a crucial simplifying role, limiting the number of possible outcomes.

3. The dynamics of economies in which scale economies and market size interact typically involve the possibility of discontinuous change: A cumulative process begins when underlying parameters cross some critical value.

4. Finally, and more subtly, the critical value for change in one direction is usually not the same as the critical value for change in the other; for example, in figure 3.1, the regional economy will not "explode" until $X > 2.5$, but it will not "implode" unless $X < 1.6$.

This last observation requires a bit more emphasis. In many of the models we discuss later in this book, we will need to distinguish between two criteria for agglomeration. On one side, we will ask when a uniform spatial economy, without agglomerations, spontaneously begins to develop concentrations of population and/or industry; this "symmetry breaking" occurs at a critical value we will refer to as the *break point*. On the other hand, agglomerations, once established, are usually able to survive even under conditions that would not cause them to form in the first place; we will refer to the critical value at which established agglomerations are no longer sustainable as the *sustain point*.

3.3 Market Potential Analysis

Producers, other things being the same, obviously prefer sites with good access to customers. But how should one measure the market access of such sites? We will see in later chapters that it is possible, within a well-defined model structure, to define market access in a precise way. For many years, however, it has been standard practice among geographers to use ad hoc but more or less reasonable measures of market potential both to describe the proximity advantages of different locations and to predict trends in actual location.

The typical market potential function measures the potential of some site r as a weighted sum of the purchasing power of all other sites s, with the weights being a declining function of distance. Thus a simple, widely used version weights purchasing power inversely to distance, so that the market potential at r is

$$M_r = \sum_s \frac{1}{D_{rs}} P_s, \tag{3.8}$$

where D_{rs} is the distance from r to s, and P_s is the purchasing power at s.

The classic market potential study was by Harris (1954), who tried to use market potential to explain the location of manufacturing in the United States. Harris used several measures of market potential, ranging from (3.8) to a measure of average distance to consumers. His results showed that the heavily industrialized regions of the United States were in general also locations with exceptionally high market potential. This was not too surprising: Precisely because a large part of U.S. population and production was concentrated in the manufacturing belt, locations in that belt had better market access than locations elsewhere in the country. But this simple observation led Harris to a suggestion similar in spirit to the exciting possibility we have already seen from considering the impact of scale economies in a base-multiplier context: that the concentration of production was self-reinforcing. Not only did firms choose to produce in regions with good access to markets, but also access to markets tended to be good in regions in which many firms chose to produce.

Like base-multiplier analysis, this is an idea that seems highly plausible on its face. Market potential analysis also seems to avoid some of the problems created by base-multiplier analysis: there is no need to distinguish between base and nonbase activities, and therefore no paradox created when one tries to think about the evolution of the geography of the economy as a whole. Moreover, market potential analysis offers a tantalizing hint of how it might be possible to think in terms of continuous space rather than prespecified regions.

3.4 Limitations of Regional Science

Regional science never quite took on the role that Isard had envisaged. The ad hoc nature of its models, their lack of closure, the general sense of loose ends left hanging prevented it from becoming a well-integrated part of mainstream economics. Indeed, regional science never even managed to become integrated with traditional urban economics.

What regional science did become was a toolbox for practical analysis: a set of methods that regional planners, transportation departments, and so on around the world could use to help guide policy decisions. For decisions must be made, even if no rigorous framework exists on which to base them, and a suggestive analysis that leaves loose ends hanging but at least addresses the right questions is better than a rigorous analysis that assumes them away.

It turns out that the key insights of central-place theory, of base-multiplier analysis, of market potential can be given a more buttoned-down justification. They do not come out exactly the way the ad hoc modelers formulated them—careful modeling has *some* payoffs—but we view our work to an important degree as a continuation, perhaps even a validation, of Isard's project.

Appendix: A Brief Introduction to Bifurcations

The base-multiplier model of section 3.2 exhibits two *bifurcations*: critical values of parameters at which the qualitative behavior of the economy's dynamics changes. Bifurcations like this are a recurring feature of the models we develop in this book. They arise because in many of our models there is a tension between centripetal forces—forces that tend to promote agglomeration—and centrifugal forces pushing the other way. Changes in factors exogenous to our models, such as transportation costs, shift the balance between centripetal and centrifugal forces; often there are critical points, bifurcations, at which this shift changes the qualitative behavior of the economy's dynamics.

Although mathematicians have studied a vast variety of bifurcations, two basic types appear repeatedly in simple models of economic geography; we offer here an informal introduction to these characteristic bifurcations.

First, let us introduce a sort of generic geography model. We imagine a setting in which something—typically manufacturing production or labor—must be allocated between two regions. We let λ be the share of manufacturing in one of the regions, with $1 - \lambda$ the share in the other; we suppose that the rate of change of λ depends on its level; and we assume that there is no inherent difference between the regions, so that the curve showing $d\lambda/dt$ is symmetric around $\lambda = \frac{1}{2}$ and passes through 0 at $\lambda = \frac{1}{2}$.

Now one might at first imagine that something like figure 3A.1 could fully represent the model's basic dynamics. Either the centrifugal forces are stronger than the centripetal, in which case $d\lambda/dt$ is downward sloping in λ and the economy converges to a symmetric equilibrium;

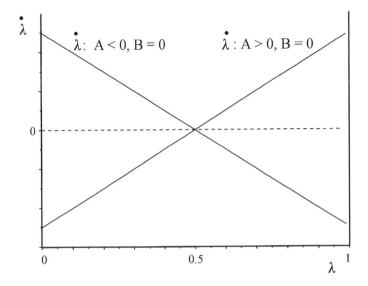

Figure 3A.1
$B = 0$

or the centripetal forces are stronger, the symmetric equilibrium is unstable, and the economy tends toward a concentration of activity in one region or the other. One need therefore only concern oneself with determining the critical point at which the slope shifts from negative to positive. Unfortunately, matters are not usually quite that simple, because the relationship between $d\lambda / dt$ and λ is not usually a straight line; it is instead a curve, symmetric around $\lambda = \frac{1}{2}$, like figure 3A.2 or figure 3A.5.

The actual equations for the curve in the models we develop later are forbiddingly complex; we invariably derive them numerically rather than analytically (although some analytical results remain possible). We may gain considerable insight into the way these models work, however, by considering the simplest possible equation that generates such a symmetric curve:

$$\dot{\lambda} = A(\lambda - 0.5) + B(\lambda - 0.5)^3, \qquad (3A.1)$$

with $0 \leq \lambda \leq 1$. (There is no λ^2 term because it would be inconsistent with symmetry around $\lambda = 0.5$.)

Two observations are immediately possible about (3A.1). First, $\lambda = 0.5$ is always an equilibrium. Second, that symmetric equilibrium is

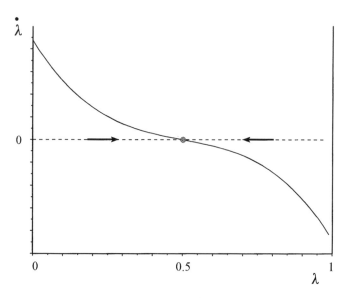

Figure 3A.2
$A < 0, B < 0$

stable (unstable) whenever $A < 0$ ($A > 0$). So if we think of the balance between centripetal and centrifugal forces as determining the value of A, there is indeed some kind of a critical point where A switches from negative to positive.

What kind of critical point turns out to depend on the curvature of the schedule relating λ to its rate of change; in terms of (3A.1), it depends on the sign of B:

1. $B < 0$: Let us look first at the case in which $B < 0$. In that case, the picture when $A < 0$ looks like figure 3A.2, with the schedule going from convex to concave. The symmetric equilibrium is both stable and unique. There are two other roots of (3A.1),

$$\lambda = 0.5 \pm \sqrt{-\frac{A}{B}}, \tag{3A.2}$$

but they are complex roots with no economic meaning.

When A becomes positive, the picture looks like figure 3A.3. The symmetric equilibrium becomes unstable but is flanked by two stable equilibria defined by the roots of (3A.2). From both the picture and the equation, these equilibria are obviously coincident at $A = 0$, then become increasingly separated as A increases.

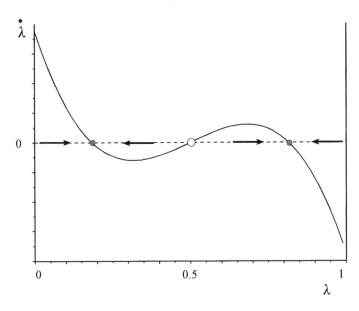

Figure 3A.3
$A > 0, B < 0$

We may therefore summarize the way that the economy's dynamics change with the bifurcation diagram figure 3A.4. In this figure we plot the equilibrium values of λ as a function of A, with stable equilibria represented by solid lines and unstable by broken lines. For A negative there is a unique, stable, symmetric equilibrium; as A increases this splits into two increasingly asymmetric equilibria. Figure 3A.4, then, illustrates the well-known *pitchfork bifurcation*.

To understand the economics of figure 3A.4, we may suppose an imaginary history in which A gradually increases over time. When the balance shifts in favor of centripetal forces, random events cause one region to attract slightly more manufacturing than the other; as A continues to rise, this advantage becomes magnified, and the regions become increasingly asymmetric.

2. $B > 0$: Although standard-looking pitchfork bifurcations emerge in some of our models, we more often find a somewhat different picture (strictly speaking a variant—subcritical—form of pitchfork bifurcation). We can understand this bifurcation by considering the version of (3A.1) with $B > 0$.

For A strongly negative, this yields a picture like figure 3A.5. This does not look very different from figure 3A.2, although the curve now

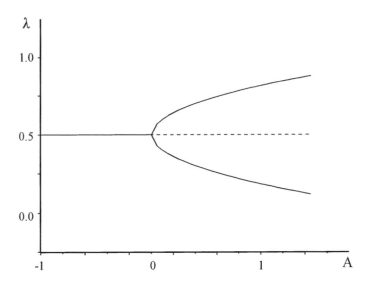

Figure 3A.4
$B < 0$: pitchfork bifurcation

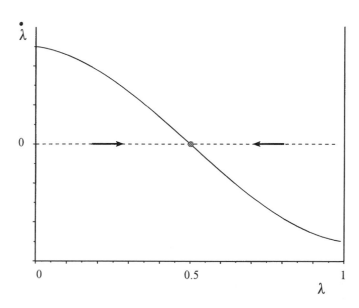

Figure 3A.5
$A \ll 0, B > 0$

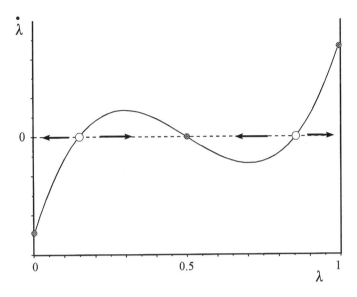

Figure 3A.6
$A < 0, B > 0$

goes from concave to convex. However, an inspection of (3A.2) reveals that the equation's two nonsymmetric roots are now real numbers. We see just one equilibrium in figure 3A.5 only because these roots lie outside the economically meaningful range $0 \leq \lambda \leq 1$.

Now suppose that A is less strongly negative. Then the picture looks like figure 3A.6. The symmetric equilibrium is still stable, but it is now flanked by two unstable equilibria. If λ should start outside the central basin of attraction, all activity will end up concentrated in one region or the other, either at an equilibrium with $\lambda = 0$ (and $d\lambda/dt < 0$) or at one with $\lambda = 1$ (and $d\lambda/dt > 0$).

From both the graph and from (3A.2), as A rises, the two unstable equilibria obviously move inward toward the center, finally disappearing when A becomes positive, at which point the picture looks like figure 3A.7.

The overall dynamic picture when $B > 0$ looks like figure 3A.8. For A sufficiently negative there is a unique, stable, symmetric equilibrium. When A passes one critical point, two stable agglomerative equilibria emerge ($\lambda = 0$ or $\lambda = 1$), but at first the symmetric equilibrium remains stable. Only when A becomes positive does full agglomeration become the unique outcome. We refer to the type of dynamic behavior shown in figure 3A.8 as a *tomahawk bifurcation*.[2]

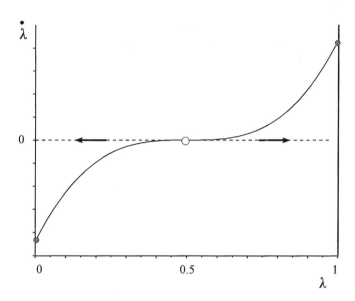

Figure 3A.7
$A = 0, B > 0$

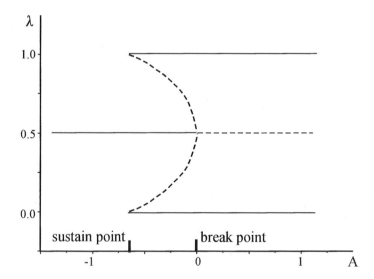

Figure 3A.8
$B > 0$: tomahawk bifurcation

When the economy exhibits tomahawk-type behavior, there are—as we suggested in chapter 1 and saw in the specific case of the base-multiplier model—two critical points in the balance between centripetal and centrifugal forces. One is the point at which a symmetric equilibrium becomes unstable and in which symmetry must therefore be broken; as noted earlier, we refer to this as the break point. The other is the point at which agglomeration, once established, is self-sustaining (i.e., where the roots in (3A.2) lie within the economically meaningful range); what we call the sustain point. When the economy is a tomahawk, it takes stronger centripetal forces to break a symmetric equilibrium than to sustain an asymmetric one: The sustain point comes before the break point.

This has a further implication: If one imagines a process in which we start with a symmetric economy, then gradually shift the balance in favor of agglomeration, the continuous change in exogenous variables produces a discontinuous change in actual outcomes—there is a "catastrophe" when the economy passes the break point.

A final observation: Alas, the dynamics our model implies are never as simple as (3A.1). However, it is usually easy to determine via numerical examples that the model implies tomahawk-type dynamics. Given that hint, it is usually possible to develop analytical expressions for the break point and the sustain point, expressions that invariably have straightforward economic interpretations.

Notes

1. In this book we pay relatively little attention to one important strand of analysis, largely inspired by the classic analyses of Weber (1909) and especially Hotelling (1929), that focuses on the strategic interactions between firms' location decisions. In essence one may say that Hotelling-type analyses treat the geographical distribution of demand and resources as exogenous and carefully analyze the strategic interactions of firms, whereas the models in this book use Dixit-Stiglitz to sterilize the strategic issues while carefully analyzing the implications of endogenous location of demand and resources. For a survey of location theory, see Beckmann and Thisse 1986.

2. The reason for this name will become apparent from figures in later chapters, for example, figure 7.6. Technically, both these bifurcations are pitchforks, the first case ($B < 0$) being a supercritical pitchfork, and the second ($B > 0$), a subcritical pitchfork. Grandmont 1988 contains a technical development of bifurcation theory.

.

II   Labor Mobility and Regional Development

4   The Dixit-Stiglitz Model of Monopolistic Competition and Its Spatial Implications

In any model in which increasing returns play a crucial role, one must somehow handle the problem of market structure. Traditional urban models deal with the issue by assuming that increasing returns are purely external to firms, allowing the modeler to continue to assume perfect competition. The approach taken in this book, however, avoids any direct assumption of external economies: Externalities emerge as a consequence of market interactions involving economies of scale at the level of the individual firm. Thus we must somehow model an imperfectly competitive market structure. The workhorse model of this kind is, of course, the Dixit-Stiglitz model of monopolistic competition (Dixit and Stiglitz 1977). Dixit-Stiglitz monopolistic competition is grossly unrealistic, but it is tractable and flexible; as we will see, it leads to a very special but very suggestive set of results.

This chapter develops a spatial version of the Dixit-Stiglitz model, that is, one with multiple locations and transport costs between those locations. This spatial Dixit-Stiglitz model is a crucial ingredient in almost everything that follows.

We consider an economy with two sectors, agriculture and manufacturing. The agricultural sector is perfectly competitive and produces a single, homogeneous good, whereas the manufacturing sector provides a large variety of differentiated goods. Of course, the label "agriculture" need not always be interpreted literally; the sector's defining characteristic is that it is the "residual," perfectly competitive sector that is the counterpart to the action taking place in the increasing-returns, imperfectly competitive manufacturing sector.

We imagine that there are a very large number of potential manufactured goods, so many that the product space can be represented as continuous, enabling us to sidestep integer constraints on the number of goods. Although each consumption and production activity takes place at a specific location, first we describe each type of activity without explicitly referring to the location.

4.1 Consumer Behavior

Every consumer shares the same Cobb-Douglas tastes for the two types of goods:

$$U = M^{\mu}A^{1-\mu}, \tag{4.1}$$

where M represents a composite index of the consumption of manufactured goods, A is the consumption of the agricultural good, and μ is a constant representing the expenditure share of manufactured goods. The quantity index, M, is a subutility function defined over a continuum of varieties of manufactured goods; $m(i)$ denotes the consumption of each available variety; and n is the range of varieties produced, often called the "number" of available varieties. We assume that M is defined by a constant-elasticity-of-substitution (CES) function:

$$M = \left[\int_0^n m(i)^{\rho}di \right]^{1/\rho}, \quad 0 < \rho < 1. \tag{4.2}$$

In this specification, the parameter ρ represents the intensity of the preference for variety in manufactured goods. When ρ is close to 1, differentiated goods are nearly perfect substitutes for each other; as ρ decreases toward 0, the desire to consume a greater variety of manufactured goods increases. If we set $\sigma \equiv 1/(1 - \rho)$, then σ represents the elasticity of substitution between any two varieties.

Given income Y and a set of prices, p^A for the agricultural good and $p(i)$ for each manufactured good, the consumer's problem is to maximize utility (4.1) subject to the budget constraint,

$$p^A A + \int_0^n p(i)m(i)di = Y.$$

This problem can be solved in two steps.[1] First, whatever the value of the manufacturing composite, M, each $m(i)$ needs to be chosen so as to minimize the cost of attaining M. This means solving the following minimization problem:

$$\min \int_0^n p(i)m(i)di \quad \text{s.t.} \quad \left[\int_0^n m(i)^{\rho}di \right]^{1/\rho} = M. \tag{4.3}$$

The first-order condition to this expenditure minimization problem gives equality of marginal rates of substitution to price ratios,

$$\frac{m(i)^{\rho-1}}{m(j)^{\rho-1}} = \frac{p(i)}{p(j)}, \tag{4.4}$$

for any pair i, j that leads to $m(i) = m(j)(p(j)/p(i))^{1/(1-\rho)}$. Substituting this equation into the original constraint,

$$\left[\int_0^n m(i)^\rho di \right]^{1/\rho} = M,$$

and bringing the common term, $m(j)p(j)^{1/(1-\rho)}$, outside the integral, we have that

$$m(j) = \frac{p(j)^{1/(\rho-1)}}{\left[\int_0^n p(i)^{\rho/(\rho-1)} di \right]^{1/\rho}} M. \tag{4.5}$$

This is simply the compensated demand function for the jth variety of manufacturing product.

We can also derive an expression for the minimum cost of attaining M. Expenditure on the jth variety is $p(j)m(j)$, so using (4.5) and integrating over all j gives

$$\int_0^n p(j)m(j)dj = \left[\int_0^n p(i)^{\rho/(\rho-1)} di \right]^{(\rho-1)/\rho} M. \tag{4.6}$$

It is now natural to define the term multiplying M on the right-hand side of this expression as a price index, so that the price index times the quantity composite is equal to expenditure. Denoting this price index for manufactured products by G we have

$$G \equiv \left[\int_0^n p(i)^{\rho/(\rho-1)} di \right]^{(\rho-1)/\rho} = \left[\int_0^n p(i)^{1-\sigma} di \right]^{1/(1-\sigma)} \tag{4.7}$$

where $\rho \equiv (\sigma - 1)/\sigma$ or $\sigma = 1/(1 - \rho)$. The price index, G, measures the minimum cost of purchasing a unit of the composite index M of manufacturing goods, so just as M can be thought of as a utility function, G can be thought of as an expenditure function. Demand for $m(i)$ can now be written more compactly (using (4.7) in (4.5)) as

$$m(j) = \left(\frac{p(j)}{G} \right)^{1/(\rho-1)} M = \left(\frac{p(j)}{G} \right)^{-\sigma} M. \tag{4.8}$$

The upper-level step of the consumer's problem is to divide total income between agriculture and manufactures in aggregate, that is, to choose A and M so as to

$$\max U = M^\mu A^{1-\mu} \quad \text{s.t.} \quad GM + p^A A = Y, \tag{4.9}$$

which yields the familiar results that $M = \mu Y/G$ and $A = (1 - \mu)Y/p^A$. Pulling the stages together, we obtain the following uncompensated consumer demand functions. For agriculture,

$$A = (1 - \mu)Y/p^A, \tag{4.10}$$

and for each variety of manufactures

$$m(j) = \mu Y \frac{p(j)^{-\sigma}}{G^{-(\sigma-1)}} \quad \text{for } j \in [0, n]. \tag{4.11}$$

Notice that, holding G constant, the price elasticity of demand for every available variety is constant and equal to σ.

We can now express maximized utility as a function of income, the price of agricultural output, and the manufactures' price index, giving the indirect utility function

$$U = \mu^\mu(1 - \mu)^{1-\mu} Y G^{-\mu}(p^A)^{-(1-\mu)}. \tag{4.12}$$

The term $G^\mu(p^A)^{(1-\mu)}$ is the cost-of-living index in the economy.

So far this is a straightforward exercise in demand theory. What is unusual in the Dixit-Stiglitz model—and plays a crucial role in our analysis—is that the range of manufactures on offer becomes an endogenous variable. This means that it is important to understand the effects on the consumer of changes in n, the number of varieties.

Increasing the range of varieties on offer reduces the manufactures' price index (because consumers value variety) and hence the cost of attaining a given level of utility. This can be seen most clearly if we assume that all manufactures are available at the same price, p^M. Then the price index, (4.7), simply becomes

$$G = \left[\int_0^n p(i)^{1-\sigma} di \right]^{1/(1-\sigma)} = p^M n^{1/(1-\sigma)}. \tag{4.13}$$

The price index's responsiveness to the number of varieties depends on the elasticity of substitution between varieties, σ, and we see that the lower is σ—the more differentiated are product varieties—the greater is the reduction in the price index caused by an increase in the number of varieties. The effect on welfare is then given by the indirect utility function, (4.12).

Changing the range of products available also shifts demand curves for existing varieties. This can be seen by looking at the demand curve for a single variety, equation (4.11). Because an increase in n reduces G, it shifts each demand curve downward. This effect is important as we come to determine the equilibrium number of varieties produced. It says that as we increase the number of varieties, product market competition intensifies, shifting demand curves for existing products downward and reducing the sales of these varieties.

4.2 Multiple Locations and Transportation Costs

Depending on what we are trying to model, it is sometimes convenient to think of the economy as consisting of a finite set of locations (regions or countries), sometimes to think of it as spread across a continuous space. For present purposes, however, it is sufficient to think in terms of discrete locations, of which we suppose there are R. For the moment, assume that each variety is produced in only one location and that all varieties produced in a particular location are symmetric, having the same technology and price. We denote the number of varieties produced in location r by n_r, and the mill or f.o.b. price of one of these varieties by p_r^M.

Agricultural and manufactured goods can be shipped between locations and may incur transport costs in shipment. To avoid modeling a separate transportation industry, we assume the "iceberg" form of transport costs introduced by von Thünen and Paul Samuelson.[2] Specifically, if a unit of the agricultural good [any variety of manufactured goods] is shipped from a location r to another location s, only a fraction, $1/T_{rs}^A$ [$1/T_{rs}^M$], of the original unit actually arrives; the rest melts away en route. The constant T_{rs}^A [T_{rs}^M] represents the amount of the agricultural [manufactured] good dispatched per unit received.

The iceberg transport technology implies that if a manufacturing variety produced at location r is sold at price p_r^M, then the delivered (c.i.f.) price, p_{rs}^M, of that variety at each consumption location s is given by

$$p_{rs}^M = p_r^M T_{rs}^M. \tag{4.14}$$

The manufacturing price index may take a different value in each location; we denote this by writing the price index for location s as G_s.

Iceberg transport costs together with the assumption that all varieties produced in a particular location have the same price mean that, using equation (4.7), this price index can be written as

$$G_s = \left[\sum_{r=1}^{R} n_r (p_r^M T_{rs}^M)^{1-\sigma} \right]^{1/(1-\sigma)}, \quad s = 1, \ldots, R. \tag{4.15}$$

Consumption demand in location s for a product produced in r now follows (from 4.11) as

$$\mu Y_s (p_r^M T_{rs}^M)^{-\sigma} G_s^{(\sigma-1)}, \tag{4.16}$$

where Y_s is income for location s. This gives consumption, but to supply this level of consumption, T_{rs}^M times this amount has to be shipped. Summing across locations in which the product is sold, the total sales of a single location r variety, denoted, q_r^M, therefore amount to:

$$q_r^M = \mu \sum_{s=1}^{R} Y_s (p_r^M T_{rs}^M)^{-\sigma} G_s^{\sigma-1} T_{rs}^M. \tag{4.17}$$

This simply says that sales depend on income in each location, the price index in each location, transport costs, and the mill price. Notice that because the delivered prices of the same variety at all consumption locations change proportionally to the mill price, and because each consumer's demand for a variety has a constant price elasticity σ, the elasticity of the aggregate demand for each variety with respect to its mill price is also σ, regardless of the spatial distribution of consumers.

4.3   Producer Behavior

Next we turn to the production side of the economy. The agricultural good, we assume, is produced using a constant-returns technology under conditions of perfect competition. Manufacturing, however, we assume to involve economies of scale. These economies of scale arise at the level of the variety; there are no economies of scope or of multiplant operation. Technology is the same for all varieties and in all locations and involves a fixed input of F and marginal input requirement c^M. Thus, assuming for the moment that the only input is labor, the production of a quantity q^M of any variety at any given location requires labor input l^M, given by

$$l^M = F + c^M q^M. \tag{4.18}$$

Because of increasing returns to scale, consumers' preference for variety, and the unlimited number of potential varieties of manufactured goods, no firm will choose to produce the same variety supplied by another firm. This means that each variety is produced in only one location, by a single, specialized firm, so that the number of manufacturing firms in operation is the same as the number of available varieties.

4.3.1 Profit Maximization

Next, consider a particular firm producing a specific variety at location r and facing a given wage rate, w_r^M, for manufacturing workers there. Then, with a mill price p_r^M, its profit is given by

$$\pi_r = p_r^M q_r^M - w_r^M (F + c^M q_r^M), \tag{4.19}$$

where q_r^M is given by the demand function, (4.17). Each firm is assumed to choose its price taking the price indices, G_s, as given. The perceived elasticity of demand is therefore σ, so profit maximization implies that

$$p_r^M(1 - 1/\sigma) = c^M w_r^M,$$
$$\text{or} \quad p_r^M = c^M w_r^M / \rho, \tag{4.20}$$

for all varieties produced at r.

We suppose that there is free entry and exit in response to profits or losses. Given the pricing rule, the profits of a firm at location r are

$$\pi_r = w_r^M \left[\frac{q_r^M c^M}{\sigma - 1} - F \right]. \tag{4.21}$$

Therefore, the zero-profit condition implies that the equilibrium output of any active firm is

$$q^* \equiv F(\sigma - 1)/c^M, \tag{4.22}$$

and the associated equilibrium labor input is

$$l^* \equiv F + c^M q^* = F\sigma. \tag{4.23}$$

Both q^* and l^* are constants common to every active firm in the economy. Therefore, if L_r^M is the number of manufacturing workers at location r, and n_r is the number of manufacturing firms ($\equiv$ the number of the varieties produced) at r, then

$$n_r = L_r^M / l^* = L_r^M / F\sigma. \tag{4.24}$$

The results (4.20) and (4.22) are somewhat odd but play a crucial role throughout our analysis. They say that *the size of the market affects neither the markup of price over marginal cost nor the scale at which individual goods are produced.* As a result, *all scale effects work through changes in the variety of goods available.* Obviously this is a rather strange result: Normally we think both that larger markets mean more intensive competition, and that one of the ways the economy takes advantage of the extent of the market is by producing at larger scale. The Dixit-Stiglitz model says, however, that all market-size effects work through changes in variety.

This result is an artifact of the constant-elasticity demand functions, together with the nonstrategic behavior implied by our assumption that firms take the price indices, G_s, to be constant as they solve their profit maximization problem. If we were to relax the assumption of nonstrategic behavior, each firm would then recognize that its choice changes the price index, and this recognition of market power would tend to reduce the firm's output and increase its price-cost margin. If we adopt a specific form of oligopolistic interaction, such as Cournot or Bertrand competition, then we can derive explicit expressions for the pricing rule, and in both these cases the price-cost margin is a decreasing function of each firm's market share.[3] Under these assumptions an increase in market size has a procompetitive effect. It causes entry of firms, which reduces price-cost margins and means that firms must operate at larger scale (and lower average cost) to break even. We have already seen (section 4.1) how variety effects create a negative relationship between market size and the price index; the procompetitive effect is a second force operating in the same direction.

Throughout our analysis, however, we choose to ignore this second effect. Having constant price-cost markups and firm scale is a dramatic simplification, allowing us to model cleanly issues that might otherwise seem quite intractable.

4.3.2 The Manufacturing Wage Equation

We have seen that the condition that firms make no profits is equivalent to the condition that they produce q^*. Using the demand functions,

(4.17), firms at location r attain this level of output if the following equation is satisfied:

$$q^* = \mu \sum_{s=1}^{R} Y_s (p_r^M)^{-\sigma} (T_{rs}^M)^{1-\sigma} G_s^{\sigma-1}. \qquad (4.25)$$

We can turn this equation around and say that active firms break even if and only if the price they charge satisfies

$$(p_r^M)^\sigma = \frac{\mu}{q^*} \sum_{s=1}^{R} Y_s (T_{rs}^M)^{1-\sigma} G_s^{\sigma-1}. \qquad (4.26)$$

Using the pricing rule (4.20) this can be expressed as

$$w_r^M = \left(\frac{\sigma-1}{\sigma c^M}\right) \left[\frac{\mu}{q^*} \sum_{s=1}^{R} Y_s (T_{rs}^M)^{1-\sigma} G_s^{\sigma-1}\right]^{1/\sigma}. \qquad (4.27)$$

We refer to this as the *wage equation* and use it often. It gives the manufacturing wage at which firms in each location break even, given the income levels and price indices in all locations and the costs of shipping into these locations. As can be seen, this wage is higher the higher are incomes in the firms' markets, Y_s, the better is the firm's access to these markets (lower T_{rs}^M), and the less competition the firm faces in these markets. (Recall that the price index is decreasing in the number of varieties sold.)

Two important observations need to be made about the wage equation. First, we assume that active firms *always* make no profits, so that this equation gives the actual manufacturing wage in any location that has a nonzero number of firms. In the long run, this wage equals the supply price of labor to manufacturing but in the short run may differ from it. Any such difference gives rise to adjustment dynamics, which are spelled out in later chapters. Essentially then, we are assuming that the entry and exit of firms occurs very fast— so profits are always 0—but relocation of workers among sectors or locations occurs more slowly, with a dynamic that we will model explicitly.

Second, the manufacturing wage as given by (4.27) is defined even in locations that have no manufacturing. It then measures the maximum wage that could be paid by a firm considering production in the location.

4.3.3 Real Wages

Real income at each location is proportional to nominal income deflated by the cost-of-living index, $G_r^\mu (p_r^A)^{1-\mu}$. This means that the real wage of manufacturing workers in location, r denoted ω_r^M, is

$$\omega_r^M = w_r^M G_r^{-\mu} (p_r^A)^{-(1-\mu)}. \tag{4.28}$$

4.4 Some Normalizations

The manufacturing price index and the wage equation pop up frequently in this book. Happily, we can simplify them if we choose units of measurement appropriately. First, notice that we are free to choose units of measurement for output—be it units, tens of units, kilos, or tons. We choose units such that the marginal labor requirement satisfies the following equation:

$$c^M = \frac{\sigma - 1}{\sigma} \ (= \rho). \tag{4.29}$$

This normalization means that the pricing equation, (4.20), becomes

$$p_r^M = w_r^M \tag{4.30}$$

and also that $q^* = l^*$.

Second, as we have seen, the number of firms is simply an interval of the real line, $[0, n]$, and without loss of generality, we can choose units of measurement for this range. For sections II and III of this book we choose convenient units by setting the fixed input requirement F to satisfy the following equation:

$$F = \mu/\sigma. \tag{4.31}$$

The number of firms in each location is related to the size of the manufacturing labor force in the location according to equation (4.24), which becomes

$$n_r = L_r^M/\mu. \tag{4.32}$$

These choices of units also set firm scale. The output level at which firms make no profit (equation (4.22)) becomes

$$q^* = l^* = \mu. \tag{4.33}$$

Using these normalizations the price index and wage equation can now be written in a more convenient form. The price index becomes

$$G_r = \left[\sum_{s=1}^{R} n_s (p_s^M T_{sr}^M)^{(1-\sigma)} \right]^{1/(1-\sigma)}$$

$$= \left[\frac{1}{\mu} \sum_{s=1}^{R} L_s^M (w_s^M T_{sr}^M)^{(1-\sigma)} \right]^{1/(1-\sigma)} . \tag{4.34}$$

The wage equation becomes

$$w_r^M = \left(\frac{\sigma - 1}{\sigma c^M} \right) \left[\frac{\mu}{q^*} \sum_{s=1}^{R} Y_s (T_{rs}^M)^{1-\sigma} G_s^{\sigma-1} \right]^{1/\sigma}$$

$$= \left[\sum_{s=1}^{R} Y_s (T_{rs}^M)^{1-\sigma} G_s^{\sigma-1} \right]^{1/\sigma} . \tag{4.35}$$

We use these two equations repeatedly, both to characterize equilibrium and to investigate its stability. Essentially we have chosen units in a way that shifts attention from the number of manufacturing firms and product prices to the number of manufacturing workers and their wage rates.

4.5 The Price Index Effect and the Home Market Effect

The price indices and wage equations (4.34) and (4.35) do not define a full economic model, but they nevertheless imply some of the most important relationships that drive the results that follow, and it is worth examining them in some detail to draw out these relationships.

Consider a two-location version of these equations. Writing the equations out in full, we have the price indices, (4.34),

$$G_1^{1-\sigma} = \frac{1}{\mu} [L_1 w_1^{1-\sigma} + L_2 (w_2 T)^{1-\sigma}],$$

$$G_2^{1-\sigma} = \frac{1}{\mu} [L_1 (w_1 T)^{1-\sigma} + L_2 w_2^{1-\sigma}], \tag{4.36}$$

and the wage equations, (4.35),

$$w_1^\sigma = Y_1 G_1^{\sigma-1} + Y_2 G_2^{\sigma-1} T^{1-\sigma},$$

$$w_2^\sigma = Y_1 G_1^{\sigma-1} T^{1-\sigma} + Y_2 G_2^{\sigma-1}, \tag{4.37}$$

where we have dropped the superscripts M, because we are looking only at manufacturing, and have denoted transport costs between locations by the single number T, and assumed, as we do throughout, that no transport costs are incurred within each location. These pairs of equations are symmetric, and so have a symmetric solution: That is, if $L_1 = L_2$ and $Y_1 = Y_2$, then there is a solution with $G_1 = G_2$ and $w_1 = w_2$. By inspection, it is easy to see that these symmetric equilibrium values satisfy the following relationships,

$$1 + T^{1-\sigma} = \frac{\mu}{L}\left(\frac{G}{w}\right)^{1-\sigma} = \frac{w}{Y}\left(\frac{G}{w}\right)^{1-\sigma} \qquad (4.38)$$

where absence of subscripts denotes that these are symmetric equilibrium values.

We can explore the relationships contained in the price indices and wage equations by linearizing them around the symmetric equilibrium. Around this point an increase in a variable in one location is always associated with a change, of opposite sign but of equal absolute magnitude, in the corresponding variable in the other country. So letting $dG = dG_1 = -dG_2$, and so on, we derive, by differentiating the price indices and wage equations respectively,

$$(1 - \sigma)\frac{dG}{G} = \frac{L}{\mu}\left(\frac{G}{w}\right)^{\sigma-1}(1 - T^{1-\sigma})\left[\frac{dL}{L} + (1 - \sigma)\frac{dw}{w}\right], \qquad (4.39)$$

$$\sigma\frac{dw}{w} = \frac{Y}{w}\left(\frac{G}{w}\right)^{\sigma-1}(1 - T^{1-\sigma})\left[\frac{dY}{Y} + (\sigma - 1)\frac{dG}{G}\right]. \qquad (4.40)$$

From the first equation, we can see the direct effect of a change in the location of manufacturing on the price index of manufactured goods. Suppose that the supply of labor to manufacturing is perfectly elastic, so that $dw = 0$. Bearing in mind that $1 - \sigma < 0$ and $T > 1$, equation (4.39) implies that a change dL/L in manufacturing employment has a negative effect on the price index, dG/G. We call this the *price index effect*. It means that the location with a larger manufacturing sector also has a lower price index for manufactured goods, simply because a smaller proportion of this region's manufacturing consumption bears transport costs.

Next, let us consider how relative demand affects the location of manufacturing. It is convenient to define a new variable, Z,

$$Z \equiv \frac{1 - T^{1-\sigma}}{1 + T^{1-\sigma}},$$

(4.41)

which is a sort of index of trade cost, with values between 0 and 1. If trade is perfectly costless, $T = 1$, then Z takes the value 0; if trade is impossible, it takes value 1. Using the definition of Z and eliminating dG/G from equations (4.39) and (4.40) gives

$$\left[\frac{\sigma}{Z} + Z(1 - \sigma)\right]\frac{dw}{w} + Z\frac{dL}{L} = \frac{dY}{Y}.$$

(4.42)

We learn a number of things from this equation.

First, suppose that our wider economic model gives us a perfectly elastic supply of labor to manufacturing, so $dw = 0$. We then have a relationship known as the *home market effect*. A 1 percent change in demand for manufactures (dY/Y) causes a $1/Z$ (> 1) percent change in the employment in, and hence production of, manufactures, dL/L. That is, other things being equal, the location with the larger home market has a more than proportionally larger manufacturing sector, and therefore also exports manufactured goods.[4]

Second, although we have just derived the home market effect for the case when labor supply is perfectly elastic, this need not be the case; if the labor supply curve slopes upward, some of the home market advantage is taken out in higher wages rather than exports. Thus, *locations with a higher demand for manufactures may pay a higher nominal wage.*[5]

But notice that we have already seen that an increase in L is, other things being the same, associated with a decrease in G. So if Y is high in some region, we may expect the real wage to be high both because the nominal wage is high and because the price index is low. Hence *locations with a higher demand for manufactures tend, other things being equal, to offer a higher real wage to manufacturing workers.*

Of course other things need not be equal, but we have just sketched out several of the key elements of the cumulative causation that, in our models, tends to lead to agglomeration. Areas with large manufacturing sectors tend to have low price indexes for manufactures, because of the price index effect; areas with large demand for manufactures tend to have disproportionately large manufacturing sectors, because of the home market effect. If we fill in just one more relationship— that manufacturing workers themselves demand manufactures, so that locations with large concentrations of manufacturing also tend to have large demand for manufactured goods—we are almost there. But let us spell out the details in chapter 5.

4.6 The "No-Black-Hole" Condition

We have seen that increasing the size of the manufacturing sector tends to raise real income. However, we often want to put an upper bound on the strength of this effect. The condition we use is best explained by looking at a closed economy: a situation where $Z = 1$.

Consider the real income of a manufacturing worker, (4.28). Suppose that the price of agricultural output is constant, and totally differentiate this to give

$$\frac{d\omega}{\omega} = \frac{dw}{w} - \mu\frac{dG}{G}, \tag{4.43}$$

where we have once again dropped the superscripts M and, because we are looking at a single economy, also the location subscripts. Now using (4.39) and (4.40) with $Z = 1$, we obtain

$$\frac{d\omega}{\omega} = (1 - \mu)\frac{dY}{Y} + \left[\frac{\mu\sigma}{\sigma - 1} - 1\right]\frac{dL}{L}$$

$$= (1 - \mu)\frac{dY}{Y} + \left[\frac{\mu - \rho}{\rho}\right]\frac{dL}{L}, \tag{4.44}$$

which says the following: Suppose that we add more workers to the manufacturing sector of a closed economy, holding expenditure on the industry constant ($dY = 0$) and hence holding constant the nominal income generated. What effect does this have on real wages of workers in the sector? Clearly, because expenditure on manufactures is held constant, so is the wage bill, implying that an increase in L reduces the wage w equiproportionately. However, the increase in manufacturing employment increases the number of varieties of manufacturing products, thus reducing G and tending to raise real income. This latter effect can conceivably outweigh the former, so that an increase in the number of workers would actually raise their real wage.

We in general are not interested in economies in which increasing returns are that strong, if only because, as we will see, in such economies the forces working toward agglomeration always prevail, and the economy tends to collapse into a point. To avoid such "black-hole location" theory, we usually impose what we call the *assumption of no black holes*:

$$\frac{\sigma - 1}{\sigma} = \rho > \mu. \tag{4.45}$$

We now have the building blocks of our approach and are ready to start examining some geography.

Notes

1. A two-stage budgeting proceduring is applicable because preferences are separable between agriculture and manufactures and M, the subutility function for manufactures, is homothetic in the quantities $m(i)$. See Deaton and Muellbauer (1980) for discussion of conditions under which two-stage budgeting is appropriate.

2. The "iceberg" transport technology was formally introduced by Samuelson (1952). Von Thünen, however, supposed the cost of grain transportation to consist largely of the grain consumed on the way by the horses pulling the wagon (von Thünen, 1826, chap. 4). Hence, the von Thünen model may be considered as the predecessor of the "iceberg" transport technology.

3. See Smith and Venables 1988 for derivation of these expressions.

4. The home market effect should apply whether or not a cumulative process of agglomeration is at work. Indeed, Krugman 1980, which originally introduced the effect, did so in the context of a model in which relative market sizes were purely exogenous. Recent work by Davis and Weinstein (1997) has attempted to measure the empirical importance of the home market effect in patterns of international trade and has found surprisingly strong impacts.

5. Because $0 \leq Z \leq 1$, the coefficient on dw/w is positive.

5   Core and Periphery

In the last chapter we laid out some basic machinery for modeling a monopolistically competitive economy—in essence, a set of technical tricks that allow us to handle the problems of market structure posed by the assumption that there are increasing returns at the level of the individual firm. We are now in a position to use that machinery to develop our first model of economic geography.

The analysis we introduce here is not intended to be realistic. Aside from the basic artificiality of the Dixit-Stiglitz model of monopolistic competition (an artificiality that is, alas, a necessary part of nearly all the models in this book), in this chapter we make a number of additional unrealistic assumptions that we drop or modify in later chapters. Our purpose here is to show, as clearly and simply as possible, how the interactions among increasing returns at the level of the firm, transport costs, and factor mobility can cause spatial economic structure to emerge and change. Some of the conclusions from this first pass turn out to be sensitive to those assumptions, but let us postpone that discussion until later. For now, let us simply get into the model.

5.1 Assumptions

We consider an economy of the type set out in chapter 4. It has two sectors, monopolistically competitive manufacturing M and perfectly competitive agriculture A. Each of these sectors employs a single resource, workers and farmers respectively, and we assume that each of these sector-specific factors is in fixed supply.

The geographical distribution of resources is partly exogenous, partly endogenous. Let there be R regions. The world has L^A farmers, and each region is endowed with an exogenous share of this world agricultural labor force denoted ϕ_r. The manufacturing labor force, by contrast, is mobile over time; at any point in time we denote the share of region r in the world worker supply L^M by λ_r. It is convenient to choose units[1] so that $L^M = \mu$, $L^A = 1 - \mu$.

Transport costs among regions take a very special form. Manufactured goods are subject to iceberg transport costs of the form introduced in chapter 4; if one unit of a good is shipped from r to s, only $1/T_{rs}$ units arrive. Shipment of agricultural goods, by contrast, is assumed costless. This is a very unrealistic assumption: In the real world, the cost of transporting one dollar's worth of raw materials is normally higher than that of transporting a dollar's worth of manufactured goods! However, assuming costless transport of food makes our life much simpler for the moment; we turn to the consequences of dropping that assumption in chapter 7.

Because agricultural goods can be freely transported, and because these goods are produced with constant returns, agricultural workers have the same wage rate in all regions. We use this wage rate as the numeraire, so $w_r^A = 1$. Wages of manufacturing workers, however, may differ both in nominal and in real terms. Let us define w_r and ω_r to be the nominal and real wage rate, respectively, of manufacturing workers in region r.

What determines how workers move between regions? Rather than try to produce a sophisticated theory of dynamics, we simply assume that they move toward regions that offer high real wages and away from regions that offer below-average real wages. Specifically, we define the average real wage as

$$\bar{\omega} = \sum_r \lambda_r \omega_r \tag{5.1}$$

and assume the ad hoc dynamics[2]

$$\dot{\lambda}_r = \gamma(\omega_r - \bar{\omega})\lambda_r. \tag{5.2}$$

(Notice that the extra λ_r is necessary to ensure that the changes in all region's shares sum to 0.)

In our model, then, the distribution of manufacturing across regions is given at any point in time but evolves over time to the extent that real wages differ across regions. Regional real wages, however, themselves depend on the distribution of manufacturing, so we turn next to that dependence.

5.2 Instantaneous Equilibrium

There are a number of different ways to describe the determination of equilibrium at a point in time. We find it most useful to think of that equilibrium as the simultaneous solution of 4R equations, which determine the income of each region, the price index of manufactures consumed in that region, the wage rate of workers in that region, and the real wage rate in that region.

5.2.1 Income

The income equation is simple. Because transportation of agricultural goods is costless, agricultural workers earn the same wage everywhere, equal to 1 because it is the numeraire. Recalling that we have chosen units so that there are μ manufacturing workers and $1 - \mu$ agricultural workers in total, the income of region r is

$$Y_r = \mu \lambda_r w_r + (1 - \mu)\phi_r. \tag{5.3}$$

5.2.2 Price Index

The second ingredient is the price index of manufactures in each location, which is as constructed in chapter 4 and given in equation (4.34). Because the number of manufacturing workers in location s is $L_s^M = \mu \lambda_s$, the price index becomes

$$G_r = \left[\sum_s \lambda_s (w_s T_{sr})^{1-\sigma} \right]^{1/1-\sigma}. \tag{5.4}$$

Equation (5.4) exhibits the price index effect that we saw in chapter 4. Suppose that wages in different regions were the same. Then it is apparent from looking at the equation that the price index in r would tend to be lower, the higher the share of manufacturing that is in regions with low transport costs to r. In particular, were there only two regions, a shift of manufacturing into one of the regions would tend, other things equal, to lower the price index in that region—and thus make the region a more attractive place for manufacturing workers to be. This is a version of the forward linkages that we discussed briefly in chapter 3, and turns out to be one of the forces that may lead to emergence of geographical structure in the economy.

5.2.3 Nominal Wages

As we saw in chapter 4, it is possible to derive the level of wages at which manufacturing in region r breaks even. This wage equation is given by equation (4.35), which we restate as,

$$w_r = \left[\sum_s Y_s T_{rs}^{1-\sigma} G_s^{\sigma-1} \right]^{1/\sigma}. \tag{5.5}$$

Like the equation for the price index, this equation is worth looking at for a moment. Suppose that the price indexes in all regions were similar. Then (5.5) would say that the nominal wage rate in region r tends to be higher if incomes in other regions with low transport costs from r are high. The reason, of course, is that firms can afford to pay higher wages if they have good access to a larger market. Thus our model exhibits a form of the backward linkages that drove the base-multiplier model sketched out in chapter 3; these reinforce the forward linkages described above.

5.2.4 Real Wages

Finally, it is straightforward to define the real wages of workers: Because manufactured goods receive a share μ of their expenditure, we have

$$\omega_r = w_r G_r^{-\mu}. \tag{5.6}$$

The nominal wage is deflated by the cost-of-living index, as in (4.28), but with the price of agriculture equal to unity everywhere.

5.2.5 Determination of Equilibrium

This model's instantaneous equilibrium can be thought of as determined by the simultaneous solution of the equations for income (5.3), the equations for price indices (5.4), the wage equations (5.5), and the real-wage equations (5.6): 4R equations in all.[3] Obviously we cannot say much about the solution of these equations in the general case. We can, however, get considerable insight by examining an obvious special case: that of a two-region economy in which agriculture is evenly divided between regions. In that special case, the obvious question is whether manufacturing is equally divided between the two regions or concentrated in one region: that is, whether the economy becomes divided between a manufacturing "core" and an agricultural "periphery." This special case has therefore come to be known as the *core-periphery model*; let us see how it works.

5.3 The Core-Periphery Model: Statement and Numerical Examples

The core-periphery model is the special case of the model described above when there are only two regions and agriculture is evenly divided between those two regions. This means that we need not explicitly write out shares of agriculture, because they are both $1/2$; and we can also simplify notation slightly by letting T be the transport cost between the two regions and letting an unsubscripted λ represent region 1's share of manufacturing (with $1 - \lambda$ representing region 2's share). Thus there are eight equations for instantaneous equilibrium:

$$Y_1 = \mu \lambda w_1 + \frac{1 - \mu}{2}, \tag{5.7}$$

$$Y_2 = \mu(1 - \lambda)w_2 + \frac{1 - \mu}{2}, \tag{5.8}$$

$$G_1 = [\lambda w_1^{1-\sigma} + (1 - \lambda)(w_2 T)^{1-\sigma}]^{1/1-\sigma}, \tag{5.9}$$

$$G_2 = [\lambda(w_1 T)^{1-\sigma} + (1 - \lambda)w_2^{1-\sigma}]^{1/1-\sigma}, \tag{5.10}$$

$$w_1 = [Y_1 G_1^{\sigma-1} + Y_2 G_2^{\sigma-1} T^{1-\sigma}]^{1/\sigma}, \tag{5.11}$$

$$w_2 = [Y_1 G_1^{\sigma-1} T^{1-\sigma} + Y_2 G_2^{\sigma-1}]^{1/\sigma}, \tag{5.12}$$

$$\omega_1 = w_1 G_1^{-\mu}, \tag{5.13}$$

and

$$\omega_2 = w_2 G_2^{-\mu}. \tag{5.14}$$

This model still does not look particularly tractable: eight simultaneous nonlinear equations! We will see shortly, however, that the core-periphery model does indeed yield clear analytical results to the determined economist. However, to know what kind of results to look for, it is very helpful to look first at some numerical examples.

Figures 5.1, 5.2, and 5.3 plot $\omega_1 - \omega_2$, the difference between the two regions' real wage rates in manufacturing, against λ, the region 1 share

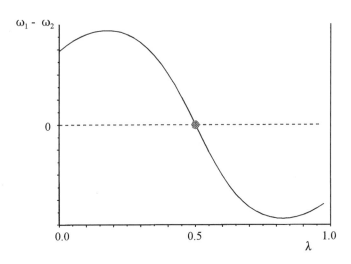

Figure 5.1
Real wage differentials, $T = 2.1$

of manufacturing. All three figures are calculated for $\sigma = 5$, $\mu = 0.4$. However, the transport cost T is different in each: Figure 5.1 shows a high transport cost case, $T = 2.1$, figure 5.2 a low case, $T = 1.5$, and figure 5.3 an intermediate case, $T = 1.7$.

In figure 5.1, the wage differential is positive if λ is less than $^{1}/_{2}$, negative if λ is greater than $^{1}/_{2}$. This means that if a region has more than

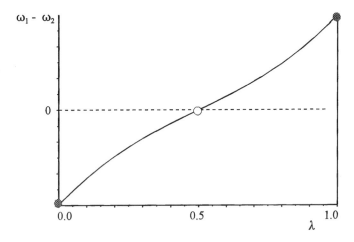

Figure 5.2
Real wage differentials, $T = 1.5$

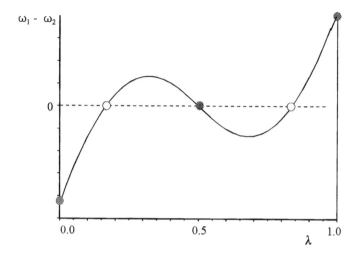

Figure 5.3
Real wage differentials, $T = 1.7$

half the manufacturing labor force, it is less attractive to workers than the other region. Clearly, in this case the economy converges to a long-run symmetric equilibrium in which manufacturing is equally divided between the two regions.

In figure 5.2, by contrast, the wage differential slopes strictly upward in λ: The higher the share of manufacturing in either region, the more attractive the region becomes. This upward slope results, of course, from the two linkage effects discussed in section 5.2: Other things equal, a larger manufacturing labor force makes a region more attractive both because the larger local market leads to higher nominal wages (backward linkage) and because the larger variety of locally produced goods lowers the price index (forward linkage). The important point here is that although an equal division of manufacturing between the two regions is still an equilibrium, it is now unstable: If one region should have even a slightly larger manufacturing sector, that sector would tend to grow over time while the other region's manufacturing shrank, leading eventually to a core-periphery pattern with all manufacturing concentrated in one region.

Finally, figure 5.3, for an intermediate level of transport costs, shows a more complicated picture. The symmetric equilibrium is now locally stable, as in figure 5.1. However, two unstable equilibria now flank it: If λ starts from either a sufficiently high or a sufficiently low initial

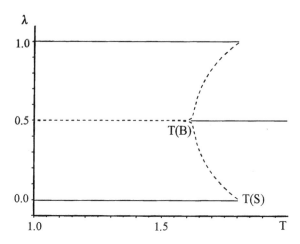

Figure 5.4
Core-periphery bifurcation

value, the economy converges not to the symmetric equilibrium but to a core-periphery pattern with all manufacturing in only one region. This picture then has five equilibria: three stable (the symmetric equilibrium and manufacturing concentration in either region) and two unstable.

From these three cases it is straightforward to understand figure 5.4, which shows how the types of equilibria vary with transport costs. As in figure 3.1, solid lines indicate stable equilibria, broken lines unstable. At sufficiently high transport costs, there is a unique stable equilibrium in which manufacturing is evenly divided between the regions. When transport costs fall below some critical level, new stable equilibria emerge in which all manufacturing is concentrated in one region. When they fall below a second critical level, the symmetric equilibrium becomes unstable.

The similarities to the base-multiplier model are clear. In particular, there are two critical points. The sustain point (labeled as point $T(S)$ in figure 5.4) is the point at which a core-periphery pattern, once established, can be sustained. And the break point $T(B)$ is the point at which symmetry between the regions must be broken because the symmetric equilibrium is unstable.

We can also now see how to approach the model analytically. We want to determine the conditions under which a core-periphery pattern is possible—the sustain point—and the conditions under which it is necessary—the break point.

5.4   When Is a Core-Periphery Pattern Sustainable?

Suppose we start with all manufacturing concentrated in one region, say region 1. To determine whether this is an equilibrium, we ask whether a small group of workers moving from region 1 to region 2 would receive a higher real wage than that received by the workers remaining behind. If so, a core-periphery geography is not an equilibrium: Manufacturing will shift over time to the peripheral region. If not, a core-periphery pattern *is* an equilibrium: The concentration of manufacturing will be self-sustaining.

In short, to assess whether a core-periphery pattern is sustainable, we need to posit a situation in which $\lambda = 1$ and ask whether in that case ω_1 is greater or less than ω_2. If $\omega_1 \geq \omega_2$, then the core-periphery pattern is sustainable, because manufacturing workers will not move out of region 1.[4]

Suppose we set $\lambda = 1$. Simply guess that $w_1 = 1$; in that case

$$Y_1 = (1 + \mu)/2, \qquad Y_2 = (1 - \mu)/2,$$
$$G_1 = 1, \qquad\qquad G_2 = T, \tag{5.15}$$

and we can then confirm from (5.11) that $w_1 = 1$ is indeed an equilibrium value. Notice that income is higher in location 1 than in location 2: It has all the income generated by manufacturing employment. And notice also that the price index is higher in 2 than in 1, because location 2 has to import all its manufactures. These two facts are the basis of the backward and forward linkages that support the core-periphery pattern.

Because $w_1 = 1$ and $G_1 = 1$, it then follows that $\omega_1 = 1$ as well. So all we need to do is determine ω_2 and see whether it is more or less than 1. Substituting into the nominal and real wage equations, (5.12) and (5.14), we have

$$\omega_2 = T^{-\mu} \left[\frac{1 + \mu}{2} T^{1-\sigma} + \frac{1 - \mu}{2} T^{\sigma-1} \right]^{1/\sigma}. \tag{5.16}$$

Equation (5.16) looks complex but lends itself immediately to interpretation in terms of forward and backward linkages. The first term in the equation, $T^{-\mu}$, represents the forward linkage: It comes from the fact that the price index in region 2 is T times as high as that in region 1 because manufactured goods must be imported. The term is less than unity: Having to import manufactures makes location 2 relatively expensive, and therefore unattractive, as a place for manufacturing workers to locate.

The second term represents the nominal wage at which a firm locating in 2 would break even. The income level in location 1 is weighted by $T^{1-\sigma}$, which is less than unity; this weighting is a result of the transport cost disadvantage that a firm in 2 would face in supplying location 1. The income level in 2 is symmetrically weighted by $T^{\sigma-1}$, greater than unity, because of the transport cost disadvantage that firms in 1 bear in supplying location 2. Although these effects are symmetric, they mean that a firm considering locating in 2 does well in the smaller market but badly in the larger; hence there is a backward linkage via demand from the concentration of production to the nominal wage rate firms can afford to pay.

What does equation (5.16) tell us about the sustainability of the core-periphery structure? First, consider the role of transportation costs. To do this it is helpful to rewrite (5.16), in the form

$$\omega_2^\sigma = \frac{1 + \mu}{2} T^{1-\sigma-\mu\sigma} + \frac{1 - \mu}{2} T^{\sigma-1-\mu\sigma}. \tag{5.17}$$

Clearly, when $T = 1$ (no transport costs), $\omega_2 = 1$: Location is irrelevant. If we consider a small transport cost increase from that point, we find (by totally differentiating (5.17) and evaluating the derivative at $T = 1$, $\omega_2 = 1$)

$$\frac{d\omega_2}{dT} = \frac{\mu(1 - 2\sigma)}{\sigma} < 0. \tag{5.18}$$

At small levels of transport costs agglomeration must therefore be sustainable, because $\omega_2 < 1 = \omega_1$.

Suppose, on the other hand, that we consider very large T. The first term in (5.17) clearly becomes arbitrarily small. There are two possibilities for the second term. If $(\sigma - 1) - \mu\sigma < 0$, then this term also becomes arbitrarily small, so ω_2 tends to 0. But recall that $(\sigma - 1)/\sigma > \mu$ is the no-black-hole condition we discussed in chapter 4. It is now clear how to interpret this alternative case: If $(\sigma - 1)/\sigma < \mu$, the agglomeration forces are so strong that a core-periphery pattern is always an equilibrium.

If the no-black-hole condition holds, so $(\sigma - 1) - \mu\sigma > 0$, then the second term in (5.17) becomes arbitrary large. Figure 5.5 shows what happens in this case. The curve defining ω_2 as a function of T slopes downward in the vicinity of $T = 1$, but then turns upward. The point where it crosses 1 defines the sustain value of T: Below this value the core-periphery pattern is an equilibrium, and above it, it is not.

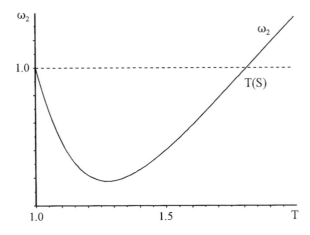

Figure 5.5
Sustain point

How does this sustain value of T depend on parameters? A lower value of σ (and ρ) stretches the curve in figure 5.5 to the right, raising the range of values of T at which the core-periphery structure is sustainable. Conversely, as σ (and ρ) get very large, the sustain value of T becomes close to unity, because very small transport costs then choke off trade, so that manufacturing must operate in both locations to supply local demand.

It is also easy to see that the likelihood that $\omega_2 < 1$, so that a core-periphery equilibrium exists, depends on a sufficiently large role of manufacturing in the economy. Suppose that $\mu = 0$, so (5.16) reduces to $[(T^{1-\sigma} + T^{\sigma-1})/2]^{1/\sigma}$. Providing $T > 1$, this is always greater than 1, so there cannot be a core-periphery pattern. More generally, at lower values of μ the curve in figure 5.5 is rotated upward, reducing the range of values of T that sustain the core-periphery geography. When the manufacturing sector is large, and so can generate significant forward linkages via supply and backward linkages via demand, it generates sufficient centripetal forces to sustain a concentrated equilibrium over a wide range of transportation costs.

5.5 When Is the Symmetric Equilibrium Broken?

We saw from figures 5.1–5.4 that the symmetric equilibrium is stable for high enough values of transport costs but becomes unstable at low values. The figures also illustrate how we can go about finding this break point: It occurs when the model's parameters are such that the $\omega_1 - \omega_2$ curve is horizontal at the symmetric equilibrium. To find it, we have to differentiate totally the equilibrium—characterized by equations (5.7)–(5.14)—with respect to λ, and hence find the equilibrium response $d(\omega_1 - \omega_2)/d\lambda$.

This task is not as formidable as it sounds, because we differentiate around the symmetric equilibrium (as we did in section 4.5). At this equilibrium we know the values of all the endogenous variables of the model. They are

$$\lambda = \tfrac{1}{2}, \quad Y_1 = Y_2 = \tfrac{1}{2}, \quad w_1 = w_2 = 1,$$

$$G_1^{1-\sigma} = G_2^{1-\sigma} = \left[\frac{1 + T^{1-\sigma}}{2} \right].$$

(5.19)

These can be checked by recalling that $\lambda = \tfrac{1}{2}$ is the definition of the symmetric equilibrium, and then seeing that equations (5.7)–(5.12) are satisfied at these values. In the subsequent discussion, we write the values of variables at the symmetric equilibrium as G, Y, etc., dropping the location subscript.

The fact that we are differentiating around the symmetric equilibrium brings another simplification. Any change in an endogenous variable in region 1 is matched by an equal but opposite sign change in the corresponding variables in region 2. This means that we do not have to keep track of region 1 and region 2 variables separately. Instead we write $dY \equiv dY_1 = -dY_2$, and similarly for changes in other variables.

To see how this works, consider the total derivative of the income equations, (5.7) and (5.8). These are

$$dY_1 = \mu w_1 d\lambda + \mu \lambda dw_1, \quad dY_2 = -\mu w_2 d\lambda + \mu(1 - \lambda)dw_2,$$

(5.20)

but around the symmetric equilibrium, these can be described by the single equation,

$$dY = \mu d\lambda + \frac{\mu}{2} dw.$$

(5.21)

Proceeding analogously, the total differential of the price indices (5.9) and (5.10) is

$$(1 - \sigma)\frac{dG}{G} = G^{\sigma-1}(1 - T^{1-\sigma})\left[d\lambda + \frac{(1 - \sigma)dw}{2} \right].$$

(5.22)

The term $1 - T^{1-\sigma}$ appears repeatedly because it captures the effects of an increase in a variable in one region and corresponding decrease in the other. We can simplify by defining a variable Z,

$$Z \equiv \frac{[1 - T^{1-\sigma}]}{[1 + T^{1-\sigma}]} = \frac{[1 - T^{1-\sigma}]}{2G^{1-\sigma}}, \tag{5.23}$$

where the second equation comes from the value of G at the symmetric equilibrium, (5.19). We have already seen Z in chapter 4. It is an index of trade barriers, taking value 0 when there are no transport costs ($T = 1$) and 1 when transport costs are prohibitive ($T \to \infty$). Using this expression, (5.22) becomes

$$\frac{dG}{G} = \frac{2Z}{1 - \sigma}d\lambda + Zdw. \tag{5.24}$$

Applying the same techniques, the total differential of the wage equations (5.11) and (5.12) and real wage equations (5.13) and (5.14) are

$$\sigma dw = 2ZdY + (\sigma - 1)Z\frac{dG}{G}, \tag{5.25}$$

$$G^\mu d\omega = dw - \mu\frac{dG}{G}. \tag{5.26}$$

We want to find $d\omega/d\lambda$, and we can do so by eliminating dG/G, dw, and dY from equations (5.21), (5.24), (5.25) and (5.26). This is a long but straightforward set of substitutions, details of which are given in the appendix. The required expression giving the change in real wages caused by a movement of workers is

$$\frac{d\omega}{d\lambda} = 2ZG^{-\mu}\left(\frac{1 - \rho}{\rho}\right)\left[\frac{\mu(1 + \rho) - Z(\mu^2 + \rho)}{1 - \mu Z(1 - \rho) - \rho Z^2}\right], \tag{5.27}$$

where we have replaced σ by ρ, $\rho = (\sigma - 1)/\sigma$. (The expression is slightly more compact this way.) The symmetric equilibrium is stable if $d\omega/d\lambda$ is negative and unstable if it is positive. We can see easily that the denominator is positive, because Z lies in the interval 0 (free trade) to 1 (autarky) and both μ and ρ are less than unity. The sign of the expression therefore depends on the numerator of the term in square brackets. When Z is close to 0 (transport costs are low), this is certainly positive, so the symmetric equilibrium is unstable. Increasing Z reduces the size of the numerator, and when $Z = 1$ (so that transport

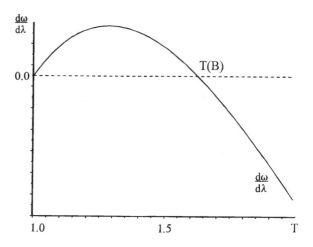

Figure 5.6
Break point

costs are infinite), the numerator is positive if $\rho < \mu$, or changes sign and becomes negative if $\rho > \mu$. This gives exactly the same two cases as we saw in our discussion of the sustain point. The symmetric equilibrium is always unstable if the no-black-hole condition fails, $\rho < \mu$. Otherwise, the symmetric equilibrium is stable at sufficiently high levels of transport costs.

Figure 5.6 gives $d\omega/d\lambda$ as a function of T, for the case in which the no-black-hole condition holds, $\rho > \mu$. At free trade ($T = 1$, $Z = 0$) relocation of labor ($d\lambda$) has no effect on the regional real wage differentials ($d\omega$), essentially because with no transport costs the regions are not economically distinct. At intermediate levels of T, the forward and backward linkages associated with the relocation of workers raise the real wage in the location to which workers are moving, so $d\omega/d\lambda > 0$ and the symmetric equilibrium is unstable. As $T \to \infty$ (autarky), an increase in one region's industrial labor force reduces the real wage there, because it increases the supply of manufactures that cannot now be exported. The break point is at point $T(B)$, where $d\omega/d\lambda$ changes sign.

We can use equation (5.27) to derive an explicit expression for the break point value of T. Setting the numerator of the term in square brackets equal to 0 and using the definition of Z, this expression is

$$\frac{d\omega}{d\lambda} = 0 \quad \text{if} \quad T^{\rho/(1-\rho)} = \frac{(\rho + \mu)(1 + \mu)}{(\rho - \mu)(1 - \mu)}. \tag{5.28}$$

Table 5.1
Critical values of T: Break points $T(B)$ and sustain points $T(S)$

	$\mu = 0.2$		$\mu = 0.4$		$\mu = 0.6$	
	$T(B)$	$T(S)$	$T(B)$	$T(S)$	$T(B)$	$T(S)$
$\sigma = 3$ ($\rho = 0.67$)	1.67	1.72	3.05	4.47	8.72	3124.7
$\sigma = 5$ ($\rho = 0.8$)	1.26	1.27	1.63	1.81	2.30	5.00
$\sigma = 7$ ($\rho = 0.86$)	1.158	1.164	1.36	1.44	1.68	2.44

The parameter values satisfying this equation define the break values at which the symmetric equilibrium becomes unstable. What do we know about these values? First, the break value of T is unique and, if we maintain the the no-black-hole condition, it occurs at a positive level of trade costs, $T > 1$. Second, the break value is increasing in μ: The larger the share of manufacturing workers in the economy, the greater the range of T in which the symmetric equilibrium is unstable. It is also decreasing in ρ (and therefore also σ), a low ρ corresponding to a high degree of product differentiation and large price cost markups, and hence strong forward and backward linkages.

The dependence of break and sustain points on parameters is most easily summarized using some numerical examples. Each cell in table 5.1 reports first the break point and then the sustain point at different values of μ and σ. Because both critical values are increasing in μ and decreasing in σ, the range of transport costs in which the core-periphery geography occurs is greater the larger is the share of manufactures in the economy, and the larger are firms' price cost markups. Notice that the sustain point always occurs at a higher value of T than does the break point, because the bifurcation is a tomahawk, as illustrated in figure 5.4.

5.6 Implications and Conclusions

One could say that the dynamic spatial model laid out in this chapter—and its two-region core-periphery version in particular—plays much the same role in our approach to economic geography that the $2 \times 2 \times 2$ model plays in constant-returns trade theory. That is, it is a model simple enough to yield readily to analysis, yet enough is going on in the model that it yields a number of suggestive and interesting conclusions. From it we learn how economies of agglomeration can emerge from the interactions among economies of scale at the level of the individual producer, transport costs, and factor mobility. We also get a clear illustration both of the tension between centripetal and centrifugal forces and of the potential for discontinuous change that tension creates. Finally, we get a first view of the way that dynamic analysis can serve as a powerful tool of simplification, allowing us to sort through and in the end limit the possibilities static analysis suggests.

For all its virtues, however, the core-periphery model—like the $2 \times 2 \times 2$ model in trade!—can be a bit too seductive: Some of its implications turn out to be sensitive to assumptions one would not want to defend. In the next two chapters we therefore push out the model's boundaries, first by considering the implications of multiple regions, then by turning to a more realistic structure of transport costs.

Appendix: Symmetry Breaking

We want to find the effect of a change $d\lambda$ on the symmetric equilibrium. In the text we totally differentiated the equilibrium around the symmetric point and derived:

$$dY = \mu d\lambda + \frac{\mu}{2} dw, \tag{5.21}$$

$$\frac{dG}{G} = \frac{2Z}{1 - \sigma} d\lambda + Z dw, \tag{5.24}$$

$$\sigma dw = 2Z dY + (\sigma - 1) Z \frac{dG}{G}, \tag{5.25}$$

and

$$G^\mu d\omega = dw - \mu \frac{dG}{G}. \tag{5.26}$$

We use (5.21) to eliminate dY from (5.25), and then write (5.24) and (5.25) as the system

$$
\begin{bmatrix}
1 & -Z \\
Z & \dfrac{\sigma - \mu Z}{1 - \sigma}
\end{bmatrix}
\begin{bmatrix}
\dfrac{dG}{G} \\
dw
\end{bmatrix}
=
\begin{bmatrix}
\dfrac{2Z}{1 - \sigma} d\lambda \\
\dfrac{2Z\mu}{1 - \sigma} d\lambda
\end{bmatrix},
\tag{5A.1}
$$

from which

$$\frac{dG}{G} = \frac{d\lambda}{\Delta} \frac{2\sigma Z}{(1-\sigma)^2} [1 - \mu Z],$$ (5A.2)

and

$$dw = \frac{d\lambda}{\Delta} \frac{2Z}{(1-\sigma)} [\mu - Z],$$ (5A.3)

with the determinant, Δ, taking the form

$$\Delta = \frac{Z^2(1-\sigma) - Z\mu + \sigma}{1 - \sigma}.$$ (5A.4)

Using these in the equation for $d\omega$, (5.26), gives

$$\frac{d\omega}{d\lambda} = \frac{2ZG^{-\mu}}{\sigma - 1} \left[\frac{\mu(2\sigma - 1) - Z(\sigma(1 + \mu^2) - 1)}{\sigma - \mu Z - Z^2(\sigma - 1)} \right].$$ (5A.5)

Equation (5.27) of the text is derived by replacing σ with $1/(1 - \rho)$ and using the definition of Z, (5.23).

Notes

1. We can choose units in which to measure each of the two different types of labor, in addition to the choice of units for output and for firms that we made in chapter 4.

2. Although we have no deep justification for this particular formulation, these dynamics are equivalent to the "replicator dynamics" routinely used in evolutionary game theory. Indeed, our model can, if one likes, be regarded as an evolutionary game. See Weibull 1995.

3. When we work with numerical examples, it is necessary to solve this system. Although it is not necessarily the most efficient procedure, simple iteration generally works: That is, start with guesses at w_r, $r = 1, \ldots , R$; calculate in sequence the implied Y and G vectors; calculate new values of w; and repeat until convergence.

4. We could of course pursue the symmetric case: set $\lambda = 0$ and see if $\omega_1 \leq \omega_2$.

6   Many Regions and Continuous Space

Chapter 5 began by developing a model of location in an economy with an arbitrary number of regions. When it came to studying that model, however, we immediately turned to a two-region special case. There are obvious advantages to "twoness," in terms of reducing the problem to a manageable size (and even the two-region case has its subtleties and surprises). Nonetheless, a theoretical analysis of economic geography must for several reasons make an effort to get beyond the two-location case. First, though the models we study here are aggressively unrealistic, they are intended to shed light on reality, and by and large real-world geographical issues cannot be easily mapped into two-region analyses. Second, at least part of the tradition in location theory is explicitly spatial, that is, it emphasizes the positioning of activities across different locations (and often does so in continuous space); though we need not be slavishly bound by tradition, there is something to be said for trying to see how much of the traditional emphasis can be saved in the new models. Third and perhaps most important, however, applying the basic approach of the last chapter to the many-region case yields some striking new results. In particular, it turns out that we can gain some unexpectedly simple insights into seemingly intractable issues using an approach borrowed from work in theoretical biology by none other than Alan Turing. Let us begin, however, with the most obvious generalization of the two-region case: to three regions.

6.1 The Three-Region Case

It is easy to write out a three-region version of the two-region model in chapter 5. Simply imagine three regions located at the corners of an equilateral triangle, with a transport cost T in each direction, and give each region an agricultural sector of size $(1 - \mu)/3$ instead

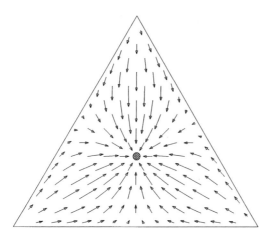

Figure 6.1
Three-region dynamics, $T = 2.5$

of $(1 - \mu)/2$. The equations are obvious and need not be written explicitly. Getting analytical results is more of a problem. It is easy, however, to solve the model numerically and to present these numerical results graphically; the results strongly suggest that the qualitative behavior of a three-region model is very similar to that of a two-region model.

The fact that any allocation of manufacturing among the three regions can be represented in two dimensions, as a point on the unit simplex, makes the three-region model relatively easy to visualize. At such a point location, r has share λ_r of workers, and these shares sum to unity. We can then get a sense of the model's dynamics by drawing a "vector field": We compute regional real wages for a number of different points $(\lambda_1, \lambda_2, \lambda_3)$ on that simplex, use those real wages to calculate (using (5.2)) the implied rates of change of the regional manufacturing shares $(\dot{\lambda}_1, \dot{\lambda}_2, \dot{\lambda}_3)$ and represent those rates of change by an arrow whose size is proportional to that vector. We can then usually get a clear picture of the model's dynamics by simply following the arrows.

Figures 6.1, 6.2, and 6.3 illustrate typical vector fields for a three-region model with $\mu = 0.4$ and $\sigma = 5$. They closely parallel figures 5.1, 5.2, and 5.3. Figure 6.1 illustrates a high transport cost case, $T = 2.5$. Clearly, there is a unique stable equilibrium with manufacturing equally divided among the regions. Figure 6.2 illustrates a low trans-

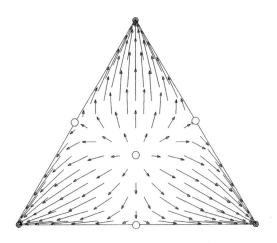

Figure 6.2
Three-region dynamics, $T = 1.5$

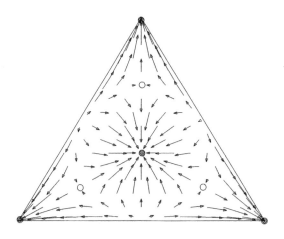

Figure 6.3
Three-region dynamics, $T = 1.9$

port cost case, $T = 1.5$. Here the equal-division equilibrium is clearly unstable; instead, manufacturing always ends up concentrated in one region. Which region depends on initial conditions: The simplex is obviously divided into three basins of attraction, each of which "drains" to one of the corners, that is, to concentration of manufacturing in one of the regions. Finally, figure 6.3 illustrates a more complex intermediate transport cost case, $T = 1.9$. In this case there are four basins of attraction: a central basin (corresponding to a fairly even initial distribution) that drains to an equal division of manufacturing among the regions, and a basin leading to concentration of manufacturing in each of the regions. Between the four stable equilibria lie three unstable ones. The qualitative similarity of these results to what we found in the two-region case is obvious. Presumably it is possible to summarize the whole sequence with a three-dimensional bifurcation diagram—but this is beyond our artistic ability.

We could clearly take the next step and examine an economy with four equidistant regions, then five, and so on; graphical analysis would be first difficult then impossible, but it should still be possible to derive some results. These extensions seem unlikely, however, to add much insight. Furthermore, whereas the case of three locations laid out in a triangle makes some intuitive sense, four locations laid out in a tetrahedron are hard to visualize in our still mainly earthbound economy.

On the other hand, a general model with many regions laid out in some arbitrary pattern seems unlikely to yield any simple results. To the extent that progress has been made in the many-region case, it has mainly been by assuming a particular unrealistic but useful "geometry": a number of regions laid out in a circle, with transportation possible only along the rim of that circle.

6.2   The Racetrack Economy

The special case we have come to think of as the "racetrack economy" maintains all of the assumptions of the many-region model introduced in chapter 5, together with the following special simplifications: the R regions are equally spaced around the circumference of a circle, with region $r + 1$ next to region r, and with region R next to region 1. Agriculture is evenly divided among the regions. Transportation must take place around the circumference, with a constant fraction τ of each manufactured good melting away per unit distance. The easiest way to represent this is by letting the transport cost between r and s be defined as

$$T_{rs} = e^{\tau |r-s|}, \tag{6.1}$$

where $|r - s|$ is the (shorter) distance around the circle from r to s. (Think of a clock face: The distance from 3 to 10 is 5—not 7—because

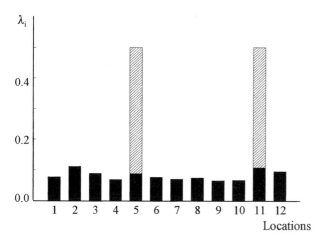

Figure 6.4
Evolution of manufacturing with twelve locations

you can get there more easily by going counterclockwise than clockwise.) It is convenient to normalize distances so that the circumference of the circle is 2π, and thus make the distance between any two neighboring regions $2\pi/R$. The longest distance in the economy then has transport cost which we shall refer to as $T_{max} \equiv e^{\tau\pi}$.

As in the two- and three-region cases, it is useful to begin analyzing this model with numerical examples. Once we go beyond three regions, however, we can no longer represent initial conditions as points in a one- or two-dimensional space and thus summarize the model's dynamics with a simple graph. Instead we must try to learn something about the model's behavior by making experiments—trying out a number of different initial conditions for a number of different parameter values, and seeing what happens.

One obvious way to do this is to start with manufacturing randomly allocated across regions. Figure 6.4 shows the results of a typical run carried out in this way, with $\mu = 0.4$, $\sigma = 5$, $T_{max} = 4$ on a twelve-region landscape. (Examples with twelve regions are often illuminating, because twelve is a fairly small number with a large number of divisors.) The solid portions of the bars show the initial, random shares of the regions in manufacturing. The shaded portions of the bars shows where the shares settle after the economy has been allowed to evolve for a while. In the case illustrated we see that all manufacturing becomes concentrated in two regions. Furthermore, the division of

λ

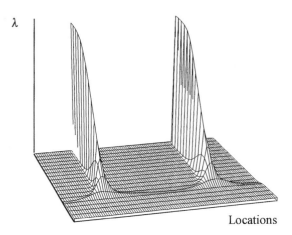

Locations

Figure 6.5
Evolution of manufacturing with many locations

manufacturing between these regions is remarkably equal, and the two regions are equally spaced: Remember that location 12 is next to location 1, so the agglomerations are at exact opposite sides of the racetrack, with five agricultural regions lying between in both directions.

The picture portrayed in figure 6.4 comes from a random initial division of manufacturing labor among regions. Repeating the experiment with the same parameter values but different initial values, we find that manufacturing almost always ends up in two regions. They are not always exactly opposite each other, nor of exactly equal size, but there is clearly a good deal of regularity.

We can make the regularity even more consistent in a somewhat surprising way. Instead of making the initial distribution of manufacturing random, make it a small random deviation from uniformity; that is, start with the distribution of manufacturing close to no structure at all. This initial position may be thought of as a small perturbation of a known equilibrium. After all, given the regions' symmetry, a position in which manufacturing is equally distributed among them —the "flat earth"—must also be a position in which real wages are the same in all locations. But the flat earth turns out to be unstable; the circular logic of concentration causes an even slightly perturbed flat earth spontaneously to develop one or more local concentrations of manufacturing. Figure 6.5 (which Northwestern University's Robert Gordon instantly dubbed the " '59 Cadillac diagram" at a seminar presentation) illustrates this process. There are now 100 regions, instead of 12, arranged along the front horizontal axis; the vertical axis measures the share of each region in the manufacturing labor force. The figure traces out the full evolution of the economy with time running back into the figure. From an almost flat but randomly perturbed initial distribution of manufacturing, the model again evolves into a structure in which all manufacturing is concentrated in only two regions. In this example, the two "winning" regions are again exactly opposite one another, and it turns out that we can guarantee this regularity as long as the initial distribution of manufacturing is sufficiently flat.

Experiments with the racetrack economy, then, offer striking examples of emergent structure. From randomness, order emerges, order that oddly seems more predictable the less structure there is in the initial conditions. What can explain this regularity?

6.3 The Turing Approach

The scenario illustrated in figure 6.5, in which an almost flat distribution of manufacturing evolves over time into a very uneven but regular structure, bears a close resemblance to the problem addressed in a classic paper in theoretical biology by none other than Alan Turing (1952): How does an embryo, an almost homogeneous group of cells, organize itself into a highly differentiated organism? Indeed, Turing's central analytical model was of a simplified embryo consisting of a ring of cells, a setup virtually identical to that of the racetrack economy. And we can therefore make direct use here of Turing's ingenious approach.

Although Turing himself stated his analysis in terms of a large but finite number of cells, the presentation of the approach is actually easier in terms of continuous space. Thus for the rest of this chapter we shift from the analysis of discrete regions to that of continuous space, with $\lambda(r)$ now the density of manufacturing at location r on the circle.

The first step in applying the Turing approach is to make a selective and unusual limitation of focus. It is natural to suppose that we must model either the whole evolution of the economy, as in figure 6.5, or at least ask where the dynamic process arrives in the end, as in figure 6.4. Turing, however, suggested that it was useful to focus instead on the beginning of the process of differentiation—on the way that the initial symmetry among cells might be broken. In our case, this means focusing on the early stages of the process illustrated in figure 6.5: on the initial divergence of the economy away from the flat earth equilibrium.

The advantage of this focus is that it allows us to linearize the model. Let us state a sort of general, reduced-form version of our model, leaving the details for later. We have a situation in which the rate of change of any one region's manufacturing sector depends on the distribution of manufacturing across all regions. We know that there is an equilibrium in which all regions have the same level of industry; call this flat earth level λ. And let us suppose that there are a very large number of regions, so that we can treat space as effectively continuous. Then a reduced-form version of our model's dynamics in the vicinity of the flat earth is

$$\dot{\lambda}(r) = \int_{-\pi}^{\pi} k(\theta)(\lambda(r + \theta) - \lambda)d\theta. \qquad (6.2)$$

That is, the rate of change of manufacturing at location r depends on the concentrations of manufacturing at all other locations, with the impact of manufacturing at another location, $r + \theta$, depending on the distance between those two locations, θ, according to the function $k(\theta)$. As long as one is willing to examine dynamics near the flat earth, then, we can study a linear system like (6.2) instead of the highly nonlinear system our model presents in the general case.

Now comes the second step in Turing analysis: realizing that the system (6.2) actually has surprisingly simple dynamic behavior. Suppose for a moment that the actual deviation of manufacturing from its flat earth value could be described by a simple sinusoidal fluctuation,[1]

$$\lambda(r) - \lambda = \delta \cos(vr), \qquad (6.3)$$

where v is an integer—so that the fluctuation goes an integer number of times around the circle—and measures the frequency of the fluctuation. We can substitute this into (6.2) to get

$$\dot{\lambda}(r) = \delta \int_{-\pi}^{\pi} k(\theta) \cos(vr + v\theta)d\theta. \qquad (6.4)$$

But this can be simplified. First, it happens to be true that $\cos(r + x) = \cos(r) \cos(x) - \sin(r) \sin(x)$. So (6.4) may be rewritten

$$\dot{\lambda}(r) = \delta \cos(vr) \int_{-\pi}^{\pi} k(\theta) \cos(v\theta)d\theta - \delta \sin(vr) \int_{-\pi}^{\pi} k(\theta) \sin(v\theta)d\theta. \qquad (6.5)$$

Second, because the effect of a manufacturing concentration depends only on how far away it is, not on which direction, $k(x) = k(-x)$. This, together with the fact that $\sin(-x) + \sin(x) = 0$, means that the second integral in (6.5) is 0. Using (6.3) in (6.5) now gives

$$\dot{\lambda}(r) = (\lambda(r) - \lambda) \int_{-\pi}^{\pi} k(\theta) \cos(v\theta)d\theta. \tag{6.6}$$

The integral in this equation is a constant, depending on neither r nor λ. It does, however, depend on the frequency of the sinusoidal deviation, v. To signal this let us call it γ_v,

$$\gamma_v \equiv \int_{-\pi}^{\pi} k(\theta) \cos(v\theta)d\theta. \tag{6.7}$$

Although there is no reason to suppose that the actual spatial distribution of manufacturing looks like (6.3), we have just shown that (6.3) defines an *eigenfunction* of the dynamic system—the continuous version of an eigenvector. Equation (6.6) expresses our system of differential equations (6.2) in terms of a differential equation for the eigenfunction (6.3) with eigenvalue given by γ_v. In fact any sinusoidal fluctuation is an eigenfunction, with an eigenvalue—a rate of growth—that depends on its frequency, v.

One analyzes a linear dynamic system, of course, by decomposing the initial vector of evolving variables into a weighted sum of eigenvectors, each of which then grows at its own characteristic rate, equal to the associated eigenvalue. One need only then decompose the distribution of manufacturing around its flat earth density into regular sinusoidal fluctuations. But this is a familiar procedure: It is precisely what one does in representing the distribution as a Fourier series.

Now comes the final step in the Turing approach. Each frequency, v, has its own eigenvalue, given by (6.7). For some frequencies this may be negative; deviations from the flat earth at these frequencies die away. If all frequencies have negative eigenvalues, then all die away, meaning that the flat earth equilibrium is stable. However, if any frequency has a positive eigenvalue, deviations at this frequency increase in amplitude over time, and the flat earth is unstable. Moreover, if we start close to the flat earth, by the time the economy has diverged sufficiently from that position, the fluctuation whose frequency has the largest positive eigenvalue—the most unstable frequency—comes to dominate all others, giving the pattern of agglomerations that develops in the economy.

Of course, this reasoning is based on the economy's local behavior in the neighborhood of the flat earth, and we cannot be certain that it predicts the system's behavior far away from the flat earth. But it seems to. Recall that figure 6.5 was constructed by starting with random perturbations and letting the economy evolve. From the randomness an extremely regular structure developed, and we now know it is because this economy has its largest eigenvalue at frequency $v = 2$.

The next step is to relate the eigenvalues, which determine the economy's dynamics, to the more fundamental parameters of tastes, technology, and transportation.

6.4   The Growth Rate of a Fluctuation

To apply the Turing approach to the racetrack economy, we need to develop an expression that determines how the growth rate of a fluctuation—a sinusoidal deviation from uniformity in the distribution of manufacturing of the form described by (6.3)—is affected by the frequency of that fluctuation. To do this, we need only to discover the pattern of real wages associated with a deviation in manufacturing employment. The reason this suffices is that we have assumed (equation (5.2)) that the growth rate of a region's manufacturing is proportional to the deviation of its real wage from the average; so whichever frequency fluctuation is associated with the greatest variation in real wages per unit amplitude defines the fastest-growing, "preferred" frequency.

To find this frequency, let us restate the racetrack model in continuous space, now allowing the economy to be a circle whose circumference is $2\pi D$, where D is the size of the economy and $T_{max} \equiv e^{\tau \pi D}$. (The reasons for not normalizing to a size 2π will become apparent below.) We choose units so that the agricultural labor force is equal to $(1 - \mu)\pi D$ and the manufacturing labor force to $\mu\pi D$. This means that the density of agricultural labor per unit space is $(1 - \mu)/2$ and, at the flat earth, the density of manufacturing is $\mu/2$. We define $\lambda(r)$ such that the density of manufacturing labor per unit space is $\mu\lambda(r)$, and at flat earth $\lambda = 0.5$.

In this economy, the equations for instantaneous equilibrium may be written

$$Y(r) = \mu\lambda(r)w(r) + \frac{1 - \mu}{2},$$

$$G(r) = \left[\int_{-\pi D}^{\pi D} \lambda(s)w(s)^{1-\sigma}e^{-\tau(\sigma-1)|r-s|}ds \right]^{1/1-\sigma},$$

$$w(r) = \left[\int_{-\pi D}^{\pi D} Y(s)G(s)^{\sigma-1}e^{-\tau(\sigma-1)|r-s|}ds \right]^{1/\sigma}, \tag{6.8}$$

and

$$\omega(r) = w(r)G(r)^{-\mu}.$$

These are just the continuous space analogues of equations (5.3)–(5.6). They do not look very appealing, but we can as usual quickly determine the flat earth equilibrium; when $\lambda = 0.5$ everywhere, we have $w = 1$, $Y = 0.5$; and the Flat Earth value of the price index is

$$G = \left[\int_0^{\pi D} e^{-\tau(\sigma-1)s}ds \right]^{1/1-\sigma} = \left[\frac{1 - e^{\tau(\sigma-1)D\pi}}{\tau(\sigma-1)} \right]^{1/1-\sigma}. \tag{6.9}$$

The next step is to linearize the model around the flat earth equilibrium, a process that turns out to very similar to the analysis of symmetry breaking in section 5.4. Let us use a prime on a variable to denote deviation from the flat earth. Totally differentiating (6.8), we derive,

$$Y'(r) = \mu\lambda'(r) + \frac{\mu}{2}w'(r),$$

$$\frac{G'(r)}{G} = -\frac{G^{\sigma-1}}{\sigma - 1}\int_{-\pi D}^{\pi D} \lambda'(r + s)e^{-\tau(\sigma-1)|s|}ds$$

$$+ \frac{G^{\sigma-1}}{2}\int_{-\pi D}^{\pi D} w'(r + s)e^{-\tau(\sigma-1)|s|}ds,$$

$$w'(r) = \frac{G^{\sigma-1}}{\sigma}\int_{-\pi D}^{\pi D} Y'(r + s)e^{-\tau(\sigma-1)|s|}ds \tag{6.10}$$

$$+ \frac{\sigma - 1}{2\sigma}G^{\sigma-1}\int_{-\pi D}^{\pi D} (G'(r + s)/G)e^{-\tau(\sigma-1)|s|}ds,$$

and

$$\omega'(r) = [w'(r) - \mu G'(r)/G]G^{-\mu}.$$

This still looks like a fairly intractable system. But now we impose the assumption that (6.3) holds: that $\lambda(r)$ is a sinusoidal fluctuation around the flat earth equilibrium, taking the form

$$\lambda'(r) = \delta_\lambda \cos(vr). \tag{6.11}$$

This generates sinusoidal fluctuations in other endogenous variables, so these take the form:

$$Y'(r) = \delta_Y \cos(vr),$$

$$\frac{G'(r)}{G} = \delta_G \cos(vr),$$

$$w'(r) = \delta_w \cos(vr), \tag{6.12}$$

and

$$\omega'(r) = \delta_\omega \cos(vr).$$

The coefficients δ_Y, δ_G, δ_w, and δ_ω are found by using (6.11) and (6.12) in the system (6.10). The resulting system can be greatly simplified, in the same way that the symmetry-breaking equations in the two-region case could be simplified, by introducing a new variable Z,

$$Z \equiv \frac{G^{\sigma-1}}{2} \int_{-\pi D}^{\pi D} \cos(vs) e^{-\tau(\sigma-1)|s|} ds, \tag{6.13}$$

or (looking up the rules for integrating functions of the form $\cos(x)e^{-x}$)

$$Z = \frac{\tau^2(\sigma - 1)^2}{\tau^2(\sigma - 1)^2 + v^2} \left[\frac{1 - \cos(v\pi D)e^{-\tau D(\sigma-1)\pi}}{1 - e^{-\tau D(\sigma-1)\pi}} \right]. \tag{6.14}$$

The system of equations (6.10) now reduces simply to[2]

$$\delta_Y = \mu\delta_\lambda + \frac{\mu}{2}\delta_w,$$

$$\delta_G = \frac{2Z}{1 - \sigma}\delta_\lambda + Z\delta_w,$$

$$\sigma\delta_w = 2Z\delta_Y + (\sigma - 1)Z\delta_G, \tag{6.15}$$

and

$$G^\mu\delta_\omega = \delta_w - \mu\delta_G.$$

This system is identical to the set of equations for symmetry breaking in the two-region case, (5.21), (5.24), (5.25), and (5.26). We can use it to derive, as we did in chapter 5, the following expression:

$$\frac{\delta_\omega}{\delta_\lambda} = 2ZG^{-\mu}\left(\frac{1-\rho}{\rho}\right)\left[\frac{\mu(1+\rho) - Z(\mu^2 + \rho)}{1 - \mu Z(1-\rho) - \rho Z^2}\right]. \tag{6.16}$$

The ratio $\delta_\omega/\delta_\lambda$ measures the effect of a small sinusoidal perturbation in manufacturing employment on the real wage, as we can see by taking the ratio of the last equation in (6.12) to (6.11), giving $\omega'(r)/\lambda'(r) = \delta_\omega/\delta_\lambda$.

We can now complete the analysis. The differential equation giving the change in manufacturing employment is $\dot\lambda(r) = \gamma[\omega(r) - \bar\omega]\lambda(r)$, equation (5.2). At the flat earth, the average real wage $\bar\omega$ is unity, and $\lambda = 0.5$, so linearizing yields

$$\dot\lambda'(r) = \gamma\omega'(r)\lambda(r) = \gamma\frac{\omega'(r)}{2}. \tag{6.17}$$

Because $\omega'(r)/\lambda'(r) = \delta_\omega/\delta_\lambda$, this becomes

$$\dot\lambda'(r) = \gamma\frac{\delta_\omega}{2}\cos(vr) = \gamma\frac{\delta_\omega}{2\delta_\lambda}\lambda'(r). \tag{6.18}$$

This says that the sinusoidal deviation $\lambda'(r) = \delta_\lambda\cos(vr)$ is an eigenfunction with eigenvalue $\gamma_v = \gamma\delta_\omega/2\delta_\lambda$, where the term $\delta_\omega/\delta_\lambda$ is given by equation (6.16). As is clear from equations (6.16) and (6.14) this depends on the parameters of the model μ, ρ, (or σ) and τ, and also on v, the frequency of the fluctuation. We must now investigate how these parameters determine the sign and magnitude of the eigenvalue, and find the preferred frequency: the value of v that gives the largest positive eigenvalue.

6.5 Determining the Preferred Frequency: The Large Economy

It is possible to derive some relatively clear results if we focus on the case of a very extensive economy, that is, one with a large D. In that case our problem becomes substantially simpler in two ways. First, Z becomes a much simpler expression: The second term in (6.14) tends toward 1, so that we have

$$Z = \frac{\tau^2(\sigma-1)^2}{\tau^2(\sigma-1)^2 + v^{2'}} \tag{6.19}$$

which is monotonically decreasing in v. Second, if the economy is large, we may guess that the preferred frequency corresponds to a wavelength that is only a small fraction of $2\pi D$. That means that the integer constraint on the allowed frequencies—the requirement that a fluctuation go an integer number of times around the circle—are much less noticeable, and we can treat v and hence Z as approximately continuous variables.

Suppose, then, that we treat Z as a continuous variable, which we know can only vary between 0 (for v extremely large) and 1 (as v approaches 0). What can we then learn from (6.16), which relates Z to the rate of growth of a fluctuation? First, we note immediately that when $Z = 0$, so is $\delta_\omega / \delta_\lambda$. Second, for small positive Z, $\delta_\omega / \delta_\lambda$ is strictly positive. That is, high-frequency, short wavelength fluctuations tend to grow over time. Third, we note that when Z approaches 1 (corresponding to very-long-wavelength fluctuations), the sign of $\delta_\omega / \delta_\lambda$ is the same as the sign of $\mu(1 + \rho) - (\mu^2 + \rho)$; this can be rearranged as $(\mu - \rho)(1 - \mu)$, which is negative provided that $\mu < \rho$. This condition is already familiar from chapters 4 and 5: It is the no-black-hole condition that says that increasing returns at the level of the economy as a whole are not so strong that manufacturing agglomerates regardless of transportation costs. Combining these statements, we can be sure that as we decrease frequency the eigenvalue first increases from 0 to a positive value, then goes negative. This means that there is a range of frequencies at which flat earth is unstable, and an interior frequency at which the eigenvalue takes its largest positive value.

The relationship between frequency and eigenvalue is illustrated in figure 6.6, which has frequency v on the horizontal, $\delta_\omega / \delta_\lambda$ on the vertical (and is computed with Z given by (6.14), not the approximation on which we based our discussion, (6.19)). It confirms the discussion, showing a range of frequencies at which the flat earth is unstable, and an interior frequency at which the eigenvalue is maximized.

We have argued that the frequency that comes to dominate is the one with the largest positive eigenvalue—frequency 2 in the example of figure 6.6. How this frequency depends on the model's parameters is best illustrated by numerical example, and table 6.1 gives the preferred frequency as a function of μ, σ, and T_{max}. We see that the higher are transport costs, the higher is the preferred frequency. This result is very natural and says that when transport costs are high, there are relatively

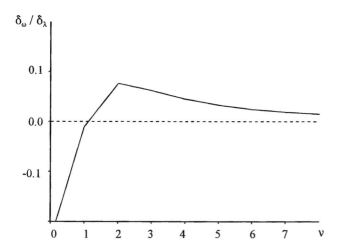

Figure 6.6
Eigenvalues as a function of frequency

Table 6.1
Preferred frequency

	$\sigma = 5$			$\sigma = 10$		
	$\mu = 0.2$	$\mu = 0.4$	$\mu = 0.6$	$\mu = 0.2$	$\mu = 0.4$	$\mu = 0.6$
$T_{max} = 2$	2	1	1	4	2	2
$T_{max} = 4$	3	2	1	7	5	3
$T_{max} = 8$	5	3	2	11	7	4

many relatively small concentrations of manufacturing activity. If there were not, the costs of supplying agricultural regions with manufactures would be prohibitive. A high value of σ has the same effect, and for similar reasons. When σ is high, trade volumes decline very rapidly as a function of distance, encouraging relatively many agglomerations.

The effect of a high share of industry in the economy, μ, is to reduce the preferred frequency, meaning that (starting from the flat earth) there are a few large agglomerations, rather than many small ones. This is because the forward and backward linkages created by concentrating industry are more powerful the greater the share of industry in the cost-of-living index (the forward linkage) and the greater the share of the population (and hence of income and demand) that is mobile (backward linkage).

6.6 From Local to Global

The Turing analysis of sections 6.3–6.5 is local; that is, it is based on a linear approximation to the model around the flat earth. This raises two questions: First, what happens as the system evolves away from the flat earth? Second, what would happen if the economy were at some point other than the flat earth, and then experienced a parameter change? We have no analytical approach to answering either of these questions, but simulation gives an answer that seems to be robust.

We can see what happens as we move away from the flat earth by comparing figures 6.6 and 6.5, both of which were constructed for the same parameter values. From figure 6.6 we see that the preferred frequency is 2. Looking at figure 6.5, we see the emergence of two agglomerations, and the advantage of the two emergent agglomerations apparently cumulates as the process continues, giving the global picture of figure 6.6. We have not found any cases in which the initial advantage predicted by the Turing analysis gets overturned.

The second question is more difficult. Suppose that some pattern of agglomeration is established, and there is then parameter change, say a continuing reduction in trade costs. What happens to the agglomeration? The existing structure is robust to parameter changes in a large interval, but may then undergo catastrophic change, as, at some parameter values, the economy reorganizes into a different structure. We address this issue more fully in chapter 17.

6.7 Conclusions

We started this chapter with a concern: that the intuition developed in chapter 5 depended too much on exercises with a two-region model, that matters might look different once we turn to multiple regions, or for that matter abandon the idea of regions entirely and deal with continuous space. And in a way these concerns are justified: Many-region models do contain possibilities excluded in the two-region case and require new tools of analysis. In particular, we are forced to shift focus from the question of whether agglomeration takes place to that of how many agglomerations form and where they are located relative to one another. We also learn, however, that much of the intuition from the core-periphery model survives. The same factors that work toward concentration of economic activity in that model tend to produce fewer, larger concentrations in a multiple-region or continuous-space model. And we find an unexpected parallel between two-region and continuous-space models: When we analyze the process of spatial differentiation using the Turing approach, the set of equations that we need to solve turns out to be isomorphic to those we used to calculate the break point in the core-periphery analysis.

Alas, beauty is not truth, in geography or in life. We have seen that much of what we learned from the core-periphery model survives a relaxation of the unrealistic assumption that there are only two regions. But how does it survive relaxation of another unrealistic assumption, that agricultural goods are costless to transport?

Appendix: Simulation Parameters

All figures have $\sigma = 5$ and $\mu = 0.4$. Figures 6.1–6.3 have $T = 2.5$, 1.5, and 1.9, respectively. Figures 6.4–6.6 have $T_{max} = 4$.

Notes

1. We state this fluctuation as a cosine wave. However, one can define any fluctuation as a sine simply by relabeling the origin on the circle.

2. We use again the properties of $\cos(vr + vs)$ that were discussed in section 6.3.

7   Agricultural Transport Costs

The analysis of preceding chapters turns on the presence of trade costs incurred in selling manufacturing output in distant locations, but we have assumed that the other sector—agriculture—incurs no such costs. This does yeoman duty as a simplifying assumption, but is clearly false. What difference does it make if both sectors' outputs bear trade costs? Intuitively, agricultural trade costs seem clearly to be a force against agglomeration. A location with a concentration of manufacturing has to import agricultural products; transport costs raise the price of these products, increasing the cost of living in the location and making immigration less likely. Can agricultural transport costs overturn the analysis of the preceding chapters?

In this chapter we investigate these issues and show how agricultural transport costs reduce the range of parameters for which agglomeration occurs. However, we also find that reductions in agricultural transport costs can cause the core-periphery geography to develop, just as a reduction in manufactures' transport costs did in chapter 5. This provides an alternative story about the trigger for agglomeration, and perhaps one more historically relevant than changes in transport costs on manufactures alone.

7.1 Trade Costs: The Realities

Because transport costs are central to our approach, we must ask how large they are in reality. There are two main sources of evidence on this question. The first is to try to measure these costs directly, and the second comes from looking at trade volumes, and seeing how rapidly they fall off over distance.

The former approach yields many estimates of transport costs. A good example is provided by Rauch (1996), who divides commodities according to whether they are homogeneous or differentiated. In the former class he places commodities for which quoted prices are available, either because they are traded on organized exchanges, or because they have a reference price. In the latter class he puts industries where product differentiation means that prices cannot be quoted without going down to the level of the individual supplying firm. Taking as an example U.S.–Japan trade, Rauch estimates transport costs (insurance plus freight costs) of around 13 percent of value for homogeneous products and 6 percent for differentiated products.

This approach has the disadvantage that the transport costs that appear in our models are only metaphorical: We are really interested in all of the costs of doing business over geographical space. In other words, we want for the theory a measure of the full cost, including all the costs of doing business at a distance—lack of face-to-face contact, more complex and expensive communications and information gathering, and possibly also different languages, legal systems, product standards and cultures. These things are difficult to measure directly but are revealed in the trade data: If the volume of trade between a pair of locations is lower the further apart they are, then presumably this is because the full cost of making the trade is higher.

The standard way of estimating the relationship between trade volumes and distance is by means of gravity models. (See Leamer and Levinsohn 1996 for an overview of these models.) Distance always appears as a highly significant determinant of trade flows, typically with the elasticity of trade with respect to distance being of the order -0.6 to -1.0.

Can gravity models provide any measure of how trade costs differ between different sectors? There is an obvious difficulty, for elasticities of demand may simply differ between sectors—so a given trade cost has a different impact on trade volumes. Rauch (1996) attempted to make such a disaggregation. He found that the distance coefficient is similar for differentiated products and homogeneous products and argued that this is because the greater complexity of gathering information about differentiated goods offsets lower transport costs on these products.

This brief overview suggests, then, that sectors other than the manufacture of differentiated products have substantial trade costs, probably at least as large as those for differentiated products. In our framework these other sectors are aggregated into "agriculture," and we now turn to analyzing the effects of such costs.

7.2 Trade Costs: The Model

We begin by assuming, as in the previous chapter, that agriculture is a homogeneous good and that one unit of agricultural labor can produce one unit of output. Each region has half the total endowment of agricultural labor, and we denote the agricultural wage in region r as w_r^A. The agricultural wage equals the price of agriculture, but these wages and prices are no longer equalized between regions because of the presence of iceberg transport costs on agriculture at the rate T^A. The difference between agricultural wages in the two regions depends on whether the region is an importer or exporter of agriculture which, given agricultural supply, depends on demand and hence income in each region. Figure 7.1 outlines the possibilities. The horizontal axis measures each region's share of income, and the solid curve traces out the agricultural wage in region 1 relative to that in region 2, w_1^A / w_2^A, as a function of income shares.

Suppose region 1 has a high share of world income (as it will if it contains manufacturing). Then we are at a point toward the right of the diagram, and $w_1^A / w_2^A = T^A$. This is because whenever region 1 imports agricultural goods, they are T^A times as expensive in 1 as in 2. Now consider the central part of the figure. If the two regions have equal incomes, then there is no agricultural trade, and agricultural

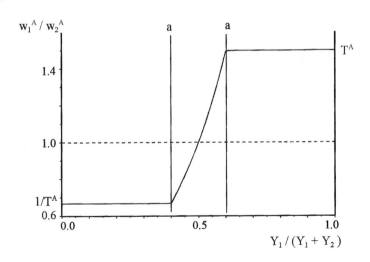

Figure 7.1
Agricultural wages and prices

wages are equal in both regions. What happens in band *aa* around this central point? Moving to the right of the symmetric equilibrium raises demand for agriculture in region 1, raising the price in 1 relative to 2. But only when w_1^A / w_2^A reaches T^A does trade commence, so in the band *aa* there is no trade in agriculture.

Given this description of agricultural prices and wages, we are now in a position to see how the presence of agricultural trade costs changes our results. We employ the model of section 5.3 but now use superscripts M and A to distinguish between variables in manufacturing and in agriculture. Letting w_r^M and w_r^A denote wages in the two sectors, income in each country takes the form

$$Y_1 = \mu\lambda w_1^M + \frac{1 - \mu}{2} w_1^A, \tag{7.1}$$

$$Y_2 = (1 - \lambda)\mu w_2^M + \frac{1 - \mu}{2} w_2^A. \tag{7.2}$$

The manufacturing sector is exactly as described in section 5.3. Superscripting manufacturing variables with M, we have price indices and wage equations in each region,

$$G_1^M = [\lambda(w_1^M)^{1-\sigma} + (1 - \lambda)(w_2^M T^M)^{1-\sigma}]^{1/1-\sigma}, \tag{7.3}$$

$$G_2^M = [\lambda(w_1^M T^M)^{1-\sigma} + (1 - \lambda)(w_2^M)^{1-\sigma}]^{1/1-\sigma}, \tag{7.4}$$

$$w_1^M = [Y_1(G_1^M)^{\sigma-1} + Y_2(G_2^M)^{\sigma-1}(T^M)^{1-\sigma}]^{1/\sigma}, \tag{7.5}$$

$$w_2^M = [Y_1(G_1^M)^{\sigma-1}(T^M)^{1-\sigma} + Y_2(G_2^M)^{\sigma-1}]^{1/\sigma}. \tag{7.6}$$

The only other modification we need to make is to allow for differing agricultural prices in the cost of living in each country. The real wages of manufacturing workers become

$$\omega_1 = w_1^M(G_1^M)^{-\mu}(w_1^A)^{\mu-1}, \tag{7.7}$$

$$\omega_2 = w_2^M(G_2^M)^{-\mu}(w_2^A)^{\mu-1}. \tag{7.8}$$

7.3 Core-Periphery or Symmetry?

How do agricultural transport costs change the structure of equilibria? We analyze this question as before, in two parts, asking if the core-periphery structure is sustainable and whether the symmetric equilibrium is stable or unstable. To investigate the stability of a core-

periphery structure we assume that such a structure is in place, then
check whether it is an equilibrium.[1]

Suppose that all manufacturing is concentrated in region 1, $\lambda = 1$.
Region 1 must then be importing agriculture, so if we use region 2
agricultural labor as numeraire, we have $w_2^A = 1$ and $w_1^A = T^A > 1$.

To find country 1 manufacturing wages, notice that world income
[adding (7.1) and (7.2)] is

$$Y_1 + Y_2 = \mu w_1^M + \frac{1 - \mu}{2}(T^A + 1). \tag{7.9}$$

The value of manufacturing output, μw_1^M, equals demand for manufactures, $\mu(Y_1 + Y_2)$, hence

$$w_1^M = \frac{1 + T^A}{2}. \tag{7.10}$$

Income levels in the two countries are therefore

$$Y_1 = \frac{T^A + \mu}{2}, \quad Y_2 = \frac{1 - \mu}{2}. \tag{7.11}$$

Given that region 2 agricultural output is used as numeraire, the agricultural trade costs increase nominal income and manufacturing
wages in region 1.

The region 2 manufacturing wage is given by the wage equation.
$\lambda = 1$ implies that price indices take values $G_1^M = w_1^M$, $G_2^M = w_1^M T^M$,
and using this together with the value of income (7.11) in (7.6) gives

$$\left(\frac{w_2^M}{w_1^M}\right) = \left[\frac{T^A + \mu}{1 + T^A}(T^M)^{1-\sigma} + \frac{1 - \mu}{1 + T^A}(T^M)^{\sigma-1}\right]^{1/\sigma} \tag{7.12}$$

The cost-of-living index in region 2 differs from that in region 1 by
factor $(T^M)^\mu (T^A)^{\mu-1}$, because region 2 has cheaper agriculture but more
expensive manufactures than region 1. The ratio of real manufacturing
wages is therefore

$$\frac{\omega_2}{\omega_1} = (T^M)^{-\mu}(T^A)^{1-\mu}\left[\frac{\mu + T^A}{1 + T^A}(T^M)^{1-\sigma} + \frac{1 - \mu}{1 + T^A}(T^M)^{\sigma-1}\right]^{1/\sigma}. \tag{7.13}$$

The core-periphery structure is an equilibrium if this is less than unity,
so that manufacturing labor has no incentive to move from region 1
to region 2.

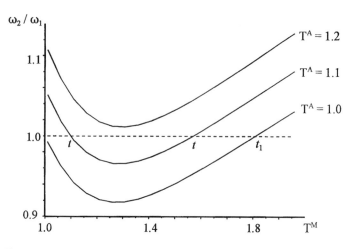

Figure 7.2
Sustain curves

This is a generalization of the sustain point condition derived in chapter 5, to which it reduces when $T^A = 1$. The presence of agricultural trade costs enters in two distinct ways. First, inside the square brackets, having $T^A > 1$ reduces the value of the expression, making it easier to sustain the core-periphery structure. This is a backward linkage effect: Because region 1 agricultural wages are higher, so is nominal income and demand in region 1, making it a more attractive location for manufacturing. The second effect comes from the term $(T^A)^{1-\mu}$, measuring the effect of the higher agricultural price on the cost-of-living index. This raises the value of the expression, making it more difficult to sustain agglomeration, because the region with manufacturing now has higher-priced agricultural products, making it more difficult for the region to hold labor and increasing the incentive for emigration.

The latter effect must dominate the former for a region importing agriculture, shifting the ω_2/ω_1 schedule upward. Figure 7.2 illustrates ω_2/ω_1 as a function of T^M for three different values of T^A. The lowest is $T^A = 1$, and the curve is exactly as in figure 5.5. The core-periphery structure is sustainable for all values of T^M less than t_1.

The second curve is for an intermediate level of T^A. We now see that the core-periphery structure is sustainable only in the interval tt, because at low levels of T^M the benefits to firms of proximity to region 1's market of manufacturing workers become relatively small; supplying from region 2 would incur only low transport costs. But manufacturing workers in region 1 have to pay the higher price for imported agricultural goods. Manufacturing workers can therefore gain by defecting to region 2.

The highest curve is drawn at a level of T^A high enough to prevent the core-periphery structure from ever being sustainable.

The precise location of these curves depends on other parameters in the sustain condition. A higher value of μ shifts the curves downward (for $T^A = 1$ this is a clockwise rotation around the origin), because a higher share of mobile workers strengthens backward linkages and supports the core-periphery structure. A lower value of σ has similar effect, again increasing the range of values of T^M for which agglomeration is sustainable.

We now turn to the question of whether the symmetric equilibrium is stable or unstable, and outline the answer. As we saw in chapter 5, we address this question by differentiating the equilibrium around the symmetric point and evaluating the differential, $d(\omega_1 - \omega_2)/d\lambda$. If the differential is positive, then the symmetric equilibrium is unstable, because adding more manufacturing workers to region 1 raises their real wages. Conducting this analysis on equations (7.1)–(7.8) proceeds similarly to the analysis of section 5.4, but now there is an extra endogenous variable, $dw^A(\equiv dw_1^A = -dw_2^A)$. We need a further equation to give us this term, and we can see where it comes from by inspection of figure 7.1. In the neighborhood of the symmetric equilibrium there is no trade in agriculture, so agricultural prices adjust to equate the value of supply and of demand in each region separately. The value of supply of agriculture in region 1 is $(1 - \mu)w_1^A/2$, and expenditure on agriculture is $(1 - \mu)Y_1$, so the equation is $dw^A = 2dY$.

Derivation of the equation for $d(\omega_1 - \omega_2)/d\lambda$ is given in appendix 7.1 (which calculates a general case, including the material of part 4 of this chapter). It turns out that providing $\rho > \mu$ (the no-black-hole condition), agricultural trade costs are sufficient to ensure that $d(\omega_1 - \omega_2)/d\lambda < 0$ for all values of $T^M > 1$, so at no point is symmetry broken. This means that starting from a high level of manufacturing trade costs at which the core-periphery structure is not sustainable, reductions in these trade costs move the economy into a region where a core-periphery structure is possible. But because there is no break point, the symmetric equilibrium never becomes unstable, and, under our simple dynamics, there is no reason to expect a core-periphery structure

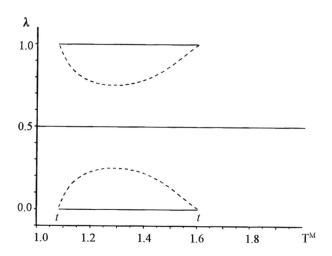

Figure 7.3
Bifurcation with homogenous agriculture, $T^A = 1.1$

to form. The intuition is straightforward. Adding a manufacturing worker to a region raises the price of agricultural products in the region. This increase is large enough to prevent migration from raising real wages.

Summarizing, the structure of equilibria takes the following form.

If there are no agricultural transport costs, $T^A = 1$, then the analysis is as in chapter 5. Both sustain and break points occur at $T^M > 1$, supporting equilibria as illustrated in figure 5.4.

If $T^A > 1$ but is not too large, then there is an interval of manufacturing trade costs (tt of figure 7.2) in which agglomeration can be sustained, but there is no break point. The configuration of equilibria is as illustrated in figure 7.3. In the interval tt, agglomeration and the symmetric equilibrium are all stable equilibria. Between stable equilibria there must be unstable equilibria, and these have been computed as the dashed lines in figure 7.3. However, the symmetric equilibrium never becomes unstable, so if we imagine a path of the economy in which T^M falls through time (exogenously), then there is no reason to believe that a core-periphery structure will form.

Finally, if $T^A > 1$ and large, then the range of values of T^M within which agglomeration can be sustained disappears. The symmetric equilibrium is unique for all levels of manufacturing transport costs.

7.4 Differentiated Agricultural Products

The analysis so far describes what happens when trade costs are imposed on an agricultural sector that produces a single type of homogeneous product. The assumption of homogeneity of agricultural output is the simplest and most natural assumption to make but is empirically unsatisfactory: Different regions usually produce different crops.

In addition to being empirically unsatisfactory, assuming homogeneity of agriculture turns out to have the peculiar implication that even infinitesimal transport costs have a major qualitative impact on the economy's dynamics: No matter how small the costs of transporting agricultural goods, introducing these costs appears to imply that a symmetric equilibrium is always stable. The reason for this stark result is, of course, that we test the stability of an equilibrium by looking at an infinitesimal deviation, $d\lambda$. The perturbation this causes lies within the band aa of figure 7.1, no matter how narrow this band may be. The change $d\lambda$ therefore has the same effect on agricultural prices and wages regardless of the magnitude of T^A, providing $T^A > 1$.

One response to this unsatisfactory implication would be to look at coordinated action by some mass of industrial workers, say $\Delta\lambda$. This could cause a movement outside the band aa, reducing the term dw^A/dY and causing the symmetric equilibrium to become unstable. The possibility that coordinated action changes the nature of an equilibrium is a more general point; as we noted in chapter 2, such coordination is a central feature of Henderson-type urban systems theory. However, our whole thrust in this book is to pursue the implications of atomistic action, so this is not a very appealing solution.

An alternative response is to remove the kinks in the relative wage schedule of figure 7.1, something that can be accomplished by letting each region produce slightly different agricultural goods. We retain the assumptions of perfect competition and constant returns to scale in agriculture, but just let each region's output be differentiated from each other—one region produces grapes, the other grain.[2] There is then trade in agriculture at the symmetric equilibrium, and changes in demand in each region produce smooth responses in trade volumes and agricultural prices.

Before we model this alternative structure in detail, it is helpful to examine how it changes the response of agriculture prices to demand shifts. Figure 7.4 is like figure 7.1 but contains three curves. These curves give the response of agricultural prices and wages to income

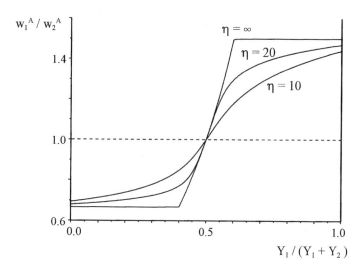

Figure 7.4
Agricultural wages and prices

differences for three different values of the elasticity of substitution (η) between the agricultural products of the two regions, and all are drawn for the same level of agricultural transport costs T^A.

The curve $\eta = \infty$ is as in figure 7.1, giving the case of a single homogeneous agricultural product. The two lower curves are for lower levels of the elasticity of substitution, $\eta = 20$ and $\eta = 10$, respectively. There are two things to note about the effect of introducing product differentiation as represented by these lower elasticities. First, for any division of world income, the regional differential in agricultural wages is reduced. And second, the gradient of this differential in the neighborhood of the symmetric equilibrium is also reduced, because consumers now demand both agricultural products, and their demand curves for each are assumed to have strictly negative and continuous gradients.[3]

Figure 7.4 suggests that agricultural product differentiation, by reducing the agricultural wage and price differentials between regions, increases the extent to which a given level of agricultural transport costs is consistent with a core-periphery structure. We must now model agricultural product differentiation formally to see if this is so.

We assume that the elasticity of substitution between the two regions' agricultural products is constant. Demand for each product is then derived from CES preferences, with a corresponding expenditure function or price index. We denote the price index of agriculture in region r as G_r^A and, borrowing the apparatus we have developed to describe demand for manufactures, this takes the form,

$$G_1^A = \left[\frac{1}{2}\left((w_1^A)^{1-\eta} + (w_2^A T^A)^{1-\eta}\right)\right]^{1/1-\eta}, \tag{7.14}$$

$$G_2^A = \left[\frac{1}{2}\left((w_1^A T^A)^{1-\eta} + (w_2^A)^{1-\eta}\right)\right]^{1/1-\eta}. \tag{7.15}$$

Supply of agriculture is perfectly competitive, and the price of region r's output is w_r^A in region r, and $w_r^A T^A$ in the other region. Each region produces an exogenously determined variety of product;[4] instead of the variable λ describing the location of production of manufacturing varieties, we now have the constant, $\frac{1}{2}$, capturing the equal division of agricultural varieties between locations.

Supply and demand determine agricultural prices and wages. The supply of each variety is $(1 - \mu)/2$ (the number of agricultural workers), and demand for the variety produced in r is

$$\frac{1 - \mu}{2}(w_r^A)^{-\eta}[Y_r(G_r^A)^{\eta-1} + Y_s(G_s^A)^{\eta-1}(T^A)^{1-\eta}].$$

Equating supply and demand gives the agricultural wage equation similar to the industrial wage equation,

$$w_1^A = [Y_1(G_1^A)^{\eta-1} + Y_2(G_2^A)^{\eta-1}(T^A)^{1-\eta}]^{1/\eta}, \tag{7.16}$$

$$w_2^A = [Y_1(G_1^A)^{\eta-1}(T^A)^{1-\eta} + Y_2(G_2^A)^{\eta-1}]^{1/\eta}. \tag{7.17}$$

One further change is needed. The cost-of-living index in each location now depends on the price index of agriculture, so equations (7.7) and (7.8), giving the real wages of manufacturing workers, become, respectively,

$$\omega_1 = w_1^M (G_1^M)^{-\mu}(G_1^A)^{\mu-1}, \tag{7.18}$$

$$\omega_2 = w_2^M (G_2^M)^{-\mu}(G_2^A)^{\mu-1}. \tag{7.19}$$

These six equations, (7.14)–(7.19), together with the income equations and description of manufacturing, (7.1)–(7.6), now define the equilibrium.

What structure of equilibria does this model support? As usual we can answer this by looking at parameters of the model for which the

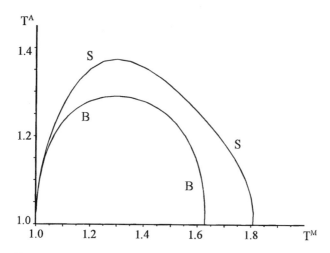

Figure 7.5
Break and sustain points

core-periphery equilibrium is sustainable, and at which the symmetric equilibrium becomes destabilized. We begin with a simulation analysis, whose results are shown in figure 7.5.[5] The horizontal and vertical axes are transport costs T^M and T^A respectively, and the curves labeled SS and BB give the sustain and break point values of these costs. The core-periphery structure is sustainable below SS and unsustainable above, and the symmetric equilibrium is stable above BB and unstable below.

The figure gives a full description of the different equilibrium configurations that arise at different values of transport costs. It is most easily interpreted by considering the effects of changing T^M at different values of T^A.

At a high level of T^A (above the maximum point on SS) there is a unique equilibrium with activity equally divided between regions. Reductions in T^M do not bring agglomeration, because agricultural trade costs are too high for a core-periphery structure to be sustainable.

At intermediate levels of T^A (below the maximum point on SS and above the maximum on BB), the structure of equilibria is qualitatively as illustrated in figure 7.3. There is an interval of values of T^M for which the core-periphery structure is sustainable, but symmetry is never broken.

At values of T^A below the maximum point on the BB curve, figure 7.6 illustrates the structure of equilibria (as a function of T^M). Once

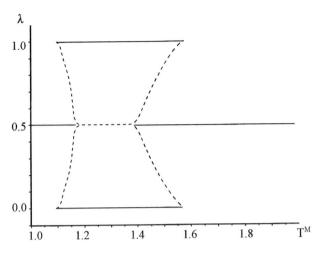

Figure 7.6
Bifurcation with product differentiation in agriculture, $T^A = 1.27$

again there is a range of values of T^M at which agglomeration is sustainable, and now there is also a pair of break points, between which the symmetric equilibrium is unstable, so agglomeration must occur. As T^M is reduced, the number of equilibria changes, 1–5–3–5–1, with agglomeration occurring at intermediate values of T^M. The reason for this structure of equilibria is that at very high T^M, the final demand from immobile agricultural workers ensures a symmetric equilibrium, as usual. And at very low T^M the backward and forward linkages operating in manufacturing are extremely weak, and agricultural transport costs therefore outweigh them. Only at intermediate levels of T^M are the backward and forward linkages strong enough to destabilize the symmetric equilibrium.

How general is the pattern suggested here? Appendix 7.1 investigates the model's break points and establishes that $d\omega/d\lambda$ is quadratic in T^M. At $T^A = 1$, $d\omega/d\lambda = 0$ has two roots, one at $T^M = 1$ and the other at $T^M > 1$, exactly as in chapter 5 (see figure 5.6). However, for T^A slightly greater than 1, there must be two roots at values of $T^M > 1$. The basic shape of the BB curve illustrated is therefore general, implying that for low values of T^A symmetric outcomes are stable both at high and at very low values of T^M.

The structure illustrated in figure 7.5 provides a substantial generalization of the model of chapter 5. It shows that reductions in agricultural trade costs as well as those on manufacturing trade can trigger the emergence of a core-periphery structure. More generally, following some path in which both agricultural and manufacturing transport costs are falling, perhaps at different rates, moves the economy across the SS and then the BB line, making a symmetric equilibrium unstable and leading to the emergence of a core-periphery structure. Agricultural transport costs, in other words, work against agglomeration, so reducing them allows agglomeration to take place.

Figure 7.5 also shows how reductions in manufacturing trade costs may lead both to the formation of a core-periphery structure and then also to its breakup. Essentially the agglomeration forces we describe throughout this book are strongest at intermediate levels of manufacturing trade costs. At high costs, the demand-side centrifugal force created by immobile consumers outweighs them, causing manufacturing to be spread out. But at low trade costs, the supply-side centrifugal force created by the need to import agricultural goods may outweigh them. The nonmonotonic effect of trade costs on the pattern of agglomeration shown in figure 7.6 is one that we will see recurring in later chapters.

7.5   Conclusions

Relaxing the model of chapter 5 to allow for transport costs on agricultural goods may seem like a minor extension; and indeed, some of the insights remain intact (and the general modeling approach is as useful here as it was there). However, adding agricultural transport costs turns out to be an important enrichment of the story, one that is more general than the specifics of our approach here. As long as agricultural transport was free, all the action—both centripetal and centrifugal forces—came from the manufacturing sector. The only question, therefore, was the direction of the forces generated by that sector: Was the pull of dispersed consumers stronger or weaker than the forward and backward linkages? By adding an additional centrifugal force, however, we become concerned not only with the direction but with the strength of the forces generated in manufacturing. Even if manufacturing on net creates a force for agglomeration, is it strong enough to do the job? We see that the answer is yes, for appropriate values of transport costs.

The role of agricultural transport costs in acting as a brake on urban development is well documented (the "tyranny of distance," as

Bairoch (1988) calls it). By enlarging our model to include agricultural transport costs, we capture this effect, and have also been able to demonstrate how reducing agricultural transport costs can cause agglomeration to occur, just as can a reduction in manufacturing transport costs. Adding costs of transporting agricultural goods not only reminds us that these costs themselves may play an important role in shaping the economy's spatial structure, it also leads us to conclude that the effects of the gradual abolition of distance—of declining transport costs— need not be monotonic: An initial decline in transport costs may foster concentration of activity, then a further decline may dissolve that very concentration. We will see that this insight allows us to tell some very interesting stories about the global economy in part III.

Appendix 7.1: Symmetry Breaking

We want to find the effect of a change $d\lambda$ on the symmetric equilibrium. We compute terms for the model with agricultural product differentiation, then specialize this for the case of homogeneous agricultural output.

Totally differentiating the equilibrium around the symmetric point in a manner analogous to chapter 5 gives:

[From (7.1)]: $dY = \mu d\lambda + \dfrac{\mu}{2} dw^M + \dfrac{1 - \mu}{2} dw^A.$ (7A.1)

[From (7.3)]: $\dfrac{dG^M}{G^M} = \dfrac{2Z}{1 - \sigma} d\lambda + Z dw^M.$ (7A.2)

[From (7.5)]: $\sigma dw^M = 2Z dY + (\sigma - 1) Z \dfrac{dG^M}{G^M}.$ (7A.3)

Turning to agriculture, we define ζ analogously to Z as

$$\zeta \equiv \frac{1 - (T^A)^{1-\eta}}{2(G^A)^{1-\eta}} = \frac{1 - (T^A)^{1-\eta}}{1 + (T^A)^{1-\eta}}$$ (7A.4)

(which also defines the symmetric equilibrium value of G^A). The variable ζ ranges from 0, when $T^A = 1$, to 1, when $T^A \to \infty$ or when $\eta \to \infty$. From (7.14) we get

$$\frac{dG^A}{G^A} = \zeta dw^A$$ (7A.5)

and from (7.16),

$$\eta dw^A = 2\zeta dY + (\eta - 1)\zeta \frac{dG^A}{G^A}. \tag{7A.6}$$

These equations implicitly give values of the five endogenous variables, dY, dG^M, dw^M, dG^A and dw^A in terms of the exogenous variable, the change $d\lambda$. We solve them by a lengthy process of substitution.

First, we use (7A.5) to eliminate dG^A/G^A from (7A.6) giving

$$\frac{dw^A}{dY} = \frac{2(1-b)}{1-\mu}, \tag{7A.7}$$

where it is convenient to introduce the constant b, defined as

$$b \equiv 1 - \frac{(1-\mu)\zeta}{\eta - \zeta^2(\eta - 1)}. \tag{7A.8}$$

Notice that b lies in the interval 1 (when $\zeta = 0$) to μ (when $\zeta = 1$). The case of homogenous agriculture arises as $\eta \to \infty$, so $\zeta \to 1$, $b \to \mu$, and $dw^A/dY = 2$, as discussed in section 7.3.

We can now solve for the manufacturing variables. Using (7A.7) in (7A.1), dY is

$$bdY = \mu d\lambda + \frac{\mu}{2} dw^M, \tag{7A.9}$$

and eliminating dY from (7A.3) gives,

$$dw\left[\sigma - \frac{Z\mu}{b}\right] + (1 - \sigma)Z\frac{dG^M}{G^M} = \frac{2Z\mu}{b} d\lambda. \tag{7A.10}$$

Equations (7A.2) and (7A.10) can be expressed as

$$\begin{bmatrix} 1 & -Z \\ Z & \dfrac{\sigma - Z\mu/b}{1-\sigma} \end{bmatrix} \begin{bmatrix} \dfrac{dG^M}{G^M} \\ dw^M \end{bmatrix} = \begin{bmatrix} \dfrac{2Z}{1-\sigma} d\lambda \\ \dfrac{2Z\mu}{b(1-\sigma)} d\lambda \end{bmatrix}, \tag{7A.11}$$

from which

$$\frac{dG^M}{G^M} = \frac{d\lambda}{\Delta} \frac{2\sigma Z}{(1-\sigma)^2}\left[1 - \frac{Z\mu}{b}\right], \tag{7A.12}$$

$$dw^M = \frac{d\lambda}{\Delta} \frac{2Z}{(1 - \sigma)} \left[\frac{\mu}{b} - Z \right], \tag{7A.13}$$

with the determinant, Δ, given by

$$\Delta = \frac{1}{1 - \sigma} \left(Z^2(1 - \sigma) - \frac{Z\mu}{b} + \sigma \right) \leq 0. \tag{7A.14}$$

Since $b \geq \mu$, $\Delta \leq 0$ for $Z \in [0, 1]$.
Substituting back into (7A.9), we obtain dY,

$$dY = \frac{d\lambda}{\Delta} \frac{\mu}{b} \frac{\sigma(1 - Z^2)}{1 - \sigma}, \tag{7A.15}$$

and hence, from (7A.7),

$$dw^A = \frac{d\lambda}{\Delta} \frac{\mu(1 - b)}{b(1 - \mu)} \frac{2\sigma(1 - Z^2)}{1 - \sigma} \tag{7A.16}$$

and from (7A.5):

$$\frac{dG^A}{G^A} = \frac{d\lambda}{\Delta} \frac{\zeta\mu(1 - b)}{b(1 - \mu)} \frac{2\sigma(1 - Z^2)}{1 - \sigma} \tag{7A.17}$$

These equations give the explicit expressions we need for the changes in endogenous variables induced by change $d\lambda$. Notice that when $T^A = 1$ and hence $b = 1$, they reduce to the same expressions as in the appendix to chapter 5.

1. Homogenous Agriculture (Section 7.3):
Differentiating the real wage equations, (7.7) and (7.8), gives

$$(G^M)^\mu d\omega = dw^M - \mu \frac{dG^M}{G^M} - (1 - \mu)dw^A. \tag{7A.18}$$

Substituting terms in (7A.18) and using the fact that as $\eta \to \infty, b \to \mu$, gives,

$$\Delta(G^M)^\mu \frac{d\omega}{d\lambda} = \frac{2(1 - Z)}{(1 - \sigma)^2}$$
$$\times [Z(1 - \sigma) - \mu\sigma Z - (1 - \mu)\sigma(1 - \sigma)(1 + Z)]. \tag{7A.19}$$

Replacing σ by $\sigma = 1/(1 - \rho)$, this becomes

$$\Delta(G^M)^\mu \frac{d\omega}{d\lambda} = \frac{2(1 - Z)}{\rho^2} (Z + \rho)(\rho - \mu). \tag{7A.20}$$

Because $\Delta < 0$, the condition $\rho > \mu$ ensures that $d\omega/d\lambda \leq 0$ for all Z in the economically relevant interval, $Z \in (0,1)$. Symmetry is never broken.

2. Differentiated Agriculture (Section 7.4):

From the real wage equation (7.18),

$$(G^M)^\mu(G^A)^{1-\mu}d\omega = dw^M - \mu\frac{dG^M}{G^M} - (1-\mu)\frac{dG^A}{G^A}. \tag{7A.21}$$

Substituting,

$$\Delta(G^M)^\mu(G^A)^{1-\mu}\frac{d\omega}{d\lambda} = \frac{2}{(\sigma-1)^2}\left[B - \frac{Z\mu}{b}(\sigma(1+b)-1)\right. \tag{7A.22}$$
$$\left. + Z^2\left(\sigma\left(1+\frac{\mu^2}{b}\right) - 1 - B\right)\right]$$

$$B \equiv \zeta\mu\sigma(\sigma-1)(1-b)/b \geq 0. \tag{7A.23}$$

If $\zeta > 0$, then $d\omega/d\lambda$ is negative at $Z = 0$ and $Z = 1$ (because $\Delta < 0$ and $b > \mu$).

To find the break points, set $d\omega/d\lambda = 0$. The right-hand side is quadratic in Z. If $\zeta = 0$ (so $b = 1$ and $B = 0$), then roots are at $Z = 0$ and $Z > 0$. If $\zeta > 0$ and small, then there are two positive real roots. Examples of these for particular parameter values are given by the BB line of figure 7.5.

Appendix 7.2: Simulation Parameters

All figures are constructed with $\mu = 0.4$, $\sigma = 5$.

Figure 7.1, $T^A = 1.5$.

Figure 7.3, $T^A = 1.1$.

Figure 7.4, $T^A = 1.5$.

Figure 7.5, $\eta = 10$.

Figure 7.6, $\eta = 10$, $T^A = 1.275$.

Notes

1. A simulation based investigation of this is contained in Calmette and Le-Pottier 1995.

2. This is the "Armington assumption" employed in many computable equilibrium trade models (Armington 1969).

3. The limiting case is when the elasticity of substitution is unity, so that each product has the same share in world income. Relative demands and prices for the two products are then unvarying, and the corresponding curve in figure 7.4 is the horizontal line at unity.

4. This can be thought of as a single variety in each region or, more accurately, as a fixed measure of product varieties.

5. Constructed with the no-black-hole condition, $\rho > \mu$.

III

The Urban System

8   Spatial Models of Urban Systems: A Heuristic Introduction

The dividing line between regional and urban economics is fuzzy at best. Nonetheless, it seems fair to say that the approach developed in part II felt more like regional than urban economics. For one thing, we mainly focused on economies with only a small number of discrete locations, rather than the continuous space that urban modelers usually assume. Also, the analysis ignored many of the characteristic concerns of urban economics: For example, how do new cities form? Why do cities of different size coexist? How do variations in transport cost, natural or artificial, affect urban location? And of course we entirely neglected that most traditional of urban economists' concerns, the role of land-rent gradients in determining location decisions.

In this part of the book we turn to a series of models that use an analytical framework very similar to that developed in part II, but whose detailed structure differs in ways that allow them to better address the issues raised by a focus on cities rather than regions. In particular, we now work mainly with continuous space, and also introduce a more realistic treatment of agriculture in which land-rent gradients play a crucial role.

This shift of focus offers a different and, we believe, valuable perspective on how economies evolve in space. In particular, one gets an exciting new way of thinking about spatial economics in terms of the coevolution of two "landscapes": the landscape defined by the current distribution of economic activity, and the implied landscape of "market potential," which determines the future evolution of that distribution. Unfortunately, however, these insights come at a cost. Spatial urban models seem unavoidably to involve more algebraic busywork than the regional models we have just seen.

And yet the difficulty of our models in this part of the book seems to us more a matter of unavoidable but not very significant technical detail than of deep economic complexity. The basic insights are quite simple. And before we get into the details it would be helpful to try to convey a sense of that underlying simplicity.

In this chapter we attempt to convey this sense by offering a heuristic approach to the spatial modeling of urban systems. This approach is in the same spirit as the regional science models described in chapter 3. That is, "heuristic" is a polite way of saying that the approach does not quite hang together: Neither budget constraints nor market structure are handled in a way that stands up to close inspection. And yet we saw in chapter 3 that some deliberate sloppiness can have its uses. The base-multiplier approach does not bear thinking about too closely, yet it is a powerful way to introduce some key intuitions about regional economics, and has even been a useful guide for empirical work; it is no substitute for the fully worked-out core-periphery model, but it is a valuable complement (and helps us understand how that more careful model works). We offer here a framework similar both in philosophy and content: an ad hoc, not quite consistent way of thinking about how producers interdependently choose locations that allows this chapter to serve as a sort of guide to the more careful analysis that follows.

Without further ado, then, let us lay out the framework and look at the stories it can be used to tell; each of these stories is, in effect, a preview of the more careful analysis in one of the chapters to come.

8.1 Location Decisions and the Distribution of Demand

Let us imagine an economy in which population and economic activity are distributed along a line. (In this case, in contrast to the Turing model described in chapter 6, we make it an ordinary line rather than a circle.) As in the regional models, the economy produces two kinds of goods: agricultural products and manufactured goods. Also, again as in the regional models, agriculture is exogenously and evenly distributed across space, whereas manufacturing is mobile.[1] And the manufacturing sector is assumed to consist of many symmetric goods, no one of which is a significant fraction of the sector.

At this point, however, we start to cheat. Rather than explicitly modeling the demand for individual manufactured goods, market structure, and the determination of prices, we blur the issue. We take the per capita consumption of each manufactured good to be a fixed number (which we can normalize to 1)—no explicit consideration of price elasticities. In fact, we do not explicitly introduce prices at all. Instead, we think of each good as being produced by a monopolist who sites one or more plants in such a way as to minimize the sum of production and transportation costs, given the geographic distribution of consumption.

Each manufacturing producer can choose to have as many plants as he wants; each additional plant, however, involves incurring a fixed cost F. Production involves a constant marginal cost c, and goods can be transported at a cost τ per unit good transported one unit of distance. What units are these costs measured in? We deliberately avoid saying.

Finally, we assume that a share μ of the population is employed in manufacturing, and thus that a share μ of the demand for each good comes from manufacturing workers, with the geographical distribution of manufacturing workers the same as that of manufacturing production. This means, of course, that manufacturing firms' location decisions are interdependent: The optimal site or sites of production for each firm depend on where other producers choose to produce.

With this admittedly very problematic and indeed not quite internally consistent set of assumptions, let us now examine a series of examples that can serve as a guide to the issues the next few chapters raise.

8.2 Sustaining and Locking In Urban Location

What holds a city together? And why are the locations of cities so persistent, even though both individuals and firms continually turn over? We can get considerable insight into these time-honored questions by considering one special case of our heuristic approach; this special case anticipates the more satisfactory approach in chapter 9.

Consider, then, an economy with a total population normalized to 1 (and thus with the consumption of each manufactured good also equal to 1) occupying a line of length 1. Farmers, who account for $1 - \mu$ of the population and consume $1 - \mu$ units of manufacturing, are spread evenly along this line. Let us also assume that the fixed cost F is sufficiently high relative to the transport cost that each producer chooses, regardless of the location of other producers, to have only one manufacturing facility. In this case, then, we are concerned only with

Figure 8.1
Plant location

the question of where plants are located, not with how many plants there are.

One possibility one might imagine is that all manufacturing is concentrated at a single urban location, say location r, where r is a number between 0 and 1. Under what conditions is such a concentration in fact an equilibrium?[2]

Each producer chooses a location—say s—to minimize the sum of production and transportation costs. As we have described the situation, however, production costs are the same regardless of the location chosen (fixed costs are given, and marginal cost is constant). Thus the problem reduces to one of minimizing transport costs.

Figure 8.1 illustrates how the total transport costs of a producer located at s may be analyzed, given that all other producers are concentrated at r. First, a fraction s of the farmers are to the "west" of the factory; because their average distance from the factory is $s/2$ and farmers account for the fraction $1 - \mu$ of demand, the transportation costs to this group are $(1 - \mu)\tau s^2/2$. Similarly, the cost of shipping to the farmers to the "east" is $(1 - \mu)\tau(1 - s)^2/2$. Finally, the urban consumers in the city consume μ units and lie at a distance $|r - s|$ away; so the cost of serving them is $\mu\tau|r - s|$. The total transport cost is therefore

$$TC = \tau\left[\frac{1 - \mu}{2}(s^2 + (1 - s)^2) + \mu|r - s|\right]. \tag{8.1}$$

Figure 8.2 shows this total transport cost as a function of s for the parameters $\tau = 0.1$, $\mu = 1/3$, under the assumption that $r = 0.4$—that is, that there is a city somewhat to the west of the country's geographical center. (The figure actually shows *minus* the transport cost, so that the firm chooses the top of the curve rather than the bottom; this is to stress the analogy with the market potential functions that will be derived in later chapters.) Clearly, in this case the point of minimum transport cost—the optimal location of a firm choosing where to locate given the locations of other firms—is at $s = 0.4 = r$. That is, each firm

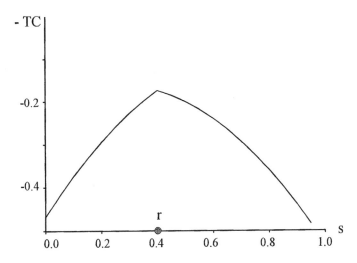

Figure 8.2
Location and transport costs

chooses to locate where all the other firms are located, and a city at $r = 0.4$, is therefore an equilibrium geography for this economy.

Why is such an off-center equilibrium possible? Nothing would be surprising about an equilibrium city at $r = 0.5$, that is, in the center of the country: Such a central location would minimize the cost of shipping goods to the agricultural population. What makes other equilibria possible is, of course, the role of the manufacturing sector as a market for itself, and the consequent incentive for each producer to get close to other producers: An off-center urban concentration drags the optimal location for each individual producer off-center as well.

And yet one might still be surprised by the economy's ability to sustain an off-center city. Imagine starting with a central city, then moving that city east or west. It is not enough that optimal manufacturing locations follow that city as it moves; they must follow it all the way. One might suppose that firms would choose locations that are a compromise between the location that minimizes the cost of shipping to farmers and the one that minimizes the cost of shipping to urban consumers. If they did, then as the hypothetical city moved off center, firms would locate somewhere between that city and the center, which means that an off-center location would not actually be an equilibrium. In fact, however, within certain limits firms do not compromise: They choose to be wherever the city is.

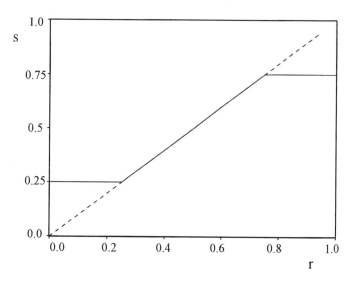

Figure 8.3
City location and plant location

Figure 8.3 illustrates this point, using the same parameters as figure 8.2. On the horizontal axis is r, the location of a hypothetical urban concentration; on the vertical axis is s, the optimal location for an individual firm calculated by minimizing (8.1). We see that for a considerable range—in fact, from $r = 0.25$ to $r = 0.75$—$s = r$; that is, the optimal decision of each firm is to locate at the city, and thus that any geography involving a city in that range is an equilibrium.

The reason for this result lies in the form of equation (8.1), which implies that there is a *cusp* in the transport cost function at r—a discontinuity in its derivative. If one imagines gradually moving the location of a plant eastward, the cost of transporting goods to the urban population falls steadily as long as one is approaching from the west, then abruptly begins rising as soon as one has reached the city and is departing to the east. This discontinuity in the derivative makes locating right at the city the cost-minimizing decision over a range of different urban locations.

This result continues to obtain in more satisfactory models. In the models developed in the next several chapters, profit maximization leads firms to choose the maximum of a fairly complex "market potential" function rather than the minimum of a simple measure of transport cost like (8.1). Nonetheless, an urban concentration normally both creates a cusp in the market potential function and is sustained by that cusp, which causes the existing urban location to be that function's maximum.

We can also step slightly outside the formal model here to see that this analysis at least suggests the reasons why cities persist despite the continual turnover of individuals and firms. Suppose that you imagine replacing one of the firms in the city with a new firm, one that may have a somewhat different market potential function than its predecessor, perhaps even one that has some bias toward a more or less easterly location. Nonetheless, its market potential still has a cusp at the city's location; and as long as the firm is not too different from the existing firms, the city thus remains its optimal location.

Of course, not any city location works. In figure 8.3 we saw that if one posits a city too far off center, firms do not choose to locate there; so only a city within a certain range is an equilibrium. We can use the idea that a city is a cusp's way of sustaining itself to establish an analytical expression for that range. Consider the left and right derivatives of TC with respect to s when $s = r$: that is, the change in total costs as one approaches the city from the west and departs to the east. These are

$$\frac{\partial TC}{\partial s} = \tau[2(1 - \mu)r - 1] \tag{8.2}$$

and

$$\frac{\partial TC}{\partial s} = \tau[2(1 - \mu)r - 1 + 2\mu]. \tag{8.3}$$

Suppose that we want to ask whether a city that is west of the center ($r < 0.5$) is an equilibrium. We need to be sure that it is not to an individual firm's advantage to locate a bit closer to the center, that is, to be sure that (8.3) is positive. This is true provided that

$$r > \frac{1 - 2\mu}{2(1 - \mu)}. \tag{8.4}$$

Similarly, if the city is east of the center, we need to be sure that it is not to an individual firm's advantage to drift a bit to the west; that is, (8.2) must be negative. This is true if

$$r < \frac{1}{2(1 - \mu)}. \tag{8.5}$$

In the case we have considered, with $\mu = 1/3$, the range of possible city locations is therefore $0.25 < r < 0.75$, which was the result we found in figure 8.3.

We have now seen how a city, once in existence, can sustain itself and lock in its location. But how do we think about the process by which cities are formed, and about the existence of a system with multiple cities?

8.3 Population Growth and City Formation

In chapter 6 we saw one way to think about the formation of population concentrations: Imagine a landscape over which manufacturing is distributed either randomly or (almost) uniformly, posit some dynamics, and trace out the process by which an organized spatial structure emerges. This can sometimes be a very helpful way of approaching the issue. When one thinks about city formation, however, it is neither an empirically compelling nor, as it turns out, an analytically helpful approach.

Instead, an approach already familiar from the urban systems literature surveyed in chapter 2 works best: Imagine an economy with an existing city or cities, and allow its population to grow. We can then consider when and where new cities emerge, using this stylized dynamic analysis to bring some order to what might otherwise be a complex taxonomy of possible spatial equilibria.

To do this properly requires being careful about market structure and general equilibrium; we provide this analysis in chapter 10. We can suggest the flavor of that analysis, however, by applying our heuristic approach.

Consider, then, an economy with the same basic setup as before, except that we no longer assume that farmers are evenly distributed along the whole line of possible locations. Instead, we assume that the line of possible locations is very long, and that only a part of it—which we may without loss of generality assume to be the section running from $-S$ to S—is currently occupied by uniformly distributed farmers. Let the population density of farmers be d. Let us also assume that there is already a concentration of all manufacturing at the center of the occupied zone, at location 0.

Now let us suppose that the population grows, but that the density of the agricultural population remains constant, so the agricultural frontier shifts outward. What happens?

Figure 8.4
Population growth and city formation

Manufacturing firms always have the option of establishing new plants somewhere away from the existing city to reduce the cost of shipment to the agricultural hinterland. Let us proceed in three stages. First, let us ask where new plants would be located if they were to be built; then let us ask when it becomes profitable to open such plants; finally, we can turn to the implications of that process.

Figure 8.4 shows how a new plant can reduce transportation costs. It shows the agricultural market to the east of the existing city, from 0 to S. Without a new plant, this entire market will be served from the existing city. If a new plant is built at location s, however, only farmers from 0 to $s/2$ will be served from that old location; the new plant will serve farmers from $s/2$ to S.

Where should the plant be located, if it is established? As in the previous section, this decision is simply a matter of minimizing transport costs. There are three groups of consumers to take into account, all farmers to the east of the city. (City residents and farmers to the west will be served from the old location.) There are $ds/2$ farmers who will continue to be served from the old location, at an average distance of $s/4$; another $ds/2$ farmers to the west of the new plant, also at an average distance of $s/4$; and $d(S - s)$ farmers to the east of the new plant, at an average distance of $d(S - s)/2$. The total transportation cost is therefore

$$TC = \tau d \left[\frac{s^2}{4} + \frac{(S - s)^2}{2} \right]. \tag{8.6}$$

The location that minimizes this cost is $s = 2S/3$: A new plant, if established, should be located two-thirds of the way to the agricultural frontier.

Should such a plant be built? Without such a plant, the dS farmers east of the center are an average distance $S/2$ from the producer, so the transport cost is $\tau dS^2/2$. With the plant, the average farmer is only $S/6$ from the producer, so the transport cost is $\tau dS^2/6$: a reduction of $\tau dS^2/3$. On the other hand, establishing a new plant involves the fixed cost F. Thus a new plant is built when

$$\tau dS^2/3 = F \qquad (8.7)$$

or when S has reached the critical value

$$S^* = \sqrt{3F/\tau d}. \qquad (8.8)$$

But the same criterion applies to all firms, and so as soon as S reaches S^*, a new manufacturing center emerges at $2S^*/3$. (In fact, even if there are some slight differences among firms, the emergence of a manufacturing center increases the size of the market and induces a cascade of movement.) And this new manufacturing center creates, in its turn, a cusp in the market potential and thus locks in its own location.

Now consider a further increase in the population. Again firms have an incentive to establish new plants as soon as the agricultural frontier reaches S^* beyond the existing cities; and so on. Thus over time a system of cities evolves in which the distance from city to city is $2S^*/3$. This distance between cities depends in a sensible way on the underlying economic parameters. From (8.8) we see that cities are further apart the larger is F, which we can loosely interpret as a measure of the importance of economies of scale; cities are closer together the larger is either the transport cost τ or the agricultural population density d.

Notice that this analysis illustrates one of the principles we suggested in chapter 1: In the presence of increasing returns and the multiple equilibria that these returns typically imply, a dynamic story is often a crucial simplifying tool. In this case it offers us an insight into the relationship between underlying parameters and the sizes and locations of cities that would be quite difficult to get out of a purely static analysis.

8.4   Urban Hierarchies

As we pointed out in chapter 3, central-place theory, with its image of a hierarchy of cities, has played a powerful role in the history of spatial economic thought. Yet until recently a central-place hierarchy had never been shown to emerge from a decentralized market process. One contribution of the approach developed here is that it at least offers some illustrative examples of how a hierarchy of central places might develop. Generating such hierarchies remains quite difficult—indeed, even in this heuristic discussion we will be a little vague—which suggests that the idea of a neat hierarchy of central places may be less compelling the harder one looks at it. Still, we can at least get a sense of what a real central-place model might require.

Imagine that there are now two types of manufacturing, 1 and 2, employing fractions of the work force μ_1 and μ_2, respectively. Suppose that the parameters of these industries differ in such a way that the S^*—the distance of the agricultural frontier at which it becomes worthwhile to set up a new plant—is several times as large for 2 as it is for 1. And suppose also that we begin with all manufacturing concentrated in a single city, then allow the population to grow.

What presumably happens is that when new cities form, they initially contain only the "lower level" industry 1. And as the agricultural frontier shifts outward, several "type 1" cities form before it becomes profitable for industry 2 firms to establish new plants.

When it does become profitable for industry 2 to establish new plants, however, it is not only to serve the agricultural population but also to get closer to the workers in these type 1 cities. And the pre-existing type 1 cities generate cusps in the market potential function for industry 2, making it likely (though not certain) that when industry 2 firms establish new plants, they do so in a location that already contains a concentration of type 1 firms. Thus we have a process in which population growth generates a pattern of several small cities containing only industry 1, followed by a larger city that contains both industries, followed by several more small cities, and so on. In short, the economy evolves a central-place hierarchy.

There is no reason to limit this story to two industries. Indeed, in chapter 11, we show an example of a three-level central-place hierarchy.

8.5   Ports and Transportation Hubs

It is obvious to even casual observation that although there may be considerable arbitrariness about urban location, many of the world's largest cities do benefit from some special natural advantage—above all, from the presence of a good harbor or access to a major waterway. We would like to be able to explain in a formal way why ports and transportation hubs tend to become urban centers; this can be done quite easily using the approach developed here.

To see why big cities tend to be ports, consider the stylized representation of the role of a transportation hub shown in figure 8.5. Here we assume that the economy is a line, but with a split in it at the point b, so

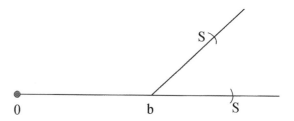

Figure 8.5
Ports and hubs

that there is potential farmland along both the northern and southern "branches" of the economy, and this land is occupied up to points S, equidistant from 0.[3] Let us suppose for the sake of argument that there is already a city at point 0, and ask where the next city appears as the population grows.

It is immediately clear that the junction point b has special advantages over other possible locations. Imagine calculating how the total transportation costs for a firm with an existing factory at 0 would vary as we shifted the location of a second factory steadily to the right. Initially, as we moved eastward from 0 the cost of shipping to farmers to the left would steadily rise, while that of shipping to farmers to the east—which includes both branches—would steadily fall. However, when we passed point b and moved the location along either branch, the cost of shipping to farmers on the other branch would be rising. Thus the junction point offers a cusp in the total transport cost curve, similar to that produced by a city.

The firms' transport costs can be expressed as

$$TC = \tau d \left[\frac{s^2}{4} + \frac{(S-s)^2}{2} + (S-b)\left(|b-s| + \frac{S-b}{2} \right) \right]. \tag{8.9}$$

This adds to the previous expression, (8.6), the transport costs incurred on the sales of the $S - b$ farmers on the new branch. Their average distance from the junction is $(S - b)/2$, and the junction is $|b - s|$ away from the plant. The left- and right-hand derivatives of this are,

$$\text{for } s < b, \quad \frac{\partial TC}{\partial s} = \tau d \left(\frac{3s}{2} + b - 2S \right) \tag{8.10}$$

and

for $s > b$, $\dfrac{\partial TC}{\partial s} = \tau d \left(\dfrac{3s}{2} - b \right)$.   (8.11)

The first of these derivatives is less than the second (unless the junction is on the very edge of the occupied area and so has no land beyond it), implying that the junction point is a cusp. Furthermore, the second (for $s > b$) is positive, establishing that it does not minimize costs to establish the plant to the right of the junction. The first of the derivatives is negative for all $s \le b$ if $b < 4S/5$. This means that if the junction is less than 80 percent of the way to the edge of the occupied area, then the cost-minimizing location is the junction. Only if this condition is violated, so the junction is close to S, will it minimize costs to build at a point other than the junction.

We see, then, that the junction point is a relatively likely place for a new city to become established. Whereas any other potential site for a new city would emerge only for very specific parameters— that is, would be chosen only for a set of measure 0 in parameter space—the junction emerges as the city site for a considerable range of parameters.

8.6 Conclusions

We have offered in this chapter a sort of teaser on the application of our basic approach to the existence and formation of cities. We have used a heuristic approach, one that does not quite work in terms of either maximization or equilibrium, to suggest why cities can exist (firms locate at a cusp in the market potential function created by a concentration of other firms), how they form (a growing and hence spreading agricultural population eventually makes it advantageous for individual producers to establish new city sites, which then become locked in via the creation of a new cusp), why cities may form a hierarchy (differences in transport costs and scale economies among goods can produce cities of different order), and how natural advantages such as the existence of harbors can catalyze the formation of cities (by creating natural cusps in market potential). The next step is to make good on those coming attractions by delivering on the details, beginning with a model of a single, isolated city: von Thünen revisited.

Notes

1. In the models developed in the rest of part III, we actually allow farmers to move, and therefore allow the location of agricultural production to be endogenous. For the purposes of this chapter, however, we leave this piece of realism on one side.

2. We do not yet consider how such a concentration might arise in the first place. One answer was given in the Turing analysis in chapter 6; another answer is given below.

3. We also assume that $2b > S$, so that if a plant is established anywhere beyond b, it minimizes cost for the plant to supply consumers along both branches of the economy.

9 The Monocentric Economy

If you want an example of how a great economist can use stark simplification to get at the essence of an issue, it is hard to beat the opening paragraph of von Thünen's classic *The Isolated State*:

> Imagine a very large town, at the centre of a fertile plain which is crossed by no navigable river or canal. Throughout the plain the soil is capable of cultivation and of the same fertility. Far from the town, the plain turns into an uncultivated wilderness which cuts off all communication between this state and the outside world. There are no other towns on the plain. The central town must therefore supply the rural areas with all manufactured products, and in return it will obtain all its provisions from the surrounding countryside.[1]

From this beginning, von Thünen developed his classic model of the joint determination of land use and land rent. Countless variants of this model have appeared since then.[2] However, for all its variety, this literature simply assumes a crucial feature of the situation: the concentration of manufacturing in the central city. To our knowledge there has never been a version of the von Thünen model that simultaneously derives the existence of the central city and the pattern of land use. In this chapter we aim to remedy that neglect.

There are several reasons for doing this. One, of course, is simply to fill in a gap in the history of thought. But there are other reasons as well. Although our eventual goal is to go beyond monocentric geographies to investigate systems of cities, the monocentric case offers us the opportunity to develop our analytical tools in a relatively simple context. Moreover, we will see in later chapters that it is helpful to think of multicity systems as emerging from an imaginary history in which a growing economy adds cities over time; the starting point for such a history must, obviously, be an economy with only one city.

The underlying structure of this chapter's model is closely related to that of the models in part II. The economy has two sectors, agriculture and manufacturing, where the former provides a single, homogeneous good, and the latter supplies a continuum of differentiated goods. As before, centripetal forces emerge from the interaction among scale economies, transport costs, and factor mobility. The main modification we make is to change the definitions of factors. We now assume that all workers in the economy are homogeneous, can move freely, and can work either in agriculture or in manufacturing. Then to introduce a new immobile factor that creates centrifugal forces, we introduce a second factor, land, used in agricultural production. This allows us to follow the spirit of the von Thünen model by introducing a land market. And for the whole of part III, we work only with models of continuous space.

How do we analyze location in continuous space? As we will see, the key concept is that of a *market potential function*, similar in spirit to though different in detail from those considered by Harris (1954) and other pioneers.

The main question we ask in this chapter is when, if ever, a von Thünen–type geography, in which all manufactured goods are produced in a single city, is in fact an equilibrium. We will see that given our usual restrictions on parameters, a monocentric geography is sustainable only if the population is less than some critical value. This insight serves as the basis for our treatment of multiple-city systems in later chapters.[3]

9.1 The Model

We consider a long, narrow economy—effectively one-dimensional—that stretches sufficiently far that we can disregard boundary conditions. Along this line lies land of homogeneous quality, with one unit of land per unit distance. The economy is also endowed with a labor force of N workers, who in this model (unlike the models of part II) are free to choose both the location and the sector in which they work. The economy's consumers consist of these workers plus a class of landlords, who for simplicity are assumed to live on their landholdings; that is, land rents are consumed where they are accrued.[4] Consumers have the same tastes we assumed in chapter 4.

The agricultural good is produced using both factors, with fixed proportions: c^A units of labor and one unit of land are required to produce one unit of output. Manufactures production requires only labor; the technology of manufactures production is the same as in part II. Finally, transport costs are the same as in chapter 6: Goods melt away at a constant proportional rate per unit distance, so that if one unit of A [M] is shipped a distance d, only $\exp(-\tau^A d)$ [$\exp(-\tau^M d)$] units actually arrive.

This model generates centrifugal and centripetal forces in much the same way that these forces arose in the models of chapters 5–7. Because agricultural production requires both land and labor, agricultural workers must be spread out along the line; this creates an incentive to disperse manufacturing as well, both to be close to the rural market and to have access to cheaper agricultural products. On the other hand, the incentive to locate close to the market provided by other manufacturing workers (backward linkage) and the supply of manufactured goods those workers produce (forward linkage), other things being the same, makes the real income of manufacturing workers higher when they are close to other manufacturing workers. The tension between these forces for and against agglomeration drives our results.

We can immediately guess that when manufactures are sufficiently differentiated from each other—and when the population of workers is not too large—centripetal forces are strong enough to outweigh the centrifugal force of dispersed farmers, allowing the agglomeration of all manufactures production in a single city. That is, the economy's geography can be *monocentric*. But if manufactures are close substitutes and/or the population is sufficiently large (and hence the agricultural hinterland of a monocentric economy would extend very far from the central city), an individual producer would have an incentive to locate far away from the city. In that case, a monocentric structure would not be sustainable, and additional cities would have to emerge. To show that these guesses are correct, we proceed in two steps. First we posit a monocentric geography and calculate the spatial distribution of activity and prices in such a von Thünen economy. Then we test that geography by asking whether any individual manufacturing firm would want to move away from the assumed agglomeration.

Before we begin, a few notational points. We continue to normalize the units in which output and the number of varieties are measured, as we did in chapter 4. We do not, however, try to normalize the units in which labor is measured, because we are examining the effects of changes in the size of the labor force in any case. Also, as in chapter 6, we slightly modify our notation to take account of the continuousness of the assumed space: Instead of denoting location with subscripts—for example, denoting the wage rate at r as w_r^M—we think of all variables as functions of continuous location, and thus write $w^M(r)$, where r is a position along the line.

9.2 The von Thünen Economy

Consider the von Thünen spatial configuration depicted in figure 9.1. In this figure, the production of all manufactures is assumed to take place in a single city; we relabel locations if necessary so as to make that urban site location 0. The agricultural area extends from $-f$ to f, where f represents the (endogenous) agricultural frontier. The city exports manufactures to its agricultural hinterland and imports agricultural goods in return. For the moment, let us simply assume that this is the economy's spatial structure and use that assumption to determine equilibrium goods prices, factor prices, and land use.

Let $p^A \equiv p^A(0)$ be the price of the agricultural good at the city. Each location in the agricultural hinterland produces one unit of agricultural output and exports to the city the surplus over local consumption. Agricultural transport costs mean that farmers receive a lower price the farther they are from the city:

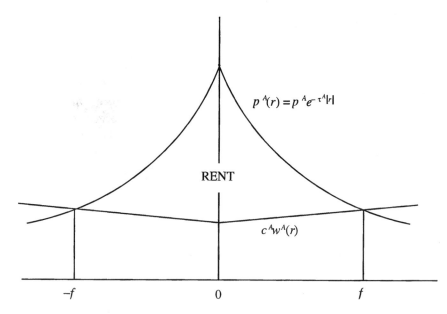

$$p^A(r) = p^A e^{-\tau^A |r|}$$

RENT

$$c^A w^A(r)$$

$-f$ 0 f

Figure 9.1
Monocentric spatial structure

$$p^A(r) = p^A e^{-\tau^A |r|}.$$ (9.1)

Let $R(r)$ and $w^A(r)$ be the land rent and wage rate for agricultural workers at location r. Rent is the value of output from each unit of land minus the wage bill for the c^A workers needed to farm that land:

$$R(r) = p^A(r) - c^A w^A(r) = p^A e^{-\tau^A |r|} - c^A w^A(r).$$

Land rents are 0 at the edge of cultivation, distance f from the city, so

$$w^A(f) = \frac{p^A e^{-\tau^A f}}{c^A}.$$ (9.2)

Both sectors generate income. In the city there are L^M manufacturing workers, so income there is the manufacturing wage bill, $w^M L^M$. Elsewhere income is the value of agricultural output, which is simply $p^A(r)$.

Turning to manufacturing, we choose the price of manufactures in the central location as the numeraire, implying that manufacturing wages in the city are also unity, by equation (4.30):

$$p^M(0) = w^M(0) = 1.$$ (9.3)

The price index $G(r)$ takes a very simple form because of the assumption that manufacturing occurs only at the central location. Using the definition of $G(r)$ from chapter 4 (equation (4.34)), we have

$$G(r) = \left(\frac{L^M}{\mu}\right)^{1/(1-\sigma)} e^{\tau^M |r|}.$$ (9.4)

The existence of manufacturing trade costs means that this index is increasing as we move to locations farther from the center. We let $G \equiv G(0)$ denote the price index at the center.

We now have all the information we need to determine equilibrium (again, simply assuming for the moment that manufacturing is concentrated in the city). We can think of equilibrium as determined by two conditions: market clearing in the market for agricultural output, and equality of real wages between farmers and workers. Let us consider these in turn.

First, income earned in the city is $w^M L^M$; a share $1 - \mu$ of that income is spent on A, so food consumption in the city will be $D^A = (1 - \mu)w^M L^M / p^A$. Meanwhile, each rural location spends a share $1 - \mu$ of its own income on food, leaving μ units to be shipped to the city. Only fraction $e^{-\tau^A |s|}$ of the units shipped from location s arrive at the city, so the supply of food to the city is $S^A = 2\mu \int_0^f e^{-\tau^A|s|}ds$. But the urban labor force is the total labor force less the number of farmers, $L^M = N - 2c^A f$, and the urban wage is unity, $w^M = 1$, so we can summarize the market-clearing condition for agriculture as a relationship between the frontier distance and the price of food:

$$p^A = \frac{(1-\mu)(N - 2c^A f)}{2\mu \int_0^f e^{-\tau^A|s|}ds}. \tag{9.5}$$

Equation (9.2) gives us the nominal wage received by the frontier farmer. His real wage, however, is

$$\omega^A(f) = w^A(f)G(f)^{-\mu}p^A(f)^{-(1-\mu)} = \frac{1}{c^A}(p^A)^\mu G^{-\mu}e^{-\mu(\tau^M+\tau^A)f}, \tag{9.6}$$

whereas the real wage of a worker in the city is

$$\omega^M = G^{-\mu}(p^A)^{\mu-1}. \tag{9.7}$$

Thus equality of real wages requires that

$$p^A = c^A e^{\mu(\tau^A+\tau^M)f}. \tag{9.8}$$

Figure 9.2 shows how the market-clearing condition (9.5) and the equal-real-wage condition (9.8) determine simultaneously the price of A and the size of the agricultural hinterland, f. It is immediately apparent that an increase in the population requires, other things equal, a rise in p^A to clear the market; as N increases, the market-clearing curve shifts up, and in equilibrium the frontier moves out.

Given relative prices and the allocation of labor between manufacturing and agriculture, everything else can be determined. Of particular interest is the real wage rate (which in equilibrium is common to all workers). By successive substitutions into the manufacturing real-wage equation (9.7), we can express that real wage as a function of the frontier distance f, which is itself monotonically related to the population size N:

$$\omega \equiv \omega^M(0) = \left[\frac{2(1 - e^{-\tau^A f})}{(1 - \mu)\tau^A}\right]^{\mu/(\sigma-1)} [c^A e^{\mu(\tau^A+\tau^M)f}]^{\mu\sigma/(\sigma-1)-1}. \tag{9.9}$$

This relationship is illustrated in figure 9.3, in which curves are constructed for several different values of $\rho(= (\sigma - 1)/\sigma)$ while holding

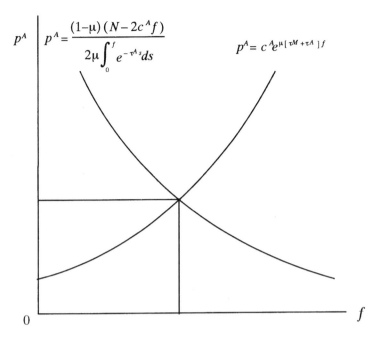

Figure 9.2
Determination of the equilibrium p^A and f

μ constant at 0.5. The main features of these curves can be established by differentiating (9.9) with respect to f to find that

$$\frac{d\omega}{df} = C\omega \left\{ \frac{\mu - \rho}{1 - \rho} + \frac{\tau^A}{\tau^A + \tau^M} \frac{e^{-\tau^A f}}{1 - e^{-\tau^A f}} \right\}, \tag{9.10}$$

where C is a positive constant.

This tells us several things. First, if the economy does not obey the no-black-hole condition that $\rho > \mu$, then $d\omega/df$ is always positive, and hence real wages are always increasing in population size. Suppose, however, that we do impose the no-black-hole condition. Then at low values of f, the slope $d\omega/df$ is unambiguously positive, whereas at high levels it becomes negative. So the relationship between population size and real wages is an inverted U. (The curves in figure 9.3 bear a more than coincidental resemblance to that in figure 2.2; in fact, we can view this analysis as one way to justify Henderson's assumption of an inverted-U relationship between city size and the utility of city residents. Notice, however, that the limit to the city size has been obtained

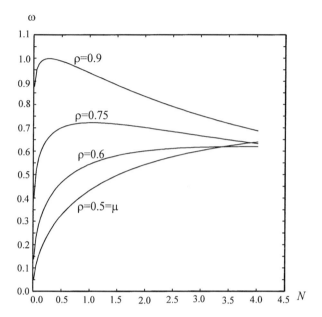

Figure 9.3
Effect of N and ρ on real wages ω

here in the absence of intra-urban commuting and land use, the standard explanation given to bound the city.) When the population increases from a low initial level, the benefits of a larger manufacturing sector dominate; but as the population continues to increase, the disadvantages of an ever more distant agricultural frontier eventually prevail. The population size that maximizes real wages behaves as one might expect: It is greater when manufactures are more differentiated; when the share of manufactures in preferences, μ, is larger; and when transport costs in both sectors are lower.

We have now set out a version of the classic von Thünen model. Our next step is to go beyond the classic treatment and justify the existence of the city itself.

9.3   The Market Potential Function

So far, we have simply assumed that manufacturing production takes place exclusively in the city. To claim, however, that this monocentric configuration is an equilibrium, we must make sure that no firm has an incentive to defect from the city. This we can do in the usual way by looking at the wages that would be paid to manufacturing workers by a zero-profit firm in some location other than the city. The configuration is sustainable if no location can offer a higher real wage than the city. It actually turns out to be convenient to work with a monotonic transformation of the potential real wage; we define the (*market*) *potential function* of manufacturing as

$$\Omega(r) \equiv \frac{\omega^M(r)^\sigma}{\omega^A(r)^\sigma}, \tag{9.11}$$

where $\omega^A(r)$ is the real wage rate of agricultural workers currently prevailing at each r (which is also the real wage of manufacturing workers at the central city), and $\omega^M(r) \equiv w^M(r)G(r)^{-\mu}p^A(r)^{-(1-\mu)}$ is the maximum real wage rate that zero-profit manufacturing firms could offer at each r.[5] Because $\omega^A(r) = \omega^M(0)$, potential is unity in the city. A monocentric geography is sustainable if and only if

$$\Omega(r) \le 1 \quad \text{for all } r. \tag{9.12}$$

that is, there is no alternative location at which zero-profit firms could offer more than workers are currently making.

To derive the potential function, we can first rewrite it as

$$\Omega(r) = \frac{\omega^M(r)^\sigma}{\omega^A(r)^\sigma} = \frac{w^M(r)^\sigma}{w^A(r)^\sigma} = w^M(r)^\sigma e^{\sigma[(1-\mu)\tau^A - \mu\tau^M]|r|} \tag{9.13}$$

This says that, at each location, the ratio of real wages equals the ratio of nominal wages, and uses the fact that agricultural nominal wages are $w^A(r) = e^{[\mu\tau^M - (1-\mu)\tau^A]r}$.[6] We now proceed in much the same way that we did in developing the core-periphery model in chapter 5. We need to know the manufacturing wage equation, and this is just the continuous-space version of (4.35):

$$w^M(r) = \left(Y(0)e^{-(\sigma-1)\tau^M|r|}G(0)^{\sigma-1} + \int_{-f}^{f} Y(s)e^{-(\sigma-1)\tau^M|r-s|}G(s)^{\sigma-1}ds \right)^{1/\sigma}. \tag{9.14}$$

To evaluate this, we need the manufacturing price index and the spatial distribution of income. We already have the price index in (9.4). As for income, in the city there are L^M manufacturing workers, so income is the manufacturing wage bill, $w^M L^M$. Elsewhere income is the value of agricultural output, which is simply $p^A(r)$. So

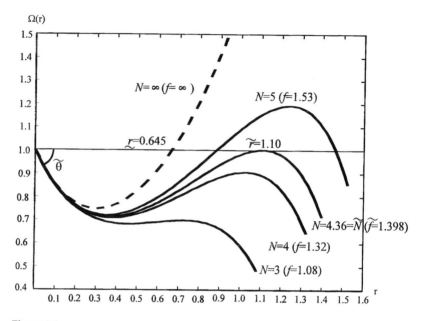

Figure 9.4
Potential curves for the monocentric system under various values of N

if $r = 0$, $Y(r) = w^M(r)L^M$,

and   (9.15)

if $r \neq 0$, $Y(r) = p^A(r) = p^A e^{-\tau^A|r|}$.

Using these components, we have all the information needed to derive the potential function.

Before we obtain a closed-form expression for the potential function, let us illustrate its structure by means of numerical simulation. Figure 9.4 illustrates $\Omega(r)$ for a constant set of parameters but several different population sizes. (We show only the curve for locations to the right of the city; it is, of course, symmetric for locations to the left.)[7] As we have argued and the figure illustrates, $\Omega(0)$ must equal 1. Moving away from the city, we see that market potential at first falls, but may then increase. This reflects the tension between the forward and backward linkages, on one side, which tend to make locations close to the city attractive, and the incentive to choose a location protected by distance from competing firms, on the other.

As long as N is sufficiently low, the potential takes on values less than unity at all locations other than the city. When this is true, a monocentric geography is an equilibrium: At no location could firms break even and pay a real wage as large as the wage that workers are already receiving. Increasing the population, however, shifts the market potential curve upward. At a *critical population*, $\tilde{N}$, the potential curve first touches unity at a location other than the existing city. We call this point $\tilde{r}$, the *critical distance* of the manufacturing sector. It is now profitable for a manufacturing firm to deviate, destroying the monocentric structure.

Once the monocentric structure is destroyed, some other structure must take its place. We postpone analysis of this transition, however, to the following chapter. Instead, let us now turn to looking at the potential curve in more detail.

9.4 The Potential Function and Sustainability of a City

Our next step is to investigate the potential function analytically. To do so, we need to evaluate the integral in the wage equation. This requires that we divide the integral into three parts, so the wage equation (9.14) becomes,

$$[w^M(r)]^\sigma = Y(0)e^{-(\sigma-1)\tau M r}G(0)^{\sigma-1} + \int_{-f}^{0} Y(s)e^{-(\sigma-1)\tau M(r-s)}G(s)^{\sigma-1}ds$$

$$+ \int_0^r Y(s)e^{-(\sigma-1)\tau M(r-s)}G(s)^{\sigma-1}ds \qquad (9.16)$$

$$+ \int_r^f Y(s)e^{-(\sigma-1)\tau M(s-r)}G(s)^{\sigma-1}ds.$$

Each part of this can be simplified using the definitions of $Y(r)$ and $G(r)$ [equations (9.15) and (9.4)] and then the equilibrium conditions from section 9.2 to eliminate p^A and L^M. We also simplify equations by exploiting the economy's symmetry to define integrals only over locations to the right of the city. Denoting the four parts on the right-hand side of (9.16) by A, B, C, and D, we can derive:

$$A = \mu e^{-(\sigma-1)\tau M r}, \qquad (9.17)$$

$$B = \frac{\mu p^A}{L^M} e^{-(\sigma-1)\tau M r} \int_{-f}^{0} e^{\tau A s}ds = \frac{1-\mu}{2}e^{-(\sigma-1)\tau M r}, \qquad (9.18)$$

$$C = \frac{\mu p^A}{L^M} e^{-(\sigma-1)\tau^M r} \int_0^r e^{[-\tau^A + 2(\sigma-1)\tau^M]s} ds$$

$$= \left(\frac{1-\mu}{2}\right) \frac{e^{-(\sigma-1)\tau^M r} \int_0^r e^{[-\tau^A + 2(\sigma-1)\tau^M]s} ds}{\int_0^f e^{-\tau^A s} ds} \qquad (9.19)$$

$$D = \frac{\mu p^A}{L^M} e^{(\sigma-1)\tau^M r} \int_r^f e^{-\tau^A s} ds = \left(\frac{1-\mu}{2}\right) \frac{e^{(\sigma-1)\tau^M r} \int_r^f e^{-\tau^A s} ds}{\int_0^f e^{-\tau^A s} ds}. \qquad (9.20)$$

Although these are individually very complex, we find that when we add the pieces back together we obtain:

$$[w^M(r)]^\sigma = A + B + C + D$$

$$= \left(\frac{1-\mu}{2}\right) e^{(\sigma-1)\tau^M r} \Psi(r, f) + \left(\frac{1+\mu}{2}\right) e^{-(\sigma-1)\tau^M r}, \qquad (9.21)$$

where the function $\Psi(r, f)$ takes the form

$$\Psi(r, f) \equiv 1 - \frac{\int_0^r e^{-\tau^A s} [1 - e^{-2(\sigma-1)\tau^M(r-s)}] ds}{\int_0^f e^{-\tau^A s} ds}. \qquad (9.22)$$

The function $\Psi(r, f)$ is increasing in f and lies between 0 and 1, as can be seen by noting that $r \le f$, and

$$1 > 1 - e^{-2(\sigma-1)\tau^M(r-s)} > 0 \qquad (9.23)$$

for $s \le r$.

We can now write the complete potential function (9.13) as

$$\Omega(r) = e^{\sigma[(1-\mu)\tau^A - \mu\tau^M]r} \left[\left(\frac{1+\mu}{2}\right) e^{-(\sigma-1)\tau^M r} + \Psi(r, f) \left(\frac{1-\mu}{2}\right) e^{(\sigma-1)\tau^M r} \right]. \qquad (9.24)$$

This bears a striking resemblance to the conditions we derived for the sustainability of a core-periphery geography in earlier chapters (i.e., (5.16) and (7.13)), to which it is clearly analogous. The first term on the right-hand side captures the fact that a firm setting up at location r has to compensate workers for the cost-of-living difference between r and the center: a higher price of manufactures and lower cost of agriculture. The term $(1 + \mu)/2$ combines the share of the economy's income at the city, μ, and to the west of it, $(1 - \mu)/2$. The first term inside the square brackets therefore measures the disadvantage that a firm at location r has when selling in the large central market and at locations to its west. The second term inside the brackets captures sales to the east of the city, so it must be adjusted according to where r is located in this eastern half, and this adjustment is made by the expression $\Psi(r, f)$.

Given this equation for the potential, what can be said about its properties? First, increases in population shift the potential curve upward. We have already seen that f is increasing in N. The variable f enters the potential only through the denominator of $\Psi(r, f)$, and hence $\Omega(r)$ is increasing in f at every $r \neq 0$. This is illustrated by the shifts in the potential function shown in figure 9.4.

Second, how does the potential depend on r, the location of a deviating firm? It is easy to establish its slope at the city, $r = 0$, at which point $\Omega(0) = \Psi(0, f) = 1$. We can derive

$$\frac{d\Omega(0)}{dr} = \sigma[(1 - \mu)\tau^A - (1 + \rho)\mu\tau^M]. \tag{9.25}$$

If this is negative, then the gradient of the potential function in the neighborhood of the city is as illustrated in figure 9.4. That is, the condition gives a strictly negative slope to the right of the city (and strictly positive to the left), so that the potential function has a cusp at the city. (We have already seen the intuition for this cusp in chapter 8.)

If (9.25) is positive, a monocentric structure can never be sustainable: Locations close to the city are able to pay higher wages and attract firms and workers. This is the case if μ is small, so that the manufacturing employment and income concentrated at the city is small; if ρ is small, so that the demand elasticity is low and the loss of sales from being far away from the city is therefore relatively low, and/or if τ^A is large compared to τ^M—as we saw in chapter 7—agricultural trade costs work against agglomeration.

This establishes the condition under which the potential slopes down at the city, a necessary condition for a monocentric geography to be possible. And of course, if N is very small, so that f is close to 0, it is also sufficient: The narrow agricultural hinterland has $\Omega(r) < 1$. Let us

Table 9.1
Sustainability of a monocentric equilibrium

$(1 - \mu)\tau^A - (1 + \rho)\mu\tau^M > 0$	$(1 - \mu)\tau^A - (1 + \rho)\mu\tau^M < 0$	
	$\mu \geq \rho$	$\mu < \rho$
Never	Always	For small N

now assume that this condition holds and see what happens at higher values of N and hence f.

This is most readily done by looking at the behavior of $\Omega(r)$ as N and hence f tend to infinity. Because the market potential $\Omega(r)$ increases with f, this *limiting curve* gives the upper limit of all potential curves, and we denote it $\overline{\Omega}(r)$. By evaluating $\Psi(r, \infty)$ (see appendix 9.2) and using the function for the potential, (9.24), we obtain

$$\overline{\Omega}(r) = Ke^{\sigma(\rho-\mu)(\tau^A+\tau^M)r} + (1 - K)e^{-[(1-\mu)(\sigma-1)\tau^M-\Omega_r(0)]r},\tag{9.26}$$

where K is a constant given by

$$K = \frac{(1 - \mu)\rho\tau^M}{(1 - \mu)\rho\tau^M + (\rho - \mu)(\tau^A + \tau^M) - \Omega_r(0)/\sigma},\tag{9.27}$$

and $\Omega_r(0)$ is the derivative given in equation (9.25). This function is always positive (as the potential function must always be, although it is not apparent from writing it this way) and takes value unity at $r = 0$. Because we are looking just at the case where $\Omega_r(0) < 0$, the function slopes downward at the origin. And because it is linear in two exponential functions in r, it has at most one turning point, implying that $\overline{\Omega}(r)$ attains value greater than unity at some value of r if and only if it is greater than unity as $r \to \infty$. By inspection of (9.26), the second exponential term goes to 0 as $r \to \infty$, so the first exponential term— and hence the no-black-hole condition—determines limiting behavior. If the no-black-hole condition is satisfied, $\rho > \mu$, then K is positive, and hence $\overline{\Omega}(r) > 1$ for sufficiently large r. The monocentric configuration therefore becomes unsustainable. But if the no-black-hole condition does not hold, then $\overline{\Omega}(r)$ is decreasing in r,[8] meaning that the monocentric structure is always sustainable: Manufacturing cannot escape from the black hole of the existing city, however large the population and agricultural area become.

Pulling together these results, we can summarize the possibilities as in table 9.1. In the left-hand column of the table, a monocentric configuration is never an equilibrium. This is the first case we looked at, in which, as we have seen, the potential function increases as we move away from the city, meaning that firms certainly move out of the city.

In the two right-hand columns, the potential function decreases as we move away from the city, and as N increases the sustainability of the monocentric configuration depends on the no-black-hole condition. If this condition is violated, $\mu \geq \rho$, then the monocentric configuration is always an equilibrium. The no-black-hole condition has already occurred repeatedly in this book: It is the condition for avoiding the situation in which an increase in the number of workers raises their real wage even given fixed expenditure (chapter 4), in which a core-periphery pattern necessarily emerges with or without transport costs on agriculture (chapters 5 and 7), in which the preferred frequency of the racetrack economy is 0 (chapter 6), and for that matter in which real wages in a monocentric economy are strictly increasing in population (section 9.2). In short, it is the case in which economies of agglomeration are so large that nothing can counter them.

Finally, consider the most interesting case given in the right-hand column of the table, in which the no-black-hole condition does hold. In this case, a monocentric geography is an equilibrium when f (which is to say N) is sufficiently small. Now, however, growth in this population eventually undermines that equilibrium, by pushing the agricultural frontier out far enough to make it profitable for firms to defect from the central city to serve this ever more remote rural market. This is the case illustrated in figure 9.4. There is a critical population, $\tilde{N}$, at which the potential curve first touches unity at a location other than the existing city, and we call this location, $\tilde{r}$, the critical distance.

What do we know about the determinants of the critical population and the critical distance? First, notice that as long as $(1 - \mu)\tau^A - (1 + \rho)\mu\tau^M$ is negative, it is never profitable to establish a manufacturing operation in the immediate vicinity of the existing city, so $\tilde{r} > 0$. That is, the city always casts an *agglomeration shadow* in its local hinterland. This shadow also has the effect of locking in the city's location: The city cannot drift to the left or right, because locations a bit to either side are strictly inferior to the city itself. Second, it is possible to show that the higher are agricultural transport costs, τ^A, the smaller are the values of both $\tilde{N}$ and $\tilde{r}$; as we saw in chapter 7, agricultural transport costs make it more difficult to support a concentration of activity.

These critical values tell us when and where it first becomes profitable to establish manufacturing production outside the existing city. In the next chapter we turn to looking in detail at the dynamics of city formation.

Appendix 9.1: On the Definition of the Market Potential Function

To see the connection between the market potential function (9.11) and the concept of market potential that has been widely used in the traditional economic geography, it is useful to rewrite (9.11) in another form. That is, first notice that if a firm locates at r and charges any mill price, p, then, using (4.17) in the present context, the firm's total sales are given by

$$q(r; p) = \mu Y(0)p^{-\sigma}e^{-(\sigma-1)\tau^M|r|}G(0)^{\sigma-1}$$
$$+ \int_{-f}^{f} \mu Y(s)p^{-\sigma}e^{-(\sigma-1)\tau^M|r-s|}G(s)^{\sigma-1}ds, \tag{9A.1}$$

and hence

$$q(r; p)p^{\sigma} = \varphi(r), \tag{9A.2}$$

where

$$\varphi(r) \equiv \mu Y(0)e^{-(\sigma-1)\tau^M|r|}G(0)^{\sigma-1} + \int_{-f}^{f} \mu Y(s)e^{-(\sigma-1)\tau^M|r-s|}G(s)^{\sigma-1}ds, \tag{9A.3}$$

which is a constant that the firm takes as given. Notice that relation (9A.2) holds under any value of p. In particular, when the firm faces the prevailing agricultural wage $w^A(r)$ there, then $p = w^A(r)$, by (4.30), and hence $q(r; w^A(r))[w^A(r)]^{\sigma} = \varphi(r)$. If the firm faces the zero-profit wage rate, $w^M(r)$, then $p = w^M(r)$ and $q(r; w^M(r)) = q^*$ by definition, and hence $q^*[w^M(r)]^{\sigma} = \varphi(r)$, where $q^* \equiv \mu$ is the zero-profit output level given by (4.33). Therefore, it follows that

$$\frac{q(r; w^A(r))}{q^*} = \frac{[w^M(r)]^{\sigma}}{[w^A(r)]^{\sigma}} = \frac{[\omega^M(r)]^{\sigma}}{[\omega^A(r)]^{\sigma}}, \tag{9A.4}$$

where the last equality holds by the definition of real wage. Thus, by (9.11), (9A.2), and (9A.3), we can obtain the following relation:

$$\Omega(r) = \frac{\omega^M(r)^\sigma}{\omega^A(r)^\sigma} = \frac{q(r; w^A(r))}{q^*}$$

$$= [w^A(r)]^{-\sigma} \left\{ Y(0)e^{-(\sigma-1)\tau^M|r|}G(0)^{\sigma-1} \right. \tag{9A.5}$$

$$\left. + \int_{-f}^{f} Y(s)e^{-(\sigma-1)\tau^M|r-s|}G(s)^{\sigma-1}ds \right\},$$

which represents the total sales of the firm (normalized by the zero-profit output q^*) that can be achieved at each location r when it pays the prevailing agricultural wage rate there.

Recall that in traditional economic geography, the market potential at each location r has been defined by equation (3.8). Equation (9A.5) is apparently a generalization of (3.8), where the former considers two additional factors of firms' competitiveness, that is, the adverse effect of the wage rate at the production site (expressed by the term $[w^A(r)]^{-\sigma}$) and the *mildness* of competition at each market (expressed by $G(s)^{\sigma-1}$). (Notice that a higher $G(s)$ implies weaker competition from other firms in market s.)

Appendix 9.2: The Limit Market Potential Function

To derive (9.26), first let $f \to \infty$ in (9.22) and integrate terms to give

$$\Psi(r, \infty) = e^{-\tau^A r} \left[\frac{2(\sigma - 1)\tau^M - \tau^A e^{-[2(\sigma-1)\tau^M - \tau^A]r}}{2(\sigma - 1)\tau^M - \tau^A} \right]. \tag{9A.6}$$

Second, notice that using (9.25) we can express the term $2(\sigma - 1)\tau^M - \tau^A$ as

$$2(\sigma - 1)\tau^M - \tau^A = (1 - \mu)(\sigma - 1)\tau^M$$

$$+ \sigma(\rho - \mu)(\tau^A + \tau^M) - \Omega_r(0) \tag{9A.7}$$

$$= \sigma[(1 - \mu)\rho\tau^M + (\rho - \mu)(\tau^A + \tau^M) - \Omega_r(0)/\sigma].$$

Using these in (9.24) gives (9.26).

Notes

1. This quotation is from the English translation of von Thünen 1826 by Wartenberg (1966, p. 7).

2. Recent general equilibrium versions include Samuelson 1983 and Nerlove and Sadka 1991.

3. For comparative static analyses of the monocentric economy, refer to section 5 of Fujita and Krugman 1995, on which the present chapter is based.

4. In a general equilibrium model with land, the question of where land rents are spent is a nuisance issue that unfortunately must be dealt with one way or another.

5. Refer to appendix 9.1 for the relation between the function (9.11) and the concept of market potential in the traditional economic geography.

6. In the city, $w^A(0) = 1$, and to hold the real wage the same throughout the agricultural hinterland, the nominal wage must move inversely to the cost-of-living index, a function of $p^A(r)$ and $G(r)$, equations (9.1) and (9.4), respectively.

7. Figure 9.4 is constructed using the following set of parameters: $\rho = 0.75$ (i.e., $\sigma = 4$), $\mu = 0.5$, $\tau^A = 0.8$, $\tau^M = 1$, and $c^A = 0.5$.

8. Since $\Omega_r(0) < 0$, if $\rho < \mu$, then both exponential terms in (9.26) go to 0 as $r \to \infty$, implying that $\overline{\Omega}(r)$ must be decreasing in all r (for otherwise it would have more than one turning point). If $\rho = \mu$, then $0 < K < 1$, and $\overline{\Omega}(r) = K + (1 - K)\exp-[(1 - \mu)(\sigma - 1)\tau^M - \Omega_r(0)]r$, which is decreasing in all $r > 0$.

10   The Emergence of New Cities

In chapter 9 we saw how a von Thünen–type spatial pattern, with an isolated city surrounded by an agricultural hinterland, could sustain itself once somehow established. But how might a city emerge, and how do we think about the structure of an economy with multiple cities? In this chapter we offer an approach that answers these questions jointly. This jointness might not seem necessary: Why should the analysis of multiple-city economies proceed in tandem with an analysis of the process of city formation? But combining the two questions substantially simplifies our analysis.

On one side, to discuss the structure of multiple-city economies in general is to risk becoming lost in an endlessly complex taxonomy. There are very many equilibria that could be sustained once established; only by telling some kind of story about which kinds of equilibria are, in fact, likely to become established can we reduce the taxonomy to manageable size. On the other side, although it is possible to imagine a discussion of city formation starting from various initial conditions—for example, from the hypothetical flat earth that we use elsewhere in this book—we find it most natural to think of new cities as emerging as an economy that already has an urban structure grows over time. This means, however, that our discussion of city formation must necessarily take place in a model of a multiple-city system.

In this chapter, then, we take the basic approach set out in chapter 9 and add two new ingredients: gradual population growth over time and a dynamic adjustment process for the location of urban manufacturing. The basic idea is simple. In chapter 9 we saw that (given certain restrictions on the parameters) a monocentric system is a possible equilibrium only when the economy's population is less than some critical value. Presumably, then, as the population grows beyond that critical value new cities emerge; when it grows beyond a further critical value, still more will emerge; and so on. To examine how that process might work, we begin this chapter by introducing an "urban" version of our usual evolutionary adjustment dynamics. We then turn to the simplest case of city formation: the transition that occurs when the population of a monocentric city system exceeds its critical value. Finally, we describe the multiple-city pattern that emerges as the population continues to grow.

10.1 Adjustment Dynamics and the Stability of the Spatial System

We imagine an economy with two sources of change over time. First, "extrinsic" dynamics arise from a steady process of population growth, which we regard as exogenous. Second, "intrinsic" dynamics come into play as workers move toward locations that offer higher wages, and by so doing in turn alter the wages offered at different locations. In general we should think of these sources of change as operating simultaneously. For the sake of simplicity, however, we instead imagine that the extrinsic change in the economy moves very slowly compared with the intrinsic adjustment process. Or to be a bit less cryptic: We think of this economy as evolving by a sort of two-step process. We start from an equilibrium spatial configuration, then increase the population a bit and hold it there; let the economy settle into a new equilibrium; then repeat.

The dynamic process we use for the adjustment of urban population is similar to that we used earlier. Let there be K city sites (existing or new—we will discuss their locations later), with the population of the kth site at a particular date being L_k, ($k = 1, 2, \ldots, K$).[1] The total number of these manufacturing workers (city residents) plus agricultural workers L^A sums to the population, N, $\Sigma_k L_k + L^A = N$. Real wages in the kth city are $\omega_k \equiv \omega_k^M$, and the average real wage in the economy is $\overline{\omega} \equiv \{L^A \omega^A + \Sigma_k L_k \omega_k\}/N$, where ω^A is the real wage common to all agricultural workers. We assume that each city's population growth is proportional to the difference between its real wage and the average in the economy as a whole,

$$\dot{L}_k = L_k(\omega_k - \overline{\omega}), \quad k = 1, 2, \ldots, K. \tag{10.1}$$

Equation (10.1) gives the dynamics of manufacturing worker migration, but what of agricultural workers? In general, we ought to think of the dynamic process of location adjustment following each population increment as involving gradual movement of all workers, both manufacturing and agricultural. To do so would, however, raise mathematical and computational difficulties we prefer not to deal with. So instead we imagine that the agricultural population moves instantaneously to equalize agricultural real wages, this giving ω^A, the real wage common to all agricultural workers.

Our choice of which hypothetical new cities to include in the system may seem arbitrary. We need not agonize over this question, however, because there are never more than a few interesting potential new cities to consider.

To identify these potential new cities, we turn to the market potential function and back to the analysis of chapter 9. The market potential $\Omega(r)$ is defined exactly as in chapter 9, so

$$\Omega(r) \equiv \frac{\omega^M(r)^\sigma}{\omega^A(r)^\sigma}. \tag{10.2}$$

Consider an urban system in which one or more cities already exist. The real wages of all agricultural workers and of all manufacturing workers in existing cities must be the same, so if a site k is occupied as a city, then $\Omega(r_k) = 1$. If this system is in spatial equilibrium, then at all other locations $r \neq r_k$, $\Omega(r) \leq 1$, so there is no other location to which a small group of workers could move and obtain higher real wages: The real wage these locations offer are less than that in agriculture or in existing cities.

But suppose now that population growth has just pushed the potential curve up to the point where it lies slightly above 1 in some locations. Then a small group of workers may gain higher wages by moving to these locations. In short, we can expect new cities to emerge when and where the market potential curve humps itself above 1.

To see how this works, let us look at what happens in the simplest case: when the population of a monocentric system grows to the point at which monocentricity is no longer sustainable. In the discussion below we always assume, for obvious reasons, that the parameters of the economy satisfy the conditions

(a) $(1 - \mu)\tau^A - (1 + \rho)\mu\tau^M < 0$,   and (b) $\mu < \rho$, $\qquad$ (10.3)

which correspond to the right-hand column of table 9.1.

10.2 From One City to Three

10.2.1 The Location of New Cities

Recall from section 9.3 that when N reaches $\tilde{N}$, the potential curve just hits 1 at the critical distance $\tilde{r}$, as illustrated in figure 9.4. This implies that even in the absence of any agglomeration there, this location has become as attractive as the existing city for the production of manufactures. And this in turn suggests that the relocation of even an arbitrarily small number of manufacturing firms from the existing city to this critical location triggers a positive feedback mechanism of spatial agglomeration, leading to the growth of a new city at that point—or rather points, because market potential at $-\tilde{r}$ is exactly the same as market potential at $\tilde{r}$. It is actually most natural to suppose that when N reaches its critical value, two new cities emerge, at $\tilde{r}$ and $-\tilde{r}$ respectively.

This needs a bit of discussion. Under the dynamics that we have specified, the simultaneous development of cities at both $\tilde{r}$ and $-\tilde{r}$ may quite possibly be unstable: If one of these cities gets marginally more population than the other, then it gets further ahead, so our dynamics might lead us from one city to two, or, more generally, through asymmetric transitions. In appendix 10.2 we consider explicitly the dynamics of a general three-city case and show that asymmetric transitions are quite possible. However, here we restrict ourselves to the case where the transition is from one city to three, that is, where two equal-sized "flankers" emerge on either side of the original center.

This restriction may be given two justifications. First, it is far simpler than the general three-city case, yet still gets at the essential economic insights. Second, although an asymmetric pattern of city emergence is literally possible given our dynamics, it produces peculiar movements in the agricultural population. Suppose that a new city emerges on only one side, say the east, of the initial city. The new two-city economy moves to an equilibrium in which the two cities are of equal size. But to support these two cities, the center of gravity of the agricultural population must suddenly shift, with farmers abandoning large amounts of land in the west and bringing large amounts in the east under cultivation. We have not specified our dynamics in such a way to rule this out, but it does seem unreasonable.

In any case, for now let us simply assume that the question is whether and when the economy makes the transition from monocentricity to a symmetric tricentricity, with the new flanking cities located at $\tilde{r}$ and $-\tilde{r}$.

10.2.2 Dynamics and Bifurcation

We want to construct a bifurcation diagram analogous to figure 5.4. To do this, we first trace out real wages in the flanking cities relative to wages elsewhere in the economy, as a function of the allocation of labor among cities (a process analogous to the construction of figures 5.1–5.3). We then use this information to show the structure of stable and unstable population distributions, and hence construct the bifurcation diagram.

Let L_1 and ω_1 respectively be the population and the real wage of workers in the central city, and L_2 and ω_2 be those of each flanking city. Then the dynamics of the economy for given N are described by

$$\left.\begin{array}{l} \dot{L}_1 = L_1(\omega_1 - \overline{\omega}) \\ \dot{L}_2 = L_2(\omega_2 - \overline{\omega}) \end{array}\right\}, \tag{10.4}$$

where

$$\overline{\omega} = \frac{(L_1\omega_1 + 2L_2\omega_2 + L^A\omega^A)}{N}, \tag{10.5}$$

$$L^A = N - L_1 - 2L_2. \tag{10.6}$$

We must then determine the values of ω_1, ω_2, and ω^A associated with any given values of L_1 and L_2 and N. The set of equations that do this are, as in earlier chapters, the price indices, the wage equations, and the real-wage equations, but now augmented by an equation giving the size of the agricultural hinterland. To simplify, we begin with a special case in which agricultural products can be freely transported, then turn to the more general case.

Suppose initially that $\tau^A = 0$. Then the agricultural price p^A is the same everywhere in the economy. Normalizing so that $w_1 = 1$, the price index of manufactures at each location s can be obtained, by using (4.34), as

$$G(s) = [(L_1/\mu)e^{-(\sigma-1)\tau M|s|}$$
$$+ (L_2/\mu)w_2^{-(\sigma-1)}(e^{-(\sigma-1)\tau M|s+\tilde{r}|} + e^{-(\sigma-1)\tau M|s-\tilde{r}|})]^{-1/(\sigma-1)}. \tag{10.7}$$

It is convenient to label the price indices in the city locations G_1 and G_2,

$$G_1 \equiv G(0) \quad \text{and} \quad G_2 \equiv G(\tilde{r}). \tag{10.8}$$

Income levels at each location are, for the cities, $Y_1 = L_1$, $Y_2 = w_2 L_2$, and for each agricultural location r, $Y(r) = p^A$. The zero-profit wage rates for manufacturing workers in each city are (using 4.35) given by

$$1 = w_1 = \left[L_1 G_1^{\sigma-1} + 2L_2 w_2 e^{-(\sigma-1)\tau M \tilde{r}} G_2^{\sigma-1} \right.$$
$$\left. + p^A \int_{-f}^{f} e^{-(\sigma-1)\tau M |s|} G(s)^{\sigma-1} ds \right]^{1/\sigma}, \tag{10.9}$$

$$w_2 = \left[L_1 e^{-(\sigma-1)\tau M \tilde{r}} G_1^{\sigma-1} + L_2 w_2 G_2^{\sigma-1} (1 + e^{-2(\sigma-1)\tau M \tilde{r}}) \right.$$
$$\left. + p^A \int_{-f}^{f} e^{-(\sigma-1)\tau M |s-\tilde{r}|} G(s)^{\sigma-1} ds \right]^{1/\sigma}, \tag{10.10}$$

where f represents the fringe distance of the agricultural area.[2] Deflating by the price indices, real income in each city is

$$\omega_1 = G_1^{-\mu} (p^A)^{-(1-\mu)}, \tag{10.11}$$

$$\omega_2 = w_2 G_2^{-\mu} (p^A)^{-(1-\mu)}. \tag{10.12}$$

Turning to agriculture, the fringe distance is given by full employment of agricultural workers, of whom there are $N - L_1 - 2L_2$, occupying land at density c^A, so

$$f = (N - L_1 - 2L_2)/(2c^A). \tag{10.13}$$

At the fringe, rent is 0, so the agricultural wage satisfies $w^A(f) = p^A/c^A$, which gives real wages in agriculture,

$$\omega^A = w^A(f) G(f)^{-\mu} (p^A)^{-(1-\mu)} = G(f)^{-\mu} (p^A)^{\mu}/c^A. \tag{10.14}$$

Given N, L_1, and L_2, the system of equations (10.7)–(10.14) defines the real wages ω_1, ω_2, and ω^A, which feed into the dynamics of L_1 and L_2 (equation 10.4). The system is too complex to study analytically, but it yields readily to numerical analysis. For a numerical example, we use the following set of parameters,

$$\rho = 0.75 \text{ (i.e., } \sigma = 4\text{)}, \mu = 0.3, \tau^A = 0, \tau^M = 1, \text{ and } c^A = 0.5, \tag{10.15}$$

for which the critical population is $\tilde{N} = 2.57$ and the critical distance, $\tilde{r} = 1.14$.

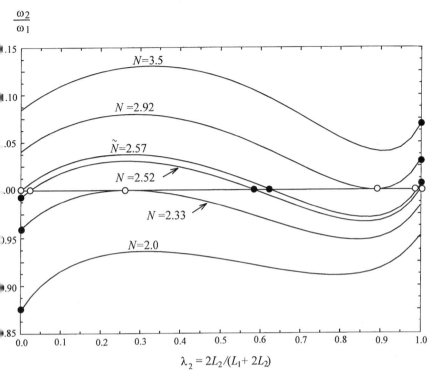

Figure 10.1
Curve ω_2/ω_1 along the locus $\omega^A = \bar{\omega}$

Figure 10.1 illustrates the system's dynamics, and hence the nature of the bifurcation that occurs as N increases. To illustrate the system on a two-dimensional diagram, the figure is constructed in the following way. The vertical axis is ω_2/ω_1, and the horizontal axis represents the share of manufacturing workers in the flanking cities, $\lambda_2 \equiv 2L_2/(L_1 + 2L_2)$.[3] Six curves are given, each corresponding to different levels of N. The curves are constructed by assigning a number of workers L_2 to each flanking city, then letting L_1 and the number of agricultural workers adjust until the agricultural real wage equals the average real wage in the economy as a whole, $\omega^A = \bar{\omega}$. Each curve gives the real wage in the flanking cities relative to that in the center, ω_2/ω_1, for the different values of λ_2 associated with each allocation L_2.

If $\omega_2/\omega_1 = 1$, we have a long-run equilibrium.[4] If $\omega_2/\omega_1 > 1$, then, from the differential equations (10.4), L_2 and λ_2 are increasing, and conversely for $\omega_2/\omega_1 < 1$. Thus the empty circles on the figure illustrate unstable equilibria, and the solid circles illustrate stable ones, either interior ($\omega_2/\omega_1 = 1$) or edge.

In figure 10.1, depending on the size of the population, there are different configurations of equilibria. At population 2.0, there is a unique equilibrium with no workers in the flanking cities ($\lambda_2 = 0$). This monocentric geography is a stable equilibrium, because any increase in λ_2 (and hence L_2) from 0 leaves $\omega_2/\omega_1 < 1$, so λ_2 moves back to 0. The same is true for any population less than $N = 2.33$.

When the population reaches $N = 2.33$, a new equilibrium emerges with workers in the flanking cities, ($\lambda_2 = 0.26$), and at N just greater than this, there are three equilibria ($\lambda_2 = 0$ and λ_2 slightly greater and slightly less than 0.26), the middle one of which is unstable. The monocentric geography is still a stable equilibrium, as is a three-city system. Increasing the population further, as N passes through $N = 2.52$, two further equilibria appear, one of which is stable and has all manufacturing concentrated in the flanking cities.

As the population passes through the critical population value, $\tilde{N} = 2.57$, so the original monocentric structure ceases to be an equilibrium. At $\tilde{N} = 2.57$, the monocentric structure ($\lambda_2 = 0$) has $\omega_2/\omega_1 = 1$, but ω_2/ω_1 is increasing in λ_2, so any small deviation of firms and workers from the central city to flanking cities is profitable and results in a catastrophic transition to a three-city equilibrium.

In the population range $2.57 < N < 2.92$, there are three equilibria. Two of these are stable, one with all three cities occupied, and one with only the two flanking cities ($\lambda_2 = 1$). Finally, above $N = 2.92$, there is a unique equilibrium, in which only the two flanking cities are occupied.

We can summarize the results with the bifurcation diagram in figure 10.2. The horizontal axis of this figure is the total population, N, and the vertical axis is the share of population in the flanking cities, $\lambda_2 \equiv 2L_2/(L_1 + 2L_2)$. The bold solid lines denote stable equilibria, and bold broken lines unstable ones. Starting at low N, the monocentric configuration is the unique (stable) equilibrium. At higher N, a three-city configuration is a stable equilibrium, although our dynamics provide no way of reaching it until $\tilde{N}$. We can view $\tilde{N}$ as a version of what we have been calling the sustain point; once we pass it, concentration of all manufacturing in the single city can no longer be sustained as an equilibrium, and the dynamics lead to a three-city equilibrium. However, given the parameters for which figure 10.2 was drawn, this con-

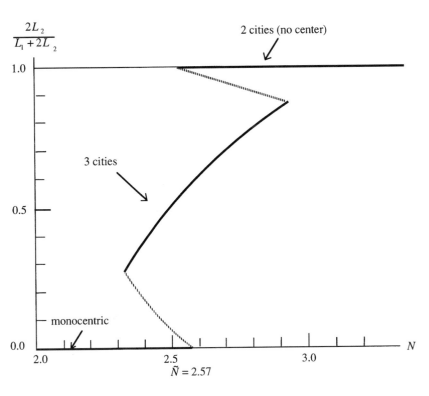

Figure 10.2
Bifurcation diagram for the three-city system

figuration also becomes unsustainable at a higher value of population, $N = 2.92$, and a two-city configuration is reached.

How general is the configuration illustrated here? First, this diagram is in a sense incomplete: There may be other equilibria, not shown, in which there are cities at locations other than $\tilde{r}$ and $-\tilde{r}$. However, because $\tilde{r}$ and $-\tilde{r}$ are the first locations at which the market potential reaches unity, we can be sure that our dynamic process first leads to this pair of cities, rather than any other. We turn to the possible emergence of additional cities in section 10.3.

In figures 10.1 and 10.2, the central city disappears at high enough N, but this is not a general property. In particular, we shall see that once we allow further cities to develop, these further cities place bounds on the size of the two flanking cities described here, making it less likely that the central city is displaced.[5]

As for the form of the bifurcation, in appendix 10.1 we establish sufficient conditions under which the bifurcation at $\tilde{N}$ must be a *tomahawk (subcritical) bifurcation*, as illustrated in the figures. This happens because in figure 10.1, when $N = \tilde{N}$, the ω_2/ω_1 curve has a positive slope at $\lambda_2 = 0$; that is, when $N = \tilde{N}$, along the locus $\omega^A = \bar{\omega}$,

$$\frac{d(\omega_2/\omega_1)}{d\lambda_2} > 0 \quad \text{at } \lambda_2 = 0. \tag{10.16}$$

Appendix 10.1 establishes sufficient conditions for this inequality to be satisfied, even in the case in which agricultural transport costs are positive.

Finally, what other differences does removing the assumption that agricultural transport costs are 0 make? When we consider the more reasonable case in which $\tau^A > 0$, the analysis becomes considerably more difficult, because we must determine to which city the agricultural good from each location is being shipped: the *flow pattern* of the agricultural good. The issue here is the following. Suppose that the two flanking cities are large and the central city quite small. Then agricultural products from land beyond the flanking cities ($|r| > |\bar{r}|$) are all consumed in the flanking cities, but so also is some of the agricultural output produced between the central and flanking cities, at locations $|r| < |\bar{r}|$. This means that the agricultural price schedule does not fall away exponentially from the central city, as we described it in equation (9.1). It also has peaks in each of the flanking cities.

Fortunately, this problem does not change the nature of the bifurcation, because the problem depends on the dynamics around $L_2 = 0$, at which point agricultural demand from flanking cities is so small that it does not disturb the price schedule. However, in the simulations of the next section, we have positive agricultural transport costs, so we have to keep track of agricultural flows and construct agricultural price functions accordingly.

10.3   Emergence of New Cities in the Long Run

We now extend the analysis beyond three cities to look at a continuing process of population growth and city formation. As population increases, we keep track of the market potential curve and, when this reaches unity at a new site, our dynamics cause a new city to be born.

Clearly we cannot expect much in the way of analytical results here. However, although different sets of parameter values generate minor differences in the result, as long as the two conditions in (10.3) are met, the long-run evolutionary process of the urban system is qualitatively the same under any parameter set. We therefore use the same parameter set we used in chapter 9, that is,

$$\rho = 0.75 \text{ (i.e., } \sigma = 4), \mu = 0.5, \tau^A = 0.8, \tau^M = 1, \text{ and } c^A = 0.5, \quad (10.17)$$

accompanied by the following critical values:

$$\tilde{N} = 4.36, \quad \tilde{r} = 1.10. \quad (10.18)$$

Given those values, figure 10.3 describes how the spatial system evolves over time as N increases gradually. We present two series of diagrams: one showing the land-rent curve, which reflects the current distribution of economic activity, and the other showing the market potential curve, which determines the future evolution of that distribution.[6] The coevolution of two curves describes how the spatial system changes in the long run through a sequence of bifurcations. First, panel (a_1) depicts the potential curve for $r \geq 0$ associated with the monocentric equilibrium under the initial population size, $N = 3$, and panel (a_2) shows the associated land-rent curve of the economy. Because $\Omega(r) < 1$ for all $r \neq r_1 \equiv 0$, this monocentric equilibrium is stable.[7]

However, as shown in panel (b_1), when N reaches the critical value, $4.36 \equiv \tilde{N}$, the potential curve hits 1 at distance $1.10 \equiv \tilde{r}$ (and at $-1.10 \equiv -\tilde{r}$); hence the monocentric system becomes unsustainable. Therefore, we transfer an arbitrarily small number of manufacturing workers (M-workers) from the existing city (at $r_1 = 0$) to each location, $r_2 = 1.10$ and $r_{-2} = -1.10$, then set off the adjustment dynamics described by (10.1). Panels (c_1) and (c_2) describe the new (stable) spatial system that has emerged at the end of this adjustment dynamics. A comparison of the two land-rent curves in panels (b_2) and (c_2) indicates that a catastrophic transformation of the spatial system has occurred at this bifurcation point. In particular, because the land rent at the location of each city is roughly proportional to the city's population,[8] panel (c_2) indicates that the new *frontier city* 2 (and *frontier city* -2) has a slightly larger population than the original city 1. (In fact, just after the bifurcation, we have that $L_1 = 0.74$ and $L_2 = L_{-2} = 0.97$.) Panels (d_1) and (d_2) describe the tricentric system at $N = 6$, which is halfway between the first bifurcation and the next bifurcation.

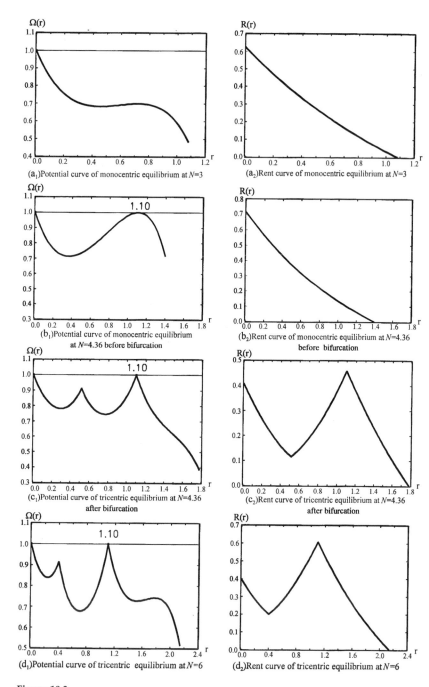

Figure 10.3
Evolutionary process of the spatial system

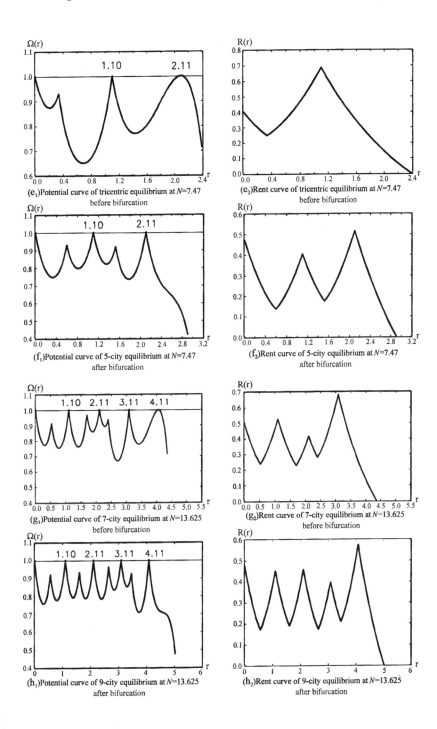

(e₁)Potential curve of tricentric equilibrium at N=7.47
before bifurcation

(e₂)Rent curve of tricentric equilibrium at N=7.47
before bifurcation

(f₁)Potential curve of 5-city equilibrium at N=7.47
after bifurcation

(f₂)Rent curve of 5-city equilibrium at N=7.47
after bifurcation

(g₁)Potential curve of 7-city equilibrium at N=13.625
before bifurcation

(g₂)Rent curve of 7-city equilibrium at N=13.625
before bifurcation

(h₁)Potential curve of 9-city equilibrium at N=13.625
after bifurcation

(h₂)Rent curve of 9-city equilibrium at N=13.625
after bifurcation

Panel (d_2) indicates that the two frontier cities have become much larger than city 1 at the center. Next, panel (e_1) shows that the second bifurcation occurs when $N = 7.47$. At this moment, the *frontier potential curve* has just hit 1 at $r_2 \equiv 2.11$ (and at $r_{-2} \equiv -2.11$), and the spatial system has become unsustainable again. As indicated by panel (e_2), just before the second bifurcation, each frontier city has a much larger population than the city at the center ($L_2/L_1 = 2.10/0.63 = 3.08$). Panels ($f_1$) and ($f_2$) describe the five-city spatial system that has emerged just after the catastrophic bifurcation.

In a similar manner, as the population $N(t)$ increases further, a pair of new frontier cities emerges periodically as the result of catastrophic bifurcations of the existing spatial system. Panels (g_1) through (h_2) in figure 10.3 describe another example of such a bifurcation, in which a seven-city system is transformed into a nine-city system when the frontier potential curve on each side hits 1 at $r_5 = 4.11$ and $r_{-5} = -4.11$, respectively.

The panels of figure 10.3 suggest that as the number of cities increases (because of increasing N), the spatial system approaches a highly regular central place system in which sizes of all cities are roughly the same. More precisely, as illustrated in panel (h_2), the two frontier cities are always the largest (because no competing city exists on their outer flank), and the two cities next to them are the smallest (reflecting the strongest competition from the frontier cities), whereas the middle cities have almost identical sizes. In particular, we can see from panel (h_1) that

$$r_2 - r_1 = \tilde{r} = 1.10, r_3 - r_2 = 1.01, r_4 - r_3 = r_5 - r_4 = r_6 - r_5 = 1.00, \quad (10.19)$$

which suggests that the distance between each pair of adjacent cities approaches a constant. Furthermore, if we measure the strength of the lock-in effect of each city k by the difference between the right- and left-hand gradients of the market potential at the cusp, $\Omega'_-(r_k) - \Omega'_+(r_k)$, then the panels indicate that the lock-in effect, too, always remains at roughly the same value, that is, $\Omega'_-(r_k) - \Omega'_+(r_k) \doteq 3.80$ for each k, which represents a very sharp cusp in the potential curve at the location of each city. Therefore, once a city is created at a location, it remains there forever, and no new cities emerge in its close vicinity.[9]

Figure 10.4 depicts the market share curve of manufactures produced by each city k ($k = 1, 2, 3, 4, 5$) in the nine-city equilibrium at $N = 13.62$, which corresponds to the spatial system represented by

market share

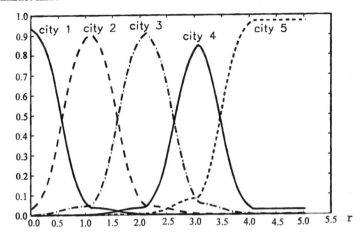

Figure 10.4
Market share curves of the nine-city equilibrium at $N = 13.62$

figure 10.3, panels (h_1) and (h_2). In figure 10.4, at each consumption location r, the market share, $MS_k(r)$, of manufactures produced in city k (in terms of delivered prices at r) can be obtained [by using (4.16) and (4.30)] as follows:

$$MS_k(r) = L_k w_k^{-(\sigma-1)} e^{-(\sigma-1)\tau M|r-r_k|} \Big/ \sum_j L_j w_j^{-(\sigma-1)} e^{-(\sigma-1)\tau M|r-r_j|}. \qquad (10.20)$$

The figure indicates that with the exception of city 4 (and city −4), each city imports less than 10 percent of its manufactures consumption from other cities (mostly from the directly adjacent cities). Because the frontier city 5 is the largest, having no competing city on its outer flank, it imports the smallest percentage of manufactures from other cities. Conversely, because city 4 is the smallest (because it is in the shadow of the frontier city 5), it imports the largest percentage of manufactures. Notice from these market share curves that the trade pattern of manufactured goods realized in our model is different from that of the classical central place theory a la Christaller and Lösch. In the former, market share curves are bell shaped, having no clear limit to the distance for trade; in the latter, each city (or central place) has a clearly defined market area for its goods. This difference arises from the fact that, in our model, each city produces a group of goods that

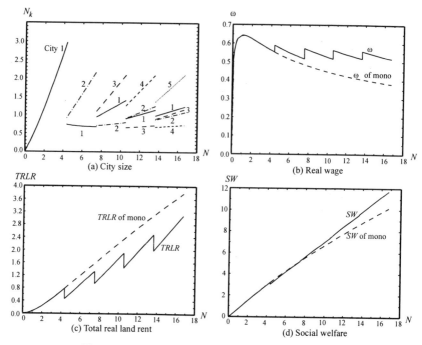

Figure 10.5. Summary measures of the evolutionary process.

are differentiated from other cities' goods, whereas in the classical central-place theory the same order of cities produce the same nondifferentiated goods.[10]

Figure 10.5 summarizes the evolutionary process. Panel (a) depicts the changes in the city size distribution along the evolutionary path. We can see that a new frontier city (more precisely, a pair of new frontier cities) is created periodically as a result of catastrophic bifurcation of the existing spatial system, and that the new frontier city is always the largest and grows fastest; but it becomes the smallest when the next new frontier city appears adjacent to it. For example, we can see in panel (a) that at $N = 7.47$, city 3 emerges as the new frontier city, and it remains the largest and grows fastest until $N = 10.52$, at which point the next new frontier city, city 4, appears as a result of a catastrophic bifurcation. The diagram also indicates that in the long run, as the number of cities increases, most cities (except the frontier city and its adjacent city) have approximately the same size.

Next, panel (b) depicts the associated cyclical change in the equilibrium real wage of workers, and shows that the real wage declines through time, but then jumps discontinuously upward when the periodic creation of new frontier cities enables the economy to overcome the diseconomies of population increase, maintaining a constant real wage in the long run. It is interesting to compare this with the broken curve, which represents the equilibrium real wage that workers would achieve if the economy were forced to remain monocentric.

Panel (c) depicts the cyclical change in the total real land rent (TRLR) defined by

$$TRLR = 2 \int_0^f R(r)G(r)^{-\mu}[p^A(r)]^{-(1-\mu)}dr. \tag{10.21}$$

Not surprisingly, each *TRLR* curve in panel (c) (the solid line for the actual spatial system and the broken one for the base case of the monocentric economy) exhibits the opposite trend to the corresponding curve in panel (b). Finally, if we define the overall social welfare of the economy by

$$SW \equiv N\omega + TRLR, \tag{10.22}$$

then the solid line in panel (d) shows that the social welfare is increasing almost proportionally with the population N. If we compare this curve with the broken line (for the monocentric case) in the same panel, we can understand that the periodic creation of new frontier cities sustains constant returns in the economy's overall performance in the long run.

10.4   Conclusions

In this chapter we have, in effect, tried to integrate von Thünen with Lösch: We have taken the framework that allowed us to give a microfoundation for the von Thünen model in chapter 9 and showed how, in the face of a growing population, that model evolves a system of central places. This evolution reflects the same logic that determined outcomes in the regional models of chapters 5–7: the tension between the centripetal forces created by backward and forward linkages, and the centrifugal force created by immobile land. And our simulations suggest that as the population grows, the distance between cities tends to approach a constant, determined by the relative strength of centripetal and centrifugal forces.

This multicity model does, we believe, represent a significant extension of the one-city von Thünen model. Yet it still has one obvious limitation: In this model all cities are basically the same. They all produce the same kinds of goods, and once the population becomes sufficiently large, almost all tend to be roughly the same size. Both in the real world and in the hypothetical world of classical central-place theory, of course, cities have very different sizes and roles. Our next step is to show that a modification of the model can indeed produce a Christaller-type urban hierarchy.

Appendix 10.1: Bifurcation with Costly Transport of Agricultural Goods

We want to establish that when N reaches the critical value $\tilde{N}$, the monocentric equilibrium is transformed to a tricentric system through a tomahawk bifurcation. This happens because in figure 10.1, when $N = \tilde{N}$, the ω_2/ω_1 curve has a positive slope at $\lambda_2 = 0$ (i.e., $L_2 = 0$); that is, along the locus $\omega^A = \overline{\omega}$, the inequality (10.16) holds. In this appendix, we obtain sufficient conditions for this inequality to be satisfied in the general case in which there are positive agricultural transport costs. Because the analysis is complex, we write down below the main lines of analysis, leaving the supplementary calculations for appendix 10.2.

When agricultural transport costs are incorporated, the first problem is to determine the flow pattern of the agricultural good (A-good). Fortunately, given that our objective is to examine the dynamics around $L_2 = 0$, this problem can be solved immediately. That is, given $N = \tilde{N}$, whenever $L_2 (= L_{-2})$ is sufficiently small, the consumption of the A-good in the flanking cities (located at $\tilde{r}$ and $-\tilde{r}$) is so small that some amount of the A-good produced in the flanking agricultural areas (A-areas), $(-f, -\tilde{r})$ and $(\tilde{r}, f)$, is transported to the central city. This implies that the excess A-good from every agricultural location must be transported in the direction of the central city; hence, the A-good price curve is given by the same equation as in (9.1). Thus, replacing p^A with $p^A(r)$ given in (9.1), the previous equilibrium conditions (10.9) through (10.12) and (10.14) are to be modified respectively as follows:[11]

$$
1 = w_1 = \left[L_1 G_1^{\sigma-1} + 2L_2 w_2 e^{-(\sigma-1)\tau M \tilde{r}} G_2^{\sigma-1} \right.
$$

$$
\left. + p^A \int_{-f}^{f} e^{-\tau A|s|} e^{-(\sigma-1)\tau M|s|} G(s)^{\sigma-1} ds \right]^{1/\sigma},
$$

(10A.1)

$$w_2 = \left[L_1 e^{-(\sigma-1)\tau M \bar{r}} G_1^{\sigma-1} + L_2 w_2 G_2^{\sigma-1}(1 + e^{-2(\sigma-1)\tau M \bar{r}}) \right.$$

$$\left. + p^A \int_{-f}^{f} e^{-\tau A |s|} e^{-(\sigma-1)\tau M |s - \bar{r}|} G(s)^{\sigma-1} ds \right]^{1/\sigma}, \tag{10A.2}$$

$$\omega_1 = G_1^{-\mu}(p^A)^{-(1-\mu)}, \tag{10A.3}$$

$$\omega_2 = w_2 G_2^{-\mu}(p^A e^{-\tau A \bar{r}})^{-(1-\mu)}, \tag{10A.4}$$

$$\omega^A = G(f)^{-\mu}(p^A e^{-\tau A f})^{\mu}/c^A. \tag{10A.5}$$

Equations (10.7), (10.8), and (10.13), however, need no change.

In (10.16), to evaluate the derivative $d(\omega_2/\omega_1)/d\lambda_2$ along the locus $\omega^A = \bar{\omega}$, after totally differentiating equilibrium equations (10.7) and (10A.1) through (10A.5), we let $L_2 = 0$. Then, as shown in appendix 10.2.a through 10.2.d, we can obtain that

$$\frac{d(\omega_2/\omega_1)}{d\lambda_2} = \frac{\mu}{2\sigma w_2^{\sigma}}$$

$$\times \left\{ -\frac{D}{2}\frac{dL_1}{dL_2} - D + w_2 \left[\frac{1+\rho}{\rho}Z + \frac{2}{\mu}w_2^{\sigma} - 2w_2^{-\sigma}e^{-2(\sigma-1)\tau M \bar{r}} - E \right] \right\}, \tag{10A.6}$$

where

$$Z \equiv e^{(\sigma-1)\tau M \bar{r}} - e^{-(\sigma-1)\tau M \bar{r}}, \quad \Lambda \equiv e^{(\sigma-1)\tau M \bar{r}} + e^{-(\sigma-1)\tau M \bar{r}}, \tag{10A.7}$$

$$D \equiv \left[\Lambda - \frac{2\mu}{1-\mu}(w_2^{\sigma}/\mu - e^{-(\sigma-1)\tau M \bar{r}}) \right] p^A e^{-\tau A f}/c^A, \tag{10A.8}$$

$$E \equiv w_2^{-\sigma}(L_1^{-1}p^A)\int_{-f}^{f} e^{-\tau A |s|}e^{2(\sigma-1)\tau M(|s|-|s-\bar{r}|)}(1 + e^{(\sigma-1)\tau M(|s-\bar{r}|-|s+\bar{r}|)})ds, \tag{10A.9}$$

$$w_2 = e^{[\mu \tau M - (1-\mu)\tau A]\bar{r}}, \quad \text{and} \quad p^A = c^A e^{\mu(\tau A + \tau M)f}. \tag{10A.10}$$

Next, totally differentiating $\omega^A = \bar{\omega}$ at $L_2 = 0$, as shown in appendix 10.2.e, we can obtain that

$$\left.\frac{dL_1}{dL_2}\right|_{\omega^A = \bar{\omega}} = -2(1 + F) \text{ at } L_2 = 0, \tag{10A.11}$$

where

$$F \equiv \frac{w_2\left[1 + \dfrac{\mu}{2(\sigma - 1)}w_2^{-\sigma}Z\right] - 1}{\dfrac{\mu}{1 - \mu} + c^A e^{\tau^{Af}}/p^A + \dfrac{\mu^2(\tau^A + \tau^M)}{(1 - \mu)\tau^A}(e^{\tau^{Af}} - 1)}. \tag{10A.12}$$

The substitution of (10A.11) into (10A.6) yields that

$$\left.\frac{d(\omega_2/\omega_1)}{d\lambda_2}\right|_{\omega^A = \bar{\omega}} = \frac{\mu}{2\sigma w_2^{\sigma - 1}} \tag{10A.13}$$

$$\times \left\{\frac{FD}{w_2} + \frac{1 + \rho}{\rho}Z + \frac{2w_2^\sigma}{\mu} - 2w_2^{-\sigma}e^{-2(\sigma - 1)\tau M_{\bar{r}}} - E\right\}.$$

Since we have, as shown in appendix 10.2.f, that

$$E < (\mu^{-1} - w_2^{-\sigma}e^{-(\sigma - 1)\tau M_{\bar{r}}})\Lambda \tag{10A.14}$$

$$= \mu^{-1}Z + 2\mu^{-1}e^{-(\sigma - 1)\tau M_{\bar{r}}} - w_2^{-\sigma} - w_2^{-\sigma}e^{-2(\sigma - 1)\tau M_{\bar{r}}},$$

it follows by (10A.13) that

$$\left.\frac{d(\omega_2/\omega_1)}{d\lambda_2}\right|_{\omega^A = \bar{\omega}} \text{(at } \lambda_2 = 0 \text{ when } N = \tilde{N}) > \frac{\mu}{2\sigma w_2^{\sigma - 1}}$$

$$\times \left\{\frac{FD}{w_2} + \left(\frac{1 + \rho}{\rho} + w_2^{-\sigma}e^{-(\sigma - 1)\tau M_{\bar{r}}} - \frac{1}{\mu}\right)Z + \frac{2}{\mu}(w_2^\sigma - e^{-(\sigma - 1)\tau M_{\bar{r}}})\right\} = \frac{\mu}{2\sigma w_2^{\sigma - 1}}$$

$$\times \left\{\frac{FD}{w_2} + \left[\frac{1 + \rho}{\rho} + w_2^{-\sigma}e^{-(\sigma - 1)\tau M_{\bar{r}}} - \frac{1}{\mu}\left(1 - \frac{2(w_2^\sigma - e^{-(\sigma - 1)\tau M_{\bar{r}}})}{Z}\right)\right]Z\right\}. \tag{10A.15}$$

Because D is always positive (see appendix 10.2.f), if both F and the quantity inside the braces above are nonnegative, then (10A.15) is nonnegative. Therefore, recalling F by (10A.12), we can conclude that the relation (10.16) always holds if the following two conditions are satisfied:

(i) $1 + \dfrac{\mu}{2(\sigma - 1)}w_2^{-\sigma}Z \geq w_2^{-1}$,

and

(ii) $\dfrac{1 + \rho}{\rho} + w_2^{-\sigma} e^{-(\sigma-1)\tau M_{\tilde{r}}} \geq \dfrac{1}{\mu}\left[1 - \dfrac{2(w_2^\sigma - e^{-(\sigma-1)\tau M_{\tilde{r}}})}{Z}\right],$

where w_2 is given in (10A.10). In particular, if $w_2 \geq 1$, that is, $\mu\tau^M \geq (1 - \mu)\tau^A$, then condition (i) always holds, and w_2 in the last term of (ii) is not less than 1. Thus, taking the safe side, we can conclude that if the following two conditions hold,

(ia) $\mu\tau^M \geq (1 - \mu)\tau^A,$

and

(iia) $\dfrac{1 + \rho}{\rho} \geq \dfrac{1}{\mu}\left[1 - \dfrac{2(1 - e^{-(\sigma-1)\tau M_{\tilde{r}}})}{e^{(\sigma-1)\tau M_{\tilde{r}}} - e^{-(\sigma-1)\tau M_{\tilde{r}}}}\right],$

then we have always the desired result, (10.16). A sufficient condition to satisfy (iia) is to assume that

$$\mu \geq \dfrac{\rho}{1 + \rho}, \qquad\qquad\qquad\qquad (10A.16)$$

which assures strong multiplier effects through the local consumption of manufactured goods (M-goods) produced in each city.[12]

   Given that these are only sufficient conditions (which have been obtained after taking the safe side many times), we can conclude that the relation (10.16) holds in a wide range of parameters in which both μ and τ^M are not too small. Thus even with costly transportation of agricultural goods there is still a wide range of parameters for which population growth eventually implies a catastrophic transition from a monocentric system to a three-city equilibrium.

Appendix 10.2: Supplementary Calculations for Appendix 10.1

We provide below a series of analyses that supplement appendix 10.1.

10.2.a   When $N = \tilde{N}$ and $L_2 = 0$, the monocentric equilibrium in chapter 9 yields, using (9.8) and the relation mentioned below (9.13), that

$$p^A = c^A e^{\mu(\tau^A + \tau^M)f}, \; w_2 \equiv w^M(\tilde{r}) = w^A(\tilde{r}) = e^{[\mu\tau^M - (1-\mu)\tau^A]|\tilde{r}|}. \qquad (10A.17)$$

Next, substituting (10.7) and (10.8) into (10A.1) and (10A.2), respectively, and letting $L_2 = 0$, we obtain the following results:

$$\int_{-f}^{f} e^{-\tau^A|s|} ds = (1 - \mu)\mu^{-1}(L_1/p^A), \tag{10A.18}$$

$$\int_{-f}^{f} e^{-\tau^A|s|} e^{(\sigma-1)\tau M(|s|-|s-\bar{r}|)} ds = (L_1/p^A)(w_2^\sigma/\mu - e^{-(\sigma-1)\tau M_{\bar{r}}}). \tag{10A.19}$$

Evaluating (10A.3) through (10A.5) at $L_2 = 0$, we have

$$\omega_1 = \omega_2 = \omega^A = (L_1/\mu)^{\mu/(\sigma-1)}(p^A)^{-(1-\mu)} \text{ at } L_2 = 0. \tag{10A.20}$$

10.2.b   Again, after the substitution of (10.7) and (10.8) into (10A.1) and (10A.2), we take the total derivative of (10A.1), (10A.2), and (10.13), and then let $L_2 = 0$. Solving these equations for df, dp^A and dw_2, then simplifying them by using (10A.18) and (10A.19), we can obtain that

$$df = -(dL_1 + 2dL_2)/(2c^A), \tag{10A.21}$$

$$dp^A = \frac{\mu}{1 - \mu}(L_1/p^A)\left\{ dL_1\left(\frac{1 - \mu}{\mu} + p^A e^{-\tau^A f}/c^A\right)\right.$$

$$\left. + 2dL_2\left(\frac{1 - \mu}{\mu}w_2 + p^A e^{-\tau^A s}/c^A\right)\right\}, \tag{10A.22}$$

$$dw_2\{(L_1/\mu)\sigma w_2^{\sigma-1}\} = -\frac{D}{2}L_1 + dL_2$$

$$\times \left\{-D + w_2\left[Z + \frac{2}{\mu}w_2^\sigma - 2w_2^{-\sigma}e^{-2(\sigma-1)\tau M_{\bar{r}}} - E\right]\right\}, \tag{10A.23}$$

where D, E, and Z are defined respectively by (10A.8), (10A.9), and (10A.7).

10.2.c   Next, totally differentiating (10A.3), (10A.4), and (10A.5) respectively, then setting $L_2 = 0$, we have that

$$\frac{d\omega_1}{\omega_1} = \frac{\mu}{\sigma - 1}(L_1/\mu)^{-1}[(dL_2/\mu) + 2(dL_2/\mu)w_2^{-(\sigma-1)}e^{-(\sigma-1)\tau M_{\bar{r}}}]$$

$$- dp^A(1 - \mu)(p^A)^{-1}, \tag{10A.24}$$

$$\frac{d\omega_2}{\omega_2} =$$

$$(10A.25)$$

$$w_2^{-1}\left\{dw_2 + \frac{\mu}{\sigma - 1}w_2(L_1/\mu)^{-1}[(dL_1/\mu) + (dL_2/\mu)w_2^{-(\sigma-1)}\Lambda]\right\},$$

$$\frac{d\omega^A}{\omega_A} = dp^A\mu(p^A)^{-1} - df\mu\tau^A + \frac{\mu}{\sigma - 1}(L_1/\mu)^{-1}$$

$$\times [(dL_1/\mu) - df(\sigma - 1)\tau^M(L_1/\mu) \qquad (10A.26)$$

$$+ (dL_2/\mu)w_2^{-(\sigma-1)}(e^{(\sigma-1)\tau M\bar{r}} + e^{-(\sigma-1)\tau M(f+\bar{r})})],$$

where Λ is defined in (10A.7).

10.2.d Because $\lambda_2 = 2L_2/(L_1 + 2L_2)$, and because $\omega_1 = \omega_2$ when $L_2 = 0$ and $N = \tilde{N}$, it follows that

$$\frac{d(\omega_2/\omega_1)}{d\lambda_2} = \frac{d\omega_2 - d\omega_1}{dL_2}\frac{L_1}{2\omega_1} \quad \text{at } L_2 = 0. \qquad (10A.27)$$

After substituting (10A.22) and (10A.23) into (10A.24) and (10A.25), respectively, we set $\omega_1 = \omega_2$. Then, further substituting the results into (10A.27), we can immediately obtain the relation (10A.6).

10.2.e Because $\omega_1 = \omega_2 = \omega^A$ when $L_2 = 0$ and $N = \tilde{N}$, the total derivative of the relation

$$\omega^A = \overline{\omega} \equiv ([L_1\omega_1 + 2L_2\omega_2 + (N - L_1 - 2L_2)\omega^A]/N) \qquad (10A.28)$$

at the equilibrium yields that

$$d\omega_1 = d\omega^A. \qquad (10A.29)$$

Thus, by substituting (10A.24) and (10A.26) into (10A.29) and using (10A.21) and (10A.22), we can readily derive the relation (10A.11).

10.2.f To show that D defined by (10A.8) is positive, first observe that

$$C \equiv \int_{-f}^{f} e^{-\tau^A|s|}e^{(\sigma-1)\tau^M(|s|-|s-\bar{r}|)}ds \qquad (10A.30)$$

$$= e^{-(\sigma-1)\tau M\bar{r}}\int_{-f}^{0} e^{-\tau^A|s|}ds + \int_{0}^{f} e^{-\tau^A|s|}e^{(\sigma-1)\tau^M(s-|s-\bar{r}|)}ds \qquad (10A.31)$$

$$< e^{-(\sigma-1)\tau\mu\bar{r}}\int_{-f}^{0} e^{-\tau^A|s|}ds + e^{(\sigma-1)\tau M\bar{r}}\int_{0}^{f} e^{-\tau^A|s|}ds$$

$$= \frac{1}{2} \int_{-f}^{f} e^{-\tau A|s|} ds \, \Lambda. \tag{10A.32}$$

Hence,

$$\Lambda > C \bigg/ \left(\frac{1}{2} \int_{-f}^{f} e^{-\tau A|s|} ds \right)$$

$$= \frac{2\mu}{1 - \mu} (L_1/p^A)^{-1} C \quad \text{[by (10A.18)]} \tag{10A.33}$$

$$= \frac{2\mu}{1 - \mu} (w_2^g/\mu - e^{-(\sigma-1)\tau M \bar{r}}) \quad \text{[by (10A.19) and (10A.30)]},$$

which implies that D defined by (10A.8) is positive. Next, to show the inequality in (10A.14), we decompose the integral in (10A.9) into two terms as follows:

$$B_1 \equiv \int_{-f}^{f} e^{-\tau A|s|} e^{2(\sigma-1)\tau M(|s|-|s-\bar{r}|)} ds$$

$$= e^{-2(\sigma-1)\tau M \bar{r}} \int_{-f}^{0} e^{-\tau A|s|} ds + \int_{0}^{f} e^{-\tau A|s|} e^{2(\sigma-1)\tau M(s-|s-\bar{r}|)} ds,$$

$$B_2 \equiv \int_{-f}^{f} e^{-\tau A|s|} e^{(\sigma-1)\tau M(2|s|-|s-\bar{r}|-|s+\bar{r}|)} ds$$

$$= 2 \int_{0}^{f} e^{-\tau A|s|} e^{(\sigma-1)\tau M(2|s|-|s-\bar{r}|-|s+\bar{r}|)} ds$$

$$= 2 e^{-(\sigma-1)\tau M \bar{r}} \int_{0}^{f} e^{-\tau A|s|} e^{(\sigma-1)\tau M(s-|s-\bar{r}|)} ds,$$

and hence, after dividing B_2 into the same two parts and rearranging terms,

$$B \equiv B_1 + B_2$$

$$= \left\{ e^{-2(\sigma-1)\tau M \bar{r}} \int_{-f}^{0} e^{-\tau A|s|} ds + e^{-(\sigma-1)\tau M \bar{r}} \int_{0}^{f} e^{-\tau A|s|} e^{(\sigma-1)\tau M(s-|s-\bar{r}|)} ds \right\}$$

$$+ \left\{ e^{-(\sigma-1)\tau M \bar{r}} \int_{0}^{f} e^{-\tau A|s|} e^{(\sigma-1)\tau M(s-|s-\bar{r}|)} ds \right.$$

$$+ \int_0^f e^{-\tau^A|s|} e^{2(\sigma-1)\tau M(s-|s-\tilde{r}|)}\, ds \Bigg\}$$

$$= e^{-(\sigma-1)\tau M\tilde{r}} C$$

$$+ \Bigg\{ e^{-(\sigma-1)\tau M\tilde{r}} \int_0^f e^{-\tau^A|s|} e^{(\sigma-1)\tau M(s-|s-\tilde{r}|)}\, ds \tag{10A.34}$$

$$+ \int_0^f e^{-\tau^A|s|} e^{2(\sigma-1)\tau M(s-|s-\tilde{r}|)}\, ds \Bigg\}$$

$$< e^{-(\sigma-1)\tau M\tilde{r}} C$$

$$+ e^{(\sigma-1)\tau M\tilde{r}} \Bigg\{ e^{-(\sigma-1)\tau M\tilde{r}} \int_0^f e^{-\tau^A|s|}\, ds + \int_0^f e^{-\tau^A|s|} e^{(\sigma-1)\tau M(s-|s-\tilde{r}|)}\, ds \Bigg\}$$

$$= e^{-(\sigma-1)\tau M\tilde{r}} C + e^{(\sigma-1)\tau M\tilde{r}} C$$

$$= C\Lambda.$$

Therefore, by (10A.9),

$$E \equiv w_2^{-\sigma}(L_1^{-1}/p^A)(B_1 + B_2)$$

$$< w_2^{-\sigma}(L_1^{-1}/p^A)C\Lambda$$

$$= w_2^{-\sigma}(w_2^{\sigma}/\mu - e^{-(\sigma-1)\tau M\tilde{r}})\Lambda \quad [\text{by (10A.19) and (10A.30)}] \tag{10A.35}$$

$$= (\mu^{-1} - w_2^{-\sigma} e^{-(\sigma-1)\tau M\tilde{r}})\Lambda,$$

which means (10A.14).

Appendix 10.3: Adjustment Dynamics of a General Three-City Case

In section 10.2, we examined the adjustment dynamics of a three-city economy in which cities are assumed potentially to exist at three locations, $-\tilde{r}$, 0, and $\tilde{r}$ (where $\tilde{r}$ is the critical distance at which the potential curve of the monocentric economy first reaches unity). In that analysis, however, we restricted ourselves to the case where two flanking cities always have the same population. In this appendix, we drop this restriction and reexamine the adjustment dynamics of the same three-

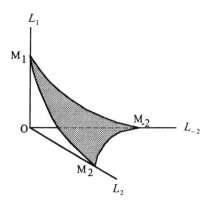

Figure 10A.1
Stable subset of the three-city system

city economy, including asymmetric transitions.[13] This more general analysis will provide us with a clearer understanding of how the initial monocentric system bifurcates to a new configuration. Because of mathematical complexity, the study is conducted through numerical analyses. In the numerical study below, we use the same set of parameters given in (10.17), accompanied by those critical numbers in (10.18). Thus, the locations of the possible three cities, city 1, city 2, and city −2, are fixed respectively at

$$r_1 = 0, r_2 = \tilde{r} = 1.10, \quad \text{and} \quad r_{-2} = -\tilde{r} = -1.10. \tag{10A.36}$$

In this context of the tricentric system, for each given value of the total population N, we set $K = 3$ in (10.1) and solve the adjustment dynamics (10.1) under every possible initial population distribution such that $L_1 + L_2 + L_{-2} < N$. The full representation of the results would involve phase diagrams in the three-dimensional space, $L_1 \times L_2 \times L_{-2}$. In practice, however, essential results can be represented in two-dimensional diagrams, because for each given value of N, there is a two-dimensional *stable subset* in the $L_1 \times L_2 \times L_{-2}$ space that contains all possible equilibria (both stable and unstable ones) of the present three-city system and to which all adjustment paths are directed.[14] In figure 10A.1, this stable subset is illustrated by a shaded surface, $M_1 M_2 M_{-2}$. It follows that to study the transitions of the three-city system in association with the total population change, it is sufficient to examine how the adjustment dynamics on this subset changes with N. Figure 10A.2 presents the results.[15]

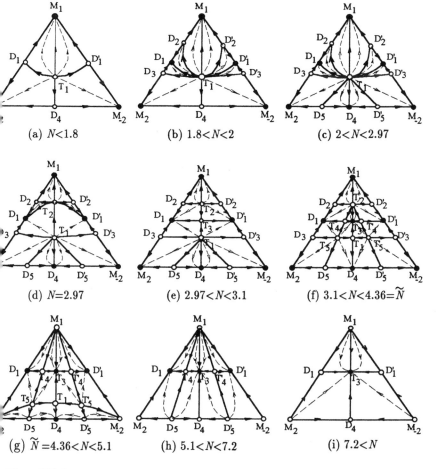

Figure 10A.2
Phase diagrams of the adjustment dynamics on the stable subsets

In each phase diagram in Figure 10A.2, solid lines depict all stable and unstable manifolds, whereas broken lines depict representative trajectories; furthermore, each filled circle represents a stable equilibrium, whereas each open circle represents an unstable equilibrium. In each panel, the monocentric equilibrium with city k ($k = 1, 2$, and -2) is denoted by M_k, which corresponds to the point M_k in figure 10A.2. The spatial configuration is duocentric along each side of $M_1M_2M_{-2}$, and it is tricentric in the interior of $M_1M_2M_{-2}$. We also note that each phase is symmetric with respect to M_1D_4, because city 2 and city -2 are located symmetrically with respect to city 1.

Panel (a) depicts the case of $N < 1.8$, where only monocentric configurations can be in stable equilibrium. Although there are symmetric duocentric equilibria at D_1, D_1', and D_4, and a tricentric equilibrium T_1, all are unstable. Thus, starting from any point in $M_1 M_2 M_{-2}$ (except those points exactly on the duocentric and tricentric equilibria), the economy eventually reaches one of the monocentric equilibria. At $N = 1.8$, new duocentric equilibria D_2 and D_3 bifurcate from D_1, making D_1 stable, whereas D_2 and D_3 inherit the instability of D_1. Panel (b) shows the case of $1.8 < N < 2$.

Next, as shown in panel (c), at $N = 2$, asymmetric duocentric equilibria D_5 and D_5' bifurcate from D_4, making D_4 stable. A further increase in N does not change the phase diagram until $N = 2.97$, at which a new tricentric equilibrium T_2 appears between M_1 and T_1, which further bifurcates into T_2 and T_3 as N increases. This process is shown in panels (d) and (e).

A comparison of panels (e) and (f) shows that at $N = 3.1$, T_4 and T_4' bifurcate from T_3, and T_5 and T_5' from T_1. In particular, the emergence of T_4 and T_4' make T_3 stable, as shown in panel (f). Now N is large enough to have a stable tricentric equilibrium, T_3. The relative city sizes, L_2/L_1, at tricentric equilibria T_1, T_2, and T_3 are respectively 4.99, 0.02, and 0.66. The dynamics is explained by panel (f) until $N = 4.36$.

When N reaches the critical size $\tilde{N} = 4.36$, major changes in the phase diagram occur. The comparison of panels (f) and (g) shows that at this critical population size, the two unstable duocentric equilibria, D_2 and D_2', and another unstable tricentric equilibrium, T_2, merge into M_1; unstable D_3 merges into M_2; and unstable D_3' merges into M_{-2}, which makes all three (previously stable) monocentric equilibria, M_1, M_2, and M_{-2}, unstable. If the economy has been previously at M_1 in panel (f), for example, then at this critical moment, the potential curve $\Omega(r)$ just reaches 1 at $r = \pm \tilde{r}$, which will trigger the formation of new cities at $\tilde{r}$ and/or $-\tilde{r}$, as explained previously. Whether one new city or two new cities emerge at this moment depends on chance. If a similar number of manufacturing firms happen to be created each at $\tilde{r}$ and $-\tilde{r}$ simultaneously, then a tricentric system is realized. Otherwise, a duocentric system is realized. Hence, history matters here.

At $N = 5.1$, tricentric equilibria T_1, T_5, and T_5' merge into duocentric equilibria D_4, D_5, and D_5', respectively. For $5.1 < N < 7.2$, panel (h) depicts the phase diagram. Finally, a comparison of panels (h) and (i) shows that at $N > 7.2$, the manifold $M_1 D_5$ [respectively, $M_1 D_5'$] merges into the manifold $M_1 M_2$ [respectively, $M_1 M_{-2}$], with only T_3 remaining as the stable equilibrium. This indicates, for example, that if the spatial system previously transformed from M_1 to the duocentric equilibrium D_1 at $N = \tilde{N} = 4.36$, it must be transformed again to a tricentric equilibrium T_3 at $N = 7.2$.[16] Notice that although panel (i) seems to indicate that the tricentric configuration T_3 would remain in equilibrium for any $N > 7.2$, this is true only if the creation of no additional new city is considered. Actually, as has been shown in section 10.3, when N reaches 7.47, the potential curve $\Omega(r)$ hits 1 again at $r = \pm 2.11$, suggesting the emergence of new cities there.

Notes

1. In a more general situation, the production of manufactures may take place not only in cities located at discrete locations, but also in a continuum of locations, that is, in an *industrial belt*. In this book we look only at discrete cities. For a study of the emergence of industrial belts, see Mori 1997.

2. In general a polycentric economy can have several agricultural areas, separated by uncultivated zones. Because we are considering a transition just after the von Thünen geography becomes unsustainable, however, we can safely assume that agriculture extends continuously from $-f$ to f.

3. In figure 10.1, the horizontal axis can be either L_2 or $\lambda_2 \equiv 2L_2/(L_1 + 2L_2)$, but we use λ_2 for normalization. That is, notice that since $\dot{\lambda}_2 = 2(L_1\dot{L}_2 - L_2\dot{L}_1)/(L_1 + 2L_2)^2$, we have:

(1) $\{\omega^A = \overline{\omega} \text{ and } \omega_1/\omega_2 < 1\} \rightarrow \omega_2 < \overline{\omega} < \omega_1 \rightarrow \{\dot{L}_1 > 0 \text{ and } \dot{L}_2 < 0\}$ by (10.4) $\rightarrow \dot{\lambda}_2 < 0$,

and

(2) $\{\omega^A = \overline{\omega} \text{ and } \omega_2/\omega_1 > 1\} \rightarrow \omega_1 < \overline{\omega} < \omega_2 \rightarrow \{\dot{L}_1 < 0 \text{ and } \dot{L}_2 > 0\} \rightarrow \dot{\lambda}_2 > 0$.

Therefore, along the locus $\omega^A = \overline{\omega}$ we have $\dot{L}_2 \gtreqless 0$ as $\dot{\lambda}_2 \gtreqless 0$.

4. Because agricultural real wages equal the average wage in the economy, $\omega^A = \overline{\omega}$, we have that $\omega_1 \gtreqless \overline{\omega}$ if and only if $\omega_1 \gtreqless \omega_2$.

5. As the next section shows, the introduction of agricultural transport costs also makes it less likely that the central city is displaced, because the agricultural transport costs work against enabling the flanking cities to grow excessively.

6. The equilibrium conditions of the spatial economy under any given N can be obtained by dropping the industry index h from all equations in the second section of chapter 11. We avoid writing them down here to save space. Refer to appendix 10.3 for a detailed analysis of the adjustment dynamics of a general three-city economy under the parameter set in (10.17).

7. Using the fact that the supply curve of the agricultural good in figure 9.2 is steeper than the demand curve at the equilibrium, it can be readily shown that the monocentric equilibrium is always stable *when the formation of no new city is considered*. Then, because $\Omega(r) < 1$ for all $r \neq 0$, the monocentric equilibrium depicted in figure 10.3 (a_1) is stable even if we consider the possible formation of new cities.

8. This is true in the same land-rent diagram. However, since the agricultural price in the city at the farthest right is always normalized to 1 in the present numerical analyses, the comparison of the absolute values of different land-rent diagrams is not meaningful.

9. More precisely, when the agricultural transport cost, $(1 - \mu)\tau^A$, is significantly large, then no existing city disappears in this evolutionary process. In contrast, when $(1 - \mu)\tau^A$ is very small in comparison with $\mu\tau^M$, some of existing cities may disappear in the long run, because when $(1 - \mu)\tau^A$ is much smaller than $\mu\tau^M$, the wage rate, $w^A(r)$, becomes much higher in frontier agricultural locations than at the frontier cities. Hence the labor cost is always much lower at frontier cities than in their forelands, which delays the emergence of a new city in either outer flank. This means that before the emergence of a new city in its foreland, each existing frontier city has a large uncontested market for its manufactures there, which makes each frontier city very large in comparison with middle cities. Hence each frontier city may eventually even absorb the middle city located directly adjacent.

10. The market area structure assumed in the classical central-place theory, called the *economic law of market areas* (*LMA*), was outlined by Launhardt (1885) and rediscovered by Fetter (1924). In contrast, the market area structure represented by equation (10.20) resembles the *law of retail gravitation* (*LRG*), which was proposed by Reilly (1931) as an empirical regularity. Hence we can consider our model (based on monopolistic competition with differentiated goods) to provide a theoretical justification for the LRG. Not surprisingly, expression (10.20) looks like the logit model that has been used in modern presentation of the LRG (refer to Anderson et al., 1992, chaps. 3 and 4).

11. Although there is no change in (10.11), we write it down below for convenience.

12. In combining (A10.16) and (b) in (10.3), we have that $\rho > \mu \geq \rho/(1 + \rho)$, which always holds if $\rho > \mu \geq 0.5$. Notice that condition (a) in (10.3) is always satisfied if (ia) holds.

13. This part of our study is based on Fujita and Mori 1997.

14. If $\tau^A = \tau^M = 0$, then the equation of this subset is given by $L_1 + L_2 + L_{-2} = \mu N$, which represents the clearance condition of the agricultural market under the assumption of the costless mobility of all goods. In the present context of positive transport costs, however, this subset is convex to the origin, located farther from the origin than the $L_1 + L_2 + L_{-2} = \mu N$ plane. This reflects the fact that if the production of manufactures is conducted on an equal scale in the two cities, for example, then the "average price" of the agricultural good in this duocentric economy is lower than that in the monocentric economy, which causes more consumption and production of the agricultural good and hence more agricultural workers in the duocentric economy than in the monocentric economy.

15. In the stability analysis below, the stability/instability of each equilibrium point is identified by using the standard method of the linear approximation of the dynamical system (10.1) at that equilibrium point.

16. Notice that our discussion here is limited to the three-city system. In general, it is also possible that D_1 is transformed into a quadricentric configuration.

11   Evolution of a Hierarchical Urban System

Chapter 10 showed how an economy could evolve from monocentrism to a multiple-city geography, but that geography was still a rather uninteresting one. Because there was assumed to be only one type of manufactured good (albeit in many varieties), all cities were doing pretty much the same thing and, as we saw, in the long run tended to be of similar sizes. Yet a major insight both of Henderson-type models and of Christaller's central-place theory is that differences in the characteristics of manufactured goods lead to the evolution of a system in which cities of different types and sizes each play distinct roles. In this chapter, we show how an economy with several different manufacturing sectors—differing in transport costs, substitution parameters, or both—can evolve a hierarchical urban system, that is, a system in which one can make a meaningful distinction between "higher-order" and "lower-order" cities: A higher-order city does everything a lower-order city does, and more.

Chapter 8 suggested—but only in a heuristic model—the basic mechanism for the emergence of such a hierarchy. Getting it right, in a full general equilibrium model with a consistent description of market structure, is much harder, but we will see that the story remains similar. Essentially, when firms find it profitable to establish a new location for the production of "higher-order goods" (goods having a lower transport cost and/or a smaller substitution parameter), they tend to choose an existing lower-order city, because of the backward-linkage effects of the consumers in such cities; so when a higher-order city emerges, it normally does so via the "upgrading" of an existing lower-order city. Repetition of this process eventually produces an ordered hierarchy of cities.

We may note that although the main concern of our study here is not on the reality of the model, the results obtained in this chapter are also helpful in understanding the evolutionary process of real-world urban systems. In particular, the evolutionary process of the hierarchical urban system simulated in section 11.5 qualitatively resembles the development process of the U.S. urban system during its westward expansion in the nineteenth century. To give some sense of this real-world background, we begin this chapter with a review of some historical data.

11.1   The Formation of an Urban Hierarchy in Nineteenth-Century America

Figure 11.1 illustrates the evolution of the U.S. urban system during the period from 1830 to 1870.[1] Over this period, the U.S. population increased threefold from approximately 13 million to 39 million, and

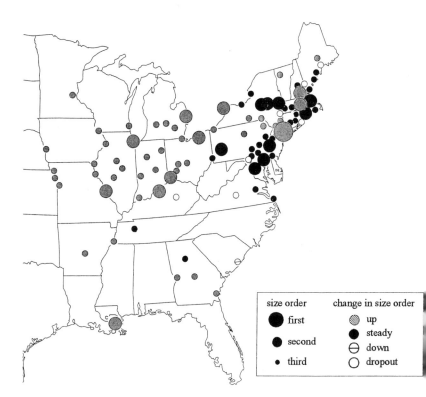

Figure 11.1
Evolution of the U.S. urban system, 1830–1870

there was a major expansion of the agricultural area toward the Great West,[2] well beyond Chicago and St. Louis. The figure shows the location of cities with a population of more than 30,000 in 1870. These cities in 1870 are classified into three *orders* such that New York, indicated by the largest circle, is the only "first-order" city, with a population of more than 1.3 million; those cities denoted by a middle-sized circle represent "second-order" cities, with population between 130,000 and 1.3 million, and those cities shown by the smallest circle belong to the "third-order" class, whose population was between 30,000 and 130,000.[3] This same figure also shows how this urban system in 1870 had evolved from that in 1830 by indicating the change in each city's size-order from 1830 to 1870.[4] That is, shaded circles denote cities that were upgraded by one or more orders, circles with a single line denote those that were downgraded in one or more orders but were still larger than or equal to the third order, open circles mark those that dropped out of the third order, and black circles show those that stayed in the same order as in 1830.

Figure 11.1 reveals several interesting facts. First, not surprisingly, most cities established before 1830 (except the steel town, Pittsburgh) were located along the northern part of the Atlantic coast or navigable rivers, reflecting the importance of waterborne transportation for trade with Europe as well as within the United States. Second, in the Midwest and Great West, a large number of new third-order cities had emerged by 1870 because of the expansion of the agricultural area toward the Great West resulting from the threefold increase of the U.S. population between 1830 and 1870. To provide farmers in the spreading agricultural area with ordinary consumption goods and farming tools, new small cities appeared, each serving a local agricultural hinterland. Third, several old third-order cities in the Midwest (such as St. Louis, Chicago, Cleveland, and Detroit) upgraded themselves to second-order cities, which were not only larger in population than third-order cities, but also played the role of regional center by supplying higher-order goods and services (such as business/trade services and sophisticated farming machines) to larger hinterlands.[5] Fourth, a previously second-order city, New York, upgraded itself to the unparalleled first-order city of the United States, providing the entire United States with the highest-order goods and services (such as major financial services and national newspapers). Finally, we can also see in the figure that although most cities that existed in 1830 still existed in 1870, several old frontier cities had disappeared (i.e., their population became smaller than the third-order threshold).

In short, as the U.S. population increased, a systematic hierarchical system of cities seems to have established itself.[6] Nobody planned this development; it was a classic case of the self-organization of a complex system.

11.2 The Model

The framework of this chapter's model is the same as that in the previous two chapters except that now we have H industries, each of which ($h = 1, 2, \ldots, H$) produces its own range of differentiated products. Hence the previous utility function (4.1) is now generalized as

$$U = A^{\mu^A} \prod_{h=1}^{H} (M^h)^{\mu^h}, \quad \mu^A + \sum_{h} \mu^h = 1, \tag{11.1}$$

where μ^h is the share of the hth industry in consumption, and M^h is the composite output of industry h [equation (4.2) with $\rho = \rho^h$ and $n = n^h$].

Each of the H industries has exactly the same form as the manufacturing sector we have studied until now, although we let the parameters describing each industry vary. Thus, the expenditure shares μ^h can vary across industries as can the substitution elasticities ($\sigma^h \equiv 1/(1 - \rho^h)$) and the transport costs, τ^h.

We can characterize equilibrium quite directly using the price indices, income statements, wage equations, and market potential functions. Consider an economy in which there are K cities located at r_k ($k = 1, 2, \ldots, K$), in the kth of which industry h employment is L_k^h. The price index for industry h products at location r, $G^h(r)$ is

$$G^h(r) = \left[\sum_{k} (L_k^h/\mu^h) w_k^{-(\sigma h - 1)} e^{-(\sigma h - 1)\tau^h |r - r_k|} \right]^{-1/(\sigma h - 1)}. \tag{11.2}$$

As before, we denote the value of the price index in city k as $G_k^h \equiv G^h(r_k)$. Income at agricultural location r is $p^A(r)$, and the size of the agricultural area we denote $|X^A|$. The full description of agriculture is complex and therefore is relegated to appendix 11.1. The complexity arises because of the problem of the flow of agricultural goods, alluded to in chapter 10. The agricultural price function $p^A(r)$ is not the simple exponential function of (9.1), and furthermore, intervals of the geographical space may be unoccupied, which is why we denote agriculture area $|X^A|$, possibly less than $2f$. As usual, the agricultural wage equals the price of agricultural output at the edge of this area.

Income in city k, Y_k, may be derived from employment in all manufacturing industries, $Y_k = \sum_h w_k^h L_k^h$, and income in each agricultural location is $p^A(r)$. The wage equation for industry h at location r is then

$$
w^h(r) = \left[\sum_k Y_k e^{-(\sigma^h-1)\tau^h|r_k-r|}(G_k^h)^{\sigma^h-1} \right.
$$

$$
\left. + \int_{X^A} p^A(s) e^{-(\sigma^h-1)\tau^h|s-r|}(G^h(s))^{\sigma^h-1} ds \right]^{1/\sigma^h}.
$$

(11.3)

This is just the natural extension of the wage equation, (4.35).

Real wages in each industry and in agriculture are

$$
\omega^h(r) = w^h(r)(p^A(r))^{-\mu^A} \prod_h (G^h(r))^{-\mu^h},
$$

(11.4)

$$
\omega^A(r) = w^A(r)(p^A(r))^{-\mu^A} \prod_h (G^h(r))^{-\mu^h}.
$$

This deflates nominal wages by agricultural prices and the price indices of each industry's manufactures, using the cost-of-living index dual to the utility function, (11.1). As before, we denote city k real wages $\omega_k^h = \omega^h(k)$.

To complete characterization of equilibrium, we need three more ingredients. Labor market clearing in the economy takes the form

$$
\sum_k \sum_h L_k^h + c^A |X^A| = N.
$$

(11.5)

Real wages must be equalized in all activities that have positive employment levels; that is,

$$
\omega_k^h = \omega^A(r) = \omega^A \quad \text{for all } h, k, \text{ such that } L_k^h > 0.
$$

(11.6)

Finally, we have to see if the equilibrium is sustainable, so no firm should be able to attain a positive profit at any possible location. This can be checked, as before, by using market potential functions, although we now have a separate function for each industry. As before, then, let us define the market potential of each industry h at each location r by

$$\Omega^h(r) \equiv \frac{[\omega^h(r)]^{\sigma^h}}{[\omega^A]^{\sigma^h}}. \tag{11.7}$$

The equilibrium is sustainable if

$$\Omega^h(r) \leq 1 \quad \text{for all } r, \tag{11.8}$$

for each industry $h = 1, 2, \ldots, H$. If, for some industry h and some new location $r = \tilde{r}^h$, $\Omega^h(\tilde{r}^h) = 1$, then we use the dynamics discussed in chapter 10 to allow a new city site to develop at $\tilde{r}^h$.

11.3 The Monocentric System

As usual, we start from a monocentric configuration. The description of this is essentially as in chapter 9. The city is centered at $r = 0$ and supplied with agricultural products from a hinterland of width $2f$. Equality of supply and demand for agricultural output and the condition that the real wage is the same for all agricultural workers as it is for manufacturing workers jointly determine the price of agricultural goods and the size of this hinterland.

The presence of multiple industries means that we distinguish between manufacturing as a whole and individual manufacturing industries. It is convenient to define μ^M, the consumption share of manufactures in aggregate, and $\bar{\tau}^M$, the consumption-weighted average of manufacturing trade costs:

$$\mu^M \equiv \sum_{h=1}^{H} \mu^h = 1 - \mu^A, \quad \text{and} \quad \bar{\tau}^M \equiv \frac{\sum_h \mu^h \tau^h}{\mu^M}. \tag{11.9}$$

We fully restate the equilibrium conditions of the monocentric economy in appendix 11.2, but for our argument we really need note only two points. First, because in the monocentric configuration all manufacturing is located in the urban center, this location has share μ^M of the economy's income. Second, if different industries have different transport costs, then the cost-of-living index now varies with distance according to the transport cost of agricultural goods and the consumption-weighted average of different manufacturing trade costs. Thus the cost-of-living index at r differs from that in the city by factor $e^{[\sum_h \mu^h \tau^h - \mu^A \tau^A]r} = e^{[\mu^M \bar{\tau}^M - \mu^A \tau^A]r}$.

These observations mean that the potential function for each industry now becomes

$$\Omega^h(r) = e^{\sigma^h[(1-\mu^M)\tau^A - \mu^M\bar{\tau}^M]r}\left[\left(\frac{1+\mu^M}{2}\right)e^{-(\sigma^h-1)\tau^h r}\right.$$

$$\left. + \psi^h(r,f)\left(\frac{1-\mu^M}{2}\right)e^{(\sigma^h-1)\tau^h r}\right], \quad (11.10)$$

where

$$\psi^h(r,f) = 1 - \frac{\displaystyle\int_0^r e^{-\tau^As}[1 - e^{-2(\sigma^h-1)\tau^h(r-s)}]ds}{\displaystyle\int_0^f e^{-\tau^As}ds}. \quad (11.11)$$

These equations are as in chapter 9, except for two points. First, they are industry specific, so elasticities and transport costs are all of the form σ^h and τ^h, respectively. However, the expenditure shares, μ^M, are not industry specific; as usual, these give total income levels in the city and outside it, and so aggregate over manufacturing industries. Second, the term outside the square brackets in (11.10) measures, as before, the difference in the cost of living between location r and the central city. Consequently, it contains the consumption-weighted average of manufacturing transport costs, $\bar{\tau}^M$.

What are the properties of these functions? Their gradient in the neighborhood of the city is easily found by differentiating to give

$$d\Omega^h(0)/dr = \sigma^h[(1-\mu^M)\tau^A - \mu^M(\bar{\tau}^M + \rho^h\tau^h)]. \quad (11.12)$$

Having a negative gradient as we move away from the city (to the right, increasing r) is a necessary condition for the monocentric structure to be sustainable, and this condition must hold for all H industries.

As population increases, so the potential functions shift upward (except at $r = 0$), and it is helpful to look at their limiting values. Constructing the limiting potential function for each industry, analogously to equation (9.26), we obtain

$$\overline{\Omega}^h(r) = K^h e^{\sigma^h[\rho^h(\tau^A+\tau^h)-\mu^M(\tau^A+\bar{\tau}^M)]r}$$

$$+ (1 - K^h)e^{-\sigma^h[(1-\mu^M)\rho^h\tau^h - \Omega_r^{h(0)}/\sigma^h]r}, \quad (11.13)$$

Table 11.1
Possibility of a monocentric equilibrium

$(1 - \mu^M)\tau^A - \mu^M(\bar{\tau}^M + \rho^h\tau^h) > 0$ for any h	$(1 - \mu^M)\tau^A - \mu^M(\bar{\tau}^M + \rho^h\tau^h) < 0$ for every h	
Never	$\mu^M\left(\dfrac{\tau^A + \bar{\tau}^M}{\tau^A + \tau^h}\right) \geq \rho^h$	$\mu^M\left(\dfrac{\tau^A + \bar{\tau}^M}{\tau^A + \tau^h}\right) < \rho^h$
	for every h	for at least one h
	Always	For small N

where K^h is a constant given by

$$K^h = \frac{(1 - \mu^M)\rho^h\tau^h}{(1 - \mu^h)\rho^h\tau^h + \rho^h(\tau^A + \tau^h) - \mu^M(\tau^A + \bar{\tau}^M) - \Omega_r^h(0)/\sigma^h}, \quad (11.14)$$

and $\Omega_r^h(0)$ is the derivative given in equation (11.12).

The behavior of equation (11.13) depends, as in the case of equation (9.26), on the first exponential term. If the exponent on the first term in (11.13) is negative, then $\overline{\Omega}^h(r)$ decreases in all $r > 0$,[7] and if this holds for all industries, then the monocentric structure is always sustainable. But if the exponent is positive for any industry (and hence K is also positive for that industry), then at some value of N the monocentric structure breaks down.

Table 11.1 summarizes the results. In the left-hand column, some industry's potential curve, $\Omega^h(r)$, has a positive slope at the edge of the city, and hence the firms in this industry certainly move out of the city, meaning that the monocentric system is never an equilibrium. In the two right-hand columns, all industries' potentials decrease as we move away from the city, and as N increases, the sustainability of the monocentric configuration depends on a variation of the no-black-hole condition. In the center column, $\mu^M(\tau^A + \bar{\tau}^M)/(\tau^A + \tau^h) \geq \rho^h$ for every h, so the limiting potential curve of every industry is below unity for all $r \neq 0$, meaning that the monocentric system is always an equilibrium, however large N becomes. That is, the centripetal force created by the agglomeration of all industries at the city is so strong that no new city can emerge, however large N becomes.

In the right-hand column, we can be sure that some industries— those satisfying $\mu^M(\tau^A + \bar{\tau}^M)/(\tau^A + \tau^h) < \rho^h$—move out of the central city at some value of N, thereby destroying the monocentric configuration. Let us then assume that every industry's potential function has a cusp at the city, then divide industries into two groups according to whether they are in the central or right-hand column. For industries $h \leq \tilde{H}$, the potential reaches unity at large enough N (they are in the right-hand column of table 11.1), whereas for industries $h > \tilde{H}$, the potential never attains unity (they are in the central column), that is,

$$\mu^M(\tau^A + \bar{\tau}^M)/(\tau^A + \tau^h) < \rho^h \quad \text{for } h = 1, 2, \ldots, \tilde{H},$$

$$\mu^M(\tau^A + \bar{\tau}^M)/(\tau^A + \tau^h) \geq \rho^h \quad \text{for } h = \tilde{H} + 1, \ldots, H,$$
(11.15)

where $1 \leq \tilde{H} \leq H$.

Thus far we have examined the behavior of potential curves separately for each industry. However, the movements of the potential curves of all H industries are synchronized through the common parameter f, the width of the agricultural hinterland, which increases monotonically with the economy's population, N. In particular, suppose that the initial value of N is sufficiently small that the economy's spatial structure is monocentric. Then as N increases gradually with time, all industries' potential curves gradually move upward, as explained before. In this context, the first new city (or the first pair of new cities) emerges when the first industry's potential curve reaches 1 at some new location, $r \neq 0$. Therefore, the crucial question is: Which industry's potential curve reaches 1 first? One might suspect that an industry "spins out" from the city sooner if it has either a high elasticity of substitution (meaning lower scale economies in equilibrium) or high transport costs (meaning that it tends to follow the agricultural frontier). And this is indeed the case. In appendix 11.3, we show the following:

Suppose that $\mu^A\tau^A \leq \mu^M\bar{\tau}^M$. Then given any pair of industries, h and g, such that $h \leq \tilde{H}$ and $g \leq \tilde{H}$ if

$$\{\rho^h > \rho^g \text{ and } \tau^h \geq \tau^g\} \quad \text{or} \quad \{\rho^h \geq \rho^g \text{ and } \tau^h > \tau^g\},$$
(11.16)

then

$$\tilde{N}^h < \tilde{N}^g, \tilde{r}^h < \tilde{r}^g, \quad \text{and} \quad \tilde{\theta}^h > \tilde{\theta}^g,$$
(11.17)

where $\tilde{\theta}^h \equiv |d\Omega^h(0)/dr|$.

In general, given a pair of industries, g and h, if ρ^g and τ^g are less than or equal to ρ^h and τ^h, respectively (and one of them is strictly less), then we say that g is *of higher order* than h. Clearly nothing says that industries must be rankable by order: An industry could have a low elasticity of substitution and high transport costs, or vice versa. But

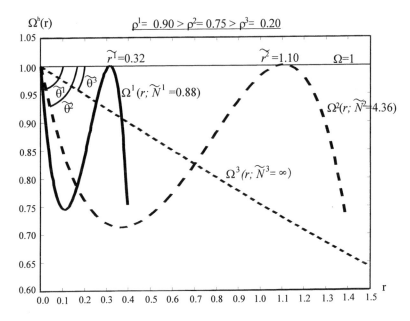

Figure 11.2
Examples of critical potential curves for the monocentric system

if industries can be ranked, and we imagine gradually increasing the population of a monocentric economy, the potential curve of a lower-order industry always humps itself above 1 sooner than that of a higher-order industry.

Figure 11.2 illustrates the impact of ρ^h on the shape of the critical potential curve, $\Omega^h(r; \tilde{N}^h)$. (The impact of τ^h is essentially the same as that of ρ^h.) Three hypothetical industries are shown, with

$$\rho^1 = 0.90 > \rho^2 = 0.75 > \rho^3 = 0.20. \tag{11.18}$$

All other parameters are fixed as follows:

$$\mu^A = 0.5, \mu^1 = \mu^2 = 0.1, \mu^3 = 0.3,$$
$$\tau^A = 0.8, \tau^h = 1 \text{ for all } h, \text{ and } c^A = 0.5. \tag{11.19}$$

Thus industry 3 is of the highest order, and industry 1 is of the lowest order. We can readily confirm that these parameters satisfy the conditions in (11.15) with $\tilde{H} = 2$. The associated critical potential curves are depicted in figure 11.2, and are accompanied by the following critical values:

$\tilde{N}^1 = 0.88 < \tilde{N}^2 = 4.36, \tilde{f}^1 = 0.40 < \tilde{f}^2 = 1.40,$

$\tilde{r}^1 = 0.32 < \tilde{r}^2 = 1.10,$ and $\tilde{\theta}^1 = 5.5 > \tilde{\theta}^2 = 1.90 > \tilde{\theta}^3 = 0.25.$

$$(11.20)$$

Therefore, among the three industries, the critical potential curve of industry 1 hits 1 first at the nearest location, $\tilde{r}^1 = 0.32$, when the economy's population reaches the smallest critical value, $\tilde{N}^1 = 0.88$.

11.4 Self-Organization toward a Hierarchical System

The discussion in the previous section suggests that the growth of an economy containing many industries of different orders naturally leads over time to the formation of a hierarchical urban system. Because of the complexity of the issue, we cannot offer any analytical confirmation. We can, however, illustrate the point with numerical simulations. To make our simulation analysis tractable, we choose parameters such that

$$\sum_{h=1}^{H} (\mu^h / \rho^h) \geq 1, \tag{11.21}$$

which ensures that the spatial structure of the economy remains *monopolar*; that is, the economy has a unique highest-order city in which all groups of M-goods are produced.[8] Lower-order cities can still emerge, however; as we will show, they do so through a series of bifurcations associated with the birth of new cities, relocation and merger of existing cities, and changes in the industrial compositions of cities. Given that the long-run evolutionary process of the spatial system is qualitatively similar as long as the parameters lie in the right-hand column of table 11.1 and satisfy condition (11.21), in the following we present the results of a representative simulation example.

Suppose that the economy has three groups of manufactured goods, $h = 1, 2, 3$. We fix parameters at those values specified in (11.18) and (11.19), which yield the critical values in (11.20). The critical potential curves of the three M-industries (associated with the monocentric configuration) can be depicted as in figure 11.2. Because (11.18) and (11.19) imply that $\{\rho^1 > \rho^2$ and $\tau^1 = \tau^2\}$ and $\{\rho^2 > \rho^3$ and $\tau^2 = \tau^3\}$, as noted before, M^3-industry is of the highest order, M^2-industry the second order, and M^1-industry the third order.

We assume that the population size of the economy, $N(t)$, increases gradually over time and examine the evolutionary process of the spatial system in the long run. In section 11.4.1, we examine in detail what happens when $N(t)$ reaches the first critical value, $\tilde{N}^1$. We show that the process of the emergence of new flanking cities may now be different from that in the single-order urban system of the previous chapter. In section 11.4.2, then, we examine the spatial system's long-run evolutionary process.

11.4.1 From One City to Three

Recall from the discussion at the end of section 11.3 that when $N(t)$ is sufficiently small ($N(t) < \tilde{N}^1 = 0.88$), all three potential curves associated with the monocentric system are strictly less than 1 everywhere outside the city at $r = 0$. Therefore, the monocentric system is a stable equilibrium, with all three groups of M-goods being produced exclusively in the single city at $r = 0$. However, when $N(t)$ reaches the smallest critical value, $\tilde{N}^1 = 0.88$, the potential curve of M^1-industry hits 1 at $\tilde{r}^1 = 0.32$ (refer to figure 11.2), resulting in the breakdown of the monocentric system.[9]

A pair of new cities then emerge at $\tilde{r}^1$ and $-\tilde{r}^1$ and, for our example, our dynamics imply that the population of these new cities grows continuously from 0 as N increases gradually beyond $\tilde{N}^1$. Hence, unlike the previous case of the single-order system in chapter 10, the new cities emerge in the form of a *pitchfork bifurcation* (i.e., a supercritical bifurcation). This is because the bifurcation occurs only for industry 1, and in our example, one industry alone does not create sufficient forward and backward linkages to lead to the discontinuous behavior we have seen previously. The new cities are completely specialized in the production of industry 1, as we can check by noting that after the bifurcation, the potential curves of M^2- and M^3-industries are strictly below 1 at $r \neq 0$.

The fact that we have a pitchfork bifurcation has two implications. First, as $N(t)$ reaches $\tilde{N}^1$, a pair of new cities must be created at $\tilde{r}^1$ and $-\tilde{r}^1$. Hence unlike before, at this moment there is no room for historical chance to affect the evolutionary process. (Recall our discussion in chapter 10 about whether one or two cities would be born as N reached its critical value.[10]) Second, during the immediate period after this bifurcation time, each frontier city is so small that it lacks enough lock-in force to stay at the same location. If each frontier city remained at the same location, then as the agricultural area expanded further, the potential curve would have a positive gradient on the frontier side of the city, thus violating the location equilibrium condition. Therefore, for the spatial system to remain in stable equilibrium, each frontier city moves continuously outward until it gains a sufficient lock-in force.[11]

It is worth briefly relating this case to that analyzed in chapter 10 and illustrated in figure 10.1. In that case, at the point where the bifurcation took place, wages in the flanking cities were strictly increasing in the proportion of the manufacturing labor force in the new cities (ω_2/ω_1 increasing in λ_2 at $\lambda_2 = 0$). But now, as N reaches $\tilde{N}^1$, so $\omega_2/\omega_1 = 1$, but is decreasing in λ_2. There is therefore no discontinuous jump in populations, but further increases in N steadily increase flanking city size. The reason is that when a city is specialized in an industry having a small expenditure share and a high substitutability (such as $\mu^1 = 0.1$ and $\rho^1 = 0.9$), further increases in the size of this industry in that city generate neither significant forward linkage effects (on the real income there) nor significant backward linkage effects (through the local demand increase for that industry's products there), but the competition among firms intensifies rapidly. (Imagine, for example, the situation in which many bakery shops appear in a small town.) Therefore, the size of the industry in each frontier city can grow only gradually as the local demand for that industry's products increases gradually in association with the expansion of the agricultural frontier.

11.4.2 Long-Run Evolution

Given the preliminary analysis above, we can now examine how the spatial system evolves over a longer run. The economy's population size, $N(t)$, is assumed to increase gradually over time, starting with a small value less than $\tilde{N}^1$. All other parameters are fixed at those values specified in (11.18) and (11.19). The result is a simulated history of city formation, occasional city extinction, and urban upgrading, eventually producing a hierarchical system. Figures 11.3 and 11.4 summarize that history; the former shows the bifurcations along the way, as $N(t)$ increases from $\tilde{N}^1 = 0.88$ to 9.79, whereas the latter depicts the changing shapes of potential curves along the evolutionary path. It is an intricate history, but worth tracing out for the insights it gives into the way the tug of war between centripetal and centrifugal forces can create spatial structure.

Recall that there are three possible city types: the highest order, with all three industries; a middle order, with industries 1 and 2; and the lowest order, with only industry 1. (Parameters are chosen for industry

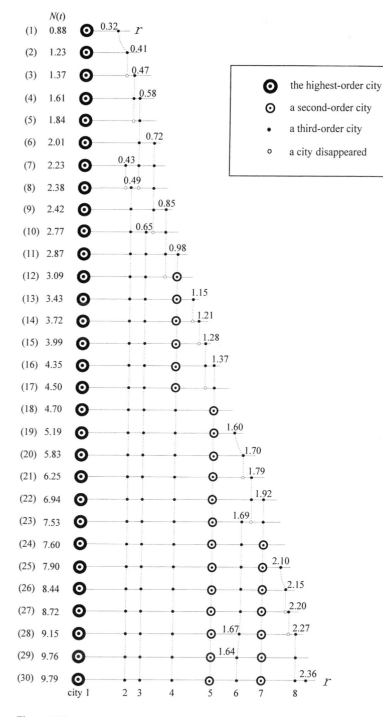

Figure 11.3
Evolutionary process of the hierarchical urban system

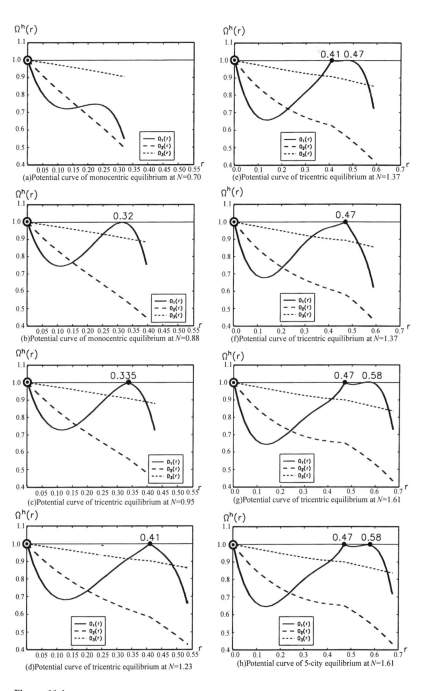

Figure 11.4
Changes in potential curves along the evolutionary path

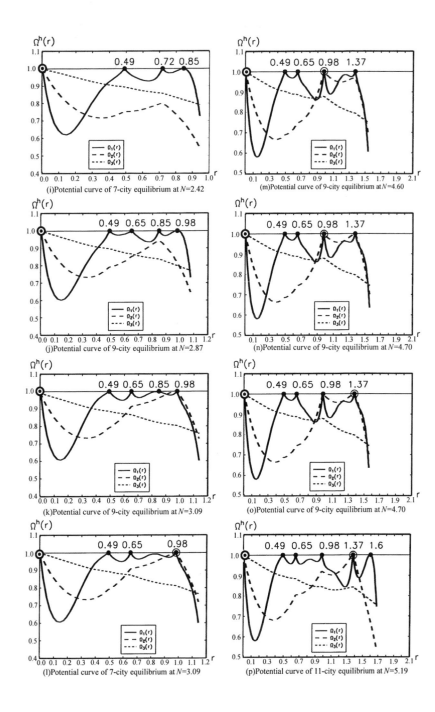

(i)Potential curve of 7-city equilibrium at N=2.42

(j)Potential curve of 9-city equilibrium at N=2.87

(k)Potential curve of 9-city equilibrium at N=3.09

(l)Potential curve of 7-city equilibrium at N=3.09

(m)Potential curve of 9-city equilibrium at N=4.60

(n)Potential curve of 9-city equilibrium at N=4.70

(o)Potential curve of 9-city equilibrium at N=4.70

(p)Potential curve of 11-city equilibrium at N=5.19

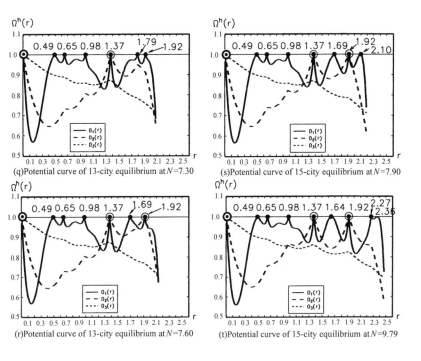

(q)Potential curve of 13-city equilibrium at $N=7.30$

(s)Potential curve of 15-city equilibrium at $N=7.90$

(r)Potential curve of 13-city equilibrium at $N=7.60$

(t)Potential curve of 15-city equilibrium at $N=9.79$

3 such that it never leaves the original central city.) In figure 11.3, given each population $N(t)$, the economy's associated spatial structure is depicted on the horizontal line. (Symmetry in the spatial structure of the economy means we need only describe its right side). For example, line 20 in figure 11.3 indicates that when $N(t) = 5.83$, the equilibrium spatial system contains a unique highest-order city at $r = 0$, a unique middle-order city (on the right half of the economy) at $r = 1.37$, and four lowest-order cities respectively at $r = 0.49, 0.65, 0.98$, and 1.70; the right-side A-fringe is at $r = 1.82$.

First, we briefly summarize what we explained in section 11.4.1 in terms of figures 11.3 and 11.4. As is illustrated in figure 11.4(a), when $N(t)$ is sufficiently small that $N(t) < \tilde{N}^1 = 0.88$, then all three potential curves associated with the monocentric system are strictly less than 1 everywhere outside the city at $r = 0$. Therefore, the monocentric system is in stable equilibrium, with all three groups of M-goods being produced exclusively at the (highest-order) city at $r = 0$. When $N(t)$ reaches the smallest critical value, $\tilde{N}^1 = 0.88$, as depicted in figure 11.4(b), the potential curve of industry 1 hits 1 at $r = \pm\tilde{r}_1 = \pm0.32$, resulting in the emergence of a pair of frontier cities there. Because these frontier cities emerge as a result of a continuous bifurcation, during the immediate period after its birth, each frontier city is so small that it lacks enough lock-in effect to stay at the same location. This point is illustrated in figure 11.4(c), which indicates that even when $N = 0.95$, the slope of the potential curve of industry 1 at the right edge of the frontier city is 0. Therefore, as indicated by the dotted curve between lines (1) and (2) in figure 11.3, in order for the spatial system to remain in stable spatial equilibrium, the frontier city must move continuously outward from $r = 0.32$ to 0.41 as $N(t)$ increases from 0.88 to 1.23. Only when N reaches 1.23 has the frontier city reached a sufficient size that its lock-in effect is strong enough to enable the city to remain at the same location (refer to panel (d) of figure 11.4).

Next, as N increases further (beyond 1.23) and hence as the frontier area keeps expanding, the frontier potential curve moves upward; it eventually hits 1 at $r = 0.47$ when $N(t) = 1.37$ (panel (e) of figure 11.4). At this moment, as the result of a (small) catastrophic bifurcation, the existing frontier city at $r = 0.41$ relocates to $r = 0.47$ (line (3) of figure 11.3 and panel (f) of figure 11.4). At $N(t) = 1.61$, as a result of a continuous bifurcation, a new frontier city starts growing at $r = 0.58$, while the old frontier city remains at 0.47 (line (4) of figure 11.3 and panels (g) and (h) of figure 11.4).[12] The old frontier city, however, is soon absorbed by the new frontier city and disappears when N reaches 1.84 (line (5) of figure 11.3). When N reaches 2.01, again as a result of a continuous bifurcation, a new frontier city starts growing at $r = 0.72$, while the old frontier city remains at 0.58 (line (6) of figure 11.3). Then after a series of maneuvers involving a creation of another lowest-order city at $r = 0.43$ (line (7) of figure 11.3), and through the merger of two existing cities, located at $r = 0.43$ and $r = 0.58$, at the new location $r = 0.49$ (line (8) of figure 11.3), the lowest-order city at $r = 0.58$ eventually relocates to $r = 0.49$. As can be seen in figure 11.3, this lowest-order city continues to remain at $r = 0.49$ thereafter. At $N = 2.42$, as the result of another continuous bifurcation, a new frontier city starts growing at $r = 0.85$ (line (9) of figure 11.3 and panel (i) of figure 11.4); at $N = 2.77$, the old frontier city (at $r = 0.72$) relocates to $r = 0.65$ (line (10) of figure 11.3). (As figure 11.3 shows, this lowest-order city continues to exist at $r = 0.65$ thereafter.) Furthermore, at $N = 2.87$, again as a result of a continuous bifurcation, a new frontier city starts growing at $r = 0.98$ (line (11) of figure 11.3).

Meanwhile, observe from panels (a) through (j) in figure 11.4 that the potential curve of industry 2 has been steadily moving upward,

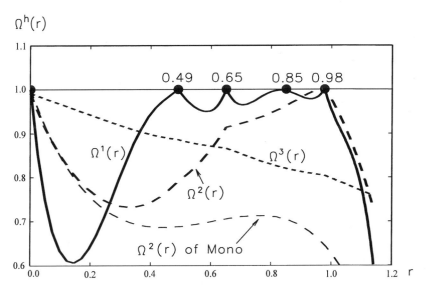

Figure 11.5
Potential curves of the nine-city equilibrium at $N = 3.09$

with kinks at the location of existing lowest-order cities. In particular, as indicated by figure 11.4(k), at $N = 3.09$, the potential curve of industry 2 first reaches 1 at the location of the frontier city (at $r = 0.98$). Hence a lowest-order frontier city becomes transformed into a middle-order city, producing both M^1-goods and M^2-goods. This arises because the demand for M^2-goods among the workers in the lowest-order cities bends and pulls upward the industry 2 potential curve. In particular, because the frontier city has the largest population among all existing lowest-order cities, the potential curve of industry 2 is most sharply kinked and uplifted toward the frontier city (refer to panel (k) of figure 11.4). Consequently, the potential curve of industry 2 reaches 1 first at the frontier city, resulting in the transformation of the frontier city to a middle-order city. Because this middle-order city has been created by adding a new industry to the second-order city, it naturally satisfies the hierarchical principle of Christaller (1933).[13]

Figure 11.5 demonstrates the strength of the demand pull of existing third-order cities on the shape of the potential curves of higher-order industries. This figure is an enlargement of figure 11.4(k), with addition of a new curve, $\Omega^2(r)$ of mono, which represents the potential curve of industry 2 associated with the hypothetical monocentric urban system (in which all M-firms are forced to locate in the city at $r = 0$) under the same population, $N = 3.09$. We can see from this figure that the demand of workers in the existing lowest-order cities (in particular, the demand of the large lowest-order city located at the frontier, $r = 0.98$) has pulled the potential curve of industry 2 up greatly.

Returning to the narrative description of figures 11.3 and 11.4, the frontier city at $r = 0.98$ is transformed to a middle-order city as the result of a continuous bifurcation. However, because it grows rapidly, it soon absorbs the nearby lowest-order city at $r = 0.85$ (panel (l) of figure 11.4). As N increases further (beyond 3.10), the frontier area expands, and a new frontier city starts growing at $r = 1.15$ when N reaches 3.43 (line (13) of figure 11.3). However, in comparison with the middle-order city at $r = 0.98$, this new frontier city is too small to gather a sufficient lock-in effect there. Hence, as the frontier area further expands, the frontier city keeps relocating (discretely) until it settles down at $r = 1.37$ (lines (13) to (17) of figure 11.3).

Observe in figure 11.4(m) that as N increases further, the potential curve of industry 2 has been gradually moving upward again in the frontier area. In particular, as shown in figure 11.4(n), at $N = 4.70$, the potential curve of industry 2 reaches 1 again at the location of the frontier city ($r = 1.37$). At this moment, the existing middle-order city (at $r = 0.98$) becomes less attractive for industry 2 (than the frontier city). Hence, as a consequence of a large catastrophic bifurcation, the whole of industry 2 at $r = 0.98$ moves to the frontier city, degrading the past middle-order city at $r = 0.98$ to a lowest-order city while upgrading the frontier city to a middle-order city (line (18) of figure 11.3 and panels (n) and (o) of figure 11.4). We can see in figure 11.3 that this change in size-order has stabilized the spatial structure in the area between the central city (at $r = 0$) and the new middle-order city (at $r = 1.37$). In the frontier area, however, the spatial structure keeps changing (lines (19) to (25) of figure 11.3 and panels (p) through (r) of figure 11.4). In particular, when N reaches 7.60, the frontier city at $r = 1.92$ is upgraded to a middle-order city. Thus, two middle-order cities now exist (in the right side of $r = 0$), with a lowest-order city locating in the middle (line (24) of figure 11.3 and panel (r) of figure 11.4). After the formation of this middle-order city at $r = 1.92$, the spatial configuration in the frontier area keeps changing as before (through the birth of new cities and relocation of existing cities), while the lowest-order city in the middle of the two middle-order cities moves to the center of them (lines (25) to (30) of figure 11.3 and panels (s) and (t) of figure

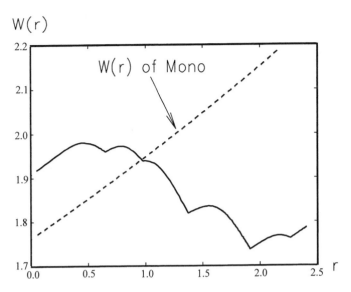

Figure 11.6
Wage curve of the fifteen-city equilibrium at $N = 9.3$

11.4). The simulation ends when N reaches 9.79, with the emergence of a quite systematic hierarchical urban system a la Christaller (line (30) of figure 11.3 and panel (t) of figure 11.4).

Next, in figure 11.6, the solid line depicts the equilibrium (nominal) wage curve when $N = 9.30$, and the broken line represents the corresponding curve associated with the (forced) monocentric system under the same population size. We can see that although all middle- and lowest-order cities are much smaller than the central city, the presence of these relatively small lower-order cities greatly affects the shape of the wage curve.[14] In particular, middle-order cities (located at $r = 1.37$ and $r = 1.92$) affect greatly the local wage rates, for each satisfies a large proportion of the local demands for M^1-goods and M^2-goods in its vicinity.

The last point above can be understood more clearly by considering figure 11.7, which depicts the trade patterns of M-goods in the context of fifteen-city equilibrium at $N = 9.30$. (In this figure, each city number coincides with that in line (30) of figure 11.3. Hence, city 1 is the highest-order city, cities 5 and 7 are the middle-order, and the rest are the lowest-order.) For each industry h at each consumption location r, the market share, $MS_k^h(r)$, of M^h-goods produced in city k (in terms of delivered price at r) can be obtained, using (4.16) and (4.30), as follows:

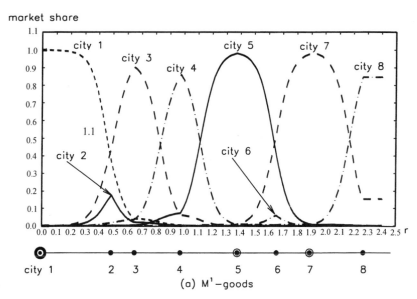

(a) M^1-goods

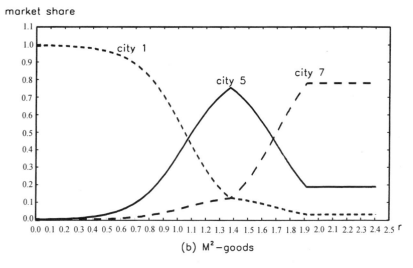

(b) M^2-goods

Figure 11.7
Market share curves of the M-goods produced in each city in the 15-city equilibrium at
$N = 9.3$

$$MS_k^h(r) = L_k^h w_k^{-(\sigma^h-1)} e^{-(\sigma^h-1)\tau^h|r-r_k|} \bigg/ \sum_j L_j^h w_j^{-(\sigma^h-1)} e^{-(\sigma^h-1)\tau^h|r-r_j|}. \qquad (11.22)$$

Setting $h = 1$ and 2 respectively, (11.22) yields the market share curve of each group of goods produced in each city. (For $h = 3$, by definition, the highest-order city at $r = 0$ has 100% share at every r.) In the middle of panel (a) in figure 11.7, for example, the bell-shaped solid-line curve shows the market share at each r of M^1-goods produced by city 5. We can see from panel (a) that except for the two smallest cities, 2 and 6, every city is almost self-sufficient in its production and consumption of M^1-goods, whereas these two small cities receive most M^1-goods from their neighboring cities. More interestingly, panel (b) shows that for M^2-goods, cities 1, 5, and 7 each have a bell-shaped market share curve covering a large number of neighboring cities. That is, not only the highest-order city, 1, but also both middle-order cities, 5 and 7, have the largest market shares of M^2-goods in their own markets, and they export significant amounts of M^2-goods to many neighboring cities. Therefore, the present hierarchical urban system also exhibits a rich spatial structure in terms of M-good trade.

Finally, figure 11.8 shows the trends of two welfare measures along the evolutionary path, which are in strong contrast to the corresponding panels, (b) and (c), in figure 10.5. Panel (a) in figure 11.8 indicates that the equilibrium utility level of each worker is increasing almost steadily with the economy's population size. In panel (b), the economy's total real land rent, defined by (10.21), is also increasing more than proportionally with the population size. Thus, the economy is in the phase of increasing returns forever. Because we have chosen a parameter set that satisfies condition (11.21), the economy maintains a monopolar spatial structure, and the population growth of large cities (in particular, that of the highest-order city) continues to propel the engine of the economy's growth through the expansion of M-good varieties.

11.5 Conclusions

Despite the intuitive appeal of the notion that cities form a spatial hierarchy, to our knowledge nobody has ever actually shown how such a hierarchy can emerge from a decentralized market process. In this chapter we have provided a demonstration in which differences among industries in scale economies and/or transportation costs define a

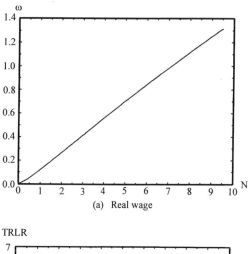

(a) Real wage

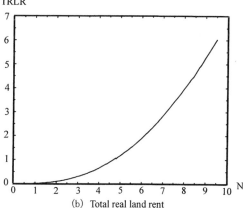

(b) Total real land rent

Figure 11.8
Trends in welfare measures along the evolutionary path

ranking of industries in terms of the tension between the pull of dispersed consumers and that of established agglomerations; this ranking of industries in turn generates a hierarchy of city types, with higher-order cities containing a wider range of industries than lower-order.

Perhaps the surprise is how difficult this demonstration is. We have definitely learned in the course of our urban modeling is that the simple ideas of central-place theory are not so simple to put into practice. Nonetheless, in a qualitative sense, our theoretical model bears out the idea that cities tend naturally to form a hierarchy both in space and in industrial structure. In addition, this model helps to explain why we do not, in practice, see a "typical" size of city: why the actual city size distribution is so wide and shows no tendency to collapse over time. In the next chapter we briefly detour from our theoretical structure to describe some of the surprising and disturbing facts about the overall urban size distribution.

Appendix 11.1: The Equilibrium of the Agricultural Market

As noted before, in the realistic case in which $\tau^A > 0$, the analysis becomes complex, because we must determine to which city the A-good from each location is being shipped—the flow pattern of the A-good. In practice, we can obtain the equilibrium flow pattern of the A-good only through trial and error, as follows.

Let $\{1, 2, \ldots, k, \ldots, K\} \equiv \mathcal{K}$ be the set of cities assumed to exist in the spatial equilibrium of the economy in section 11.2, and $(r_1, r_2, \ldots, r_k, \ldots, r_k)$ be their location. To obtain the equilibrium flow pattern of the A-good in this economy, the first step is to assume a regional division of the economy, $\{A_1, A_2, \ldots, A_l, \ldots, A_R\}$, in terms of A-good trade. Here, each regional area, $A_l = [f_l^-, f_l^+] \subset X$, is supposed to represent a minimum interval of X ($\equiv$ the location space of the economy) in which the A-good trade is balanced. For convenience, region 1 is assumed to locate at the farthest left, region 2 at the next farthest left, and so on, which implies that $f_1^- < f_1^+ \leq f_2^- < f_2^+ \leq \cdots f_R^- < f_R^+$. Because each regional area A_l is supposed to be a minimum interval of X in which the A-good trade is balanced, there must exist a city $k(l)$ in A_l, called the *central city* of region l, such that all flows of the excess A-good (from all agricultural locations) are directed toward this city. Let $p^A(s)$ denote the A-good price at each location $s \in X$. Then to support this flow pattern of the A-good in region l, the A-price curve in the region must be such that

$$p^A(s) = p^A(r_{k(l)})e^{-\tau^A|s - r_{k(l)}|} \quad \text{for} \quad s \in A_l, \tag{11A.1}$$

where $p^A(r_{k(l)})$ represents the A-good price at the central city $k(l)$, which is an unknown that will be determined later. That is, the A-good price curve is single-peaked in each region. Furthermore, when two regions are adjacent to each other, the A-price curve must be continuous at the boundary: $p^A(f_l^+) = p^A(f_{l+1}^-)$ if $f_l^+ = f_{l+1}^-$ for $l = 1, 2, \ldots, R - 1$.

Because the entire surplus generated from A-good production goes to the landlords at each location s, the land rent $R(s)$ there can be obtained as

$$R(s) = \max\{p^A(s) - c^A w(s), 0\} \quad \text{for} \quad s \in X, \tag{11A.2}$$

which implies that $R(f_1^-) = 0$ and $R(f_R^+) = 0$; $R(f_l^-) = 0$ if $f_l^- > f_{l-1}^+$ for $l = 2, 3, \ldots, R$; and $R(f_l^+) = 0$ if $l_l^+ < f_{l+1}^-$ for $l = 1, 2, \ldots, R - 1$. That is, if a border location is adjacent to vacant land, the land rent there must be 0. It can also be readily verified that in equilibrium, no vacant land remains inside any region.

Next, in each region l, the equality of the demand and supply of the A-good must hold. To express this condition, notice that the excess supply of the A-good per unit distance at each noncity location s equals $1 - (\mu^A Y(s)/p^A(s)) = 1 - \mu^A$ [because $Y(s) = c^A w(s) + R(s) = p^A(s)$ by (11A.2)]. Let $\mathcal{K}(l)$ be the set of cities in region l. Then, by (11A.1), the demand for the A-good among workers in each city $k \in \mathcal{K}(l)$ equals $\mu^A Y_k/p^A(r_k) = \mu^A L_k w_k/p^A(r_k)$. Because all excess supply of the A-good is transported toward the city at $r_k(l)$, considering the consumption of the A-good in transportation, the equality of the demand and supply of A-good at city $r_k(l)$ can be expressed as

$$\mu^A \left(\sum_{k \in K(l)} L_k w_k \right) \bigg/ p^A(r_{k(l)}) = (1 - \mu^A) \int_{A_l} e^{-\tau^A |r_k(l) - s|} ds,$$
$$\tag{11A.3}$$
$$\text{for} \quad l = 1, 2, \ldots, R.$$

In addition, for the A-good flow assumed to be feasible in each region l, it must be confirmed that at any other city in region l, the total supply of the A-good to that city must not be less than the demand of the A-good there.

If no equilibrium solution satisfies all equilibrium conditions (noted in section 11.1 and above), we must consider a new regional division and/or a new set of central cities.

Appendix 11.2: The Equilibrium Conditions of the Monocentric Economy

The central city is located at $r = 0$, and to normalize prices, we set the wage rate at the city equal to 1. Then, because for every $L_1^h > 0$ for every h, it follows that $w_1 = w_1^h = 1$ for every h. The agricultural price function takes the same form as in equation (9.1),

$$p^A(r) = p^A e^{-\tau^A |r|}. \tag{11A.4}$$

The agricultural wage on fringe land is, as in equation (9.2),

$$w^A(f) = \frac{p^A e^{-\tau^A f}}{c^A}. \tag{11A.5}$$

We can now solve for p^A and f exactly as we did in chapter 9. Equating supply and demand for agricultural output gives

$$p^A = \frac{\mu^A(N - 2c^A f)}{2(1 - \mu^A) \displaystyle\int_0^f e^{-\tau^A s} ds}. \tag{11A.6}$$

Equating real wages for manufacturing workers and the fringe agricultural worker proceeds as follows. City workers have nominal wage 1, and the fringe agricultural worker nominal wage is given by (11A.5). The cost-of-living index at f differs from that in the city by factor $e^{[\Sigma_h \mu^h \tau^h - \tau^A \mu^A]f}$, so equality of real wages means

$$p^A = c^A e^{[\Sigma_h \mu^h \tau^h + (1-\mu^A)\tau^A]f} = c^A e^{\mu^M[\bar{\tau}^M + \tau^A]f}, \tag{11A.7}$$

where μ^M and $\bar{\tau}^A$ are defined in (11.9). These equilibrium conditions are clearly exactly analogous to those of chapter 9, the only difference being the consumption-weighted average of manufacturing trade costs appearing in (11A.7). Given values of p^A and f implicitly defined by (11A.6) and (11A.7), equilibrium values of other variables can be found. In particular, by eliminating p^A from equations (11A.6) and (11A.7), we have

$$\mu^A(N/c^A - 2f)e^{-\mu^M[\bar{\tau}^M + \tau^A]f} = 2(1 - \mu^A)\int_0^f e^{-\tau^A s} ds, \tag{11A.8}$$

which determines f uniquely as an increasing function of N, as in chapter 9.

Finally, to assure that no firm has an incentive to defect from the city, all industries must meet the sustainability condition, (11.8), where the potential function for each industry h is defined by (11.10).

Appendix 11.3: The Proof that (11.16) Implies (11.17)

We prove that (11.16) implies (11.17) through several steps of analysis.

11.3.a   First, we rewrite the potential function, (11.10), in a more convenient form for the present purpose. Taking the negative exponential term, $\exp - (\sigma^h - 1)\tau^h r$, outside the brackets of (11.10), and expressing the potential explicitly as a function of two parameters, r and f, we have that

$$\Omega^h(r;f) = e^{-\eta^h r}\left[\frac{1 + \mu^M}{2} + \Psi^h(r,f)\left(\frac{1 - \mu^M}{2}\right)e^{2(\sigma^h - 1)\tau^h r}\right], \qquad (11A.9)$$

where

$$\eta^h \equiv \sigma^h[\mu^M\bar{\tau}^M - \mu^A\tau^A] + (\sigma^h - 1)\tau^h. \qquad (11A.10)$$

After the substitution of (11.11) into (11A.9), we use the following identity,

$$e^{[2(\sigma^h - 1)\tau^h - \tau^A]r} = 1 + [2(\sigma^h - 1)\tau^h - \tau^A]\int_0^r e^{[2(\sigma^h - 1)\tau^h - \tau^A]s}ds, \qquad (11A.11)$$

and arrange terms appropriately. Then we can eventually obtain the new expression of the potential function as follows:

$$\Omega^h(r;f) =$$

$$e^{-\eta^h r}\left[1 + \mu^A(\sigma^h - 1)\tau^h\int_0^r e^{2(\sigma^h - 1)\tau^h s}\left(1 - \frac{1 - e^{-\tau As}}{1 - e^{-\tau Af}}\right)ds\right]. \qquad (11A.12)$$

11.3.b Next, in the context of section 11.2, take any industry $h \leq \tilde{H}$, and let $\tilde{f}^h$ be the critical fringe distance associated with the critical population, $\tilde{N}^h$. Then the critical potential curve, $\Omega^h(r;\tilde{f}^h)$, is tangent to the horizontal line having height 1 at the critical distance $\tilde{r}^h$ (refer to figure 11.2). Hence, the pair $(\tilde{r}^h, \tilde{f}^h)$ must satisfy the following two relations,

$$\Omega^h(\tilde{r}^h;\tilde{f}^h) = 1, \qquad (11A.13)$$

and

$$\partial\Omega^h(\tilde{r}^h;\tilde{f}^h)/\partial r = 0, \qquad (11A.14)$$

where $\tilde{r}^h > 0$ and $\tilde{f}^h > 0$. For convenience, let us define

$$v^A(s) \equiv 1 - g^A(s), \ g^A(s) \equiv e^{-\tau As}, \qquad (11A.15)$$

$$v^h(s) \equiv 1 - g^h(s), \ g^h(s) \equiv \frac{\eta^h}{\mu^A(\sigma^h - 1)\tau^h}e^{-2[(\sigma^h - 1)\tau^h - \eta^h]s}. \qquad (11A.16)$$

By solving (11A.13) for the term, $1 - e^{-\tau A\tilde{f}^h}$, we have that

$$1 - e^{-\tau A\tilde{f}^h} = \int_0^{\tilde{r}^h} e^{2(\sigma^h - 1)\tau^h s}v^A(s)ds\left/\int_0^{\tilde{r}^h} e^{2(\sigma^h - 1)\tau^h s}v^h(s)ds.\right. \qquad (11A.17)$$

Condition (11A.14) yields that

$$1 - e^{-\tau A \tilde{f}^h} = v^A(\tilde{r}^h)/v^h(\tilde{r}^h).$$ (11A.18)

Hence, if we define

$$Q^h(r) \equiv \int_0^r e^{2(\sigma h - 1)\tau h s} v^h(s) ds/v^h(r) - \int_0^r e^{2(\sigma h - 1)\tau h s} v^A(s) ds/v^A(r)$$

$$= \int_0^r e^{2(\sigma h - 1)\tau h s} \frac{v^A(s)}{v^h(r)} \left(\frac{v^h(s)}{v^A(s)} - \frac{v^h(r)}{v^A(r)} \right) ds,$$ (11A.19)

then, by (11A.17) and (11A.18), $\tilde{r}^h$ must be such that

$$Q^h(\tilde{r}^h) = 0,$$ (11A.20)

and $\tilde{r}^h > 0$. It is not difficult to show that equation (11A.20) has a unique positive solution. (For a proof of this statement, see Fujita, Krugman, and Mori 1995, pp. 74–76.)

11.3.c To be explicit about the parameters involved, let us rewrite (11A.19) as follows:

$$Q(r; \mu^A, \tau^A, \Delta T, \sigma^h, \tau^h) \equiv \int_0^r e^{2(\sigma h - 1)\tau h s} \frac{v^A(s)}{v^h(r)} \left(\frac{v^h(s)}{v^A(s)} - \frac{v^h(r)}{v^A(r)} \right) ds,$$ (11A.21)

where

$$\Delta T \equiv \mu^M \bar{\tau}^M - \mu^A \tau^A = \sum_h \mu^h \tau^h - \mu^A \tau^A,$$ (11A.22)

$$\eta^h \equiv \sigma^h \Delta T + (\sigma^h - 1)\tau^h,$$

$$v^A(s) \equiv v^A(s; \tau^A) \equiv 1 - e^{-\tau A s},$$ (11A.23)

and

$$v^h(s) \equiv v^h(s; \mu^A, \tau^A, \Delta T, \sigma^h, \tau^h)$$

$$\equiv 1 - [\eta^h / \{\mu^A(\sigma^h - 1)\tau^h\}] e^{-[2(\sigma h - 1)\tau h - \eta^h]s}.$$ (11A.24)

Then, as noted above, there exists a unique positive $\tilde{r}^h \equiv \tilde{r}(\mu^A, \tau^A, \Delta T, \sigma^h, \tau^h)$ such that

$$Q(\tilde{r}^h; \mu^A, \tau^A, \Delta T, \sigma^h, \tau^h) = 0.$$ (11A.25)

11.3.d Next, focusing on the parameter $\sigma^h [\equiv \rho^h/(1 - \rho^h)]$, the total derivative of (11A.25) with respect to $\tilde{r}^h$ and σ^h leads to

$$\frac{d\tilde{r}^h}{d\sigma^h} = -\frac{\partial Q/\partial\sigma^h}{\partial Q/\partial\tilde{r}^h},$$ (11A.26)

where

$$\frac{\partial Q}{\partial\tilde{r}^h} = \left\{\int_0^{\tilde{r}^h} e^{2(\sigma^h-1)\tau hs} v^h(s)ds / v^h(\tilde{r}^h)\right\}[2(\sigma^h - 1)\tau^h - \eta^h]$$

$$\times \frac{g^h(\tilde{r}^h)}{v^h(\tilde{r}^h)}\left\{\frac{\tau^A}{2(\sigma^h - 1) - \eta^h} - \frac{v^A(\tilde{r}^h)g^h(\tilde{r}^h)}{v^h(\tilde{r}^h)g^A(\tilde{r}^h)}\right\},$$ (11A.27)

$$\frac{\partial Q}{\partial\sigma^h} = \int_0^{\tilde{r}^h} 2\tau^h s e^{2(\sigma^h-1)\tau hs} \frac{v^A(s)}{v^h(\tilde{r}^h)}\left(\frac{v^h(s)}{v^A(s)} - \frac{v^h(\tilde{r}^h)}{v^A(\tilde{r}^h)}\right)ds$$

$$+ [v^h(\tilde{r}^h)]^{-2}\int_0^{\tilde{r}^h} e^{2(\sigma^h-1)\tau hs} C^h(s)ds,$$ (11A.28)

in which

$$C^h(s) \equiv \left[\frac{\Delta T}{(\sigma^h - 1)\eta^h} + (\tau^h - \Delta T)s\right]g^h(y)v^h(\tilde{r}^h)$$

$$- \left[\frac{\Delta T}{(\sigma^h - 1)\eta^h} + (\tau^h - \Delta T)\tilde{r}^h\right]g^h(\tilde{r}^h)v^h(s).$$ (11A.29)

11.3.e It is not difficult to show that $\partial Q/\partial\tilde{r}^h$ is always positive (see Fujita, Krugman, and Mori 1995, p. 75). We can also show (see Fujita, Krugman, and Mori 1995, pp. 77–78) that

$$\Delta T \geq 0 \to C^h(s) > 0 \quad \text{for} \quad s \in (0, \tilde{r}^h).$$ (11A.30)

Therefore, because the first term of the right side of (11A.28) is always positive, it follows from (11A.28) and (11A.30) that $\{\Delta T \geq 0 \to \partial Q/\partial\tilde{r}^h > 0\}$, and hence we can conclude by (11A.26) that

$$\Delta T \geq 0 \to \frac{d\tilde{r}^h}{d\sigma^h} \equiv \frac{\partial\tilde{r}(\mu^A, \tau^A, \Delta T, \sigma^h, \tau^h)}{\partial\sigma^h} < 0.$$ (11A.31)

Next, if we substitute $\tilde{r}^h \equiv \tilde{r}(\mu^A, \tau^A, \Delta T, \sigma^h, \tau^h)$ into (11A.18), $\tilde{f}^h$, which is denoted by $\tilde{f}(\mu^A, \tau^A, \Delta T, \sigma^h, \tau^h)$, can be uniquely determined. It is not difficult to show by using (11A.31) that

$$\Delta T \geq 0 \rightarrow \frac{d\tilde{f}^h}{d\sigma^h} \equiv \frac{\partial \tilde{f}(\mu^A, \tau^A, \Delta T, \sigma^h, \tau^h)}{\partial \sigma^h} < 0. \tag{11A.32}$$

If we replace f in equation (11A.8) with $\tilde{f}^h \equiv \tilde{f}(\mu^A, \tau^A, \Delta T, \sigma^h, \tau^h)$, then $\tilde{N}^h \equiv \tilde{N}(\mu^A, \tau^A, \Delta T, \sigma^h, \tau^h)$ is uniquely determined. Then because the relation (11A.8) determines f as an increasing function of N, we can conclude by (11A.32) that

$$\Delta T \geq 0 \rightarrow \frac{d\tilde{N}^h}{d\sigma^h} \equiv \frac{\partial \tilde{N}(\mu^A, \tau^A, \Delta T, \sigma^h, \tau^h),}{\partial \sigma^h} < 0. \tag{11A.33}$$

11.3.f Next, although ΔT ($\equiv \sum_h \mu^h \tau^h - \mu^A \tau^A$) contains each τ^h, here we treat ΔT as a constant. (Notice that our objective here is not the comparative statics of critical values, but the ordering of critical values for different industries under a fixed set of parameters. When parameters are fixed, ΔT becomes a fixed number.) Then, in a manner similar to that employed in appendix 11.3.e, we can show that

$$\Delta T \geq 0 \rightarrow \frac{d\tilde{r}^h}{d\tau^h}\bigg|_{\Delta T=\text{const}} \equiv \frac{\partial \tilde{r}(\mu^A, \tau^A, \Delta T, \sigma^h, \tau^h)}{\partial \tau^h} < 0, \tag{11A.34}$$

$$\Delta T \geq 0 \rightarrow \frac{d\tilde{f}^h}{d\tau^h}\bigg|_{\Delta T=\text{const}} \equiv \frac{\partial \tilde{f}(\mu^A, \tau^A, \Delta T, \sigma^h, \tau^h)}{\partial \tau^h} < 0, \tag{11A.35}$$

$$\Delta T \geq 0 \rightarrow \frac{d\tilde{N}^h}{d\tau^h}\bigg|_{\Delta T=\text{const}} \equiv \frac{\partial \tilde{N}(\mu^A, \tau^A, \Delta T, \sigma^h, \tau^h)}{\partial \tau^h} < 0. \tag{11A.36}$$

11.3.g Now we fix all parameters of the model (and hence, the value of ΔT) and assume that the assumption (11.15) holds and that $\Delta T \geq 0$. In this context, take any $h \leq \tilde{H}$ and $g \leq \tilde{H}$, and suppose that

$$\rho^h > \rho^g \text{ (i.e., } \sigma^h > \sigma^g) \text{ and } \tau^h \geq \tau^g. \tag{11A.37}$$

Then, it follows that

$$\tilde{r}^h = \tilde{r}(\mu^A, \tau^A, \Delta T, \sigma^h, \tau^h) < \tilde{r}(\mu^A, \tau^A, \Delta T, \sigma^g, \tau^h) \quad \text{by (11A.33)}$$

$$\leq \tilde{r}(\mu^A, \tau^A, \Delta T, \sigma^g, \tau^g) \quad \text{by (11A.34)} \tag{11A.38}$$

$$= \tilde{r}^g.$$

We can show similarly that (11A.37) also implies that $\tilde{f}^h < \tilde{f}^g$ and $\tilde{N}^h < \tilde{N}^g$. In the same way, we can also show that if $\rho^h \geq \rho^g$ (i.e., $\sigma^h \geq \sigma^g$) and $\tau^h > \tau^g$, then $\tilde{r}^h < \tilde{r}^g$, $\tilde{f}^h < \tilde{f}^g$, and $\tilde{N}^h < \tilde{N}^g$. Finally, it follows immediately by definition that (11A.37) implies $\tilde{\theta}^h > \tilde{\theta}^g$. Therefore, summarizing the results, we can conclude that (11.16) implies (11.17).

Notes

1. For an elaboration of this empirical study (including figure 11.1), see Fujita, Krugman, and Mori 1995.

2. The Great West is the nineteenth-century name for the area that represents the vast interior region of the United States west of the Ohio River or Lake Michigan (Cronon 1991).

3. Figure 11.1 was created by adapting figures 5 to 8 in Borchert 1967. Based on the rank size distribution of 178 U.S. cities in 1960, Borchert defined four thresholds of population size (at which the slope of the rank-size distribution changed noticeably). Then, for the years before 1960, each ith size-order threshold, T_{is}, in year s ($s = 1830$ or 1870) was defined by relationship, $T_{is} = T_{io}(N_s/N_o)$, where T_{io} is the ith threshold population in 1960, and N_s [respectively, N_o] is the U.S. population in year s [respectively, 1960]. In developing figure 11.1, for simplicity, we combined the original second- and third-order cities; the cities of the original fourth and fifth orders were also combined to form the new third order.

4. The threshold population for each size-order in 1830 is given as follows: The first-order cities were those with a population beyond 530,000 (which actually did not exist), the second-order cities had populations between 90,000 and 530,000, and the third-order cities were those populations between 15,000 and 90,000.

5. These second-order cities, of course, also provided nearby hinterlands with most goods and services that were provided elsewhere by third-order cities. In other words, they upgraded themselves to second-order cities by adding functions to those of third-order cities. The same note applies to the highest-order city. Hence, the entire system has, roughly speaking, a hierarchical structure in which a higher-order city supplies its own goods as well as most goods supplied in lower-order cities.

6. This story is not unique. A similar urbanization process took place in Europe in the twelfth century as its population increased rapidly. For a comprehensive study of urban development in Europe and the United States, see, for example, Marshall 1989.

7. This can be shown essentially the same way as in the case of equation (9.26).

8. Condition (11.21) is evidently related to the no-black-hole condition. If $H = 1$, then (11.21) implies that the no-black-hole condition is not satisfied, and so ensures a monocentric structure for all N. When $H > 1$, the condition is clearly weaker. It does not prevent new cities from forming, but it is sufficient for monopolarity.

9. More precisely, at this moment the monocentric system becomes structurally unstable, implying that any small increase of N beyond $\tilde{N}^1$ makes the monocentric system unstable (in the usual sense).

10. In the previous case of chapter 10, when a single new city is born (as N reaches the critical value), the two cities come to have the same size, which in turn makes the spatial

system stable. In the present context, however, if only a single (very small) city emerged at $\tilde{r}^1$, for example, then the resulting two-city system would be asymmetric, which in turn would make the system unstable. This is because the existence of any small number of M^1-firms at $\tilde{r}^1$ enhances significantly the competition of M^1-industry there, even though it does not create a significant new demand there. In this situation, for a potential entrant into M^1-industry, the opposite location, $-\tilde{r}^1$, becomes more attractive than $\tilde{r}^1$ because of the absence of (competing) M^1-firms there. Hence, as N reaches $\tilde{N}^1$, the spatial system can remain stable only when a pair of (symmetric) cities emerges at $\tilde{r}^1$ and $-\tilde{r}^1$.

11. In reality, cities rarely relocate marginally. Introducing urban infrastructure into our model would eliminate this odd phenomenon.

12. Unlike the first frontier city, this second frontier city (on the right side of $r = 0$) stays at the same location, although it emerges as a result of a continuous bifurcation. In general, when a new frontier city emerges next to a large (highest- or medium-order) city, it grows slowly and relocates continuously outward for a while. In contrast, if a new frontier city emerges next to a lowest-order city (which is always small), it grows very rapidly and remains at the same location from the beginning.

13. Christaller's *hierarchical principle* states that a higher-order central place shall provide its own order of consumption goods as well as all consumption goods that are provided at any lower-order central places.

14. In terms of the city-index, $k = 1, 2, \ldots, 8$, indicated in line (30) of figure 11.3, when $N = 9.30$, the population of each city is as follows: $N_1 = 6.42$, $N_2 = 0.00691$, $N_3 = 0.0722$, $N_4 = 0.0478$, $N_5 = 0.167$, $N_6 = 0.000763$, $N_7 = 0.138$, $N_8 = 0.0240$.

An Empirical Digression:
The Sizes of Cities

The empirical motivation for the analysis in chapter 11 was, of course, the observation that real cities come in a wide variety of sizes and types. As we saw, differences among industries in scale economies and/or transport costs can indeed produce a hierarchical urban system, vindicating the classic analysis of Christaller (1933). However, we must now admit that we—along with all other urban economists and geographers—nonetheless continue to have a problem in the match between the theory and the data, a problem of a quite unusual kind.

Attempts to match economic theory with data usually face the problem that the theory is excessively neat, that theory gives simple, sharp-edged predictions, whereas the real world throws up complicated and messy outcomes. When it comes to the size distribution of cities, however, the problem we face is that the data offer a stunningly neat picture, one that is hard to reproduce in any plausible (or even implausible) theoretical model.

12.1 The Size Distribution of Cities

It has been known for at least seventy years that the distribution of larger cities in the United States is surprisingly well described by a power law; that is, the number of cities with a population larger than S is approximately proportional to S^{-a}, with a quite close to 1. (See Carroll 1982 for a survey of the massive empirical literature on city size distributions.) To get an idea of how well this works, consider that in 1991 there were forty U.S. metropolitan areas with more than one million people, twenty with more than two million, and nine with more than four million. (Houston was just a bit too small.) Figure 12.1 plots the log of metropolitan area size against the log of rank (i.e.,

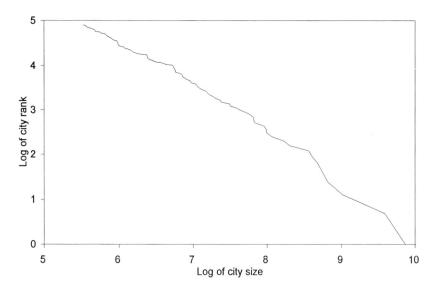

Figure 12.1
U.S. city size

New York = 1, Los Angeles = 2, etc.) for the 130 such areas listed in the *Statistical Abstract of the United States*; the near linearity, and the approximately 45-degree slope, are remarkable. And more formal statistical analysis confirms this visual impression. Let $N(S)$ be the number of cities of population S or greater; then a log-linear regression finds

$$\ln(N) = 10.549 - 1.004 \ln(S)$$
$$(.010)$$

Nor is this just a fact about a single time and place. As already suggested, the distribution of city sizes in the United States has been well described by a power law with an exponent close to 1 at least for the past century. Dobkins and Ioannides (1996) have reassembled U.S. historical data on "urban places"—that is, cities under a single jurisdiction—back to 1900 into data on metropolitan areas more or less along modern definitions, and estimated a for each census year; the estimate for 1900 is 1.044, and in no year is it very far from 1.[1] International data are more problematic, in particular because it is difficult to assemble comparably defined metropolitan areas. However, the classic study by Rosen and Resnick (1980) suggests that a power law with an exponent

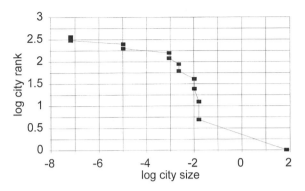

Figure 12.2
Evolved city size

not too far from 1 well describes most national metropolitan size distributions, and that the exponent gets closer to 1 the more carefully the metropolitan areas are defined.

There is, in short, something suspiciously like an empirical law regarding the size distribution of cities. Indeed, the proposition that city sizes follow a power law with exponent 1 is often referred to as Zipf's Law, after eccentric author George Zipf, whose *Human Behavior and the Principle of Least Effort* (1949) collected a number of apparent empirical regularities in the social sciences. An alternative name is the *rank-size rule*: If a power law with exponent 1 held exactly, the second-largest city would have one-half the population of the largest, the third, one-third that population, etc.

12.2 Do Urban Theories Predict the Rank-Size Rule?

The urban hierarchy model developed in chapter 11 has no automatic tendency to produce anything resembling the rank-size rule. We can see this by examining directly the results from our simulation exercises. Figure 12.2, analogously to figure 12.1, plots the "data" for the fifteen-city urban hierarchy we evolved in chapter 11. Clearly these data do not even reproduce the log-linearity of the real data, let alone the exponent of 1. It might be possible to find some parameter combination that would produce a closer fit to the rank-size rule. However, the key feature of that rule is its apparent robustness: its consistent validity over a century of U.S. data and its rough applicability across a broad cross-section of countries as well. This means that any explanation ought to be similarly robust, not dependent on parameters lying within some narrow range.

The same objection applies to attempts to explain the rank-size rule using other models of urban size distribution. The main contender here would be Henderson-type urban system models of the kind described in chapter 2. Recall from that chapter that such models generate a size distribution via the following argument: External economies tend to be specific to particular industries, but diseconomies tend to depend on a city's overall size, whatever it produces. This asymmetry has two consequences. First, because there are diseconomies to city size, it makes no sense to put industries without mutual spillovers in the same city—if steel production and publishing generate few mutual external economies, steel mills and publishing houses should be in different cities, where they do not generate congestion and high land rents for each other. So each city should be specialized (at least in its export industries) in one or a few industries that create external economies. Second, the extent of these external economies may vary greatly across industries: A textile city may have little reason to include more than a handful of mills, whereas a banking center might do best if it contains practically all of a nation's financial business. So the optimal size of a city depends on its role.

It is an impressively concise and clean analysis. It makes the sizes of cities an economic variable that depends on forces that can, in principle, be measured (and Henderson's model has given rise to extensive empirical work, such as Henderson 1988); it also helps explain why the actual distribution of cities contains a wide size range that shows no signs of collapsing.

It is hard to see, however, why this model should generate anything that looks like a power law. Suppose that the optimum banking city has four million people, the optimum high-tech manufacturing city two million, the optimum low-tech city one million; why should the economy require the same ratio of banking to high-tech cities as of high-tech to low-tech? And because the Henderson model generates a size distribution out of a tension between external economies and diseconomies—both of which presumably depend on the technologies of production, communication, transportation, and so on—one would surely predict from this model that the size distribution would change over time, rather than show the mysterious stability it exhibits in practice.

In short, the regularity of the urban size distribution poses a real puzzle, one that neither our approach nor the most plausible alternative approach to city sizes seems to answer.

12.3 Can Random Growth Explain the Rank-Size Rule?

Both our spatial model of urban hierarchy and Henderson-type urban system models, although they rely on some rudimentary dynamics to limit the range of possible outcomes, are essentially tales about static trade-offs: the trade-off between external economies and diseconomies in the Henderson model, the trade-off between economies of scale and distance in central-place theory as formalized in chapter 11. There is, however, an alternative tradition, due mainly to Herbert Simon, which views the existence of a wide size range of cities (or for that matter of business firms) as evidence that there really are no trade-offs—that size is more or less irrelevant. And Simon argued that precisely because size is irrelevant, a process of random growth can produce a huge range of sizes whose upper tail is well described by a power law.

Simon's original exposition of a random-growth model (Simon 1955; Ijiri and Simon 1977) has had surprisingly little impact on economic thinking, perhaps because it is nihilistic about the economics, giving us little more to say, but also in part because the exposition is peculiarly dense. Here we offer a streamlined version that serves to highlight both the insightfulness and the weakness of the model.

12.3.1 Simon's Model

As a starting point, it is useful to consider an alternative statement of the power law on urban sizes. We know that the upper tail is well described by a relationship of the form $N = kS^{-a}$, where N is the number of cities with populations greater than S. We may therefore also say that the *density* of city sizes is $n = akS^{-a-1}$. Finally, in what turns out to be the most useful statement, we may say that the elasticity of the density of cities with respect to size is $-a - 1$:

$$\frac{dn}{dS}\frac{S}{n} = -a - 1. \tag{12.1}$$

We can now turn to Simon's urban growth model. Simon envisaged a process in which the urban population grows over time by discrete increments—call them "lumps," and let the population at any point in time, measured in lumps, be P. Where does a new lump go when it arrives? Simon supposes that with some probability π, it goes off to a previously unpopulated location; that is, it creates a new small city. With probability $1 - \pi$, it attaches itself to an existing city, with the probability that any particular city gets the next lump proportional to its population.

This is an extremely nihilistic and simplistic model. It supposes that there are neither advantages nor disadvantages to city size: A city is simply a clump of lumps whose expected growth rate is independent of size. If you like, you may think of a lump as an industry; in this case, Simon's model says that industries are equally likely to give birth to other industries in the same city regardless of the city's size.

There would be little reason to take such a model seriously, except for one thing: The size distribution of cities does follow a power law, and Simon's model both predicts this result and gives at least a hint why the size distribution might have remained stable despite huge changes in technology and economic structure.

To analyze the model, we provisionally assume that over time the urban size distribution converges to a steady state. That is, the ratio of the number of cities of size S, n_S, to the population tends toward a constant. The ratio n_S/P can change for three reasons. A city of size $S - 1$ may expand by one lump, which increases n_S; there are n_{S-1} such cities, and the probability of this happening for a single one of these is $(1 - \pi)(S - 1)/P$. A city of size S may expand by one lump, with probability $(1 - \pi)S/P$, which reduces n_S. And the overall population is increasing, which reduces n_S/P. If we write the expected change in n_S/P when P increases and are carefully sloppy about the discrete nature of the change in P, we find

$$\frac{Ed(n_S/P)}{dP} = \frac{1}{P^2}[(1 - \pi)(S - 1)n_{S-1} - (1 - \pi)Sn_S - n_S]. \tag{12.2}$$

If the city size distribution is to approach a steady state, however, in the long run this expected change must be 0, giving us a relationship in steady state between the number of cities of sizes S and $S - 1$:

$$\frac{n_S}{n_{S-1}} = \frac{(1 - \pi)(S - 1)}{(1 - \pi)S + 1}. \tag{12.3}$$

This may be rewritten as

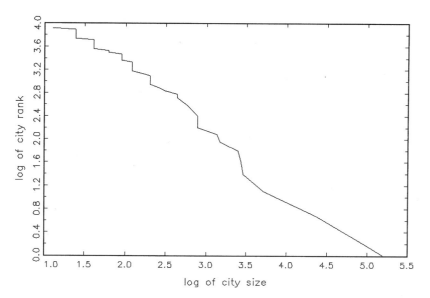

Figure 12.3
City size from random growth

$$\frac{n_S - n_{S-1}}{n_{S-1}} = \frac{\pi - 2}{(1 - \pi)S + 1}.$$

(12.4)

We now focus only on the upper tail of the distribution, for which
S is large. In this case, it is possible to approximate the discrete distribution of city sizes by a smooth distribution $n(S)$, with

$$\frac{dn/dS}{n} \cong \frac{n_S - n_{S-1}}{n_{S-1}} = \frac{\pi - 2}{(1 - \pi)S + 1}.$$

(12.5)

And we can then derive the elasticity of n with respect to S,

$$\frac{dn}{dS}\frac{S}{n} = \frac{\pi - 2}{1 - \pi + 1/S} \cong \frac{\pi - 2}{1 - \pi},$$

(12.6)

which by (12.1) tells us that the upper tail of the city size distribution
is characterized by a power law with exponent $a = 1/(1 - \pi)$.

Does this really work? Yes, it does. Figure 12.3 shows the results of
a simulation run in which π was set equal to 0.2, and in which we
started with 10 seeds of one lump each and allowed the population to
grow by a factor of 100. The figure shows the rank-size relationship
for the top 50 cities; it is reasonably log-linear, with a slope not too far
from the predicted value.

If your concern is with the seeming universality of a power law on city sizes, with an exponent that is stable across time and space, Simon's model represents a big improvement over the "economistic" models, for at least three reasons:

1. It predicts a power law, whereas the urban system and central-place models do not.

2. The parameter that determines the exponent on the power law is the probability of forming a new city, which seems less obviously something that must have changed drastically over the past century than variables like economies of scale or urban commuting costs.

3. The mysterious exponent of 1, which seems so hard to justify, has a natural interpretation here: It is what you get when increments to urban population usually attach themselves to existing cities rather than forming new cities.

So Simon's model seems to get us much closer to the grail of understanding the power law on city sizes. One might object to its lack of economic content. However, even if one is willing to let that slide, there is a further problem.

12.3.2 The Degeneracy Problem

In the derivation of the power law result in Simon's model, the crucial first step was the assumption that the urban size distribution tends to approach a steady state. Yet this can never be exactly true: The size of the largest city has no upper bound and therefore always tends to rise. The model nonetheless works because the largest city tends in the long run to have an ever smaller share of the total population, and therefore an ever smaller share of the increment in population goes to making that biggest city bigger. Suppose that the distribution really followed a power law throughout (it actually does so only for the upper tail, but this is good enough), and let S_{min} be the size of the minimum possible city. Then it is straightforward to show that the share of the population in cities larger than any given size S is $(S/S_{min})^{1-a}$. Because this is a constant, the share of the growth in population going to make the biggest cities bigger eventually becomes negligible, justifying the steady-state assumption.

This works only if $a > 1$, which is true as long as $\pi > 0$. If $a = 1$, then Simon's process does not produce a power law—as one might expect, because with $a = 1$, a power law would predict that the population of cities of size larger than any given size S would be infinite. But unfortunately, the data tell us that a is extremely close to 1, implying that π is essentially 0.

One might think that we can evade this problem by assuming that π is only close to 0, but not exactly 0. However, intuition suggests that when π is very small it requires a very large increase in the urban population to produce a smooth power law. Simulation experiments confirm this intuition: With π anywhere close to 0, the distribution tends to approach a steady state only after a massive increase in population. Indeed, figure 12.3 shows the results of a simulation with π still an unacceptably large 0.2; to get the fairly smooth distribution shown, the urban population had to increase by a factor of 100, and the fit to a power law is still not nearly as smooth as the one we see in the actual data.

It is true that U.S. urban population has increased by a factor of approximately 50 since the mid-nineteenth century. However, as we noted earlier, a power law on U.S. city sizes—with a very close to 1—has prevailed at least since 1890. Moreover, the rank-size rule works fairly well for countries whose populations have grown by much less than that of the United States.

Incidentally, a power law with an exponent of 1 does not imply an infinite population in the real data because we are saved from absurdity by an integer constraint. A continuation of the power law for the United States would predict 0.5 cities with twice the population of New York, 0.25 cities with four times the population, and so on, with an implied infinite population; but because fractional cities are impossible, this is not a real problem. This observation should send chills down the spine of anyone who knows something about the history of physics: The need to impose an integer constraint to avoid predicting infinite black-body radiation led to the discovery of the quantum nature of energy. It is deeply suggestive that the exponent of the power law on city sizes should be precisely at the point at which the indivisible nature of cities is necessary for the distribution to make sense. But what it suggests is still a mystery.

12.3.3 Other Stochastic Models

Some other kind of stochastic model might possibly explain the remarkable tenacity of Zipf's Law. A number of analysts have suggested that an approximate power law might emerge from *Gibrat's Law*: the assumption that the expected rate of growth of a city is independent of its size. Recently Gabaix (1997) has shown more precisely what is required to make this work. He supposed that over some range of city sizes both the expected growth rate of a city's population and the variance of that growth rate are independent of size, and that the expected growth rate is 0. This produces a steady-state distribution that approximates a power law over that range, and with an exponent of 1. A simple example is the following: Suppose that cities can come in sizes 1, 2, 4, 8, 16, 32, 64; and suppose that for all sizes except the top or bottom a city has a one-third chance of doubling in population, a two-thirds chance of halving, so that the expected population growth is 0. (At the bottom, cities have some probability of staying where they are, otherwise they double in population; at the top, the same, except that they halve instead of doubling). It takes only a few minutes with a spreadsheet to demonstrate that this rule does in fact produce Zipf's Law.

Is this a solution to the riddle? Our view is that it is ingenious but not entirely satisfactory. It is easy, if disturbing, to suppose that there are really constant returns to city size, so that the expected rate of growth is independent of size. But Gibrat's Law requires also that the variance of that growth rate be independent of city size, which is harder to understand: If a city consists of a simple assortment of industries, with neither positive nor negative spillovers between them, shouldn't the variance of the growth rate decline with size simply as a matter of diversification? The economics of the phenomenon remain puzzling.

Krugman 1997 makes yet another suggestion: The randomness that creates the power law may not involve random growth but random "connections" in space. For example, imagine port cities that serve the interior along a transport network formed by random connections among transport nodes, with the direction of the preferred connections reflecting accidents either of history or of geography. Alternatively, we could suppose that the connections lie in some abstract space of industry linkages. In either case, the size distribution of the hinterlands would then reflect the principles of "percolation theory," a well-studied area in the physical sciences. (The original motivating example was the size distribution of connected areas in porous rocks.) Percolation models easily produce power laws; indeed, the distribution of river sizes, as measured by volume of flow, fits Zipf's Law quite well! A percolation model might provide a way around the problems with Simon's model. However, all this is purely speculative.

12.4   Conclusions

At this point we have no resolution to the explanation of the striking regularity in city size distributions. We must acknowledge that it poses a real intellectual challenge to our understanding of cities, in at least two ways. The first is that at this point nobody has come up with a plausible story about the process that generates the rank-size rule, although Simon's early analysis and later variants do provide some insight into the kind of process that might be involved.

But there is also a more profound issue: The stochastic models that have been proposed all rely fundamentally on the assumption of constant returns to city size, so that a city's expected growth rate is independent of its size. Yet all existing economic models of cities involve returns that are anything but constant. Rather, they involve a tug-of-war between increasing returns and decreasing returns, which for any given type of city (industry specialization in Henderson-type models, order in the central-place model of chapter 11) determines a characteristic size. Perhaps there is some way that we do not currently understand to reconcile the tension between centripetal and centrifugal forces that we believe determines city sizes at the micro level, and the as-if-constant-returns dynamics that seem to apply at the macro level. We hope that future research will resolve this puzzle.

Note

1. Dobkins and Ioannides actually estimate a for all cities; most other estimates use only the upper tail. For example, their estimate for 1990 covers 334 metropolitan areas, not the 130 in our own regression. Both practical experience and the theoretical analysis below suggest that their already striking results would be even more striking had they restricted themselves to the larger areas.

Ports, Transportation Hubs, and City Location

In a way, we have allowed von Thünen's agenda to dictate our discussion of cities up to this point: We tried to explain the emergence of spatial structure on a one-dimensional version of his "fertile plain which is crossed by no navigable river or canal." Yet in reality any schoolchild can tell you that many cities owe their origin precisely to their position on rivers, canals, good harbors, and so on. Indeed, most of the world's great cities are located at transportation hubs of one sort or another.

In chapter 8 we suggested that a way to introduce the effect of such hubs without sacrificing the simplicity of the linear economy is to imagine that the economy branches at some point, forming something like the letter Y—or, more generally, something like an asterisk (*). In this chapter we apply the same model developed in chapters 9 and 10 to such a branching geometry and show why and in what sense the point of branching—the crotch of the Y—is an especially likely place for a city to emerge.

Figure 13.1 illustrates the geometry of our modified world. As before, there is one-dimensional land of uniform quality stretching indefinitely along a line, but this line splits into two indistinguishable branches at the *branch point*, labeled *b*. Although the easiest interpretation of the figure may be as one in which three branches of a valley converge at some point, we view it as a metaphorical representation for any sort of transportation hub, whether created by the crossing of transportation routes or even by the availability of a port through which goods may be shipped to and from distant regions.[1]

It is immediately apparent that the branch point has a sort of special claim to be an urban location. As one moves away from *b* down any of the branches, one gets closer to consumers along that branch, but one moves away from consumers along *two* (or more, if the economy

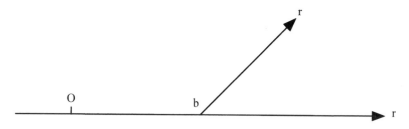

Figure 13.1
The new location space ($k = 1$)

is an asterisk) branches. Thus other things being the same, one would expect b to be a point of especially good market access.

To be more precise, we will show that when the agricultural area of the economy extends into all three branches of land, the market potential curve for manufacturing has a cusp at the branch point, even when there is no city there. As a result, the branch point is likely to be a local maximum for the market potential curve, and therefore likely to be a place at which a new city emerges when population grows large enough.

We use the word "likely" advisedly. A city need not develop at b. If the branch point lies in the agglomeration shadow of a preexisting city, the process of city formation may bypass it. (A possible real-world example: South Korea's largest city, Seoul, is not a port. Although the seaport at Inchon, about 100 kilometers from Seoul, is Seoul's gateway to the rest of the world, Seoul's lock-in effect has been so strong that Inchon has never become a full-fledged city). But whereas most points along the line develop only under very specific combinations of parameters and initial conditions—normally, for a set of measure 0 in the relevant space—there is always a range of parameters and initial conditions under which a city develops at the branch point. Thus emergence of a city there is in this sense "likely."

13.1   The Monocentric Economy

We begin with a hypothetical economy with a small population, and with a single existing urban center that happens not to be at the branch point. It will turn out to be helpful to take whatever branch of the Y (or asterisk) that the preexisting city is on, together with one other branch (it does not matter which) and call the two combined the *baseline* of the economy, the line along which we will calculate market potential. We define the location of this initial city as the origin of that line. In figure 13.1, the existing city's location is indicated by 0.

We have drawn figure 13.1 for an economy with three branches, that is, with one branch in addition to the baseline. At no real cost we can, however, just as well imagine an asterisk-shaped economy in which there are k branches in addition to the baseline. When $k = 0$, we have the linear location space of chapter 9. When $k = 1$, we have the Y-shaped location space of figure 13.1. We will use the city at 0 as the origin for measuring location on all branches; thus for all branches other than the one on which the city sits (and for that branch as well between the city and the junction point), the location coordinate is also the distance to the city.

Except for the introduction of a branching location space, this mono-centric world is identical to that discussed in chapter 9. Thus we need not spend much time describing it; we need only think through the small differences.

When the population is sufficiently small, agriculture takes place only near the existing city, and the model is indistinguishable from that of chapter 9. As population continues to increase, however, the agricultural frontier moves away from the city. Because the attractiveness of farming land depends only on how far it is from the city, not on which direction, agriculture spreads up all branches; in particular, once the frontier distance f exceeds the distance to the branch point b, agriculture extends a distance $f - b$ up each nonbaseline branch. For convenience, let us introduce a new variable, δ, such that

$$\delta = \begin{cases} 0 & \text{for } f \leq b, \\ 1 & \text{for } f > b. \end{cases} \tag{13.1}$$

The cultivated area on the baseline is always equal to $2f$; that in the nonbaseline branches is $\delta k(f - b)$; thus, the total cultivated area is $2f + \delta k(f - b)$. Except for this change, we have the same equilibrium conditions for the monocentric economy as in chapter 9. It is straightforward to show that, as in chapter 9, f is an increasing function of N, going to infinity as N does; and as before, everything in the monocentric economy can be expressed as a function of f.

It is when we turn to the implied market potential function that the branching makes a difference. As before, we define the market potential as a transform of the ratio of the wage that zero-profit manufacturing could pay to the wage rate in agriculture:

$$\Omega(r) \equiv \frac{[\omega^M(r)]^\sigma}{[\omega^A(r)]^\sigma} = \frac{[w^M(r)]^\sigma}{[w^A(r)]^\sigma}$$

$$= [w^M(r)]^\sigma e^{\sigma[(1-\mu)\tau^A - \mu\tau^M]|r|}. \tag{13.2}$$

Now, however, the wage equation becomes

$$[w^M(r)]^\sigma = L^M w(0) e^{-(\sigma-1)\tau M|r|} G(0)^{\sigma-1}$$

$$+ \int_{-f}^{f} p^A(s) e^{-(\sigma-1)\tau M|r-s|} G(s)^{\sigma-1} ds \tag{13.3}$$

$$+ \delta k \int_{b}^{f} p^A(s) e^{-(\sigma-1)\tau Md(r,s)} G(s)^{\sigma-1} ds,$$

where $d(r,s)$ is the distance to farmers off the baseline, determined by

$$d(r, s) = \begin{cases} s - r & \text{for } r \le b, \\ (r - b) + (s - b) & \text{for } r > b. \end{cases} \tag{13.4}$$

The crucial difference from chapter 9 (equation 9.14) is the third term in (13.3), which represents the impact on the zero-profit wage rate of access to the market provided by the off-baseline farmers. The important point to notice is that as one approaches the junction point from the city, the distance to farmers off the baseline is steadily decreasing; but as soon as one passes the junction, it is increasing. This, of course, is what creates the cusp in market potential.

To fill in the market potential, recall the expressions for the price index and agricultural prices in the monocentric equilibrium (equations (9.4) and (9.1), respectively). Substituting them in the wage equation and rearranging terms, we get

$$[w^M(r)]^\sigma = \mu e^{-(\sigma-1)\tau M|r|} + \left(\frac{\mu p^A}{L^M}\right)\left[2\int_0^f e^{-\tau^A s} e^{(\sigma-1)\tau M[s-|r-s|]} ds\right.$$

$$\left. + \delta k \int_b^f e^{-\tau^A s} e^{(\sigma-1)\tau M[s-d(r,s)]} ds\right]. \tag{13.5}$$

Let us define

$$A(f) \equiv 2\int_0^f e^{-\tau^A s} ds + \delta k \int_b^f e^{-\tau^A s} ds. \tag{13.6}$$

Then the supply of agricultural goods to the city is $\mu A(f)$. Since agricultural market clearing implies, analogously to equation (9.5), that $\mu p^A / L^M = (1 - \mu)/A(f)$, we can rewrite (13.5) as follows:

$$[w^M(r)]^\sigma = \mu e^{-(\sigma-1)\tau M|r|} + \frac{(1 - \mu)}{A(f)}\left[2\int_0^f e^{-\tau As} e^{(\sigma-1)\tau M(s-|r-s|)} ds \right.$$

$$\left. + \delta k \int_b^f e^{-\tau As} e^{(\sigma-1)\tau M[s-d(r,s)]} ds \right].$$

(13.7)

Hence, substituting this into (13.2), the market potential at each location is given by

$$\Omega(r) = e^{\sigma[(1-\mu)\tau A - \mu\tau M]|r|}\left\{ \mu e^{-(\sigma-1)\tau M|r|} + \frac{(1 - \mu)}{A(f)} \right.$$

$$\times\left(2\int_0^f e^{-\tau As} e^{(\sigma-1)\tau M(s-|r-s|)} ds \right.$$

(13.8)

$$\left.\left. + \delta k \int_b^f e^{-\tau As} e^{(\sigma-1)\tau M[s-d(r,s)]} ds \right)\right\}.$$

A monocentric geography can be sustained only if this potential curve nowhere exceeds 1.

13.2 The Impact of a Transportation Hub on the Market Potential Function

It turns out to be helpful to divide the market potential function into two pieces, that to the left and that to the right of the junction point:

$$\Omega(r) = \begin{cases} \Omega_1(r) & \text{for } r \leq b, \\ \Omega_2(r) & \text{for } r \geq b. \end{cases}$$

(13.9)

Then if we calculate each integral in (13.8) along the same lines as in the derivation of function (9.24), we find that for $0 \leq r \leq b$,[2]

$$\Omega_1(r) = e^{\sigma[(1-\mu)\tau A - \mu\tau M]r}\left[\left(\frac{1 + \mu}{2} - \frac{(1 - \mu)\phi(f)}{2} \right)e^{-(\sigma-1)\tau Mr} \right.$$

(13.10)

$$\left. + \Psi(r, f)\left(\frac{1 - \mu}{2} \right)e^{(\sigma-1)\tau Mr} \right],$$

and for $r \geq b$,

$$\Omega_2(r) = e^{\sigma[(1-\mu)\tau^A - \mu\tau M]r}$$

$$\times \left\{\left(\frac{1+\mu}{2} - \frac{(1-\mu)\phi(f)}{2}\right)e^{-(\sigma-1)\tau Mr} + \Psi(r,f)\left(\frac{1-\mu}{2}\right)\right. \quad (13.11)$$

$$\left. \times e^{(\sigma-1)\tau Mr} - (1-\mu)\phi(f)e^{(\sigma-1)\tau Mr}[1 - e^{-2(\sigma-1)\tau M(r-b)}]\right\},$$

where

$$\phi(f) \equiv \delta k \int_b^f e^{-\tau A_s} ds/A(f), \quad (13.12)$$

$$\Psi(r,f) \equiv 1 + \phi(f) - 2\int_0^r e^{-\tau A_s}[1 - e^{-2(\sigma-1)\tau M(r-s)}]ds/A(f). \quad (13.13)$$

Here $\phi(f)$ is the proportion of the city's agricultural supply that comes from nonbaseline branches.

When $f < b$, we have $\delta = 0$ and hence $\phi(f) = 0$; thus, the potential function above becomes identical to (9.24), as expected. When $f > b$, $\phi(f)$ increases as f increases, and hence the potential function becomes increasingly different from that in chapter 9.

Figure 13.2, which has been constructed under the same set of basic parameters used for the construction of fig. 9.4, with additional geographical parameters $k = 2$ and $b = 0.5$ (implying that two "valleys"

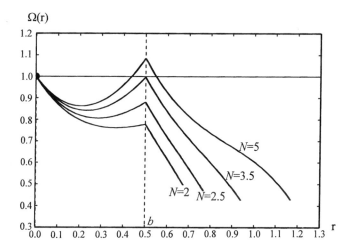

Figure 13.2
Potential curves under the influence of hub effects

branch off from the baseline at a distance 0.5 from the city), illustrates the shape of potential curves when $f > b$. In contrast to what we saw in figure 9.4, the potential curves now have sharp cusps at b. We can evaluate this cuspiness by differentiating $\Omega_1(r)$ and $\Omega_2(r)$ respectively at $r = b$, to find that

$$\Omega_1'(b) - \Omega_2'(b) = \phi(f)2(1-\mu)(\sigma-1)\tau^M e^{(\sigma-1)\tau M b} e^{\sigma[(1-\mu)\tau^A - \mu\tau^M]b} > 0. \quad (13.14)$$

Thus the derivative of the potential curve has a discontinuity at the branch point. Because $\phi(f)$ increases with f, this effect becomes stronger as the agricultural area expands farther beyond b. Notice also that $\phi(f)$ increases when k increases. Hence, the more branches, the stronger the attraction of the branch point.

Recall from figure 9.4 that in the monocentric economy of chapter 9, as f increases, the potential curve shifts upward everywhere except at $r = 0$. In the present context, the situation is a bit more complex. Locations less than $2b$ to the right of the city always become more attractive as f increases. However, locations at a distance greater than that have worse access to the off-baseline branches than the original city, so they can actually lose market potential as the population of those branches grows.[3] Except for this technical detail, however, the effect of growing N on the market potential curve is as in chapter 9: we can think of the curve as humping itself upward as the population grows, as illustrated in figure 13.2.

And figure 13.2 immediately gives us the punchline: Because of the cuspiness of the potential curve, it is indeed likely that when the population reaches the critical level at which a new city emerges, that new city emerges precisely at the branch point b—Likely, but not certain. Let us conclude this chapter by summarizing the possible patterns of spatial evolution in this model.

13.3   Patterns of Spatial Evolution

To think about the economy's possible spatial development, let us hold the parameters of the economy constant and imagine varying just one thing: the location of the branch point, b. The economy's spatial evolution then follows one of the three basic patterns indicated in figure 13.3.[4]

First, suppose that b is much smaller than $\tilde{r}$, where $\tilde{r}$ is the critical distance from the nonbranching model of chapter 9 (illustrated in figure 9.4). Then as the population increases gradually, we see pattern

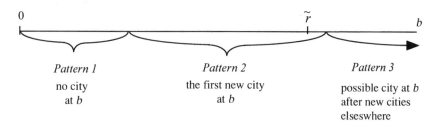

Figure 13.3
Possible patterns of spatial evolution

1: The junction never develops a city. Instead, the first new city (or cities) emerges somewhere beyond b. The junction never develops as a city because it is too close to the existing city, and hence it remains in the agglomeration shadow of that city. Panel (a) in figure 13.4 depicts the critical potential curve assocated with pattern 1, which has just reached 1 at distance r_1 from the existing city. At this point, because the market potential becomes 1 at $k + 1$ new locations simultaneously, as many as $k + 1$ new cities will emerge through a catastrophic bifurcation. Although it is difficult to determine precisely how many new cities will emerge at this moment, eventually every branch of land will have many cities as N continues to increase. The original city at 0 will, however, have a continued advantage from its proximity to the junction: Even though it is actually not right at b, it has managed to preclude the emergence of a competitor there, and thus grows as the dominant city by using that junction as the gateway to other branches.

Second, if b is neither too large nor too small we get pattern 2—the case illustrated in panel (b) of figure 13.4—in which the next city does emerge at the branch point. In this two-city economy, the new city at the branch point is always larger than the original city at 0. The original city may disappear completely when the new city emerges. In effect, the economy remains monocentric, but finally manages to break the forces that locked its city in the wrong location.[5]

Finally, suppose that the branch point is very far away from the existing city, giving rise to pattern 3. Then as the critical potential curve depicted in panel (c) of figure 13.4 indicates, the first new city will emerge at a location to the left of the branch point. Thereafter, this new city plays the role of the original city at 0, and the basic analysis is repeated.

The important point to make, as suggested before, is that whereas an ordinary point along the baseline will be the site of a new city only

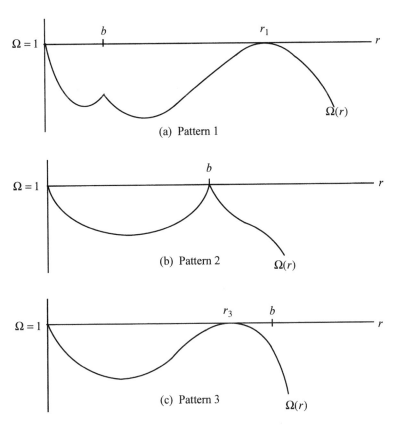

Figure 13.4
Critical potential curve associated with each pattern

under very specific conditions—indeed, only if the original city is at exactly the right point—there is always a range of conditions under which the branch point becomes a city. In effect, the cuspiness introduced by the branch gives someone trying to make the economy build a city there wiggle room in all directions; and in that sense the branch point is indeed a likely, though not certain, point for a city to develop.

13.4 Conclusions

When one of the authors mentioned to a noneconomist friend that we had managed to show why ports and other transportation hubs become sites for cities, his reaction was disbelief: "Didn't we already know that?" Well, we did—but it had never been formalized. We have seen in this chapter how the same analytical framework we have used to model the emergence of cities in a featureless landscape can be used to step away from those assumptions and examine how transportation hubs change that spatial evolution. The important point to make here is that as we see it, the main function of a hub in city location is catalytic. The hub provides some continuing advantages to a city, but the main thing it does is provide the city's site with an advantage over other sites during that critical period when the economy's growth has made the emergence of a new city necessary. And our theory thus neatly deals with a paradox about the world's great cities: Nearly all are major ports (or were at one time), but many have long since ceased to be mainly port cities. Our model, in other words, finds nothing paradoxical in the fact that the Erie Canal made New York—and is now no more than a tourist attraction.

Notes

1. That is, figure 13.1 may be interpreted as saying that the "old world" represented by the horizontal line is connected with the "new world" (shown by the diagonal half-line) through ports at zero transport costs. See Fujita and Mori 1996 for a study of the hub effect of ports in a more realistic situation with positive transport costs between ports.

2. When $f \leq b$, $\phi(f) = 0$, and hence $\Omega(-r) = \Omega(r)$ for all r; that is, Ω is symmetric with respect to $r = 0$. When $f > b$, $\Omega(-r) < \Omega(r)$ for all $r > 0$. Therefore, when we study the formation of new cities (which occurs at locations where $\Omega(r) = 1$), it is sufficient to focus on $r \geq 0$.

3. Recall that the market potential is normalized such that $\Omega(0) \equiv 1$. Hence, the market potential at any location is always relative to the city location.

4. The following discussion is based on the results of simulations under the technological/taste parameters given in footnote 7 in chapter 9.

5. Numerical simulations under the set of parameters given for figure 9.4 show that if $k \geq 2$, then the original city always disappears whenever the new city emerges at b.

IV

International Trade

14   International Specialization

More than sixty years ago, Bertil Ohlin concluded his seminal book on international trade theory—entitled, by the way, *Interregional and International Trade*—with the declaration that international trade theory is simply international location theory. Yet in practice, over the past 170 years, the two subfields have barely communicated with each other. One of our objectives is to help remedy that breach; in this part of the book we show how the same basic approach we have applied to the study of regions and cities can yield important insights into the processes that drive specialization and trade among nations.

But what, in economic terms, *is* a nation? As we move across geographical space, what is special about crossing a national boundary? A national boundary is, of course, a point at which political jurisdictions change. But we have not put government into our models and will not introduce it here.

One might well argue that in practice national boundaries are associated with de facto barriers to the flow of goods—not only explicit barriers like tariffs and import quotas, but also implicit obstacles imposed by language differences, inconsistent standards, and the sheer nuisance associated with border crossing. Evidence from Canadian-U.S. trade suggests that even that most innocuous of borders has a huge impact (McCallum 1995; Helliwell 1997): On average, the exports of Canadian provinces to other Canadian provinces are some twenty times larger than their exports to equivalently situated U.S. states, and evidence from urban price movements suggests that the border imposes barriers to arbitrage comparable to 1,700 miles of physical space (Engel and Rogers 1996).

Although such limits to trade are a crucially important consequence of borders in practice, they do not introduce qualitatively new issues from those we discussed in parts II and III of this book, and we will not try to model the effects of borders on the "geometry" over which flows of goods take place. Instead we will focus on a different kind of barrier that national boundaries normally present: a barrier to the movement of people. Whereas advanced countries nowadays generally have quite low formal barriers to trade in goods, they universally impose strict restrictions on immigration, and evidence suggests that even where the immigration regime is relatively open and there are no language barriers, international migration is far smaller than migration within countries. Helliwell (1997, p. 20) writes, "For every resident in a Canadian province who was born in a U.S. state, how many will you meet who were born in some other Canadian province (other than Quebec) of similar size, distance, and personal income per capita? The current answer appears to be close to 100." And as a result, differences in wage rates and per capita income are far larger between than within countries: Although the European Union is similar to the United States in population and far more compact geographically, it has twice as much regional dispersion in per capita income.

In short, national boundaries are associated with barriers to labor mobility, and we take this as the defining characteristic of "nations." That is, in this and succeeding chapters we move from the assumption that labor moves over time to equalize real wages in all locations to the other extreme, and assume that labor is immobile between distinct national units.

Without labor mobility, of course, one cannot have agglomeration in the usual sense; nor does the cumulative process of geographical concentration we have described in earlier chapters operate in the same way. However, a process of international specialization whose logic is very similar to that of classic agglomeration can emerge through the joint role of manufacturing as a producer and consumer of intermediate goods. A region with a relatively large manufacturing sector typically offers a greater variety of intermediates, implying lower costs of production for final goods, that is, forward linkages. Conversely, a large final goods sector in manufacturing provides a large local market for intermediates, that is, backward linkages. The result of these linkages cannot be concentration of population in particular countries, but it can lead to a process of specialization that concentrates manufacturing or particular industries in a limited number of countries.

In this chapter we develop a two-country model in which intermediate goods play a role closely parallel to that played by labor mobility in the two-region model developed in chapter 5. Having set out the model in section 14.1, we turn in section 14.2 to an investigation of the patterns of industrial specialization that the model generates. In section 14.3 we show that the model yields some highly suggestive insights into the effect of global economic integration on real incomes; in section 14.4 we slightly generalize the model in a way that, we believe, suggests a broader interpretation of the relationship between trade costs and national inequalities.

14.1   A Model with Intermediate Goods

When economists discuss intermediate goods, they normally think of many industrial sectors linked through an input-output matrix. Some sectors are relatively upstream, producing intermediate goods, and others downstream, with most of their production going for final consumption. Although the input-output structure of production can be important (and will be discussed in later chapters), it also adds complications that we might want to avoid if possible. Luckily, as long as we are in a Dixit-Stiglitz world in which manufacturing miraculously manages to be a single sector of many goods, we can use a clever trick to introduce input-output linkages without actually introducing any additional industries. We simply assume that manufacturing uses itself (in addition to labor) as an input, that is, that the same aggregate of manufacturing varieties demanded by consumers is also an input into the production of each variety. Thus the same industry is both downstream, producing output for final consumption, and upstream.

To see how this works, consider the technology of each manufacturing firm. Until now we have assumed that production uses a single input: labor, at location r price w_r. We now modify the manufacturing production function so that the input becomes a composite of labor and intermediate goods. Rather than stating the production function explicitly, we can define it indirectly in terms of the relevant price indices.[1] Let the price of the intermediate goods in location r be G_r; we then assume that the input composite is a Cobb-Douglas function of labor and intermediates with intermediate share α, so that the price of the input is $w_r^{1-\alpha} G_r^\alpha$. This input is used in both the fixed cost of production and the marginal cost and, as before, we choose units such that the marginal input requirement equals the price-cost markup ($c = \rho$) to ensure that firms set price according to

$$p_r = w_r^{1-\alpha} G_r^\alpha. \tag{14.1}$$

The intermediate, in turn, is assumed to be a CES function of the varieties available;[2] thus the price index for that intermediate, G_r at location r, takes the form

$$G_r = \left[\sum_s n_s (p_s T_{sr})^{1-\sigma} \right]^{1/(1-\sigma)}, \tag{14.2}$$

where n_s is the numbers of varieties produced in location s, p_s the f.o.b. price, and T_{sr} the transport cost. This is exactly as in chapter 4 (equation 4.15) and implies that the same price index is the appropriate one both in consumer preferences and in firms' technologies.[3] In other words, the assumed elasticity of substitution among varieties of manufacture is the same for firms as it is for consumers. This simplifying assumption is not central to our results but does a great deal to keep analysis manageable.[4]

An implication of this technology is that firms use all varieties of manufactured products as intermediate goods in production and gain from having a wider range of varieties produced in the world. This creates a forward linkage: Access to a greater variety of intermediate products reduces the price index and hence the costs of production of firms that use those intermediates. Furthermore, the more varieties are available locally, the lower are costs, as there is a saving on intermediates' transport costs.

Turning to sales, part of each firm's output now goes to consumers as final consumption and part to firms for intermediate usage. Demand for manufactures in each location thus comes from both sources. We define location r's expenditure on manufactures, E_r, as

$$E_r = \mu Y_r + \alpha n_r p_r q^*. \tag{14.3}$$

The first term on the right-hand side of this equation is demand from consumers; as before, μ is the share of manufactures in consumption and Y is income. The second is intermediate demand. Assuming that firms are at zero-profit equilibrium with sales q^*, the total costs of location r firms equal the total value of their production, $n_r p_r q^*$. A share α of these costs consists of the purchase of intermediates, and this is the source of the backward linkage among firms. The more firms that produce at location r, the larger the intermediate demand, and thus, other things equal, the larger the total expenditure on manufactures.

We now imagine a world of two countries and set the total labor supply in each country equal to 1. Within each country, we assume that labor is intersectorally mobile between manufacturing and agriculture. The share of country r's labor force in manufacturing we denote λ_r. The total value of manufacturing output in country r is $n_r p_r q^*$, so the manufacturing wage bill in country r is a share $(1 - \alpha)$ of this,

$$w_r \lambda_r = (1 - \alpha) n_r p_r q^*. \tag{14.4}$$

We choose units such that $q^* = 1/(1 - \alpha)$, so that

$$n_r = \frac{w_r}{p_r} \lambda_r. \tag{14.5}$$

As in previous chapters, we want to direct attention to the allocation of labor among sectors, λ (rather than the number of firms), and to wages (rather than to prices). Using (14.5) and (14.1) in the price index (14.2), we can write the price indices for each country as

$$G_1^{1-\sigma} = \lambda_1 w_1^{1-\sigma(1-\alpha)} G_1^{-\alpha\sigma} + \lambda_2 w_2^{1-\sigma(1-\alpha)} G_2^{-\alpha\sigma} T^{1-\sigma}, \tag{14.6}$$

$$G_2^{1-\sigma} = \lambda_1 w_1^{1-\sigma(1-\alpha)} G_1^{-\alpha\sigma} T^{1-\sigma} + \lambda_2 w_2^{1-\sigma(1-\alpha)} G_2^{-\alpha\sigma}. \tag{14.7}$$

These expressions are similar to the analogous expressions in earlier chapters (e.g., equations (5.9) and (5.10)), but now the price indices depend not just on wages in each location but also on price indices, for these enter marginal cost and hence the prices firms charge.

Firms make zero profits when the price they charge is such that they sell $1/(1 - \alpha)$ units of their output. As before, this defines the manufacturing wage that is consistent with zero profits. These wage equations now take the form

$$\frac{(w_1^{1-\alpha} G_1^\alpha)^\sigma}{1 - \alpha} = E_1 G_1^{\sigma-1} + E_2 G_2^{\sigma-1} T^{1-\sigma}, \tag{14.8}$$

$$\frac{(w_2^{1-\alpha} G_2^\alpha)^\sigma}{1 - \alpha} = E_1 G_1^{\sigma-1} T^{1-\sigma} + E_2 G_2^{\sigma-1}. \tag{14.9}$$

Like the price equations, these resemble the analogous equations we have seen earlier (e.g., 5.11 and 5.12) but also contain some differences. First, expenditures on manufacturing in each location are now given by the terms E_1 and E_2 (instead of μY_1 and μY_2). Second, our choice of firm scale, $1/(1 - \alpha)$, accounts for the term in the denominator of the left-hand side. Finally, the numerator of the left-hand side gives the price that must be charged if firms are to make zero profits, which now depends on both the wage rate and the price index in each location. We have already seen that expenditure comes both from consumers (share μ of income) and from firms demanding intermediates (share α of output), and using (14.4) in (14.3) we derive

$$E_1 = \mu Y_1 + \frac{\alpha w_1 \lambda_1}{1 - \alpha}, \qquad E_2 = \mu Y_2 + \frac{\alpha w_2 \lambda_2}{1 - \alpha}. \tag{14.10}$$

Both manufacturing and agriculture generate income. Agricultural output we take as freely tradeable and use as numeraire, but we allow for a more general agricultural production function than we have used up to now. Agricultural output depends on the amount of labor employed in the sector, $1 - \lambda$, according to the increasing and concave production function $A(1 - \lambda_r)$. Income in each country is therefore

$$Y_1 = w_1 \lambda_1 + A(1 - \lambda_1), \qquad Y_2 = w_2 \lambda_2 + A(1 - \lambda_2). \tag{14.11}$$

The agricultural wage is the marginal product of labor, $A'(1 - \lambda_r)$, and the wage gap between sectors we define as v_r,

$$v_1 \equiv w_1 - A'(1 - \lambda_1), \qquad v_2 \equiv w_2 - A'(1 - \lambda_2). \tag{14.12}$$

Given the shares of each country's labor force in manufacturing, λ_1, λ_2, equations (14.6)–(14.12) characterize the short-run equilibrium and give the wage levels and the wage gap between agriculture and industry in each country. We assume a simple adjustment dynamic in which, within each country, labor moves from agriculture to industry if v_r is positive, and vice versa. The long-run equilibrium occurs either when v_r is 0 in both countries, or at a corner point, when one sector has contracted to 0 in one country. Long-run equilibrium manufacturing wages therefore satisfy

$$w_r = A'(1 - \lambda_r), \qquad \lambda_r \in (0, 1),$$

$$w_r \geq A'(1 - \lambda_r), \qquad \lambda_r = 1, \tag{14.13}$$

$$w_r \leq A'(1 - \lambda_r), \qquad \lambda_r = 0.$$

In words, when both sectors operate, wages are equalized; an economy that has only manufacturing may have manufacturing wages greater than the agricultural marginal product; if there is no manufacturing, then the manufacturing wage must be less than or equal to the agricultural wage.

14.2 The Structure of Equilibria

To understand the locational forces at work in this model, consider the effects of increasing the amount of labor operating in country 1 manufacturing, λ_1. Does this raise the wage gap, $w_1 - A'(1 - \lambda_1)$—in which case it encourages further increases in λ_1—or decrease it? Four forces are at work. The first is the response of the marginal product of labor in agriculture; if the agricultural production function is strictly concave, a decline in agricultural employment raises the marginal product, and this reduces the incentive for a further movement of labor into manufacturing. The second force is product market competition. An increase in λ_1 is associated with the supply of more varieties and this, as usual, reduces the price index G_1. This shifts the demand curve for each firm's output downward and reduces the manufacturing wage. (This effect occurs via the price index terms on the right-hand side of the wage equation (14.8).)

Both the agricultural wage response and product market competition effects are stabilizing forces, working against agglomeration. Working in the opposite direction are forward and backward linkages. The forward linkage arises as the reduction in G_1 associated with an increase in λ_1 reduces the cost of intermediates, tending to increase the instantaneous equilibrium wage. (This effect shows up via the G_1 term on the left-hand side of the wage equations.) The demand or backward linkage arises as a higher value of λ_1 raises expenditure on manufactures in country 1 (E_1 in equation (14.10)), shifting firms' demand curves up and tending to raise the manufacturing wage (equation (14.8)).

The tension among these forces is the subject of this chapter, but we start with a simplification. We initially switch off the agricultural wage effect by making two assumptions. The first is that the agricultural production function is linear in output: $A(1 - \lambda_r) = (1 - \lambda_r)$. This implies that the agricultural wage is unity, and hence that—as long as there is some agricultural employment in the economy—the equilibrium manufacturing wage is also unity. The second assumption is that the share of manufactures in consumption, μ, is not more than $1/2$. This says that the level of demand for manufactures is small enough for all

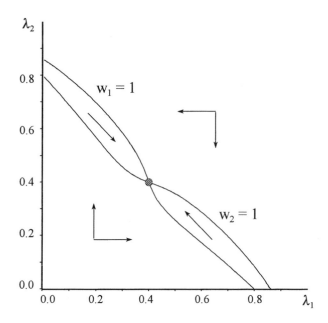

Figure 14.1
Manufacturing employment and wages, $T = 3$

of manufacturing to fit in one country, and thus ensures that, even if all manufacturing is concentrated in a single country, this country also has some agriculture. The two assumptions together ensure that equilibrium wages in both countries are equal to unity. Manufacturing can therefore draw labor from agriculture at a constant wage, neutralizing any factor market competition effects.

To understand the structure of equilibria we commence with simulation analysis, the results of which are illustrated in figures 14.1–14.3. The axes are the shares of each country's labor force in manufacturing, λ_1 and λ_2. The curve $w_1 = 1$ gives combinations of λ_1 and λ_2 at which the manufacturing wage in country 1 equals unity, the agricultural wage. To the right of this curve the wage is less than unity; to the left it is more. Our assumption that manufacturing employment falls or rises according to intersectoral wage differences means that the horizontal arrows on the figure indicate the evolution of λ_1. The curve $w_2 = 1$ gives analogous information for country 2, and vertical arrows show the corresponding dynamics.

The three figures are drawn for high, low, and intermediate levels of trade costs, respectively, giving the following structure of equilibria.

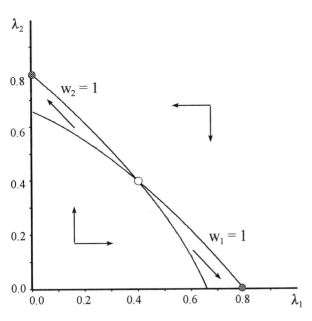

Figure 14.2
Manufacturing employment and wages, $T = 1.5$

At high trade costs (figure 14.1), the $w_1 = 1$ curve is relatively steep, and $w_2 = 1$ relatively flat. (The intuitive reason for this can be seen by thinking about autarky, in which case $w_1 = 1$ is vertical, and $w_2 = 1$ horizontal.) Consequently, there is a unique and stable equilibrium at $\lambda_1 = \lambda_2 = \mu$. Manufacturing is equally divided by locations, and the two economies are symmetric.

At lower trade costs, the $w_1 = 1$ curve becomes flatter, and $w_2 = 1$ steeper. Figure 14.2 shows a case in which the direction in which the curves intersect is reversed, and there are three equilibria. The symmetric equilibrium is now unstable, whereas full concentration of industry in either country 1 or country 2 is a stable equilibrium.

At intermediate trade costs, the pattern is as given in figure 14.3, with five equilibria. The symmetric equilibrium is stable, as is concentration of manufacturing in either country 1 or country 2. Between these stable equilibria there are unstable equilibria.

This should sound familiar from chapter 5: Just as we did there, we find that for sufficiently low trade costs, geographical concentration of manufacturing becomes possible; at somewhat lower trade costs, it becomes inevitable. Thus our analytical tasks are to find the sustain

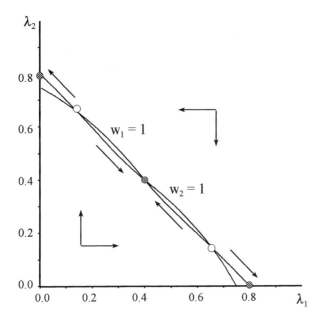

Figure 14.3
Manufacturing employment and wages, $T = 2.15$

point, at which the concentrated equilibria of figures 14.2 and 14.3 exist, and the break point, at which the symmetric equilibrium becomes unstable.

To find the sustain point, we start by assuming that manufacturing is concentrated in country 1, so $\lambda_2 = 0$. Wages in both countries are unity, because of our assumption that constant returns to scale agriculture is operating in both countries, so income in both countries is also unity. This means that $\lambda_1 = 2\mu$, that is, the manufacturing wage bill λ_1 equals the value of manufactures supplied to consumers in the two countries, 2μ. The price indices ((14.6) and (14.7)) therefore take values

$$G_1 = (2\mu)^{1/(1-\sigma(1-\alpha))}, \qquad G_2 = G_1 T. \tag{14.14}$$

Because income in both countries is 1, the manufacturing expenditure levels (14.10) reduce to

$$E_1 = \frac{\mu(1 + \alpha)}{1 - \alpha}, \qquad E_2 = \mu. \tag{14.15}$$

Substituting these in the country 2 wage equation (14.9) gives country 2 manufacturing wage:

$$w_2^{1-\alpha} = T^{-\alpha} \left[\frac{1 + \alpha}{2} T^{1-\sigma} + \frac{1 - \alpha}{2} T^{\sigma-1} \right]^{1/\sigma}.$$ (14.16)

Concentration of manufacturing in country 1 is an equilibrium providing that this is less than or equal to the agricultural wage, unity, so that there is no movement of country 2 workers to manufacturing.

It is striking that this expression for the sustain condition is identical to that in chapter 5, except that the share of the mobile factor in the economy (μ in chapter 5) is now replaced by the share of intermediates in production, α. The term $T^{-\alpha}$ captures the forward linkages foregone if a firm establishes in country 2—it bears transport costs T on its intermediates, which account for share α of costs. The term in square brackets is the backward linkage. Country 1 has share $(1 + \alpha)/2$ of world expenditure on manufactures, and this is weighted by $T^{1-\sigma}$; this weighting captures the transport cost disadvantage that a firm in country 2 would have in supplying country 1. Country 2 has share $(1 - \alpha)/2$ of manufacturing expenditure, and the term is weighted by $T^{\sigma-1}$, representing the disadvantage that firms in country 1 face in supplying the country 2 market.

We do not need to spend time studying the shape of the relationship given in (14.16), because it is exactly as described in chapter 5 and figure 5.5. Providing that $(\sigma - 1)/\sigma = \rho > \alpha$, there is a unique sustain value of $T > 1$, below which agglomeration of manufacturing in a single country is sustainable. The inequality $\rho > \alpha$ is of course a restatement of the no-black-hole condition.

We now turn to the point at which symmetry is broken. At the symmetric equilibrium, manufacturing wages in each country equal the marginal product of labor in agriculture (equation (14.13)), and the equilibrium is stable if increasing manufacturing employment drives manufacturing wages below agricultural, and unstable otherwise. We must therefore evaluate the following derivatives:

$$\frac{dv_1}{d\lambda_1} = \frac{dw_1}{d\lambda_1} + A''(1 - \lambda_1), \qquad \frac{dv_2}{d\lambda_2} = \frac{dw_2}{d\lambda_2} + A''(1 - \lambda_2).$$ (14.17)

Because we assume in this section that agriculture has constant returns to scale in its single input, labor, the term A'' is equal to 0. To evaluate $dw_r/d\lambda_r$, we have to totally differentiate the equilibrium defined by equations (14.6)–(14.11). As we have seen in earlier chapters, the fact that the calculation is around the symmetric equilibrium greatly simplifies this. First, we can easily calculate the symmetric equilibrium values of endogenous variables; they are

$$\lambda = \mu, \qquad Y = 1, \qquad w = 1,$$

$$G^{1-\sigma(1-\alpha)} = \mu[1 + T^{1-\sigma}], \qquad E = \mu/(1 - \alpha), \tag{14.18}$$

where the absence of subscripts denotes symmetric equilibrium values. Second, we can look at a symmetric perturbation of the equilibrium, $d\lambda \equiv d\lambda_1 = -d\lambda_2$, which causes equal and opposite changes in the values of variables at each location, so we can work with $dG \equiv dG_1 = -dG_2$, $dE \equiv dE_1 = -dE_2$, and so on.

Totally differentiating the price indices, (14.6) or (14.7), gives

$$[(1 - \sigma)G^{1-\sigma} + \mu\alpha\sigma(1 - T^{1-\sigma})G^{-\alpha\sigma}]\frac{dG}{G} =$$

$$G^{-\alpha\sigma}(1 - T^{1-\sigma})d\lambda + \mu G^{-\alpha\sigma}(1 - T^{1-\sigma})[1 - \sigma(1 - \alpha)]dw. \tag{14.19}$$

As in earlier chapters, it is convenient to define a parameter Z,

$$Z \equiv \frac{1 - T^{1-\sigma}}{(1 + T^{1-\sigma})} = \frac{\mu(1 - T^{1-\sigma})}{G_1^{1-\sigma(1-\alpha)}}, \tag{14.20}$$

and using this, equation (14.19) becomes

$$[1 - \sigma + \alpha\sigma Z]\frac{dG}{G} = \frac{Z}{\mu}d\lambda + [1 - \sigma(1 - \alpha)]Zdw. \tag{14.21}$$

Differentiating the wage equations, (14.8) or (14.9), with similar substitutions, yields

$$\sigma dw + \left[\frac{\alpha\sigma - (\sigma - 1)Z}{1 - \alpha}\right]\frac{dG}{G} = \frac{Z}{\mu}dE. \tag{14.22}$$

Turning to expenditure on manufactures, we substitute the definition of income (14.11) into the equation for expenditure (14.10), giving

$$E_1 = \left[\mu + \frac{\alpha}{1 - \alpha}\right]w_1\lambda_1 + \mu A(1 - \lambda_1),$$

$$E_2 = \left[\mu + \frac{\alpha}{1 - \alpha}\right]w_2\lambda_2 + \mu A(1 - \lambda_2), \tag{14.23}$$

and differentiating these,

$$\frac{dE}{\mu} = \left[\mu + \frac{\alpha}{1 - \alpha}\right]dw + \frac{\alpha}{1 - \alpha}\frac{d\lambda}{\mu}. \tag{14.24}$$

Eliminating dE and dG from (14.21), (14.22), and (14.24), we derive the required expression for $dw/d\lambda$:

$$\frac{dw}{d\lambda} = \frac{-Z}{\mu\Delta}\left[\frac{\alpha(1 + \rho) - Z(\alpha^2 + \rho)}{1 - \rho}\right]. \tag{14.25}$$

Full details of the derivation are given in appendix 14.1, where an expression for Δ is also given.

With constant returns in agriculture, the symmetric equilibrium is stable or unstable according to whether $dw/d\lambda$ is negative or positive. The term Δ in the denominator of equation (14.25) is negative providing $\alpha < \rho$, the no-black-hole condition. Stability therefore depends on the numerator of (14.25), which takes exactly the same form as the analogous symmetry-breaking equation of chapter 5 equation (5.27). As in that chapter, the point of symmetry breaking can be found explicitly, using the definition of Z, and it is

$$T^{\rho/(1-\rho)} = \frac{(\rho + \alpha)(1 + \alpha)}{(\rho - \alpha)(1 - \alpha)}. \tag{14.26}$$

Pulling together the sustain condition and the symmetry-breaking condition, we now know what the structure of equilibria must be. At high transport costs, the symmetric equilibrium is unique, because each country must have manufacturing to supply its local consumers. At low transport costs, forward and backward linkages dominate, and manufacturing agglomerates in a single country. And there is an intermediate range (between the sustain and the break values) at which there are three stable equilibria. The bifurcation diagram of chapter 5 (figure 5.4) applies, with the single modification that the vertical axis is now the share of manufacturing in employment in one of the countries (either λ_1 or λ_2).

14.3 Agglomeration and National Inequalities

In the preceding section we made two assumptions ($A' = 1$ and $\mu < \frac{1}{2}$) that combined to ensure wage equality between countries, even when one country had a labor demand from manufacturing and the other did not. More generally, however, we might expect an expansion in manufacturing employment to raise wage rates. How does this change the analysis? We answer this question in two stages. First we try maintaining the assumption that the marginal product of labor in agriculture is constant but let $\mu > \frac{1}{2}$, and second (in the next section) we let the marginal product of labor in agriculture increase smoothly as labor is withdrawn.

If manufacturing expenditure exceeds half of income, then manufacturing cannot all be fitted into a single economy at equal wages in both countries. If the world economy tries to concentrate manufacturing, wages in the country with the incipient manufacturing concentration will be bid up. And because of this wage differential, some manufacturing activity may continue to take place in the other economy.

To analyze this more systematically, consider first the symmetric equilibrium and the point at which symmetry is broken. Analysis of this is exactly as in the previous section. Because we are maintaining the assumption that $A'(1 - \lambda_r) = 1$ and $A''(1 - \lambda_r) = 0$, wages are equal to unity in the neighborhood of the symmetric equilibrium, and the previous analysis applies. Equation (14.26) gives the point at which symmetry is broken.

Now consider the sustainability of a concentration of manufacturing in country 1. Here we have to be a bit careful about defining what we mean by "concentration." *Both* countries could be specialized—1 in manufacturing, 2 in agriculture. However, for large μ, in the more usual configuration, one country produces only manufacturing, but there is also a smaller-scale (and lower-wage) manufacturing sector in the other. Let us consider only that case, that is, a case in which equilibrium is determined by equations (14.6)–(14.11); but whereas previously we posited $\lambda_1 = 2\mu$, $w_1 = 1$, and $\lambda_2 = 0$, we now tie the model down by positing $\lambda_1 = 1$ and $\lambda_2 < 1$ (which by (14.13) implies $w_2 = 1$). This situation is not an equilibrium when it implies a country 1 wage of less than 1, so that workers would defect to the agricultural sector. That is, the sustain point is that point at which, given $\lambda_1 = 1$ and $w_2 = 1$, we also have $w_1 = 1$, so that beyond this point country 1 no longer specializes in manufacturing. There is no simple analytical expression for this sustain point, so we instead illustrate the structure of equilibria numerically.[5]

Figure 14.4 traces out equilibrium values of λ_1 and λ_2 as functions of the level of trade costs. Solid lines are stable equilibria and dashed, unstable. At high values of T the symmetric equilibrium is unique and stable. As T drops below level $T(S)$, specialization of one country (we assume country 1) in manufacturing becomes sustainable. At $T(B)$, the symmetric equilibrium becomes unstable. The qualitative configuration of the sustain and break points is as in section 14.2, but the higher share of manufacturing in consumption means that, although country

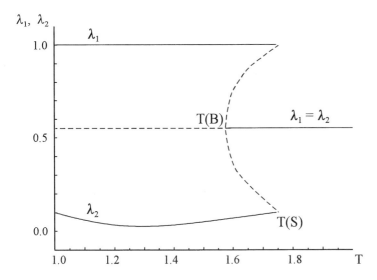

Figure 14.4
The bifurcation diagram

1 is specialized in manufacturing, country 2 also produces some manufacturing, as illustrated by the positive levels of λ_2 in the figure.

Figure 14.5 gives the real wages, $\omega_1 = w_1 G_1^{(\mu-1)}$, $\omega_2 = w_2 G_2^{(\mu-1)}$, corresponding to figure 14.4 (and reports only stable equilibria). We see that agglomeration of manufacturing in country 1 causes a discontinuous upward jump in real wages in country 1 and a fall in country 2. Two forces underlie these real income changes. First, the labor demand generated by manufacturing raises the country 1 wage, measured relative to agricultural goods. And second, the country with manufacturing has a lower cost-of-living index, because it does not have to pay transport costs on imported manufactures. This effect amplifies the country 1 gain and also drives the decline in real wages in country 2. The size of the wage gap between the two countries may continue to increase over some interval of trade costs. Eventually, however, the wage gap declines with transport costs; in the limit, as these costs go to 0, factor prices are equalized.

The structure of equilibria shown in these figures suggests a story we have referred to elsewhere (Krugman and Venables 1995) as "History of the World, Part I." Call country 1 North and country 2 South, and imagine a long-term secular fall in transport costs (first caravels, then steamships and railroads, then air freight, . . .). From an initial

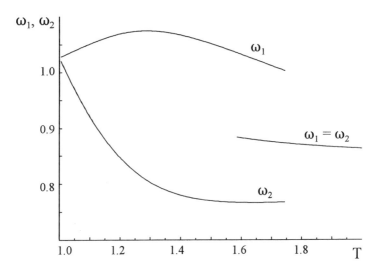

Figure 14.5
Real wages

position in which the two countries are identical, an international division of labor spontaneously arises through a process of uneven development. North immediately gains from this division of labor, while
South, which suffers deindustrialization, initially loses. The world
economy then necessarily has a core-periphery structure, with manufacturing concentrated in North; low wages in South are not enough
to attract manufacturing because of the lack of sufficient forward and
backward linkages. Eventually, however, further reductions in transport costs move the world into a globalization phase. The value of
proximity to customer and supplier firms diminishes as transport costs
fall, and so the sustainable wage gap between North and South narrows; in the limit of perfectly costless trade, we go to factor price equalization. During this globalization phase North may suffer a real as well
as a relative income decline, as illustrated in figure 14.5.

The qualitative structure of equilibria in figures 14.4 and 14.5 is general, as is the discontinuous increase in real income in North and the
fall in South at the point where specialization occurs. Figures 14.6 and
14.7 illustrate the quantitative dependence of real wages on parameters. In figure 14.6, the strength of linkages is increased: The parameter
α, giving the share of intermediates in production, is increased from
0.4 to 0.5. This increases the range of transport costs at which agglomer-

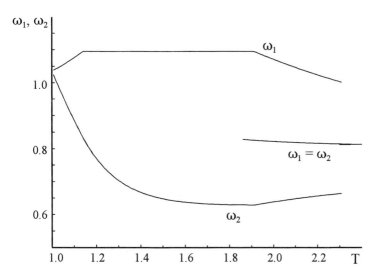

Figure 14.6
Real wages with high α

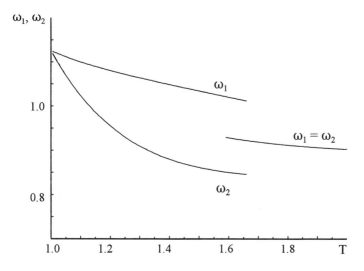

Figure 14.7
Real wages with high μ

ation occurs and also the absolute magnitude of the wage gap. It also creates a range of transport costs at which $\lambda_2 = 0$. This shows up as the flat segment of the ω_1 curve: Transport cost reductions do not change real income in country 1 when there is no import competition. In figure 14.7, α is returned to its previous value, and μ, the share of manufactures in consumption, is increased (from 0.55 to 0.7). This allows country 2 to hold more manufacturing. It also means that country 1 does not suffer a real wage decline in the globalization phase. Real wages increase steadily as transport costs are reduced, because country 1 imports a substantial share of its manufactures, and so benefits from the falling transport costs.

14.4 Decreasing Returns in Agriculture

We now generalize further by making agricultural wages a decreasing function of agricultural employment, that is, making the production function $A(1 - \lambda_r)$ strictly concave. This means that the labor supply curve to manufacturing always slopes upward. An expansion of manufacturing employment may increase the manufacturing wage, but it also increases the agricultural wage, so the stability of equilibrium depends on the relative movements of these wages.

Analysis of this is a generalization of the work already done in section 14.2. The stability of the equilibrium depends on the sign of $d\upsilon_1/d\lambda_1 \,(= d\upsilon_2/d\lambda_2)$, given by

$$\frac{d\upsilon_1}{d\lambda_1} = \frac{dw_1}{d\lambda_1} + A''(1 - \lambda_1), \tag{14.27}$$

which is equation (14.17). In section 14.2, agricultural technology was such that the second term was 0. It is now strictly negative. How does this affect our results?

The first point to note is that the symmetric equilibrium must now be stable at very low levels of transport costs. We know from the preceding analysis that as $T \to 1$, so $dw_1/d\lambda_1 \to 0$ (equation (14.25), with $Z \to 0$), while A'' remains negative. A verbal argument makes the intuition clear and also provides a stronger result. The value of forward and backward linkages with local firms goes to 0 as transport costs become very small, so as $T \to 1$, manufacturing wages in the two countries tend to equality. But with a strictly concave agricultural production function, agricultural wages are the same only if agricultural employment is the same in both countries, $\lambda_1 = \lambda_2$. Thus, as $T \to 1$, the equilibrium with dispersed activity is not only stable, but also unique.

This suggests that as we reduce T, we may go through the following stages. At very high T, activity is dispersed, and the symmetric equilibrium is stable and unique. At intermediate levels of T, agglomeration takes over, and the symmetric equilibrium is unstable. But at low enough levels of T, the symmetric equilibrium becomes stable once again. This pattern is confirmed by the simulations we undertake using an agricultural production function taking the form

$$A(1 - \lambda_r) = \frac{K}{\eta}\left(\frac{1 - \lambda_r}{K}\right)^{\eta}, \qquad (14.28)$$

where η is the share of labor in agriculture, and K is a constant chosen such that the symmetric equilibrium agricultural wage is unity. (K could be interpreted as the stock of an agriculture-specific factor such as land.)

The simulation output is reported in the bifurcation diagram (figure 14.8), which shows the share of manufacturing employment in the two countries as a function of trade costs. Figure 14.9 depicts the corresponding real-wage information, showing how the country with the

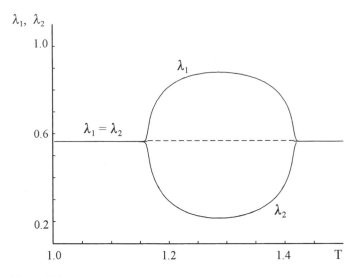

Figure 14.8
Bifurcation with diminishing returns in agriculture

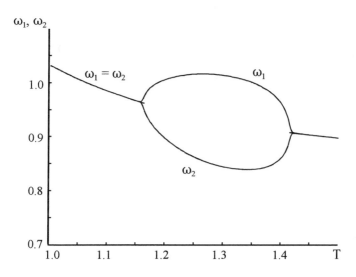

Figure 14.9
Real wages with diminishing returns in agriculture

larger share of manufacturing has the higher manufacturing wage and the lower consumer price index, generating the real-wage paths illustrated.

Appendix 14.1 analyzes the two bifurcations. We find that the equation for the break point, at which the symmetric equilibrium goes from stability to instability, is quadratic in T. Providing the absolute value of A'' is not too large, there are two positive real roots. The larger is the absolute value of A'', the narrower is the range in which agglomeration occurs, and if this value is large enough, the symmetric equilibrium is stable for all values of trade costs.[6]

The presence of these two distinct break points confirms our conjecture that, as transport costs are reduced, the equilibrium goes through three stages. We believe that this nonmonotonic effect of transport costs on industrial location is actually a fairly general insight. It is similar to our findings in chapter 7, in which trade costs in agriculture provide a countervailing force to agglomeration. At high trade costs, the dominant force in determining location is the need to be close to final consumption, preventing any strong geographical concentration of manufacturing. At low trade costs, the dominant determinant of location is wage costs, again mandating dispersed manufacturing to keep labor costs down. Therefore the linkage forces that can cause agglomeration are strongest relative to other forces at intermediate values of trade costs. Thus there is, we believe typically, an inverted-U relationship between trade costs and geographic concentration of industry. Figures 14.8 and 14.9 are also novel insofar as the bifurcations are smooth pitchfork bifurcations, not the tomahawk variant we usually find. This makes little difference to our main qualitative results—the presence of a range of values at which manufacturing agglomeration occurs. It arises because of the way we have modeled agriculture in equation (14.28). Evidently, with an iso-elastic production function, there will always be some agriculture in both locations, because the marginal product rises without limit as agricultural employment goes to 0. It turns out that with the particular functional form for agriculture given in equation (14.28), the curvature of the agricultural marginal product schedule is such that the bifurcation is a pitchfork.[7]

14.5 Conclusions

In a world of countries—which we think of as geographical units that can trade, but among which labor does not move—agglomeration in the sense of population concentration cannot occur. However, linkages among industrial sectors can still lead to a process of industrial concentration that is conceptually very similar to the stories about agglomeration we told in our regional and urban analyses. And the geographic structure of production in the international economy, like that within nations, can experience qualitative changes when parameters, especially the level of transport costs, change.

So far we have shown that a geographical approach to world trade can indeed be conducted using the same tools we have applied to cities and regions, and that structure of this analysis is indeed at an abstract level almost exactly the same as what we have done before. There are, however, two important differences. First, where linkages in parts II and III led to an unequal distribution of population across space, we now see the possibility not only of an uneven distribution of manufacturing, but also of the spontaneous emergence of inequalities in wage rates and living standards. We would not claim that this story is the sole or even the major explanation of the division of the world's nations into rich and poor, but it does offer the interesting suggestion that uneven development may have been a predictable consequence of growing world integration. Even more interesting, the same analysis suggests that the recent narrowing of income gaps between the advanced nations and (some) developing countries might be partially attributable to the continuation of the same trend toward integration: Declining trade costs first produce, then dissolve, the global inequality of nations.

All this is obviously a mere speculation based on an appealing but untested model. And there are other possible stories, even within a geographical framework, about the spread of industry to newly emerging economies; such an alternative story is the subject of chapter 15.

Appendix 14.1: Symmetry Breaking

In this appendix we derive the point of symmetry breaking for the model. To find the point at which symmetry is broken, we must differentiate around the symmetric equilibrium and compute $dv/d\lambda$. From the text we have equations (14.21), (14.22), and (14.24):

$$[1 - \sigma + \alpha\sigma Z]\frac{dG}{G} = \frac{Z}{\mu}d\lambda + [1 - \sigma(1 - \alpha)]Zdw, \qquad (14.21)$$

$$\sigma dw + \left[\frac{\alpha\sigma - (\sigma - 1)Z}{1 - \alpha}\right]\frac{dG}{G} = \frac{Z}{\mu}dE, \qquad (14.22)$$

$$\frac{dE}{\mu} = \left[\mu + \frac{\alpha}{1 - \alpha}\right]dw + \frac{\alpha}{1 - \alpha}\frac{d\lambda}{\mu}. \qquad (14.24)$$

Eliminating dE/μ, the first two of these equations can be written as

$$\begin{bmatrix} \sigma(1 - \alpha) - Z[\mu(1 - \alpha) + \alpha] & \alpha\sigma + (1 - \sigma)Z \\ [\sigma(1 - \alpha) - 1]Z & 1 - \sigma + \alpha\sigma Z \end{bmatrix}$$

$$\times \begin{bmatrix} dw \\ dG/G \end{bmatrix} = \begin{bmatrix} Z\alpha d\lambda/\mu \\ Zd\lambda/\mu \end{bmatrix}, \qquad (14A.1)$$

from which

$$\frac{dw}{d\lambda} = \frac{-Z}{\mu\Delta}[\alpha(2\sigma - 1) - Z(\sigma(1 + \alpha^2) - 1)]$$

$$= \frac{-Z}{\mu\Delta}\left[\frac{\alpha(1 + \rho) - Z(\alpha^2 + \rho)}{1 - \rho}\right], \qquad (14A.2)$$

where the Δ is the determinant, so

$$\Delta = Z^2[\sigma((\sigma - 1)(1 - \alpha) - \alpha^2 - \mu\alpha(1 - \alpha)) + 1 - \sigma]$$
$$+ Z[\alpha(2\sigma - 1) + \mu(\sigma - 1)(1 - \alpha)] + \sigma(1 - \sigma)(1 - \alpha)$$

$$= \frac{1}{(1 - \rho)^2} \{Z^2[\rho(\rho - \alpha) - \alpha(1 - \rho)(\alpha + \mu(1 - \alpha))]$$

$$+ Z(1 - \rho)[\alpha + \rho(\alpha + \mu(1 - \alpha))] - (1 - \alpha)\rho\}. \tag{14A.3}$$

The determinant Δ is negative for all $Z \in [0,1]$ if the no-black-hole condition is satisfied, $\alpha < \rho$.

The required stability condition is the change in manufacturing wages compared to agricultural given a change $d\lambda$, that is,

$$\frac{d\upsilon}{d\lambda} = \frac{dw}{d\lambda} + A''. \tag{14A.4}$$

If $A'' = 0$, then the condition under which $d\upsilon/d\lambda = 0$ comes from (14A.2), giving a unique break point value of Z and hence of T (compare (14A.2) with (5A.5)).

If $A'' < 0$ then $d\upsilon/d\lambda < 0$ at $Z = 0$ and $Z = 1$. The equation for $d\upsilon/d\lambda$ is a quadratic in Z that has two positive real roots for small enough A''.

Appendix 14.2: Simulation Parameters

Figures 14.1–14.3: $\sigma = 5$, $\alpha = 0.5$, $\mu = 0.4$, $T = 3$, 1.5, and 2.15 respectively.

Figures 14.4–14.5: $\sigma = 5$, $\alpha = 0.4$, $\mu = 0.55$.

Figure 14.6: $\sigma = 5$, $\alpha = 0.5$, $\mu = 0.55$.

Figure 14.7: $\sigma = 5$, $\alpha = 0.4$, $\mu = 0.7$.

Figures 14.8–14.9: $\sigma = 5$, $\alpha = 0.4$, $\mu = 0.55$, $\eta = 0.95$.

Notes

1. The production function for a single firm in country s is, instead of $F + cq_s = l_s$ (equation 4.18),

$$F + cq_s = \alpha^{-\alpha}(1 - \alpha)^{\alpha-1}l_s^{1-\alpha}\left[\sum_r n_r \tilde{x}_{rs}^\rho\right]^{\alpha/\rho},$$

where l_s is labor input and $\tilde{x}_{rs}$ is the input of each variety produced in country r. The final term on the right-hand side is a CES aggregator on intermediate inputs, analogous to the quantity index given in equation 4.2.

2. This is a formulation due to Ethier (1982), drawing on Dixit and Stiglitz (1977), and has been widely used in new growth theory.

3. For consumers, the price index is an expenditure function, and for producers, it is a cost function.

4. This is within a single manufacturing industry. We shall come to multi-industry settings in chapter 15 and make the distinction between upstream and downstream industries.

5. At this point, equality of supply and demand for manufactures means that $\lambda_2 = 2\mu - 1$. The sustain value of T can be found by using these facts in equilibrium conditions (14.6)–(14.11).

6. At large enough $|A''|$, the roots are imaginary. At lower values of μ, the curves on this figure are shifted apart, and there may be an interval within which $\lambda_2 = 0$.

7. Recall from the appendix to chapter 3 that the character of a bifurcation depends on the curvature of the schedule relating the level of λ to its rate of change. At the critical point, we know that we have

$$\frac{dv_1}{d\lambda_1} = \frac{dw_1}{d\lambda_1} + A''(1 - \lambda_1) = 0.$$

The critical point is a point of inflection, so

$$\frac{d^2v_1}{d\lambda_1^2} = \frac{d^2w_1}{d\lambda_1^2} - A'''(1 - \lambda_1) = 0.$$

The function goes from concave to convex if

$$\frac{d^3v_1}{d\lambda_1^3} = \frac{d^3w_1}{d\lambda_1^3} + A''''(1 - \lambda_1) < 0,$$

and conversely if the expression is positive. It turns out that $d^3w_1/d\lambda_1^3$ is negative. The pitchfork bifurcation arises when the function goes from convex to concave, so occurs if the fourth derivative of the agricultural production function is positive and sufficiently large to overturn the first term. A positive fourth derivative, in turn, is a property that just happens to hold for the iso-elastic form of the agricultural production function that we used in our examples.

Economic Development and the Spread of Industry

Any economist familiar with the standard argument that trade leads to factor price equalization realizes that he must somehow account for the stark fact that factor prices—above all wages—are very much *not* equalized. To make sense of the world, we need to have a story about how nations that participate in the same markets can pay wages that differ by a factor of five, ten, or twenty. On the other hand, the most striking feature of the world economy in the last generation has been the narrowing of the gap between at least some low-wage countries and the advanced West. For example, wages in Taiwan went from only 6 percent of the U.S. level as recently as 1975 to 34 percent in 1995; in South Korea, the numbers were 6 and 43 percent respectively. What can explain both the origins of such international inequality and the ability of some countries to move rapidly up the economic ladder?

In chapter 14 we already saw one answer, in our "History of the World, Part I": In a model in which linkages give rise to external economies, a secular decline in transport costs can first create a world divided between a wealthy core and a poorer periphery, then cause that division to collapse. In this chapter we pursue an alternative though closely related story in which the source of international economic inequality is the same, but a secular rise in the demand for manufactured goods drives change. In brief, the story runs as follows: We imagine a world economy in which some one region has initially managed to get a self-reinforcing advantage in manufacturing, an advantage that allows it to pay higher wages than other countries. Over time, however, the world's demand for manufactures rises. This increases the level of activity in the manufacturing region, reinforcing the agglomeration and also increasing wages. As this process continues, the wage gap between regions may become too large to be sustainable. It is then profitable for individual firms to set up manufacturing in a second region, which begins to develop self-reinforcing advantages of its own and thus has a surge in wages. Then at a later date, a third region goes through the same process, and so on. This story not only offers a possible explanation of rapid growth in the Third World, but also offers a clue as to why at any given time certain regions of the developing world appear to be surging while others lag behind.

A further elaboration of the model allows for multiple industries that differ in labor intensity, input-output structure, and so on. In this case we observe the emergence of a characteristic life cycle of development, in which countries that industrialize first do so by developing industries that are especially labor-intensive or that are weakly linked to other sectors, before eventually developing a mature industrial structure. In some cases we see in particular a pattern reminiscent both of the past industrialization of Japan and current industrialization in China and other low-wage manufacturing exporters: On the way to full maturity they experience a temporary phase of producing labor-intensive, weak-linkage goods not only for their home market but for the world as a whole.

15.1   Growth and Sustainable Wage Differentials

We begin with a model that is as close as possible to that introduced in chapter 14. As before, we suppose a two-sector economy in which the presence of intermediate goods creates forward and backward linkages within manufacturing. But we now add a growth process that acts as the driving force behind economic change. Because we are concerned with the spatial implications of growth, not with its origins, we take this process as exogenous: We simply assume that technical progress steadily augments all primary factors. We can put this in the model by measuring primary factors in efficiency units and denoting this efficiency level L. Thus $L\lambda_r$ and $(1 - \lambda_r)L$ are the number of efficiency units of labor operating in country r manufacturing and agriculture respectively, and w_r now denotes the wage per efficiency unit of labor.

We also change the formulation of consumer demand. For our story, we need demand for manufactures to increase more rapidly than potential supply in the currently industrialized nations. But increases in L raise both supply and demand. To get some action out of growth, we replace Cobb-Douglas consumer preferences between agriculture and manufactures with a formulation under which manufactures account for a growing share of expenditure as income rises. The simplest formulation that does the job is a linear expenditure system in which consumers are assumed to have a minimal "subsistence" level of food consumption. Thus if a consumer's income (measured in terms of agriculture) is Y, all of that individual's income below some level $\overline{Y}$ is spent on agriculture. Of income above $\overline{Y}$, we assume that a proportion μ is spent on manufactures, and $1 - \mu$ on agriculture.[1] The consequence of this assumption is that as L increases through time, so does household income (each household is endowed with more efficiency units of primary factors), and so therefore does the share of income devoted to manufactures. This expansion of demand for manufactures relative to agriculture provides the driving force in our analysis.

The following equations rewrite the model of chapter 14 to incorporate these assumptions. Writing these equations for an arbitrarily large number of countries, the price indices are,

$$G_r^{1-\sigma} = \sum_s L\lambda_s w_s^{1-\sigma(1-\alpha)} G_s^{-\alpha\sigma} T_{sr}^{1-\sigma}. \tag{15.1}$$

Notice that it is employment in efficiency units, $L\lambda_s$, that is relevant, because this determines the number of varieties of manufactures produced. The wage equations, for efficiency units of labor, are

$$\frac{(w_r^{1-\alpha} G_r^{\alpha})^{\sigma}}{1 - \alpha} = \sum_s G_s^{\sigma-1} E_s T_{rs}^{1-\sigma}. \tag{15.2}$$

Expenditure on manufactures comes from our representative consumer and from firms demanding intermediates,

$$E_r = \mu(Y_r - \overline{Y}) + \frac{\alpha w_r L\lambda_r}{1 - \alpha}, \tag{15.3}$$

in which the fact that demand for manufactures comes only from income in excess of $\overline{Y}$ modifies the consumer demand term. Income in each country is given by

$$Y_r = w_r L\lambda_r + A(1 - \lambda_r)L, \tag{15.4}$$

where the first term is income from manufacturing employment, and the second is the value of agricultural output. The rate of technical progress is the same in both sectors and for all primary factors (land as well as labor), so L enters both terms in (15.4) multiplicatively, and the agricultural wage per efficiency unit of labor is $A'(1 - \lambda_r)$. We assume throughout the chapter that $A(1 - \lambda_r)$ is strictly concave, as in section 14.4, so agriculture always operates in all countries. An economy that also has manufacturing has the same wages per efficiency unit of labor in both sectors, so

$$w_r = A'(1 - \lambda_r). \tag{15.5}$$

We start from a position in which manufacturing is concentrated in a subset of countries, and we want to find the point at which it starts spilling out from this existing industrial center to other countries. We can of course do this by finding the sustain point. Suppose that there are just two countries and that manufacturing is concentrated in country 1, so $\lambda_1 > 0$ and $\lambda_2 = 0$. With this pattern of specialization we can derive relative manufacturing wages in the two countries, from (15.1) and (15.2), as

$$\left(\frac{w_2}{w_1}\right)^{(1-\alpha)\sigma} T^{\alpha\sigma} = \frac{E_1 T^{1-\sigma} + E_2 T^{\sigma-1}}{E_1 + E_2}. \tag{15.6}$$

Country 1 has $w_1 = A'(1 - \lambda_1)$. In country 2, $\lambda_2 = 0$, and this is sustainable provided $w_2 \leq A'(1)$, so the sustain condition takes the form

$$A'(1) \geq A(1 - \lambda_1)' \left[\left(\frac{E_1}{E_1 + E_2} T^{1-\sigma} + \frac{E_2}{E_1 + E_2} T^{\sigma-1} \right) T^{-\alpha\sigma} \right]^{1/(1-\alpha)\sigma}. \tag{15.7}$$

This is of course similar to sustain conditions we have derived in other chapters, although it contains endogenous variables on the right-hand side. We can derive the equilibrium values of these variables in a fairly straightforward way. Since production in country 1 meets total demand for manufactures, the country 1 wage bill satisfies

$$w_1 L\lambda_1 = (1 - \alpha)(E_1 + E_2). \tag{15.8}$$

Expenditure on manufactures in countries 1 and 2 are (from (15.3) and (15.4), with $\lambda_2 = 0$)

$$E_1 = \mu[w_1 L\lambda_1 + A(1 - \lambda_1)L - \overline{Y}] + \frac{\alpha w_1 L\lambda_1}{1 - \alpha},$$

$$E_2 = \mu(A(1)L - \overline{Y}), \tag{15.9}$$

so adding these and using them in (15.8),

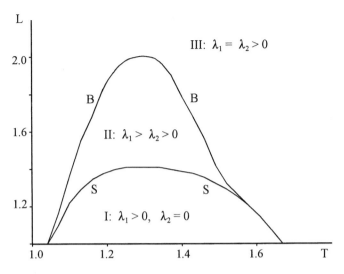

Figure 15.1
Break and sustain points

$$w_1 L \lambda_1 (1 - \mu) = \mu[A(1)L + A(1 - \lambda_1)L - 2\overline{Y}]. \tag{15.10}$$

(Although we have derived this equation via manufacturing expenditures, it can also be interpreted as equality of supply and demand for agriculture.) This equation, together with

$$w_1 = A'(1 - \lambda_1), \tag{15.11}$$

determines w_1 and λ_1. Expenditure levels in each country can then be solved from (15.9), giving all the information needed to evaluate the sustain condition, (15.7).

The curve SS in figure 15.1 illustrates the sustain curve. Axes of this figure are the parameters T and L, and the curve is the locus of these parameters at which the concentrated equilibrium (with manufacturing wages, employment levels, and expenditures given by (15.9)–(15.11)) satisfy the sustain condition (15.7) with equality. Below the curve, concentration of manufacturing in country 1 is sustainable, and above it, it is not.

The hump shape of the sustain curve reflects that fact that, as usual, it is relatively difficult to sustain agglomeration at very low and at very high levels of trade costs, exactly as we found in sections 14.3 and 14.4. The role of forward and backward linkages can be seen by looking at the equation for the sustain curve, (15.7).[2] Forward linkages are captured by the term $T^{-\alpha\sigma}$, which represents the fact that firms in country 2 have to pay T more for their intermediate inputs than do firms in country 1, and this penalty is worse the higher is T. The term in square brackets captures backward-linkage effects. Raising T switches expenditure in the country 2 market toward country 2 firms, and has the opposite effect in the country 1 market.

Our focus in this chapter, however, is not on changing trade costs, but on changes in L, the efficiency parameter. Figure 15.1 indicates that as L increases, agglomeration of manufacturing in country 1 eventually becomes unsustainable, because when $\overline{Y} > 0$, raising L increases both w_1 and λ_1, as can be established by totally differentiating (15.10) and (15.11). The reason is that income growth increases demand for manufactures relative to agriculture, and this manufacturing growth is concentrated in country 1. This then has two effects on the sustain condition. One the one hand, because it increases the country 1 wage, it makes it more attractive for manufacturing to set up in country 2. But on the other hand, precisely because country 1 is manufacturing more and paying higher wages, the share of country 1 in world manufacturing expenditure rises, and this strengthens backward linkages and reinforces the existing agglomeration. In terms of the sustain equation, $E_1/(E_1 + E_2)$ rises, the corresponding country 2 share declines, and because $T^{\sigma-1} > T^{1-\sigma}$, the term in square brackets decreases.

The net effect therefore depends on the tension between changing relative wages and stronger backward linkages. In figure 15.1 the former dominate, pushing the economy through the SS curve. However, this need not necessarily be the case. For example, if the share of manufactures in consumption, μ, is very low, then the limiting values of λ_1 and w_1 as $L \to \infty$ are relatively small, so the sustain point is never reached. (In terms of figure 15.1, the SS curve has two sections that become vertical, so that there is a range of T below SS for all L). Generally, the SS curve is higher (hence agglomeration is sustainable for longer) the smaller is the share of manufactures, μ, and the larger the input-output linkage, α; higher α means that a larger wage differential is required to compensate for linkages foregone in moving out of the existing manufacturing center.

As we pass through the SS curve, what happens? It depends on whether the bifurcation is a tomahawk or a pitchfork. In the former case there is a discontinuity, and the economies jump to full conver-

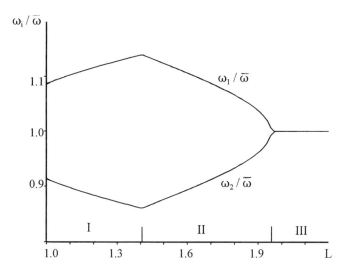

Figure 15.2
Relative real wages, two country model

gence, $\lambda_1 = \lambda_2$. In the latter, λ_1 and λ_2 move continuously with L, so we enter a region in which $\lambda_1 > \lambda_2 > 0$, as illustrated in region II in the figure. Moving up across the region has the effect of raising λ_1, and we eventually reach a point of full convergence, $\lambda_1 = \lambda_2 > 0$. The locus of such points is the BB curve, which is, provided the bifurcation is a pitchfork, simply the point of symmetry breaking. (We are now passing through this point in the opposite direction from earlier chapters; it is now the point of symmetry *restoration*.)

We can now pull all these elements together and see the development path these economies follow if the technical efficiency factor, L, continues to increase. This is best illustrated by tracing out relative real wages (the real wage in each country relative to the average for both) as L increases, and is shown in figure 15.2, which takes as given a value of $T = 1.3$.

In phase I, when L is in the interval I on the horizontal axis, manufacturing is concentrated in country 1, and the country 1 wage is higher than the country 2 wage (both in real terms and in terms of agricultural output). Growth of L raises demand for manufactures, and this builds up pressure in the country 1 manufacturing agglomeration and causes contraction of country 1 agriculture and an increase in its wage. In this phase, we therefore see a divergence of economic structure and income levels between countries.

Country 2 industrialization takes place during phase II. It starts when the wage gap between countries is large enough for it to be profitable for some firms to move out of country 1, even though they forego linkage benefits with other firms. Increasing L within phase II narrows the wage gap between countries, and this narrowing occurs at an increasing rate. The reason is of course that as industry expands in country 2 it creates its own linkages, feeding an accelerating process of convergence. During this process the share of industry in country 1 falls and real wages per worker may increase or decrease, depending on the alternative employment opportunities (here represented by the shape of the agricultural production function), the change in the price index arising from availability of cheaper imported manufactures, and the underlying rate of technical change.

Finally, as L increases still further, we enter phase III. This is the mature phase, at which point the economies have attained full convergence.

15.2 Many Industries and Many Countries

We now turn to a situation in which there are many countries and many industries. Having many countries allows us to address the geographical pattern of spread of industry from country to country. If we start in a situation where industry is concentrated in a single country, does it spread evenly to all the others, or does it spread first to one, then the next, and so on?

Having many industries allows us to address a number of questions concerning the industrial structure and trade patterns of countries during their period of industrialization. Different industries face ties of different strength to an existing agglomeration, through the linkage benefits they receive, so what can be said about which industries are first to move out of an established agglomeration? From this, can we identify how a country's industrial structure is likely to change during its industrialization phase, and also during its mature phase, as it loses industrial activity to newly industrializing economies? Because industries differ in the linkages they create for other industries, how does the pace and character of industrialization depend on which industries are the first to start to relocate in the industrializing economy?

We have tried to gain some insight into the answers to these questions by conducting simulation analysis in a five-country and seven-industry model. The structure is exactly as in the previous section, and the generalization to many industries is given in appendix 15.1. We assume that the countries are identical in their underlying structure of preferences, technologies, and endowments, and start from a position in which all industry is concentrated in a single country—call it country 1. We then trace the process of the spread of industry to the other economies. The seven industries have different characteristics, and could potentially differ in the extent of their increasing returns, in their transport costs, in the sources of demand for their output, and in the composition of their inputs. To try to isolate some of the key forces at work, we focus on the effect of differences in industries' input-output coefficients and proceed by tracing the industrialization process under a series of different hypothetical input-output matrices.

15.2.1 Differing Labor Intensities

The simplest case, with which we begin, is one in which industries are identical in all key respects except their labor intensity.[3] Industry 1 is the most labor intensive, and industry 7 the least. Figures 15.3 and 15.4 present the evolution of three of the economies under this condition.[4]

The first question is, because there are several countries, does industry spread to countries simultaneously or sequentially? We can answer

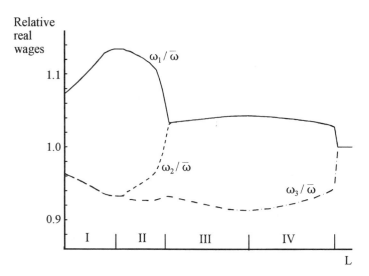

Figure 15.3
Relative real wages, multicountry model

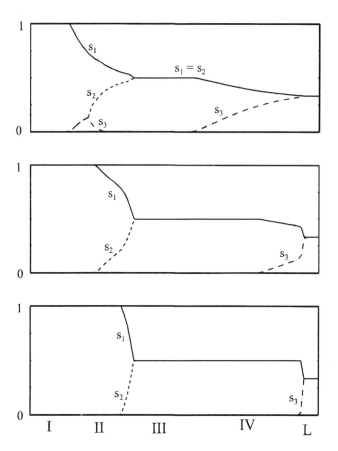

Figure 15.4
Industry shares; top panel most labor intensive industry

this by looking at the evolution of relative real wages per efficiency unit of labor as a function of L, the efficiency level,[5] as we do in figure 15.3, on the horizontal axis of which the main phases of development are marked out. In phase I, all industry is located in country 1, and there is a wage gap between country 1 and countries 2 and 3. Increases in L increase the magnitude of this gap, until it becomes profitable for some industry to relocate—and phase II begins. Phase II is the period in which country 2 starts to industrialize, and we see the wage gap between countries 1 and 2 narrowing at an increasing rate during the interval, until the two countries converge.

The behavior of the country 3 wage relative to the country 2 wage during this period gives the answer to our question about whether the spread of industry is uniform to all countries or consecutive, spreading to each country in turn. At the beginning of phase II both countries 2 and 3 start to industrialize; the $\omega_2 / \overline{\omega}$ and $\omega_3 / \overline{\omega}$ curves coincide for a very short interval at the beginning of phase II. However, as linkages within countries 2 and 3 become stronger, the equilibrium in which they both have the same industrial structure becomes unstable. If one country gets marginally ahead, its advantage is amplified, and the other country drops behind, which is what we see occurring. Although in the present framework there is nothing to say which country takes off and which lags (we simply label them 2 and 3 respectively), the presence of even small differences between the countries might have large effects, by giving one country an edge over the other at the crucial moment.

By the end of phase II, country 2 has completely caught up with country 1. There is a wage gap between these countries and country 3, and this gap starts to widen. During this phase (marked as III) manufacturing employment in country 1 and 2 is increasing, and this drives the increasing wage gap. At some point the gap becomes too large to be sustainable, and country 3's process of industrialization starts (phase IV). Country 3 wages start to catch up with those in 1 and 2, in an accelerating (and eventually discontinuous) process.

The main point to draw from this figure is that the process of industrialization is not uniform across countries. Instead, it proceeds in a series of waves, with countries successively undergoing rapid industrialization as each establishes a critical mass of industry. Successful industrialization, however, raises wages—given our continuing growth of demand for manufactures—and thus eventually prepares the way for the spread of industry to yet another country.

Figure 15.4 gives some of the industrial detail associated with this process. There are seven industries, and the three panels of figure 15.4 illustrate industries 1, 4 and 7—the most, the average, and the least labor intensive. The horizontal axis is once again the technical efficiency level, L, whereas the vertical axis is each country's share in the output of the industry. (Thus the three lines in each panel, s_i, $i = 1, 2, 3$, sum to unity, the height of the panel.) There are two main things to note from this figure. First, the most labor-intensive industry is the first to leave country 1 and become established in 2 and 3—unsurprisingly, because high wages cause the relocation of industry.[6] Second, later industries—the less labor-intensive industries—enter more rapidly than the earlier ones, and possibly discontinuously, because the earlier industries create forward and backward linkages that facilitate entry of firms in other industries. This accounts for accelerating industrialization.

15.2.2 Forward and Backward Linkages

We now turn to the way in which the interindustry structure of the input-output matrix determines the process of the spread of industry. To simplify the various ways in which industries' input output coefficients may differ we proceed in several stages.

Sales Orientation

The first possibility is to suppose that all industries have the same cost structure but differ in their sales orientation: the extent to which their sales go to firms or to final consumers. In terms of the coefficients of the interindustry transactions part of the input-output matrix, all columns are identical, but the rows differ. Because industries all use the same inputs, they all *create* the same backward linkages (and receive the same forward linkages). However, an industry with small row elements *receives* few backward linkages (and creates few forward ones), because most of its output is used as final consumption, not as intermediates.[7]

The pattern of development in this case is that consumption-oriented industries are the first to move from the established agglomeration. Because a high proportion of demand for these industries' output comes from final demand, not from other firms, their demand is less concentrated in country 1, making them the first to move away from country 1. The overall pattern of development remains qualitatively similar to that outlined for the case of differing labor intensities. Industry spreads first to country 2, which fully converges to country 1, and then spreads to country 3, and so on.

Input Orientation

What if each industry has the same pattern of sales to industrial and final consumers but different intermediate input requirements? In terms of the input-output matrix, rows are now identical, but columns differ, industries with small column elements drawing less of their inputs from other imperfectly competitive industries, and so benefiting less from forward linkages and creating fewer backward linkages.[8] Unsurprisingly, these industries with low intermediate input requirements are the first to leave; because they are less dependent on supply from other firms, their location is more responsive to wage differences.

15.2.3 Upstream/Downstream

The preceding examples allowed industries to vary either in the forward linkages (different rows) or the backward linkages (different columns) they create. What if they differ in both? We shall look at two possible cases. In the first, there is a perfect negative rank correlation between the forward and backward linkages each industry creates. There is then an unambiguous "most upstream" industry, which creates strong forward linkages (its sales are industrially oriented, so it has the largest row elements) and weak backward linkages (smallest column elements). Conversely, there is a "most downstream" industry with weak forward linkages and strong backward linkages.[9]

The changing industrial structure is illustrated in figure 15.5, in which the top panel is the most upstream industry, and the bottom, the most downstream. Two features stand out. First, the upstream industry is the first to leave. And second, each country's development process, once it has gotten under way, is extremely rapid. Both these phenomena have the same fundamental cause. In this model forward linkages are stronger than backward. The upstream industry uses few manufactures as intermediates, and so receives few forward linkages, which means it is the first industry to become detached from an existing agglomeration. However, it creates the strongest forward linkages, attracting entry by firms in other industries. This makes for the rapid transition we see in figure 15.5.

15.2.4 Linkage Strength

In the converse case (the second of the two mentioned at the beginning of the previous section), there is a perfect positive rank correlation between the forward and backward linkages each industry creates. We can now rank industries from the most weakly linked—in both directions—through to the most strongly linked. Outcomes are shown in figure 15.6. Unsurprisingly, the order of movement runs from the most weakly linked (industry 1, top panel) through to the most strongly linked.

The process of development is slower in this case than in the preceding one, as the first industries to move to a new country not only receive

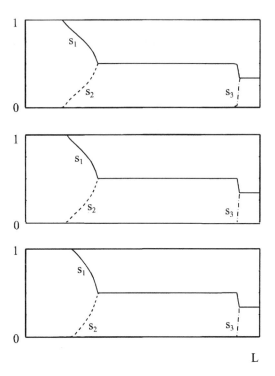

Figure 15.5
Industry shares; top panel most upstream industry

few linkages but also transmit few. In this case we also get a kind of "overshooting" of industrial structure, with newly industrializing countries (country 2 then country 3) taking the largest share of world output in sectors with weak linkages. Although all fully industrialized countries have the same industrial structure (so the only trade between them is intra-industry trade), during the transition phases the newly industrializing country goes from being a net exporter of agriculture to being a net exporter of weakly linked manufacturing goods, before settling down to a mature trading pattern.

Comparison of the fate of country 3 during phase II is also noteworthy. Whereas in the upstream/downstream case, country 3 has no industry during almost all this interval, in this case, country 3's development of the most weakly linked industry (industry 1) runs parallel to country 2's for much of phase II. The advantage of cheap country 3 labor is more valuable to industry 1 than the absence of its (weak) links to other country 3 industry.

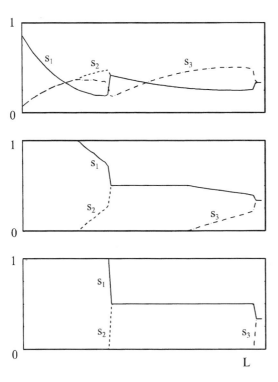

Figure 15.6
Industry shares; top panel most weakly linked industry

15.3 Conclusions

In this chapter, we have managed to use a slightly modified version of our basic model to tell a story of breathtaking scope: a story in which industrialization in the world economy occurs via a series of dramatic developmental spurts, with a few countries at any given time experiencing surging production and wages while others are for the time being left on the sidelines. Economic growth does not take the form of smooth convergence of all countries in the world economy, but instead there is a group of rich countries and a group of poor ones. Development involves countries in turn making a fairly rapid transition from one group to the other.

When we consider multiple industries that vary in their characteristics, we also get a suggestive, even exciting story about the natural life cycle of development, in which countries typically develop through the production of certain goods, then move "upscale" as they cede those sectors to the nations that come after.

As in chapter 14, some caution is in order. We do not really believe that this model captures all or even most of the forces actually driving development in the modern economy. It does, however, show the ability of a geographical approach to generate surprisingly complex and yet strongly suggestive behavior out of very simple elements.

Appendix 15.1: The Multicountry, Multi-industry Model

To derive the full multicountry and multi-industry model, it is helpful to start, as we did in chapter 4, by focusing on numbers of firms and prices of individual varieties, before making the substitutions to focus on employment levels and wages. The number of countries is denoted R, and subscripts refer to country. The number of industries is denoted H, and industry-specific variables are superscripted.

We start with the definition of the price index:

$$G_r^i = \left[\sum_{s=1}^{H} n_s^i (p_s^i T_{s,r})^{(1-\sigma)} \right]^{1/(1-\sigma)}, \quad i = 1 \dots H, \quad r, s = 1 \dots R. \quad (15A.1)$$

Prices charged by firms in country r industry i take the following form:

$$p_r^i = (w_r^i)^{\alpha^i} \prod_{j=1}^{H} (G_r^j)^{\alpha^{ji}}. \quad (15A.2)$$

The right-hand side of (15A.2) is a Cobb-Douglas cost function over labor and intermediates in which α^i is the labor share, and α^{ji} gives the value of the input of an intermediate good from industry j per unit cost industry i. $\sum_j \alpha^{ji} - \alpha^i \leq 1$, and if this holds with strict inequality, then some of the agricultural good is used an intermediate, so that input shares sum to unity. As previously, we choose units of measurement for output such that the the markup cancels out with a cost parameter.

Demand in country s for a unit of industry i output produced in country r is

$$q_{r,s}^i = (p_r^i)^{-\sigma} \left(\frac{T_{r,s}}{G_s^i} \right)^{(1-\sigma)} E_s^i, \quad (15A.3)$$

where E_s^i is country s expenditure on the products of industry i. The zero-profit condition sets an equilibrium output level per firm which, by choice of units, is $1/\alpha^i$, so

$$q_r^i \equiv \sum_{s=1}^{R} q_{r,s}^i = 1/\alpha^i. \tag{15A.4}$$

Expenditure on each industry's products in each country is

$$E_r^i = \mu^i(Y_r - \overline{Y}) + \sum_{j=1}^{H} \alpha^{ij} n_r^j p_r^j q_r^j. \tag{15A.5}$$

The wage bill in each sector is

$$L\lambda_r^i w_r^i = \alpha^i n_r^i p_r^i q_r^i = n_r^i p_r^i, \tag{15A.6}$$

and income is

$$Y_r = \sum_{j=1}^{H} L w_r^j \lambda_r^j + A\left(1 - \sum_{j=1}^{H} \lambda_r^j\right) L. \tag{15A.7}$$

As elsewhere, we can eliminate terms in n_r^i and p_r^i. Using (15A.2) and (15A.6), the price index, (15A.1) becomes

$$(G_r^i)^{1-\sigma} = \sum_{s=1}^{H} L\lambda_s^i T_{sr}^{1-\sigma} (w_s^i)^{1-\sigma\alpha^i} \prod_{j=1}^{H} (G_s^j)^{-\sigma\alpha^{ji}}. \tag{15A.8}$$

Using (15A.2), (15A.3), and (15A.4) gives the wage equation:

$$\left[(w_r)^{\alpha^i} \prod_{j=1}^{H} (G_r^j)^{\alpha^{ji}}\right]^{\sigma} = \alpha^i \sum_{s=1}^{R} (T_{rs}/G_s^i)^{1-\sigma} E_s^i. \tag{15A.9}$$

Expenditure, (15A.5), becomes

$$E_r^i = \mu^i(Y_r - \overline{Y}) + \sum_{j=1}^{H} L\lambda_r^j w_r^j \alpha^{ij}/\alpha^i. \tag{15A.10}$$

These three, together with the income equation, (15A.7), determine the equilibrium values of the price indices, wages, expenditure, and income, given an allocation of labor across industries. In the long run, this adjusts to equate wages across different sectors.

Appendix 15.2: Simulation Parameters

All simulations use the equations in the text plus the iso-elastic agricultural production function equation from chapter 14. Parameter values are

Figure 15.1: $\sigma = 5$, $\alpha = 0.4$, $\mu = 0.9$, $\eta = 0.95$, $\overline{Y} = 0.67$.

Figure 15.2: $\sigma = 5$, $\alpha = 0.4$, $\mu = 0.9$, $\eta = 0.95$, $\overline{Y} = 0.67$,
$\quad\quad T = 1.3$ and 1.5.

Figure 15.3–15.6: $\sigma = 5$, $\eta = 0.94$, $\overline{Y} = 0.7$, $T = 1.2$.

Figure 15.3, 15.4:

Demand shares: $\mu^i = 0.086$, $i = 1 \ldots 7$.

Labor shares: $\alpha^i = 0.67, 0.61, 0.56, 0.51, 0.45, 0.4, 0.34$.

Manufacturing
intermediate shares: $\alpha^{ij} = 0.0471$, $i = 1 \ldots 7$, $j = 1 \ldots 7$.

Figure 15.5:

Demand shares: $\mu^i = 0.083, 0.088, 0.094, 0.10, 0.105, 0.111, 0.116$.

Labor shares: $\alpha^i = 0.5$, $i = 1 \ldots 7$.

Manufacturing intermediate shares:

$$
\alpha^{ij} = \begin{bmatrix}
.042 & .049 & .056 & .063 & .070 & .077 & .084 \\
.038 & .045 & .051 & .058 & .064 & .070 & .077 \\
.035 & .041 & .047 & .052 & .058 & .064 & .070 \\
.031 & .037 & .042 & .047 & .052 & .058 & .063 \\
.028 & .032 & .037 & .042 & .047 & .051 & .056 \\
.024 & .029 & .033 & .037 & .041 & .045 & .049 \\
.021 & .024 & .028 & .031 & .035 & .038 & .042
\end{bmatrix}
$$

This matrix is constructed so that industry 1 is upstream: Its column elements are half those of industry 7, and its row elements are twice those of industry 7.

Figure 15.6:

Demand shares: $\mu^i = 0.117, 0.112, 0.106, 0.101, 0.095, 0.090, 0.084$.

Labor shares: $\alpha^i = 0.5$, $i = 1 \ldots 7$.

Manufacturing intermediate shares:

$$\alpha^{ij} = \begin{bmatrix}
.021 & .024 & .028 & .031 & .035 & .038 & .042 \\
.024 & .029 & .033 & .037 & .041 & .045 & .049 \\
.028 & .033 & .037 & .042 & .047 & .051 & .056 \\
.031 & .037 & .042 & .047 & .052 & .058 & .063 \\
.035 & .041 & .047 & .052 & .058 & .064 & .070 \\
.038 & .045 & .051 & .058 & .064 & .070 & .077 \\
.042 & .049 & .056 & .063 & .070 & .077 & .084
\end{bmatrix}$$

This matrix is constructed so that industry 1 is weakly linked. Both its row and column coefficients are half those of industry 7.

Notes

1. Because preferences are no longer homothetic, construction of the aggregate demand function requires that we assume that all households in the economy have the same income, implying that rent from land is equally distributed.

2. It is easy to see how T enters the sustain condition, particularly because w_1, λ_1, E_1, and E_2 do not depend on T (see equations (15.9)–(15.11)).

3. To make variations in labor input shares across industries consistent with the same input-output coefficients among industrial sectors, we allow industries to use agriculture as an input. Thus, an industry with a low labor input share has a correspondingly high agriculture input share. Because the price of agriculture is the same in all countries, this enables us to present the experiment in as pure a form as possible.

4. We concentrate on just three of the five economies, raising L only far enough for three economies to industrialize.

5. Figure 15.3 gives wages in terms of the numeraire. Real wages trend upward because of benefits from increasing product varieties and display larger cross-country differences. The cross-country real-wage gap is larger because of international differences in price indices.

6. Notice that at the beginning of phase II, industry 1 starts to develop in country 3, but because simultaneous development of both countries is unstable, it then drops back.

7. We scale industries such that they are all the same size in the initial equilibrium. The demand parameter μ^i varies to offset the effects of cross-industry variations in intermediate demands.

8. All industries have the same labor input coefficients; once again, agriculture is used as an input to ensure input shares sum to unity.

9. The actual input-output matrix and details of its construction are given in appendix 15.2.

16   Industrial Clustering

Although grand issues such as the division of the world between high- and low-wage countries are both fascinating and a useful proving ground for our modeling approach, many of the likely policy issues involving economic geography are more modest in their scale. Few people think that closer integration of the European market is likely to deindustrialize either the periphery or the core of the continental economy. On the other hand, there are real issues concerning the impact of lower trade costs on which industries are located where. For example, Europe currently maintains several distinct national centers of production in many industries, from automobiles to financial services, whereas the United States has a single dominant producing region. As the European market becomes more closely integrated, will the polycentric geography of its industries unravel, giving way to American-style concentration? Will high-technology industries concentrate in some European Silicon Valley? Will the financial services sector maintain its current polycentricity, or will it concentrate in London (or Frankfurt)? These are questions about *industrial clustering*; and they are questions that can, we believe, usefully be addressed using our basic approach to economic geography.

To do so, we must enrich the economy's input-output structure, and in this chapter we focus on models with two or more manufacturing sectors. This enables us to study the forces for agglomeration within each industry as well as within the manufacturing sector as a whole. It allows us to move from the question "Where will manufacturing concentrate (if it does)?" to the question "What manufacturing will be concentrated where?"

In this chapter we develop a series of models to address this question. We now imagine economies that are already completely industrialized; the constant-returns agricultural sector is simply dropped from the story. Of course, we still need to make some assumptions to keep the analytics manageable; our main simplifying device is the imposition of symmetry both in the parameters of industries and on the assumed input-output matrices. Not too surprisingly, these assumptions allow us to address the question of specialization in ways that bear a strong resemblance to the analysis of earlier chapters.

The first model we develop has two countries, two industries, and a single factor of production. We establish conditions under which each industry agglomerates in a single country, and trace the implications of changes in trade costs for industrial location and for real income. In the second model, we add a second production factor, and thereby link our approach to a $2 \times 2 \times 2$ Heckscher-Ohlin trade model. Finally, we move to having many industries. Each industry agglomerates in a single country, but the number of industries in each country may be indeterminate. One country may have a higher proportion of world industry than the other, and consequently also higher wages. We can, however, define bounds on the sustainable degree of difference between the countries.

16.1   Industrial Clusters: The Evidence

A good deal of evidence indicates that industries are more highly clustered than standard theories of comparative advantage might predict. We have already alluded to Silicon Valley and some of the world's financial districts, and industry centers such as Hollywood spring to mind. Geographical clustering of industries is central to Porter's (1990) view of competitive advantage. He undertook case studies of selected industrial clusters—German printing equipment, Italian ceramic tiles, Japanese robotics, and American health care equipment—and documented the clustering of internationally competitive industries in a number of countries.

Statistical evidence on geographic concentration is provided by Krugman (1991b), who used United States data to look at industrial localization. He computed locational Gini coefficients for three-digit manufacturing industries across U.S. states and found surprisingly high levels of concentration.[1] Taking as benchmark the U.S. automotive industry (with half its employment still in the Detroit area), nearly half of other industries have higher locational Gini coefficients. Kim (1995) looked at a longer time series, 1860–1987, and showed that the rapid increase in industry regional specialization occurred before the First World War, at the same time as the United States was developing its transport system and becoming an integrated national economy. Since the interwar years, regional specialization has been falling. This work is nicely mirrored by work on European data, suggesting that as European integration has proceeded, regional concentration of industry and divergence of countries' industrial structures have recently increased (Amiti 1997; Brulhart and Torstensson 1996).

Of course, any theory of interregional or international trade and specialization is likely to predict that regions or countries have different industrial structures, and the studies referred to above do not provide a rigorous test of an agglomeration-based theory of location against some other theory, although Ellison and Glaeser (1997) did test agglomeration against chance. They pointed out that random chance may mean that industries turn out to be concentrated, even if there are no underlying forces for concentration—particularly if internal increasing returns to scale are such that there are few plants in the industry. However, using U.S. state data, they found that the actual pattern of U.S. plant location is considerably more concentrated than chance alone would explain.

Accepting then that industrial clustering is a significant empirical phenomenon, let us move to constructing a theory to show how it can emerge.

16.2   Industrial Clusters: The Model

We initially work with two countries, two industries, and a single factor of production, labor. Each country is endowed with one unit of labor, which is assumed to be internationally immobile and may be employed in either of the two manufacturing industries. (We assume that there is no agricultural sector.) Keeping track of the two manufacturing industries requires some extra notation, which we handle by using superscripts 1 and 2 to label the industries. To prevent notation from getting too complex, we set out the model for a single country— "Home"—and do not use country subscripts. Where it is necessary to distinguish the "Foreign" country, we do so by placing a tilde ($\sim$) over the variable.

The two industries are both monopolistically competitive as described in earlier chapters. They are also symmetric in the following sense: On the demand side, both have identical consumer demand parameters, each taking half of consumers' expenditure and having the same demand elasticity σ. Looking at technology, they both have the same fixed costs and equilibrium firm scale, and utilize Cobb-Douglas technologies employing labor and intermediate goods both from their own industry and from the other industry. The input-output matrix, giving the value of different inputs per unit cost, has the following form:

	Industry 1	Industry 2
Industry 1	α	γ
Industry 2	γ	α
Labor	β	β

The interindustry part of the transactions matrix is symmetric, so for each industry, inputs from the other industry account for a share γ of costs, and inputs from the same industry account for a share α. As we will see, $\alpha > \gamma$ means that intra-industry linkages are more powerful than interindustry linkage. The share of labor is β, and of course, $\alpha + \beta + \gamma = 1$.

Choosing units such that the marginal input requirement equals the price-cost markup ($c = \rho$), this technology means that the prices charged by Home firms in industry 1 and 2 are

$$p^1 = (w^1)^\beta (G^1)^\alpha (G^2)^\gamma, \tag{16.1}$$

$$p^2 = (w^2)^\beta (G^2)^\alpha (G^1)^\gamma, \tag{16.2}$$

where G^1 and G^2 are the Home price indices and w^1 and w^2 the Home wage rates in each industry. The amount of Home labor employed in each industry is λ^i; the Home labor force is unity, ($\lambda^1 + \lambda^2 = 1$); and we choose firm scale $q^* = 1/\beta$ so that the total value of the wage bill in industry i is $w^i \lambda^i = \beta n^i p^i q^* = n^i p^i$. We can now write expressions for each industry's price index (see, for reference, equation (14.6)). They take the form

$$G^1 = [\lambda^1 (w^1)^{1-\beta\sigma} (G^1)^{-\alpha\sigma} (G^2)^{-\gamma\sigma}$$
$$+ \tilde{\lambda}^1 (\tilde{w}^1)^{1-\beta\sigma} (\tilde{G}^1)^{-\alpha\sigma} (\tilde{G}^2)^{-\gamma\sigma} T^{1-\sigma}]^{1/(1-\sigma)}, \tag{16.3}$$

$$G^2 = [\lambda^2 (w^2)^{1-\beta\sigma} (G^2)^{-\alpha\sigma} (G^1)^{-\gamma\sigma}$$
$$+ \tilde{\lambda}^2 (\tilde{w}^2)^{1-\beta\sigma} (\tilde{G}^2)^{-\alpha\sigma} (\tilde{G}^1)^{-\gamma\sigma} T^{1-\sigma}]^{1/(1-\sigma)}. \tag{16.4}$$

Notice that each price index now depends on the price indices of both industries in both countries (Home G^i and Foreign $\tilde{G}^i$), because these feed into the costs and prices of manufacturing firms. Analogous equations can be written for the price indices in the Foreign economy, $\tilde{G}^1$ and $\tilde{G}^2$.

The wage equations in the Home economy take the form

$$[(w^1)^\beta (G^1)^\alpha (G^2)^\gamma]^\sigma = \beta[E^1(G^1)^{\sigma-1} + \tilde{E}^1(\tilde{G}^1)^{\sigma-1} T^{1-\sigma}], \tag{16.5}$$

$$[(w^2)^\beta (G^2)^\alpha (G^1)^\gamma]^\sigma = \beta[E^2(G^2)^{\sigma-1} + \tilde{E}^2(\tilde{G}^2)^{\sigma-1}, T^{1-\sigma}]. \tag{16.6}$$

These are similar to the wage equations used previously (e.g., (14.8) and (14.9)) and can be thought of as determining the level of the wage in each industry, w^1, w^2, that gives a product price such that firms in the industry make zero profits.

Expenditure on each industry is given by

$$E^1 = \left[\frac{w^1\lambda^1 + w^2\lambda^2}{2}\right] + \left[\frac{\alpha w^1\lambda^1 + \gamma w^2\lambda^2}{\beta}\right], \tag{16.7}$$

$$E^2 = \left[\frac{w^1\lambda^1 + w^2\lambda^2}{2}\right] + \left[\frac{\alpha w^2\lambda^2 + \gamma w^1\lambda^1}{\beta}\right]. \tag{16.8}$$

Income is equal to the sum of the wage bills in each sector, and consumer preferences are such that half of income goes to each industry, thus giving the term in the first square brackets. The second bracketed term gives the intermediate demands, depending on the wage bill in each industry and technological coefficients.

For a given allocation of labor between industries, λ^1, λ^2, equations (16.3)–(16.8) define the instantaneous equilibrium for the Home country, and an analogous set apply for the Foreign country, generating twelve equations in twelve unknowns (price indices, wages, and expenditure levels in both industries and both countries). In the long run, labor moves between industries in response to wage differences, although we maintain the assumption that labor is internationally immobile.

16.3   Concentration or Dispersion?

What equilibria does this model support? One possibility is dispersion: Each country has half of each industry. Another is geographic concentration: clustering of firms in each industry, so that each industry localizes in only one country. We can apply our techniques to establish circumstances in which these configurations are equilibria.

We start by looking at the sustainability of concentration. Although this model seems quite complex, we have built in a double symmetry that makes analysis relatively straightforward. The double symmetry comes from the fact that both the countries and the industries are symmetric. To see the force of this assumption, suppose that industry 1 is concentrated in Home, so $\lambda^1 = 1$. Then Foreign has industry 2, so

$$\lambda^1 = \tilde{\lambda}^2 = 1, \text{ and } \lambda^2 = \tilde{\lambda}^1 = 0. \tag{16.9}$$

This symmetry extends to other endogenous variables, so that values for Home industry 1 are the same as those for Foreign industry 2, and so on; that is,

$$G^1 = \tilde{G}^2, G^2 = \tilde{G}^1, \quad E^1 = \tilde{E}^2, E^2 = \tilde{E}^1, \quad w^1 = \tilde{w}^2, w^2 = \tilde{w}^1. \tag{16.10}$$

Of course, this implies that real wage levels in the two economies are identical. Home workers are all employed in industry 1 earning w^1, and Foreign workers in industry 2 earning $\tilde{w}^2$.

We can now examine the equilibrium conditions when industry is agglomerated and establish parameter values under which agglomeration is sustainable. Looking first at the price indices, (16.3) and (16.4), if industry 1 operates only in Home and industry 2 only in Foreign, we have the following cross-country relationship between price indices,

$$\tilde{G}^1 = TG^1, \quad G^2 = T\tilde{G}^2. \tag{16.11}$$

Using the symmetry described in equation (16.10), this extends to

$$\tilde{G}^1/G^1 = G^2/\tilde{G}^2 = G^2/G^1 = \tilde{G}^1/\tilde{G}^2 = T. \tag{16.12}$$

(The values of the price indices are given in appendix 16.1; the argument here requires only ratios.)

Now taking the ratio of the two wage equations (dividing (16.6) by (16.5) and using (16.12)) gives

$$\left(\frac{w^2}{w^1}\right)^{\beta\sigma} T^{(\alpha-\gamma)\sigma} = \left[\frac{\tilde{E}^2 T^{1-\sigma} + E^2 T^{\sigma-1}}{E^1 + \tilde{E}^1}\right]. \tag{16.13}$$

If industries are concentrated, expenditure levels are

$$E^1 = \tilde{E}^2 = w^1\left(\frac{1}{2} + \frac{\alpha}{\beta}\right), \quad E^2 = \tilde{E}^1 = w^1\left(\frac{1}{2} + \frac{\gamma}{\beta}\right). \tag{16.14}$$

Using these in (16.13), together with the fact that $\alpha + \beta + \gamma = 1$, gives

$$\left(\frac{w^2}{w^1}\right)^{\beta\sigma} T^{(\alpha-\gamma)\sigma} = \left(\frac{\beta + 2\alpha}{2}\right) T^{1-\sigma} + \left(\frac{\beta + 2\gamma}{2}\right) T^{\sigma-1} \qquad (16.15)$$

or

$$\left(\frac{w^2}{w^1}\right)^{\beta} = T^{-(\alpha-\gamma)} \left[\left(\frac{1 + \alpha - \gamma}{2}\right) T^{1-\sigma} + \left(\frac{1 + \gamma - \alpha}{2}\right) T^{\sigma-1}\right]^{1/\sigma}. \qquad (16.16)$$

Equation (16.16) expresses w^2/w^1 as a function of parameters, and agglomeration of industry 1 in Home is sustainable if industry 2 does not pay higher wages, that is, if $w^2 \leq w^1$.

Readers will not be surprised to see that this is exactly the same condition as we derived in chapters 5 and 14. But once again, the interpretation of the parameters has changed, with $\alpha - \gamma$ (the difference between the diagonal input-output coefficient and the off-diagonal) now playing the critical role.

Why should $\alpha - \gamma$ have replaced μ (chapter 5) and α (chapter 14) in an otherwise identical equation for the sustain condition? As usual, the term outside the square brackets captures forward linkages; if an industry 1 firm were to locate in Foreign, it would find its inputs from industry 1 relatively more expensive and those from industry 2 cheaper, and the cost shares of these inputs are α and γ, respectively. Inside the square brackets are the backward-linkage effects, where Home has share $(1 + \alpha - \gamma)/2$ of world expenditure on industry 1 and share $(1 + \gamma - \alpha)/2$ of expenditure on industry 2.

The interpretation of the sustain condition is quite natural. If $\alpha - \gamma$ is negative, then linkages between industries are stronger than those within industries. The right-hand side of (16.16) is then less than unity for all $T > 1$, and concentration is never sustainable: Because firms derive their most important locational benefits from linkages with firms in the other industry, nations tend to develop a diversified industrial mix. Conversely, if $\alpha - \gamma$ is positive, then the within-industry linkages are stronger than those between industries. Geographic concentration of industry is then sustainable for a low enough value of T, in line with the discussion of earlier chapters. The range of T within which agglomeration is sustainable is wider, the larger is $\alpha - \gamma$, although we bound this by $\alpha - \gamma < \rho = (\sigma - 1)/\sigma$, the new version of the no-black-hole condition.

Turning to the break point, we want to find how a reallocation of labor between industries changes wages in each sector. We can evaluate changes around the symmetric equilibrium, at which $\lambda^1 = \lambda^2 = \frac{1}{2}$. It is easily checked that at the symmetric equilibrium,

$$w = 1, \quad E = 2/\beta, \quad G^{1-\sigma\beta} = (1 + T^{1-\sigma})/2. \tag{16.17}$$

As usual we have to totally differentiate equilibrium conditions (equations (16.3)–(16.8)) around this equilibrium, but as we differentiate, the double symmetry property applies. For each variable, an increase in industry 1 at Home is accompanied by a decrease in industry 2, and also by a decrease in Foreign industry 1 and increase in Foreign industry 2. In other words, derivatives satisfy

$$d\lambda \equiv d\lambda^1 = d\tilde{\lambda}^2 = -d\lambda^2 = -d\tilde{\lambda}^1, \tag{16.18}$$

and similarly for other variables.

We want to find the total differential $dw/d\lambda$; calculations and an explicit expression are given in appendix 16.1. We find that the set of parameter values at which $dw/d\lambda = 0$ and at which symmetry is broken are given by

$$T^{\rho/(1-\rho)} = \frac{(\rho + \alpha - \gamma)(1 + \alpha - \gamma)}{(\rho - \alpha + \gamma)(1 - \alpha + \gamma)}. \tag{16.19}$$

This condition too is exactly analogous to that derived in chapters 5, 7, and 14, meaning that the structure of equilibria is just as we have seen before. At high trade costs, both industries operate in both economies, but at lower trade costs, concentration becomes first possible, then necessary. Because of the symmetry we have built in, the two economies always have the same wages and income levels, but they have come totally to specialize despite the absence of any differences in technology, preferences, or endowments.

It is extremely tempting to think of this model as suggesting the reasons why the industrial geographies of the United States and Europe, economies of similar size and technological development, look so different. As we pointed out, U.S. industries are typically monocentric, concentrated in and around a Silicon Valley, Detroit, or Wall Street. Often those same industries have three or four major centers in Europe. The obvious explanation for the difference is that the higher de facto trade costs posed by Europe's borders have blocked continental-scale industrial clustering. And our model therefore suggests that the growing integration of the European market could break the symmetry of

Europe's multiple-industry geography, leading to a cumulative process of concentration that produces American-style monocentricity.

But isn't this a good thing? Should European policy makers be concerned?

16.4 Adjustment and Real Income

We have been suggesting that a model of this type might yield insights about the effects of economic integration among regions—perhaps within the European Union or the North American free-trade area. So far, however, our analysis has been all positive; what about the normative implications? That is, what does the model say about the economic costs and benefits of reductions in trade barriers if they lead to the sort of reorganization of economic geography demonstrated in the previous section?

Figure 16.1 illustrates the Home country's real wages in each industry as a function of λ^1, the share of the Home labor force in industry 1. Real wages are nominal wages deflated by the consumer price index; that is,[2]

$$\omega^i = w^i(G^1G^2)^{-1/2}. \tag{16.20}$$

The figure illustrates only the Home economy but is constructed with international symmetry, so $\lambda^1 = \tilde{\lambda}^2$, and so on. The solid lines depict

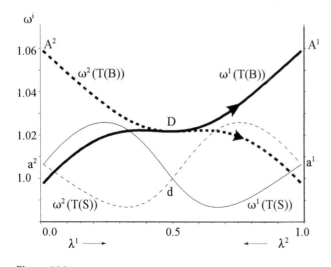

Figure 16.1
Sectoral employment and wages

real wages in industry 1, and the dashed, real wages in industry 2. The curves are drawn for two values of trade costs. The lower pair of curves (the two that intersect at points a^2, d, and a^1) have trade costs set at exactly the level at which agglomeration becomes sustainable ($T(S)$ = 1.8). The upper pair (in bold, intersecting at D) have lower trade costs, set at the level at which the symmetric equilibrium becomes unstable ($T(B)$ = 1.625).

Looking first at the lower pair of curves, the equilibrium at d is stable (because an increase in λ^1 implies $\omega^1 < \omega^2$). Points a^1 and a^2 are also equilibria, with Home having industry 1 or 2 respectively, because $\omega^1 = \omega^2$ at these end points. (Recall that the curves are constructed for the sustain point level of T; at higher trade costs, agglomeration is not sustainable because $\omega^1 < \omega^2$ at $\lambda^1 = 1$, and at lower trade costs $\omega^1 > \omega^2$ at $\lambda^1 = 1$.) The point to note from these curves is that agglomeration, were it to occur, would bring a real income gain: Points a^1 and a^2 are above point d. Agglomeration means that more trade costs are incurred in shipping final products to consumers, this tending to lower welfare. But trade costs are saved on intermediate products as firms benefit from agglomeration. If agglomeration is sustainable, the latter effect dominates, and the net effect is the real income gain illustrated. (Appendix 16.2 gives expressions for welfare in the two cases and establishes that agglomeration yields higher real income than diversification for small values of T.)

As trade costs fall, the real wage curves of figure 16.1 shift upward and rotate. For trade costs between the sustain and break values, there are five equilibria (edge points, the symmetric equilibrium lying between d and D, and two unstable equilibria flanking the symmetric equilibrium). At the break point, the intersection of the real-wage curves at D changes direction, as illustrated by the tangency of ω^1 to ω^2 at point D.

If trade costs fall steadily, then the economy tracks up from d to D. When D is reached, diversification becomes unstable, and agglomeration occurs. Let us suppose that Home attracts industry 1. λ^1 therefore starts to rise, and as this happens workers in industry 1 get steadily better off: Their wages move along from D to A^1, as illustrated by the arrow on the ω^1 curve. What about workers in industry 2? Their real wages follow the path illustrated by the arrow on the ω^2 curve in the figure. They suffer declining real income—although the number of workers in this category is of course falling to 0 as λ^1 increases to unity.

The message therefore is clear. If falling trade costs bring agglomeration, then the aggregate gain from the reduction in these costs is amplified: Real-income gains flow from clustering of industries. However, there are adjustment costs on the way. In our simple model, half the labor force has to change jobs, and these workers suffer a real-income loss in the process. Of course, the magnitude of the real-income loss depends on the speed at which adjustment occurs, and also on other labor market imperfections that we have not tried to describe.

16.5 Multiple Factors: Industrial Clustering in a Heckscher-Ohlin World

Up to this point we have worked with a model that has only a single factor of production—in effect a sort of Ricardian model of international trade, even if the source of specialization is linkage-driven agglomeration rather than exogenous comparative advantage. Trade theorists have long known, however, that models with multiple factors of production typically soften the extreme specialization results of Ricardian models. Is the same true here? More generally, what happens to the model's results when we move to a framework with two or more factors of production?

To answer these questions while preserving as much of the model's basic simplicity as we can, we adopt a device introduced to trade theory by Kenen (1965). We now think of the "primary" inputs used in the production of each good not as factors of production, but themselves as produced from more basic factors. That is, we now suppose that λ^1 and λ^2 are "produced" from primary factors such as labor and capital, and that they differ in their factor intensities, so that the economy has a strictly concave production possibility frontier (PPF) for the creation of these inputs. Figure 16.2 illustrates such a frontier; it is identical to the PPF between quantities of output that obtains in a standard two-good competitive model, such as Heckscher-Ohlin. Because factor markets are perfectly competitive and firms are cost minimizing, its construction is the same as that for a PPF on final output space. As usual, the gradient of the PPF gives the marginal rate of transformation between the quantities λ^1 and λ^2, and with competitive factor markets this is equal to their price ratio. Thus, the gradient of the PPF at a given point measures the relative prices of λ^1 and λ^2 at that point, and we call this price ratio v^2/v^1. These prices are constructed from the prices of the underlying primary factors in the economy, but for

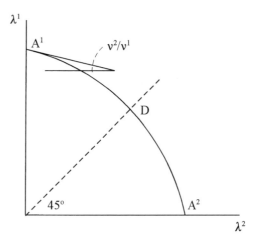

Figure 16.2
Production possibility frontier with two factors

our immediate purposes, we do not need to go back to these factor prices.

Rather than working with a completely general PPF, we maintain the assumption (surprise!) that the two industries are symmetric, giving rise to a PPF that is symmetric around the 45° line. In a Heckscher-Ohlin framework, this means that if units are chosen such that the economy is equally endowed with capital and labor, then at all factor prices, the capital-labor ratio in industry 1 is the reciprocal of the capital-labor ratio in industry 2. We also scale units such that endpoints of the PPF are at $\lambda^1 = 0$, $\lambda^2 = 1$, and $\lambda^1 = 1$, $\lambda^2 = 0$.

With this reinterpretation of λ^1 and λ^2 we can easily see how our analysis of agglomeration carries over to economies with concave PPFs. Suppose that the equilibrium involves agglomeration of industry 1 in Home and industry 2 in Foreign, so we are at point A^1 on figure 16.2 with $\lambda^1 = 1$, $\lambda^2 = 0$. From section 16.3, we know that the prices Home firms are offering for inputs λ^2 and λ^1 are, in ratio form, w^2/w^1, given by equation (16.16):

$$\left(\frac{w^2}{w^1}\right)^\beta = T^{-(\alpha-\gamma)}\left[\left(\frac{1+\alpha-\gamma}{2}\right)T^{1-\sigma} + \left(\frac{1+\gamma-\alpha}{2}\right)T^{\sigma-1}\right]^{1/\sigma}. \qquad (16.21)$$

However, the equilibrium price ratio for these inputs is v^2/v^1, given by the slope of the PPF at point A^1. The agglomeration is therefore

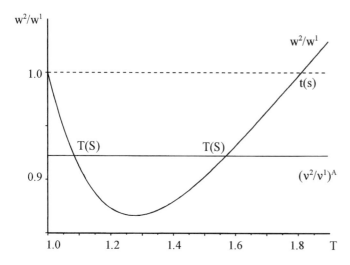

Figure 16.3
Sustain points

sustainable if $w^2/w^1 \leq v^2/v^1$; if this inequality holds it is not profitable for factors to move into industry 2.

This is illustrated in figure 16.3, where the curve is the relationship between w^2/w^1 and T and has a familiar shape (see, for example, figure 5.5). With a single factor of production, the PPF is a straight line with gradient -1, so the sustain condition is exactly as described in section 16.3; it is illustrated on the figure as point $t(s)$. However, the strictly concave PPF means that at point A^1, we have $v^2/v^1 < 1$, so that agglomeration becomes more difficult to sustain. The horizontal solid line in figure 16.3 is drawn at height v^2/v^1 and consequently gives two sustain points, $T(S)$. We see that, provided the gradient v^2/v^1 is not too low, there is an interval of trade costs at which agglomeration is sustainable, but agglomeration is unsustainable both at low and at high values of T. The intuition is straightforward. If only one industry is active in the economy, then the factor intensive in this industry is expensive, and the factor intensive in the other industry is cheap (this showing up in $v^2/v^1 < 1$). These factor price differences make entry by a firm in the other industry relatively attractive. In particular, such factor price differences are unsustainable at perfectly free trade—where factor price equalization will certainly hold—so that agglomeration is impossible at (and in the neighborhood of) $T = 1$.

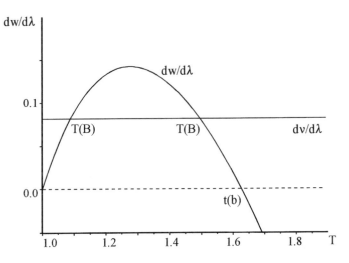

Figure 16.4
Break points

What about the break point? The diversified equilibrium becomes unstable where an increase in λ^1 enables industry 1 to pay more for its inputs than their going price. At the symmetric equilibrium (point D on figure 16.2) we have

$$\frac{w^2}{w^1} = \frac{v^2}{v^1} = 1. \tag{16.22}$$

Writing (as usual) $d\lambda = d\lambda^1 = -d\lambda^2$, $dw = dw^1 = -dw^2$, and $dv = dv^1 = -dv^2$, the symmetric equilibrium is unstable if

$$\frac{dw}{d\lambda} > \frac{dv}{d\lambda}. \tag{16.23}$$

The expression for $dw/d\lambda$ is exactly as outlined in section 16.3 and given in the appendix; it is illustrated in figure 16.4. With the straight-line PPF of section 16.2, the right-hand side of (16.23) is 0 and the critical point is as before—equation (16.19)—and illustrated at point $t(b)$ of figure 16.4. Curvature of the PPF means that $dv/d\lambda$ is positive, so providing that the curvature is not too great, there are two break points, $T(B)$. Intuitively, the factor price changes associated with changing the sizes of the two industrial sectors are stabilizing forces that offset—but do not necessarily overturn—the destabilizing forces forward and backward linkages create.

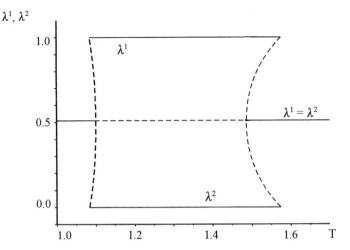

Figure 16.5
Bifurcation with two factors

Figure 16.5, which gives the allocation of labor between industries as a function of trade costs, shows the full bifurcation picture. We see that at high and at low trade costs, each country employs half its labor force in each industry: at high trade costs because of the need to serve final consumers, and at low trade costs because of factor supply considerations. In between there is a range in which agglomeration is sustainable, and a narrower range in which the diversified equilibrium is unstable.

All of this should look familiar from chapters 7 and 14. In both of those chapters we found that when centrifugal forces besides transport costs were at work on manufactured goods, the relationship between those transport costs and agglomeration tended to be an inverted U: no agglomeration at high transport costs, the emergence of a core-periphery pattern at intermediate costs (where being close to the final consumer had become less important but linkages were still powerful), and finally a reversion to dispersed manufacturing to take advantage of low wages or food costs at low transport costs. We suggested that this might be a fairly general pattern, and indeed we see it here again.

How does the configuration illustrated in figure 16.5 depend on the production functions for primary factor usage in the two industries? Figures 16.3–16.5 were constructed for a two-factor Heckscher-Ohlin-type model, in which the two industries have Cobb-Douglas technologies with different factor intensities, details of which are given in appendix 16.2. Making the factor intensities of the two industries more different has the effect of narrowing the range in which agglomeration occurs (pushing (v^2/v^1) downward in figure 16.3, and $dv/d\lambda$ upward in figure 16.4).

Cobb-Douglas technologies generate (in all the examples we computed) the double tomahawk configuration illustrated in figure 16.5. It is easy to see that other functional forms generate different configurations. For example, fixed-coefficient technologies imply a PPF that has two straight segments and a kink at the symmetric equilibrium. With such a technology, the symmetric equilibrium never becomes unstable, but agglomeration may be sustainable. (The bifurcation diagram is like that in figure 7.3.) At the other extreme, consider a PPF that is linear (with gradient -1) in the neighborhood of the symmetric equilibrium but has strictly concave segments close to the axes. For some parameters, such a technology may cause the symmetric equilibrium to be unstable, but agglomeration (with full specialization) to be unsustainable. We then have a standard pitchfork rather than a tomahawk configuration, with asymmetric interior equilibria, as we saw in chapter 14 (figure 14.8). Once again, whether the equilibrium configuration is pitchfork or tomahawk depends not on our modeling of behaviour in manufacturing, but instead on the curvature of the technology between the industries.

Finally, it is worth drawing out the implications of this analysis for the prices of the underlying factors of production. The model generates the possibility that trade liberalization may, over some range, have the effect of disequalizing factor prices. Factor price equalization obtains at very low trade costs and, because the economies are by construction identical, also at very high trade costs. But if a reduction in trade costs brings about agglomeration, say to point A^1 in figure 16.2, then it raises the price of λ^1 relative to λ^2 in the Home economy, with the converse effect in the Foreign economy. Any differences in these prices cause magnified differences in the prices of the underlying factors as Stolper-Samuelson effects come into play.

16.6 Multiple Industries and Sustainable Cross-Country Differences

We now return to the assumption of a single primary factor but allow for the existence of many (more than 2) industries. When agglomeration occurs, how many industries—what proportion of the total number—are located in each country? With just two industries, the answer is one industry in each country, implying (given the symmetry between industries) that the two countries have the same wages and income levels. But in a many-industry model, the division need not be half and half. One economy may have more industries than the other, and if it does, it will also have higher real wages.[3] As we shall see, there is a range within which the actual division of industries among countries is indeterminate, and within this range there may be incentives for countries to try to attract as many industries as possible. Our first task in this section is to characterize this range of indeterminacy, and we can do this in the familiar way, by establishing what patterns of agglomeration are sustainable.

Analysis is based on modification of the model of section 16.2 to accomodate many industries. We assume that all industries are symmetric and let the number of industries be H. We also set the off-diagonal elements of the input-output matrix, γ, equal to 0, so that there are only intra-industry linkages, $\alpha > 0$, and $\alpha + \beta = 1$. This assumption is not necessary for the results but greatly simplifies the expressions that follow. With these assumptions, the price set by a Home firm in industry i is, for each $i = 1 \ldots H$,

$$p^i = (w^i)^\beta (G^i)^\alpha. \tag{16.24}$$

We can restate the price indices and wage equations (from equations (16.3–16.4), and (16.5–16.6)) as

$$G^i = [\lambda^i(w^i)^{1-\beta\sigma}(G^i)^{-\alpha\sigma} + \tilde{\lambda}^i(\tilde{w}^i)^{1-\beta\sigma}(\tilde{G}^i)^{-\alpha\sigma}T^{1-\sigma}]^{1/(1-\sigma)}, \tag{16.25}$$

and

$$[(w^i)^\beta(G^i)^\alpha]^\sigma = \beta[E^i(G^i)^{\sigma-1} + \tilde{E}^i(\tilde{G}^i)^{\sigma-1}T^{1-\sigma}], \tag{16.26}$$

for each $i = 1 \ldots H$. Expenditure on each industry comes from equations (16.7) and (16.8) and takes the form

$$E^i = \frac{1}{H}\sum_{j=1}^{H} w^j\lambda^j + \frac{\alpha w^i\lambda^i}{1-\alpha}, \tag{16.27}$$

where consumers spend a fraction $1/H$ of their income on each industry's output, and the summation gives the total wage bill in the home economy.

We focus on the sustainability of an equilibrium in which each industry is agglomerated in one country. As usual, then, we assume a division of industries between countries and check to see whether it is sustainable. Suppose that industries are partitioned into sets I and II, located in Home and Foreign, respectively. The number of industries in set I is denoted h, and the number in set II, $\tilde{h}$, so $h + \tilde{h} = H$. We use superscripts I and II to denote variables for industries in each set, so, for example, λ^I is Home country employment in one industry in set I. Each economy fully employs its endowment of one unit of labor in its set of industries, so the partition implies that

$$\lambda^I = 1/h, \quad \lambda^{II} = 0,$$
$$\tilde{\lambda}^I = 0, \quad \tilde{\lambda}^{II} = 1/\tilde{h}.$$

(16.28)

The first row says that the Home country has no employment in industries in set II and that its total labor force (of unity) is equally divided between the h industries in set I. The second line gives the corresponding employment levels in Foreign. Notice that if $h > \tilde{h}$ then $\lambda^I < \tilde{\lambda}^{II}$. Thus, if Home has more than half of world industry, then employment in each of the Home industries is less than in each of Foreign's.

Conditional on this distribution of industries, what does the equilibrium look like? First, it is easy to derive relative wages in the industries active in each country, $w^I / \tilde{w}^{II}$. Each industry takes the same share of world income and has the same share of wages in costs, implying that the wage bill is the same in all industries. But as we have seen, employment levels depend on the distribution of industries (equation (16.28)), so wages vary inversely, meaning that

$$w^I / \tilde{w}^{II} = h / \tilde{h}.$$

(16.29)

Thus, if Home has twice as many industries as Foreign, then it has twice the wage; high wages match low per industry employment levels to give an equal value of output in all industries.

These relationships allow some simplification of the expressions for manufacturing expenditure, (16.27), which become,

$$E^I = w^I \left[\frac{1}{H} + \frac{\alpha}{(1-\alpha)h} \right], \quad E^{II} = \frac{w^I}{H},$$

$$\tilde{E}^{II} = \tilde{w}^{II} \left[\frac{1}{H} + \frac{\alpha}{(1-\alpha)\tilde{h}} \right], \quad \tilde{E}^I = \frac{\tilde{w}^{II}}{H}.$$

(16.30)

We also need expressions for the price indices. Because each industry operates in just one country, the price index equations (16.25) become,

$$G^{\mathrm{I}} = w^{\mathrm{I}}(\lambda^{\mathrm{I}})^{1/[1-\sigma(1-\alpha)]}, \quad G^{\mathrm{II}} = T\tilde{G}^{\mathrm{II}}$$
$$\tilde{G}^{\mathrm{II}} = \tilde{w}^{\mathrm{II}}(\tilde{\lambda}^{\mathrm{II}})^{1/[1-\sigma(1-\alpha)]}, \quad \tilde{G}^{\mathrm{I}} = TG^{\mathrm{I}} \tag{16.31}$$

We can now test for sustainability of our assumed division of industry. To do this, we have to compare wages in industries operating with the wages that could be paid by a firm entering another industry. For the Home economy, we must therefore compare wages paid by industries in set I with those that would be paid by a potential entrant from a set II industry. From (16.26), the ratio of the wage equations for industries in set I and in set II is

$$\left(\frac{w^{\mathrm{II}}}{w^{\mathrm{I}}}\right)^{\beta\sigma} T^{\alpha\sigma} = \left(\frac{G^{\mathrm{I}}}{\tilde{G}^{\mathrm{II}}}\right)^{[1-\sigma(1-\alpha)]} \left[\frac{\tilde{E}^{\mathrm{II}}T^{1-\sigma} + E^{\mathrm{II}}T^{\sigma-1}}{E^{\mathrm{I}} + \tilde{E}^{\mathrm{I}}}\right]. \tag{16.32}$$

Using equations (16.28)–(16.31), we can reduce this to

$$\left(\frac{w^{\mathrm{II}}}{w^{\mathrm{I}}}\right)^{\beta} = T^{-\alpha}\left(\frac{\tilde{h}}{h}\right)^{\beta}\left[\frac{\tilde{h} + h\alpha}{H}T^{1-\sigma} + \frac{(1-\alpha)h}{H}T^{\sigma-1}\right]^{1/\sigma}. \tag{16.33}$$

If this expression is less than unity, then $w^{\mathrm{II}} < w^{\mathrm{I}}$, so workers in set I industries do not want to move into industries in set II.

This condition has a structure similar to other sustain conditions, and when $h = \tilde{h} = H/2$, it collapses back to the simple sustain condition of section 16.2 (equation (16.16)). The shape of this relationship is illustrated by the solid curve on figure 16.6, which has transport costs on the horizontal axis and, country 1's share of world industry on the vertical axis, and maps out values of these variables at which equation (16.33) is unity. At values of h/H above the line, no firm from a set II industry wants to enter the Home economy ($w^{\mathrm{II}} < w^{\mathrm{I}}$), whereas below the solid line, h/H is unsustainable ($w^{\mathrm{II}} > w^{\mathrm{I}}$).

The curve derives its shape from the following forces. The first term on the right-hand side of (16.33), $T^{-\alpha}$, captures forward linkages, as usual; a potential deviant has to import all its intermediates from Foreign suppliers and pay transport costs on so doing. The final term (in square brackets) captures backward linkages and is increasing in h; having more industries raises income and enlarges the market, making it more attractive for firms from industries in set II to become

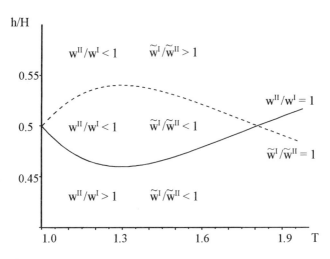

Figure 16.6
Set of sustainable equilibria

established in the Home country. But the middle term $(\tilde{h}/h)$ reflects relative wages in the two locations (see equation (16.29)) and is decreasing in h; a larger number of industries in Home raises wages, making entry of further industries less attractive. Combining these effects, the right-hand side as a whole is decreasing in h, so the higher is h, the less likely it is that a further industry becomes established in Home.

For the equilibrium to be sustainable, we have to establish both that entry of industry II firms in Home is not profitable, and that entry of industry I firms in Foreign is unprofitable. A second sustain equation must therefore be derived for Foreign; it is like (16.33) but gives $\tilde{w}^I/\tilde{w}^{II}$ and has h and $\tilde{h}$ interchanged. It is illustrated by the dashed line on figure 16.6, above which Foreign wages are sufficiently low that entry by an industry I firm is profitable $(\tilde{w}^I/\tilde{w}^{II} > 1)$.

Putting the curves together, any division of industry between countries is sustainable as long at it lies in the area between these curves and to the left of their intersection. The T value at which the curves intersect is just the usual sustain point, as can be seen by giving each country half of the world industries and comparing equation (16.33) with the sustain equation of section 16.2 (equation (16.16)). At transport costs above this point, no agglomeration at all is possible. At the other end, when $T = 1$, factor prices must be equalized, and this forces the number of industries in each country to be the same. As usual, then, the scope for agglomeration is greatest at intermediate values of trade costs, and the width of the range of equilibria that can be sustained is also largest there.

At a given level of transport costs, the width of the range of sustainable allocations of industries, and hence of international wage differences, is larger the stronger are the intra-industry linkages, α. Figure 16.6 was computed with $\alpha = 0.4$. Increasing α widens the sustainable range considerably: With $\alpha = 0.67$, one economy may have three times as many industries as the other. Generalizing the model to have positive interindustry linkages ($\gamma > 0$), it can be shown that for agglomeration to be sustainable, $\alpha - \gamma$ must be greater than 0, and the range of sustainable allocations is wider, the larger is $\alpha - \gamma$.

Although the model says nothing about what determines the actual division of industries among countries, there is clearly a potential conflict of interest among countries, insofar as each may want to attract a disproportionate share of the set of industries. By doing so, a country raises its nominal wage and reduces the proportion of its consumption on which it has to bear transport costs. But two forces are pulling in the other direction. One is that the number of varieties produced by each industry in the Home country falls as more industries are packed in; the other is that as Foreign economy shrinks, so the volume of trade falls and the gains from trade are lost. Putting this differently, the terms of trade start to deteriorate as the level of Foreign demand for Home output falls.

What is the net effect of attracting industries on real income? We have derived an explicit expression for real income as a function of the division of industries among countries, but the expression is far from transparent, and we relegate it to appendix 16.4. However, simulation indicates that within the range of sustainable equilibria, each country's real income is strictly increasing in its share of manufacturing industry. That is, although in principle it may not be in a country's interest to push a policy of "industry grabbing" too far, our simulations suggest that, within the relevant range, there are gains to grabbing as many as you can.

16.7 Conclusions

The models examined in this chapter have, we believe, illustrated both the flexibility and the surprising generality of the approach taken in this book. The original core-periphery model introduced in chapter 5 may have seemed rather specific in its focus: It was about regional agglomeration within a country, and about agriculture versus manufacturing as an aggregate. Now we have seen not only that very similar models can be applied to cities and nations as well as regions, but also that many of the same insights carry over with suitable reinterpretation to issues involving the geographical concentration of particular industries, and provide an explanation of the observed clustering of industries.

The issues raised in this chapter have interesting policy dimensions. Although the model says nothing about what determines the actual division of industries among countries, the location of a particular industry clearly may be subject to hysteresis. Suppose that one economy experiences a temporary adverse shock, causing it to lose industries to the other country; there is then no mechanism for the return of these industries once the shock is reversed. And as we have seen, conflicts of interest can arise among nations even when all industries are assumed to be symmetrical, and these conflicts are likely to be exacerbated if some industries are regarded as strategic, with relatively strong links to other sectors.

Appendix 16.1: Symmetry Breaking

Sustainability
The equilibrium values of variables in the equilibrium with agglomeration are $\lambda^1 = \tilde{\lambda}^2 = 1$, $\lambda^2 = \tilde{\lambda}^1 = 0$ (equation 16.9) and $w^1 = \tilde{w}^2 = 1$. Price indices and expenditure levels are

$$G^1 = \tilde{G}^2 = T^{\gamma\sigma/(\beta\sigma-1)},$$

$$G^2 = \tilde{G}^1 = T^{(\beta\sigma+\gamma\sigma-1)/(\beta\sigma-1)}, \tag{16A.1}$$

$$E^1 = \tilde{E}^2 = \left(\frac{1}{2} + \frac{\alpha}{\beta}\right), \quad E^2 = \tilde{E}^1 \left(\frac{1}{2} + \frac{\gamma}{\beta}\right).$$

Stability Analysis
At the symmetric equilibrium, we have $\lambda = \frac{1}{2}$ and

$$w = 1, \quad E = 2/\beta, \quad G^{1-\sigma\beta} = (1 + T^{1-\sigma})/2. \tag{16A.2}$$

Defining Z,

$$Z \equiv \lambda \frac{1 - T^{1-\sigma}}{G^{1-\sigma\beta}} = \frac{1 - T^{1-\sigma}}{1 + T^{1-\sigma}}, \tag{16A.3}$$

and totally differentiating the price indices gives

$$[1 - \sigma + \sigma(\alpha - \gamma)Z]\frac{dG}{G} = Z\frac{d\lambda}{\lambda} + (1 - \beta\sigma)Zdw. \tag{16A.4}$$

From the wage equations,

$$\sigma\beta dw = Z\frac{dE}{E} + [(\sigma - 1)Z - \sigma(\alpha - \gamma)]\frac{dG}{G}, \tag{16A.5}$$

and from expenditure,

$$\frac{dE}{E} = (\alpha - \gamma)\left[\frac{d\lambda}{\lambda} + dw\right]. \tag{16A.6}$$

Eliminating dE, the system becomes

$$\begin{bmatrix} \sigma\beta - Z(\alpha - \gamma) & (\alpha - \gamma)\sigma + (1 - \sigma)Z \\ (\sigma\beta - 1)Z & 1 - \sigma + (\alpha - \gamma)\sigma Z \end{bmatrix}$$

$$\times \begin{bmatrix} dw \\ dG/G \end{bmatrix} = \begin{bmatrix} Z(\alpha - \gamma)d\lambda/\lambda \\ Zd\lambda/\lambda \end{bmatrix}, \tag{16A.7}$$

from which

$$\frac{dw}{d\lambda} = -\frac{Z}{\lambda\Delta}[(\alpha - \gamma)(2\sigma - 1) - Z(\sigma(1 + (\alpha - \gamma)^2) - 1)]$$

$$= -\frac{Z}{\lambda\Delta}\left[\frac{(\alpha - \gamma)(1 + \rho) - Z((\alpha - \gamma)^2 + \rho))}{1 - \rho}\right], \tag{16A.8}$$

where

$$\Delta = \sigma(1 - \sigma)\beta + Z(\alpha - \gamma)(2\sigma - 1)$$

$$- Z^2[\sigma(\alpha - \gamma)^2 - (\sigma - 1)(\beta\sigma - 1)], \tag{16A.9}$$

which is negative if $(\sigma - 1)/\sigma \equiv \rho > \alpha - \gamma$.

Appendix 16.2: Adjustment and Real Income

Real income is

$$\omega^i = w^i(G^1G^2)^{-1/2}. \tag{16A.10}$$

Using values of the price indices and wages, real income at the symmetric and agglomerated equilibria are, respectively, $\omega(d)$ and $\omega(a)$:

$$\omega(d) = [(1 + T^{1-\sigma})/2]^{1/(\beta\sigma-1)},$$

$$\omega(a) = T^{[1-(\beta+2\gamma)\sigma/2(\beta\sigma-1)]}.$$

(16A.11)

These are equal at $T = 1$. Differentiating with respect to T in the neighborhood of $T = 1$ establishes that if $\alpha > \gamma$, then $\omega(a) > \omega(s)$ for some interval of $T > 1$.

Appendix 16.3: The Production Possibility Frontier

Let the endowments of the primary factors be denoted $k1$, $k2$ with prices $r1$, $r2$. Industry technologies are defined by cost functions for the composite primary inputs:

$$v^1 = r1^\delta r2^{1-\delta}, \quad v^2 = r1^{1-\delta} r2^\delta.$$

(16A.12)

If $\delta = \frac{1}{2}$, the two sectors have the same technology, and the further is δ from $\frac{1}{2}$, the more different are the sectors. Factor market clearing can be expressed in value terms as

$$r1k1 = \delta v^1 \lambda^1 + (1 - \delta)v^2 \lambda^2,$$

$$r2k2 = (1 - \delta)v^1 \lambda^1 + \delta v^2 \lambda^2.$$

(16A.13)

Defining relative factor prices, $R \equiv r1/r2$, and using (16A.12) in (16A.13), we can derive

$$Rk1 = \delta R^\delta \lambda^1 + (1 - \delta)R^{1-\delta}\lambda^2,$$

$$k2 = (1 - \delta)R^\delta \lambda^1 + \delta R^{1-\delta}\lambda^2.$$

(16A.14)

These two equations implicitly define the PPF (obtained by eliminating R). We set endowments at

$$k1 = k2 = \delta^\delta(1 - \delta)^{1-\delta}.$$

(16A.15)

The gradient of the PPF is $v^2/v^1 = R^{1-2\delta}$. If $\lambda^1 = 1$, then $R = \delta/(1 - \delta)$, and $v^2/v^1 = (\delta/(1 - \delta))^{1-2\delta}$. At the symmetric equilibrium, $\lambda = k1$, $R = 1$, and $\lambda dv/d\lambda = (2\delta - 1)^2/(4\delta(1 - \delta))$.

Appendix 16.4: Multiple Industries

Real income in Home is $w_1[(G^I)^h(G^{II})^{\tilde{h}}]^{-1/H}$. We can use Home labor as numeraire, so $w_1 = 1$. From (16.31) with (16.28) and (16.29),

$$G^I = h^{1/(\beta\sigma-1)}, \quad G^{II} = T\tilde{h}^{1/(\beta\sigma-1)}\tilde{h}/h,$$

(16A.16)

from which an explicit expression for real income as a function of the allocation of industries, h, $\tilde{h}$, can be derived.

Appendix 16.5: Simulation Parameters

Figure 16.1: $\sigma = 5$, $\alpha = 0.4$, $\beta = 0.6$, $\gamma = 0$, $T = 1.8$ and $T = 1.625$.

Figure 16.2: Not drawn from simulation.

Figures 16.3–16.5: $\sigma = 5$, $\alpha = 0.4$, $\beta = 0.6$, $\gamma = 0$, $\delta = 0.4$.

Figure 16.6: $\sigma = 5$, $\alpha = 0.4$, $\beta = 0.6$, $H = 100$.

Notes

1. If s_j^i denotes the share of state j in employment in industry i, Krugman computed, for each industry i, the Gini coefficient across states j of the variable $s_j^i / \sum_i s_j^i$.

2. Because labor is mobile only within countries, analysis of the structure of equilibria can use either w^i or ω^i. In section 16.3 it was simplest to use w^i. Now we want to draw out real income implications, so we use ω^i.

3. This analysis is somewhat similar in spirit to Baumol and Gomory 1987.

17   A Seamless World

International economics has traditionally focused, for good reasons, on trade flows as they cross national boundaries. Boundaries are the points at which data is collected, and national boundaries seem to matter a great deal for trade flows, even when formal trade barriers are low. Nonetheless, one might think of a general theory of trade as explaining trade flows across a geographical space, not just those flows that happen to cross arbitrary lines called borders. In this chapter we construct a model of specialization and trade in a "seamless" world, one in which national boundaries are ignored, and even economic regions—which are typically fuzzy edged areas rather than points—are observed rather than defined ex ante.

It would be straightforward to construct a comparative advantage–based model of trade in a seamless world, although we are not aware of any studies that do so. Imagine, for example, a Ricardian model in which a continuum of locations is arrayed in a line from north to south and climate and therefore the relative productivity of labor in wine as opposed to wheat production varies smoothly with latitude. Then one would immediately have a model in which equilibrium in the world economy could be thought of in terms of the boundary between wheat and wine areas rather than in terms of the specialization of nations. It would be natural to think of this world as consisting of two regions, one producing wheat and the other producing wine, but the boundary between these regions would be endogenous rather than specified in advance.

For some purposes this approach to modeling a seamless world might well prove useful; comparative advantage still explains much, perhaps most of world trade. But rather than follow this approach, we abstract from underlying differences in comparative advantage, as we have throughout this book. Instead, we suppose that there are two (or more) manufacturing industries, and ask whether these industries organize into distinct regions of specialization. The framework is that of the preceding chapter, so linkages among firms create forces for industrial clustering. In a seamless world, do these forces lead to the formation of specialized economic regions, and if so, how large are these regions, and how many of them form? We developed the tools for answering these questions in chapter 6: the Turing analysis of emergent structure. We will see that a regular structure of specialization emerges, involving the formation of regions specializing in each industry. We then turn to a second set of issues. As parameters of the model change, what happens to this structure? For example, as trade costs fall, an existing pattern of regional specialization may become, in some sense, less appropriate to the new circumstances, but the very existence of the structure creates a lock-in effect: Firms are unwilling to move away from an existing region of specialization because of the linkages that they would forego. There is therefore a tension between the circular causation that sustains an existing structure and the pressure for change falling transport costs create. How is this tension resolved? The answer is that geographical change is characterized by "punctuated equilibrium."[1] A structure of regional specialization, once established, persists for some time even as the economy's parameters change, but eventually a critical point is passed, and a bifurcation occurs: The structure becomes unsustainable and another economic geography develops.

Finally, with an eye (as in chapter 16) to the effects of European integration, we abandon our assumption of symmetry of locations and industries to consider a geometry that makes an inherent distinction between central and peripheral regions. We show that for any given level of trade costs, there is a characteristic distribution of industry between center and periphery, but that this distribution can change, and even reverse, as transport costs fall.

17.1 The Model

We begin with a version of the racetrack economy of chapter 6. That is, locations are spread around the circumference of a circle of radius D, and are labeled $r, s \in [0, 2\pi D]$.

The industrial structure is the same as that of the previous chapter: There is no agricultural sector, but instead two monopolistically competitive industries, with firms linked through the production and use of intermediate goods. We continue to assume, as we did at the end of that chapter, that each firm uses as intermediates only products from its own industry—that the input-output matrix has nonzero elements only on the main diagonal—although this assumption would be fairly easy to relax. We also return to the production structure of section 16.5, in which inputs are generated from primary factors along a concave production possibility frontier for input into each industry. For computational convenience, however, we derive the PPF not from a Heckscher-Ohlin-type two-factor model, but from a Cobb-Douglas version of the Ricardo-Viner model (as in Jones 1971; Samuelson 1971), in which a mobile factor must be allocated between employment in two industries, each with its own specific factor.

Let us then denote the price of the industry i–specific factor at location r as $y^i(r)$, its share in costs κ, and each location's endowment as k^i. The prices charged by location r firms in industry i therefore take the form

$$p^i(r) = [w^i(r)]^\beta[G^i(r)]^\alpha[y^i(r)]^\kappa, \quad i = 1, 2, \tag{17.1}$$

where β is the share of labor, α is the share of intermediates from the same industry, κ is the share of the industry-specific factor, and $\alpha + \beta + \kappa = 1$. These parameters are the same for both industries: As in the previous chapter, the industries are symmetrical.

Factors are geographically immobile, and their prices adjust to secure their full employment at each location. With Cobb-Douglas technologies, it is easy to find an expression for the prices of the specific factors. If the wage bill in industry i at location r is $w^i(r)\,\lambda^i(r)$, then the equilibrium value of specific factor inputs, $y^i(r)k^i$, satisfies $y^i(r)\,k^i = w^i(r)\,\lambda^i(r)\kappa/\beta$. We choose units of measurement for the specific factors such that endowment levels are $k^i = \kappa/\beta$, $i = 1, 2$, meaning that the price of the specific factor is $y(r)^i = w(r)^i\,\lambda(r)^i$. Using this in equation (17.1), we can restate the prices charged by location r firms in each industry as,

$$p^1(r) = [w^1(r)]^{\beta+\kappa}[G^1(r)]^\alpha[\lambda^1(r)]^\kappa, \tag{17.2}$$

$$p^2(r) = [w^2(r)]^{\beta+\kappa}[G^2(r)]^\alpha[\lambda^2(r)]^\kappa. \tag{17.3}$$

The effect of the specific factor is apparent. If $\kappa > 0$, then expanding an industry (i.e., increasing $\lambda^i(r)$) encounters diminishing returns, pushing up costs and prices. We shall see, as in some previous chapters, that this factor supply effect enters as a centrifugal force, working against agglomeration of industry.

We can now write down the model's equations. Each location is endowed with one unit of labor, so $\lambda^1(r) + \lambda^2(r) = 1$. The price indices for each industry's products in each location take the form

$$[G^1(r)]^{1-\sigma} = \int_{-\pi D}^{\pi D} [w^1(s)]^{1-\sigma(\beta+\kappa)}[G^1(s)]^{-\alpha\sigma}[\lambda^1(s)]^{1-\kappa\sigma}e^{-\tau(\sigma-1)|r-s|}ds, \qquad (17.4)$$

$$[G^2(r)]^{1-\sigma} = \int_{-\pi D}^{\pi D} [w^2(s)]^{1-\sigma(\beta+\kappa)}[G^2(s)]^{-\alpha\sigma}[\lambda^2(s)]^{1-\kappa\sigma}e^{-\tau(\sigma-1)|r-s|}ds. \qquad (17.5)$$

The wage equations are

$$([w^1(r)]^{\beta+\kappa}[G^1(r)]^{\alpha}[\lambda^1(r)]^{\kappa})^{\sigma} = \beta\int_{-\pi D}^{\pi D} [G^1(s)]^{\sigma-1}E^1(s)e^{-\tau(\sigma-1)|r-s|}ds, \qquad (17.6)$$

$$([w^2(r)]^{\beta+\kappa}[G^2(r)]^{\alpha}[\lambda^2(r)]^{\kappa})^{\sigma} = \beta\int_{-\pi D}^{\pi D} [G^2(s)]^{\sigma-1}E^2(s)e^{-\tau(\sigma-1)|r-s|}ds. \qquad (17.7)$$

Expenditure on each industry at location r is given by

$$E^1(r) = \left(\frac{\beta+\kappa}{2\beta}\right)[w^1(r)\lambda^1(r) + w^2(r)\lambda^2(r)] + \left[\frac{\alpha w^1(r)\lambda^1(r)}{\beta}\right], \qquad (17.8)$$

$$E^2(r) = \left(\frac{\beta+\kappa}{2\beta}\right)[w^1(r)\lambda^1(r) + w^2(r)\lambda^2(r)] + \left[\frac{\alpha w^2(r)\lambda^2(r)}{\beta}\right]. \qquad (17.9)$$

The coefficient on the first term in the expenditure equations reflects the fact that there is income from labor and from the specific factors; thus total income is $(\beta + \kappa)/\beta$ times the wage bill. The second term is the backward linkage of intermediate demand from the same sector.

Finally, we assume that, whereas all factors of production are geographically immobile, labor can move between industries at a location. This adjustment follows a dynamic of the form

$$\dot{\lambda}^1(r) = (w^1(r) - \overline{w}(r))\lambda^1(r), \qquad (17.10)$$

where $\overline{w}(r)$ is the average wage in the two sectors at location r. The quantity $\lambda^2(r)$ adjusts in an equal and offsetting way to hold total employment at unity.

17.2 The Frequency of Agglomeration

What can be said about the equilibria of this model? First, there is certainly a flat earth equilibrium in which both industries have an equal presence in all locations. At the flat earth, $\lambda = \frac{1}{2}$, $w = 1$ (dropping location and industry-specific notation), and we see from inspection of the equilibrium conditions that $E = 1/2\beta$ and

$$G^{1-\sigma+\alpha\sigma} = \left(\frac{1}{2}\right)^{1-\kappa\sigma} \int_{-\pi D}^{\pi D} e^{-\tau(\sigma-1)s} ds. \tag{17.11}$$

The flat earth may or may not be stable, and to find out, we look at eigenvalues of the differential equation (17.10). We know how to do this from the Turing analysis of chapter 6. We are concerned only with local stability, so we linearize and look at small deviations around the flat earth; and we need look only at sinusoidal fluctuations, because any sinusoidal fluctuation is an eigenfunction of the system, and any deviation from the flat earth can be represented as a sum of sinusoidal fluctuations.

Expressing deviations from the flat earth by placing a prime on variables, the deviation in employment shares is

$$\lambda^1(r)' = -\lambda^2(r)' = \delta_\lambda \cos(vr), \tag{17.12}$$

where v is the frequency of the deviation and δ_λ measures its amplitude. These perturbations in $\lambda^i(r)$ induce changes in other endogenous variables that are also sinusoidal and have the property that an increase for one industry is a decrease for the other, so they must take the form

$$\frac{G^1(r)'}{G} = -\frac{G^2(r)'}{G} = \delta_G \cos(vr),$$

$$w^1(r)' = -w^2(r)' = \delta_w \cos(vr), \tag{17.13}$$

$$E^1(r)' = -E^2(r)' = \delta_E \cos(vr).$$

The ratios δ_G/δ_λ, δ_w/δ_λ and δ_E/δ_λ give the changes in, respectively, $G^i(r)$, $w^i(r)$, and $E^i(r)$ associated with the perturbation $\lambda^i(r)$ and can be found by totally differentiating the equilibrium conditions, (17.4), (17.6), and (17.8), and using (17.12) and (17.13). In particular, we are interested in the change in wages in each sector induced by a change in employment, the term δ_w/δ_λ. This is derived in appendix 17.1 and takes the form,

$$\frac{\delta_w}{\delta_\lambda} = 2\left[\frac{Z(1-\rho)(\alpha(1+\rho)-Z(\alpha^2+\rho))-\kappa(1-Z^2)\rho}{\rho(1-\alpha)-Z\alpha(1-\rho^2)-Z^2(\rho^2+\alpha^2\rho-\alpha\rho-\alpha^2)}\right], \quad (17.14)$$

where

$$Z \equiv \frac{\displaystyle\int_{-\pi D}^{\pi D}\cos(vs)e^{-\tau(\sigma-1)|s|}ds}{\displaystyle\int_{-\pi D}^{\pi D}e^{-\tau(\sigma-1)|s|}ds} \qquad (17.15)$$

$$= \frac{\tau^2(\sigma-1)^2}{\tau^2(\sigma-1)^2+v^2}\left[\frac{1-\cos(v\pi D)e^{-\tau D(\sigma-1)\pi}}{1-e^{-\tau D(\sigma-1)\pi}}\right].$$

To look at the stability of the flat earth, we have to use this information in the differential equation for $\lambda^i(r)$, equation (17.10). Linearizing this and substituting from (17.12) and (17.13), it becomes

$$\dot\lambda^1(r) = \lambda w^1(r)' = \frac{\delta_w}{2}\cos(vr) = \frac{1}{2}\frac{\delta_w}{\delta_\lambda}\lambda^1(r)', \quad (17.16)$$

so $\delta_w/2\delta_\lambda$ is the eigenvalue. This depends on the frequency of the perturbation, v; if any frequency has a positive eigenvalue, then flat earth is unstable, and industrially specialized regions form at the frequency with the largest eigenvalue, which we call, as in chapter 6, the preferred frequency.

To establish the preferred frequency, we need to look at two relationships. Equation (17.15) determines Z in terms of v and τ, and equation (17.14) gives the eigenvalue, $\delta_w/Z\delta_\lambda$, in terms of Z. Let us assume for a moment, as we did in chapter 6, that D is very large. In that case v can be treated as a continuous variable, and Z becomes a much simpler expression: The second term in (17.15) tends toward 1, so that we have

$$Z = \frac{\tau^2(\sigma-1)^2}{\tau^2(\sigma-1)^2+v^2} = \frac{(\sigma-1)^2}{(\sigma-1)^2+(v/\tau)^2} \quad (17.17)$$

The variable Z, then, can take on any value between 0 (for v extremely large) to 1 (as approaches 0). What can we then learn from (17.14)? The denominator of the equation is strictly positive, provided, as usual, the no-black-hole condition is satisfied, $\rho > \alpha$. The numerator then gives the sign of the eigenvalue; that is,

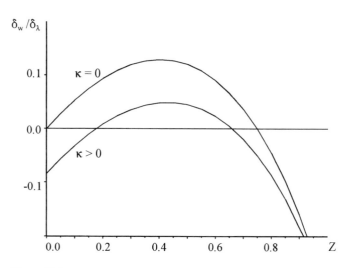

Figure 17.1
Eigenvalues

$$sign[\delta_w / \delta_\lambda] = sign[Z(1 - \rho)(\alpha(1 + \rho) - Z(\alpha^2 + \rho))$$
$$- \kappa(1 - Z^2)\rho]. \tag{17.18}$$

Consider first the case in which industry does not use specific factors, so $\kappa = 0$. Inspection of this expression indicates that the eigenvalue is 0 at $Z = 0$ and positive at small Z, so that high-frequency, short-wavelength fluctuations certainly tend to grow over time. However, at $Z = 1$, the expression is negative—providing the no-black-hole condition $\rho > \alpha$ holds. Thus the relationship between the eigenvalue and Z must look like the upper curve in figure 17.1: At some interior level of Z, the rate of growth of a fluctuation is maximized; this level of Z, in turn, corresponds to the preferred frequency, which determines the distance between incipient regions of industrial specialization.

We can also immediately confirm that the size of these incipient industrial regions depends on transport costs; in fact, the preferred frequency is exactly proportional to τ. This can be seen by looking at (17.17) and noting that v always enters in the form v / τ.

If industry does use specific factors, $\kappa > 0$, the relationship between the eigenvalue and Z shifts downward. There may then be *no* frequency of fluctuation with a positive eigenvalue; in that case, the flat earth is stable, and regions of industrial concentration never form. In the case illustrated by the lower curve in figure 17.1, however,

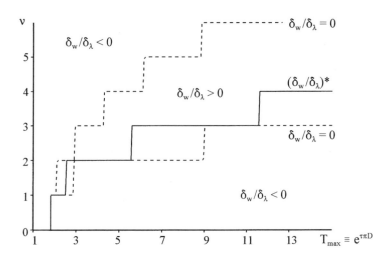

Figure 17.2
Unstable frequencies

fluctuations with intermediate values of Z, and hence intermediate frequencies—not too high, not too low—will grow.

Notice that in this latter case, if we consider a fluctuation of a given frequency and imagine varying the transport cost τ, we have our usual inverted-U relationship between transport costs and agglomeration. For τ very high, Z is close to 1; for τ very low, Z is close to 0. So any given frequency fluctuation tends to grow only if τ is in an intermediate range.

Figure 17.2 shows the relationship between the preferred frequency and τ using a numerical example (calculated, owing to the finiteness of our computers, for a finite-sized economy) with $\kappa = 0.025$, $\sigma = 5$, and $\alpha = 0.4$. The units on the horizontal axis are the transport costs on the longest distance in the economy, $T_{max} \equiv e^{\tau \pi D}$. The solid line in the figure, $(\delta_w / \delta_\lambda)^*$, shows the preferred frequency, which has the largest possible eigenvalue, and the two broken lines show, for each level of transport costs, the pair of frequencies at which the eigenvalue is 0. To interpret the figure, pick a frequency and move horizontally across the diagram. There are two critical values of trade costs between which the eigenvalue is positive, so agglomeration occurs, similar to what we saw in section 5 of chapter 16. As we would expect, at low trade costs, factor supply acts against agglomeration; at high trade costs, the need to supply immobile consumers acts against agglomeration; and at in-

termediate values, the benefits of agglomeration—at the selected frequency—dominate.[2]

17.3   From Local to Global

As usual, our analytical results are based on behavior in the immediate
vicinity of the flat earth, but simulation confirms that the locally preferred frequencies do in fact come to determine the long-run equilibrium. The full evolution of the equilibrium is given in figure 17.3, which
has employment in industry 1 on the vertical axis, locations on the
front horizontal axis, and model time running back into the diagram.
It is computed with the same parameter values as figure 17.2, and with
$T_{max} = 4$, so from figure 17.2 we can see that the preferred frequency is
2. The initial position is one in which there are only very small random
deviations from the flat earth (giving the apparently flat front edge of
the surface). Over time regions of economic specialization emerge, and
a remarkably smooth and evenly spaced structure develops. There are
two peaks of industry 1 activity, and the industry 1 troughs are of
course peaks of industry 2 activity.

It is worth looking at the characteristics of the long-run equilibrium
in greater detail. Long-run values of endogenous variables are illustrated in figure 17.4, which has locations on the horizontal axis. The
higher amplitude curves give the division of the labor force between

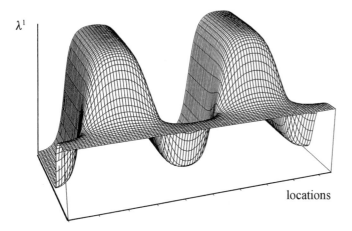

locations

Figure 17.3
The evolution of manufacturing

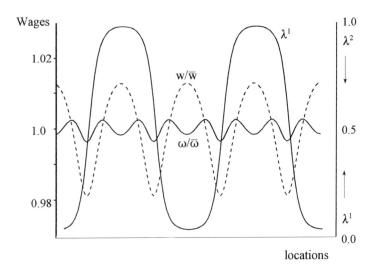

Figure 17.4
Equilibrium employment and wages

the two industries, with λ^1 measured on the right-hand scale, and $\lambda^2 = 1 - \lambda^1$. Clearly there are two equally spaced regions specializing in industry 1 and two specializing in industry 2. Because of the presence of the specific factors, no location fully specializes, and if the specific factor is made more important (κ is increased) then the amplitude of the curve is decreased (assuming it is not set so large as to prevent agglomeration from developing at all). Conversely, as $\kappa \to 0$, the regions become increasingly specialized, and the λ^1 curve in figure 17.4 tends toward a step function, demarcating regions of total specialization.

The smaller-amplitude curves mark out nominal and real wages in each location. The nominal wage curve, $w/\overline{w}$, gives the wage relative to its average value in the economy as a whole, and we see that this has frequency 4. The wage is highest at the most specialized locations—be it specialization in industry 1 or industry 2—and lower in the intermediate mixed regions; this simply reflects the benefits to producing in the center of a specialized region. The real wage line, $\omega/\overline{\omega}$, $\omega \equiv w(G^1G^2)^{-1/2}$ is rather more curious. It contains four equal global minima. These are in the intermediate regions, as we saw for the nominal wage. However, in the most specialized regions, real wages attain local minima. The reason is that the other industry's price index is quite high in these regions, depressing real wages. The net effect is to produce eight regions of maximum real wages, on the shoulders of regions of specialization. Workers here benefit both from high manufacturing wages and from relatively low cost-of-living indices.

17.4 Punctuated Equilibrium

Up to this point we have examined a hypothetical history in which a flat earth organizes itself into different manufacturing regions. Real history, however, is as Henry Ford described it: one damn thing after another. We cannot hope to capture the richness of that succession, but we can at least try to get some insight into how changes in underlying parameters alter the pattern of trade and specialization in a world already differentiated into industrial regions. In particular, what happens to the pattern of specialization as the world economy becomes increasingly well integrated over time?

We address this question by carrying out the following experiment. We reduce transportation costs in a series of small steps, and following each step allow the model economy to evolve until it reaches a steady state; then take the next step. Anyone who has read earlier chapters in this book can guess what happens in such an experiment. As transport costs fall—in effect, as the world gets smaller—the model eventually reaches a bifurcation point, at which the equilibrium structure of manufacturing regions changes. At that point the structure unravels, giving rise to a new structure with fewer (and therefore larger) manufacturing regions. As we continue to reduce transport costs, this new structure persists for a time; then it in turn collapses, and so on.

Figure 17.5 summarizes the results of such an experiment (constructed with the same parameter values as figures 17.3–17.4). The solid lines give the "preferred" frequencies that are reached starting from the flat earth equilibrium. The dashed lines and downward-pointing arrows show the effects of starting with high transport costs and multiple industrial regions and progressively reducing transport costs.

Suppose, then, that initially transport costs are high enough for a five-region structure (i.e., five industry 1 regions, and five industry 2 regions) to exist. As transport costs fall, this regional structure remains in place, until a critical point is reached (T_{max} of around 9.5) at which the five-region structure collapses into a three-region structure. This then collapses into a two-region structure and then into a world with each industry occupying a single region. Notice that in this fictitious

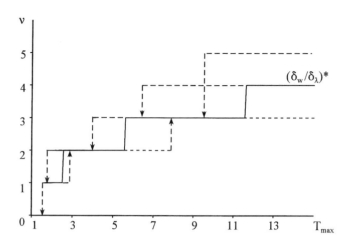

Figure 17.5
Punctuated equilibria

history, the four-region structure is leapfrogged, although if a four-region structure existed, it too would collapse down to three regions as transport costs fall (a transition that is also illustrated on the figure). We find, then, that even if the change in underlying parameters is gradual, the evolution of the world's spatial structure is characterized by "punctuated equilibrium." Long stretches of stability are interrupted by episodes of discontinuous change.

We should also note that the equilibria that the model "visits" as we reduce transport costs do not coincide with the equilibria attained starting from a flat earth, so there is a path dependence in the structure of equilibria. This is emphasized further if we run history backwards: Start with the one-manufacturing-region equilibrium and gradually increase T_{max}, an evolution illustrated by the dashed lines and upward pointing arrows in figure 17.5. The model retraces its steps, from one to two and then to three industry 1 regions, but transitions do not occur at the same levels of transport costs. Clearly these ranges are overlapping. We see, then, that this model exhibits a considerable degree of path dependence. Even in the story of self-organization from a near-uniform world, which locations have which industries depends on details of the initial conditions. But beyond this, as the economy evolves over time, even gross features of the spatial structure of production may depend on where the economy has come from.

Figure 17.5 does not reveal where new concentrations of each industry are sited. However, our simulations indicate that one of the concentrations of industry 1 activity is always based on an old concentration. The overall pattern of concentrations is evenly spaced, with other concentrations fitting on or between earlier ones.

Finally, we have seen in earlier chapters that bifurcations occur in our models for two distinct reasons. An equilibrium may become unstable or may simply cease to be an equilibrium (it becomes unsustainable). Which is happening here? The answer can be found by computing the eigenvalues of the system of differential equations at each step in the process. Away from one of the critical points, there are no positive eigenvalues, so the structure is stable.[3] As we reach a critical point, we find that some of the eigenvalues of the system become positive, so the structure becomes unstable. The bifurcations in the geographical structure are therefore due to instability of an existing structure as the critical value of transport costs is reached.

17.5 Multiple Industries

In the analysis above we worked with just two industries. What difference does it make if there are many? The Turing analysis of this case is remarkably straightforward. Inspection of equations (17.4)–(17.8) indicates that for a particular industry—say the first—the price index and the wage equation depend only on the level of employment, the price index, the wage level, and the expenditure level in that industry. The expenditure level includes total income, which depends on variables from both industries. But as we differentiate in the neighborhood of the symmetric equilibrium, total income is unchanged (see equation (17A.4)). This means that the Turing analysis for this model can be performed at the level of a single industry, and that the results we derive hold regardless of the number of industries there are. Thus a particular set of industry parameters and transport costs implies the same preferred frequency of agglomeration for each industry, regardless of the number of industries.

In simulations we have examined, this local result also holds for the global properties of the equilibrium. Figure 17.6 was simulated for a three industry model in which all industry parameters are as in earlier figures. The vertical axis registers total employment, and the curves give the cumulative employment shares of each industry (λ^1 the dashed

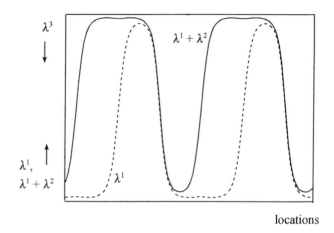

locations

Figure 17.6
Equilibrium employment with three industries

line, $\lambda^1 + \lambda^2$ the solid). We see that each industry is concentrated at two locations, just as in figure 17.4. All three industries have the same locational pattern; changing the order in which the curves are represented would change only the phase of the picture, not the shape of the curves.

Although the number of concentrations of each industry is independent of the number of industries, the number of economic regions in the world is not. If there are H industries and the preferred frequency is v, then this analysis says that the world divides up into H times v specialized economic regions.

17.6   Center and Periphery

Our usual procedure in this book has been to assume that all locations are identical, as a way of isolating the pure forces of geographic self-organization rather than adulterating our analysis with inherent locational distinctions. However, in real life not all locations are symmetrical, and we would like to take at least an occasional look at the way these asymmetries might affect the emergent locational pattern. Of particular interest is the interaction between natural geography and industrial structure. If both regions and industries have some inherent differences, what types of industries locate in what sorts of regions, and how might this pattern of specialization change if trade costs are

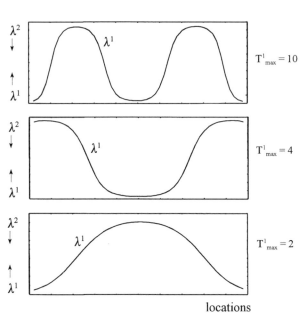

Figure 17.7
Industrial employment in central and peripheral locations

reduced? We have no analytical results on this issue, but simulation reveals some suggestive patterns.

Let us consider then as our geographical space a line of given length, each point of which is endowed with the same quantity of labor and specific factors. However, we no longer make this a racetrack economy: This world line has ends, so that the economy has a priori central and peripheral locations. With this geography, central locations have an automatic leg up in terms of access both to markets and to suppliers and consequently pay higher wages than do peripheral ones. How does this affect the geography of industrial specialization?

There are two industries, as in early sections of this chapter, but as a first experiment, suppose that the two industries differ in their transport cost parameter; to be precise, assume that trade costs in industry 1 are always twice those in industry 2. Figure 17.7 has the regions on the horizontal and marks out the regions occupied by industry 1. It does this for three different levels of the industries' transport costs (maintaining the 2:1 transport cost difference between the industries), with lower values on the lower panels. The upper panel was evolved from the flat earth; the lower two were evolved by reducing trade costs incrementally. Thus there is a punctuated equilibrium story underlying the panels, although because we only illustrate the structure at three distinct points, this is not apparent.

Looking at the three panels, we observe two things. First, as we move from higher to lower trade costs, we move to lower frequency agglomeration, exactly as we would expect. Second, the frequency change is associated with dramatic changes in the location of industry. In particular, looking at the lower two panels, we see that industry 2 (with relatively lower trade costs) goes from occupying the central region to occupying the periphery. The reason for this inversion of industrial structure can be understood in terms of forces we have already seen. Agglomeration forces, and the market access considerations driving them, are strongest at levels of transport costs that are, in some sense, intermediate. In the middle panel, the lower-trade-cost industry (industry 2) has transport costs that are intermediate, so it occupies the center ground. But in the bottom panel, trade costs in both industries are reduced, so the higher-trade-cost industry (industry 1) is now intermediate and occupies the center, with the low-trade-cost industry locating in the lower-wage periphery. Essentially, trade costs in industry 2 become low enough that agglomeration forces are relatively unimportant, and the industry relocates to the periphery to benefit from lower wages.

What about other differences in industry characteristics? Suppose that one industry has a lower input-output coefficient α and correspondingly higher labor input coefficient β. This industry is the more *local* labor intensive. (It also uses labor embodied in intermediates, but some of these are imported from other regions.) Consequently, we see that this industry occupies the peripheral locations, where wages are lowest. If transport costs are low, then it occupies peripheral locations only, and the central region is occupied by the industry with the stronger linkages. But at higher transport costs, this leaves each industry too far away from some of its consumers. We therefore see the lower-α industry occupying edge sites, plus some other zones, including perhaps the central regions.

The combination of even the simplest physical geography—the fact that there are ends to the line—with the economic geography of agglomeration, seems then to produce a complex set of interactions in which reductions in trade costs can change the location of industry dramatically.[4]

17.7   Conclusions

The real world is anything but seamless: It remains separated by oceans and deserts, by cultural and language differences, and by national boundaries that continue to impose substantial practical obstacles to trade even when there are no formal trade barriers. Still, it is interesting both as a theoretical exercise and as a preview of what a more perfectly integrated world might look like to investigate the geography of an economy with space but without distinct spatial units.

We find that even in the absence of prespecified regions, the world tends to organize itself into zones of industrial specialization: Spatial structure need not be imposed, because it evolves of its own accord. Furthermore, this spatial structure is robust to changes in the model's parameters, because the economic geography is locked in by the interdependence of firms' location decisions. But the lock-in effect can only hold up to some threshold, and changes in parameters beyond this threshold trigger abrupt changes in economic geography: punctuated equilibria. The shifts in economic geography may be dramatic, causing the specialization of many regions to change.

One gratifying feature of the analysis in this chapter is that it bridges an ancient divide in economics, between location theorists (who normally think in terms of continuous space) and trade theorists (who tend to treat countries as discrete points). The models developed here are not, by any means, realistic, but they are general-equilibrium models of global specialization and trade that are also as continuously spatial as a location theorist could want. At least within the special assumptions we use to make the analysis tractable, the merger between trade and location theory turns out to be . . . seamless.

Appendix 17.1: Symmetry Breaking

To analyze the dynamics we need to linearize the model around the flat earth equilibrium. At the flat earth, $w = 1$, $\lambda = \frac{1}{2}$ and $E = 1/2\beta$. G is

$$G^{1-\sigma+\alpha\sigma} = \left(\frac{1}{2}\right)^{1-\kappa\sigma} \int_{-\pi D}^{\pi D} e^{-\tau(\sigma-1)s} ds. \tag{17A.1}$$

As we differentiate the equilibrium, we use flat earth values of variables and exploit symmetry so that, for example, $\lambda(r)' \equiv \lambda^1(r)' = -\lambda^2(r)'$. Differentiating the price indices, (17.4) and (17.5):

$$(1 - \sigma)\frac{G(r)'}{G}G^{1-\sigma} = \int_{-\pi D}^{\pi D} [2(1 - \kappa\sigma)\lambda(s)' + (1 - \sigma(\beta + \kappa))w(s)'$$
$$- \sigma\alpha G(s)'/G]G^{-\alpha\sigma}\lambda^{1-\kappa\sigma}e^{-\tau(\sigma-1)|r-s|}ds. \tag{17A.2}$$

The wage equations, (17.6) and (17.7):

$$\left[\sigma(\beta + \kappa)w(r)' + \sigma\alpha\frac{G(r)'}{G} + 2\kappa\sigma\lambda(r)'\right]G^{-\alpha\sigma}\lambda^{\kappa\sigma}$$

$$= \frac{1}{2}\int_{-\pi D}^{\pi D} [(\sigma - 1)G(s)'/G + 2\beta E(s)']G^{\sigma-1}e^{-\tau(\sigma-1)|r-s|}ds. \tag{17A.3}$$

Manufacturing expenditure:

$$E(r)' = \frac{\alpha}{\beta}\left[\frac{w(r)'}{2} + \lambda(r)'\right]. \tag{17A.4}$$

Using (17A.4) to eliminate δ_E, and equations (17.13) and (17.15), gives

$$\begin{bmatrix} \sigma(\beta - \kappa) - Z\alpha & \sigma\alpha + (1 - \sigma)Z \\ [\sigma(\beta + \kappa) - 1]Z & 1 - \sigma + \alpha\sigma Z \end{bmatrix}$$

$$\times \begin{bmatrix} \delta_w \\ \delta_G \end{bmatrix} = \begin{bmatrix} 2(\alpha Z - \kappa\sigma)\delta_\lambda \\ 2Z(1 - \kappa\sigma)\delta_\lambda \end{bmatrix}, \tag{17A.5}$$

from which we obtain

$$\frac{\delta_w}{\delta_\lambda} = \frac{2}{\Delta}[Z(\alpha(1 - 2\sigma) + Z(\alpha^2\sigma + \sigma - 1)) + \kappa\sigma(\sigma - 1)(1 - Z^2)], \tag{17A.6}$$

$$\Delta = \sigma(1 - \sigma)(\beta + \kappa) + Z\alpha(2\sigma - 1)$$
$$- Z^2[\sigma\alpha^2 - (\sigma - 1)((\beta + \kappa)\sigma - 1)]. \tag{17A.7}$$

Replacing σ by ρ ($\sigma = 1/(1 - \rho)$) gives equation (17.17).

Appendix 17.2: Simulation Parameters

Figure 17.1: $\sigma = 5$, $\alpha = 0.4$, $\beta = 0.575$, $\kappa = 0$ and $\kappa = 0.025$.

Figure 17.2: $\sigma = 5$, $\alpha = 0.4$, $\beta = 0.575$, $\kappa = 0.025$.

Figure 17.3–17.6: $\sigma = 5$, $\alpha = 0.4$, $\beta = 0.575$, $\kappa = 0.025$, $T_{max} = 4$.

Figure 17.7: $\sigma = 5$, $\alpha = 0.4$, $\beta = 0.575$, $\kappa = 0.025$.

top panel: $T^1_{max} = 10$, $T^2_{max} = 6$.

midde panel: $T^1_{max} = 4$, $T^2_{max} = 2.5$.

bottom panel: $T^1_{max} = 2$, $T^2_{max} = 1.5$.

Notes

1. The term was coined by evolutionary theorists Stephen Jay Gould and Niles Eldredge. We should note that other evolutionists have been known to refer to the concept as "evolution by jerks."

2. In figure 17.2 we see that at very low transport costs no frequency has a positive eigenvalue. Looking at (17.17) and (17.18) this may seem hard to understand: Can't we always match any fall in τ with an equiproportional reduction in v? But in a finite economy, you cannot have fluctuations of frequency less than 1! The economic intuition here is that when τ is very low, even a monopoly on the world market is not enough to get a fluctuation going.

3. Figure 17.5 was computed using sixty locations. The eigenvalues are those of the 60 × 60 differential equation system, and since we are not looking just at sinusoidal deviations around flat earth, they are not the eigenvalues of the Turing system of section 17.2.

Even when the equilibrium is stable (has no positive eigenvalues) there are always one or more zero eigenvalues. The eigenvector associated with a zero eigenvalue simply takes the form of adding industry 1 employment to one side of each industry 1 region and removing it from the other; that is, it rotates the existing industrial structure around our racetrack economy. This, of course, corresponds exactly to the fact that the actual location of manufacturing regions is indeterminate.

4. Further numerical explorations of a variant of this model are contained in Venables 1998.

External Trade and Internal Geography

In this book we have developed three kinds of models: "regional" models (in which manufacturing production is mobile but agriculture is not), "urban" models (in which everything except land is mobile), and "international" models (in which factors do not move, but the role of intermediate goods nonetheless creates backward and forward linkages). In principle, of course, there is no reason why we cannot mix assumptions—for example, by allowing intermediate goods to play a role in regional divergence.[1] And there is no question that in the real world our artificial divisions do not apply. Nonetheless, the distinction among types of models has proved useful as a way of limiting each analysis to the minimum necessary number of moving parts. Empirical applications do, of course, require complicating the models, but mixed urban-regional-international theoretical analysis should, we believe, be undertaken only if it is essential to tell some empirically motivated story.

One such story was suggested in recent work by Hanson (1993), who was examining changes in the location of Mexican industry following changes in the trade regime. Prior to the late 1980s, Mexico followed a classic strategy of industrial development through import substitution; the result was the emergence of an inward-looking economic base, much of it concentrated in the immediate vicinity of Mexico City. In the second half of the 1980s, however, Mexico began a dramatic process of liberalization, culminating in the North American Free Trade Agreement. Associated with this process was a noticeable decentralization of Mexican industry, away from Mexico City and toward centers in the north of the country. This decentralization was obviously linked to a shift in focus away from the domestic market and toward exports to the United States. But why did it involve a shift of industry away from Mexico City?

The simplest answer, which is surely part of the truth, involved proximity: Most of the rapidly growing centers of industry in Mexico have been closer to the U.S. border than the capital. Hanson, however, suggested that this was not the whole story. Rather, he argued, trade liberalization would have led to decentralization in any case. The reason was that Mexico's internal core-periphery geography—the concentration of industry in Mexico City—has historically been sustained, despite the high costs of operating in a congested metropolis, by forward and backward linkages: In an inward-looking economy, the capital district is where firms have the best access both to domestically produced inputs and to the domestic market. Once the economy has turned outward, however, these linkages become less important: A plant that receives most of its intermediate inputs from abroad and sells most of its output to foreign markets has little incentive to locate in the domestic core, and the diseconomies of agglomeration outweigh the remaining linkage advantages of a core location.

It is a provocative story that links urban economics and international trade policy. Some empirical evidence supporting the story has also been offered by Ades and Glaeser (1997) who, in a sample of eighty-five countries, found that the population of the largest city was negatively related to the share of imports in GNP and positively related to tariff barriers. An initial formalization of Hanson's story was offered in Krugman and Livas 1996. Here we offer a simplified version of the Krugman-Livas model intended to stress the parallels with our general approach.

Hanson also found that the changing pattern of industrial location was not uniform across industries. Some sectors found the pull to border regions stronger than others, and there is some evidence of increasing regional specialization.[2] This raises the question of whether external trade policy interacts with industrial clustering of the sort we analyzed in chapter 16. Does external trade liberalization promote or inhibit internal regional specialization?

In this chapter, we show how our theory suggests that external trade liberalization, although it brings a spatial deconcentration of industry as a whole, may also bring spatial clustering of particular industries, as locations come to specialize. As we argue, both these effects provide sources of welfare gain from international openness, over and above the usual gains from trade.

18.1 Urban Concentration in an Open Economy

We consider a world economy consisting of three locations: 1, 2, and 0 (for the outside economy). All three locations can trade with each other, but labor is mobile only between the "domestic" locations, 1 and 2.

Labor is the only factor of production; and we let location 0 labor be the numeraire. The labor force in 0 we denote L_0, and we choose units so that the total domestic labor force is 1, with a share λ in location 1, $1 - \lambda$ in location 2. The incomes of the three regions can then be written

$$Y_0 = L_0, \tag{18.1}$$

$$Y_1 = \lambda w_1, \tag{18.2}$$

$$Y_2 = (1 - \lambda) w_2. \tag{18.3}$$

Initially we assume a single manufacturing sector that uses labor to produce differentiated goods with the usual Dixit-Stiglitz setup. (Notice that, in contrast with chapter 5, there is no agricultural sector in this economy; in the notation of that chapter, we have set $\mu = 1$.) It is costly to ship goods in all directions. We assume that if a good is shipped between either of the two domestic locations, only a fraction $1/T$ arrives; if a good is shipped between either domestic location and the outside world, only a fraction $1/T_0$ arrives. This external transport cost is the same for both internal locations, so we are not allowing one location the advantage of proximity to location 0.

This implies price and wage equations of the usual form:

$$G_0 = [L_0 + \lambda(w_1 T_0)^{1-\sigma} + (1 - \lambda)(w_2 T_0)^{1-\sigma}]^{1/1-\sigma}, \tag{18.4}$$

$$G_1 = [L_0 T_0^{1-\sigma} + \lambda w_1^{1-\sigma} + (1 - \lambda)(w_2 T)^{1-\sigma}]^{1/1-\sigma}, \tag{18.5}$$

$$G_2 = [L_0 T_0^{1-\sigma} + \lambda(w_1 T)^{1-\sigma} + (1 - \lambda)w_2^{1-\sigma}]^{1/1-\sigma}, \tag{18.6}$$

$$w_1 = [Y_0 G_0^{\sigma-1} T_0^{1-\sigma} + Y_1 G_1^{\sigma-1} + Y_2 G_2^{\sigma-1} T^{1-\sigma}]^{1/\sigma}, \tag{18.7}$$

$$w_2 = [Y_0 G_0^{\sigma-1} T_0^{1-\sigma} + Y_1 G_1^{\sigma-1} T^{1-\sigma} + Y_2 G_2^{\sigma-1}]^{1/\sigma}. \tag{18.8}$$

As we have set it up so far, this model contains no form of diminishing returns. Because there is only one factor of production, and it is mobile between the two domestic locations, there is no apparent reason why all labor should not concentrate in one location or the other. To produce an interesting tension between centripetal and centrifugal forces, then, we must introduce some countervailing force. Once such force would be the existence of immobile factors, such as land; indeed, that is how we have created a tension in other models. For simplicity, however, in this case we simply postulate the existence of some kind of congestion diseconomy to city size and put it directly into the real-wage equation.[3] We therefore write real wages in each location as

$$\omega_1 = w_1(1 - \lambda)^\delta / G_1, \tag{18.9}$$

$$\omega_2 = w_2\lambda^\delta / G_2. \tag{18.10}$$

The terms $(1 - \lambda)^\delta$ and λ^δ capture the congestion cost in each location, and we assume that $\delta \in (0, 1)$.[4] This means that as a location's population increases (other things equal), its real wage falls at an increasing rate, going to zero if the location has the country's entire population. The regional allocation of labor, λ, adjusts according to the difference between the real wage in each region and the average for the economy as a whole.

We are now in a position to ask the following question: How does the integration of the domestic economy with the outside world, as measured by the cost T_0, affect the equilibrium allocation of labor between the two domestic locations?

18.2   The Effects of Trade Liberalization

We begin with a numerical analysis. Figure 18.1 illustrates the equilibrium location of the domestic labor force, measured by λ, as a function of the external trade cost, T_0. As usual, stable equilibria are marked with solid lines, and unstable with a dashed line. We see that an equal division of population between the two sites occurs at low values of the external trade cost, T_0, whereas at higher values the two sites have different populations.

The easiest way to get intuition on this is to consider the stability of the equilibrium in which population is evenly divided between the locations. At low values of T_0, the economy is outward oriented, with domestic producers in each location selling a high proportion of their output to the external market. If we move a unit of labor from location 2 to location 1, this enlarges the market in location 1 and reduces it in 2, tending to make 1 a more attractive location, but this backward-linkage effect is quite weak—because such a high proportion of firms'

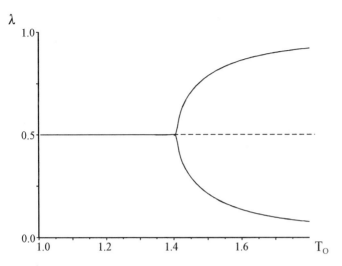

Figure 18.1
The bifurcation diagram

sales are directed not to these markets, but to the external market. Pulling in the other direction is the congestion cost, and this is the more powerful force. The equilibrium is therefore stable.

The difference at high T_0 is now apparent. At high T_0, firms are more dependent on the internal market, so movement of labor creates more powerful backward-linkage effects. This makes the equilibrium with two equal-sized production centers unstable.

If having two equal-sized production centers does not lead to a stable equilibrium, what then happens? From our modeling of congestion costs, it is clear that the economy does not end up at a corner solution, with the entire population in a single location: If this happened, the cost of living in this location would be infinite and the real wage 0; see equations (18.9) and (18.10). Instead, then, we have two centers of production, but they are of unequal sizes. One is large, with the benefits of linkages but the costs of congestion, and the other smaller.

Figure 18.1 allows us to read off the fictitious history of a trade liberalization's effects on the internal geography. We see that starting from a high value of external trade barriers, liberalization brings a steady narrowing in the difference in size of the two locations. Access to external markets reduces the smaller location's disadvantage and permits its growth. This process occurs at an accelerating rate until the bifurcation point is reached and the two locations become of equal size.

Let us now characterize this bifurcation point analytically. As usual, we can do this by linearizing the model around the symmetric equilibrium $\lambda = 0.5$ and deriving an expression for $d\omega/d\lambda$ (using the notation $d\omega = d\omega_1 = -d\omega_2$, and so on). It is not possible to derive simple closed-form solutions for the domestic price and wage at the symmetric equilibrium, G and w, but they are implicitly defined by equations given in appendix 18.1. In that appendix, we derive

$$\frac{d\omega}{d\lambda}\frac{\lambda}{\omega} = \frac{Z(2\sigma - 1)}{[\sigma + Z(\sigma - 1)](\sigma - 1)} - \delta$$

$$= \frac{Z(1 - \rho)(1 + \rho)}{\rho(Z\rho + 1)} - \delta, \tag{18.11}$$

where Z is defined by

$$Z \equiv \frac{1}{2}\left[\frac{G}{w}\right]^{\sigma-1}(1 - T^{1-\sigma}). \tag{18.12}$$

This result has an immediate interpretation. The first term should look familiar: It is a version of our standard expression for forward and backward linkages. (Compare this with equation (5.27) with $\mu = 1$.) In this particular version, the first term is always positive and captures the centripetal forces in the model. The second term represents the diseconomies of urban concentration.

The symmetric equilibrium is unstable if $d\omega/d\lambda$ is positive. We can see immediately that this expression is negative when $Z = 0$ and is increasing in Z, becoming positive providing that congestion costs, δ, are not too large.

Z depends on parameters directly, and through the expressions for G and w given in appendix 18.1. If we focus on external transport costs, then it can be shown that Z is increasing in these costs, because G and w are respectively increasing and decreasing in T_0. (A higher value of external transport costs raises the price of imports, so raising the price index, and reduces export opportunities, so reducing the wage.) The fact that Z is increasing in T_0 means that higher external trade costs may destabilize the symmetric equilibrium and lead to an asymmetric equilibrium with two unequal-sized cities. In other words, provided δ is not too large, the configuration of equilibria is as illustrated in figure 18.1. Making the economy more open also makes its internal structure less geographically concentrated.

It is worth making several further remarks on the implications of this model. The first concerns the comparative statics of the critical point. The critical value of T_0 is higher (so the economy is more likely to have cities of equal size) the higher is δ, the higher is L_0, and the lower is T. Unsurprisingly, higher congestion costs deter agglomeration, and a larger foreign population is like being more open: It raises the share of exports in each firm's sales. Lower internal transport costs weaken the agglomeration forces inside the economy, again making it more likely that the economy has two cities of equal size.

The second remark concerns the type of bifurcation. The model produces a pitchfork, but as usual this is sensitive to the modeling of the centrifugal force (here the congestion costs). Suppose that the relationship between real wages and congestion, instead of taking the form $\omega_1 = w_1(1 - \lambda)^\delta / G_1$, is linear in the congestion externality, so $\omega_1 = w_1/G_1 - \delta\lambda$. Simulating this case, the bifurcation turns out to be a tomahawk. Clearly, wages do not go to infinity as λ goes to one, and more fundamentally, the third derivative of ω with respect to λ is positive, so the function passes from concave to convex at the point of symmetry breaking.

18.3   Industrial Clustering and External Trade

We have just seen that increased openness to external trade may cause the spatial deconcentration of internal population and of manufacturing activity as a whole. What does it do to the concentration of particular industries? Do firms in particular industries tend to cluster in a single location or be dispersed among locations?

The two-sector model of industrial specialization developed in chapter 16 provides the apparatus for answering this question. Recall that in this model industrial linkages create the centripetal force—firms benefit from proximity to their industrial suppliers and customers—and the centrifugal force arises from final consumer demand in each location.[5] As we open the economy to external trade, both these forces are weakened. Firms use more imported intermediates and sell a larger proportion of their output as exports, and consumers derive a higher proportion of their consumption from imports. But how does the balance between these forces change?

We answer this question in two stages. First, we assume that domestic population is evenly divided between two domestic locations and see whether external trade liberalization promotes the clustering of industries. Second, we go on to combine this with the model of earlier sections of this chapter, adding congestion costs and permitting labor mobility between locations. We find a startlingly rich set of outcomes. There is a hierarchy of domestic locations, in which locations have different population sizes and different industrial structures. External trade liberalization causes deconcentration of population and simultaneously, the clustering of particular industries.

Starting with a fixed internal population distribution requires only a relatively minor generalization of the model of chapter 16. Let there be two industries and three regions, two internal and one external, as in section 18.1. Industries are referred to by superscripts and location by subscripts, so for example, industry i employment in region j is L_j^i. We hold the industrial composition of the outside region constant by fixing $L_0^1 = L_0^2 = L_0/2$. Initially we assume that each internal location has a fixed population, set at one-half the domestic economy's population (of unity). Thus for each domestic location, $j = 1, 2$, we have

$$L_j^1 + L_j^2 = 0.5. \tag{18.13}$$

Within each of these domestic locations, labor moves between industries according to the wage difference which, because all workers within the same region face the same cost-of-living index, is just the nominal wage difference.

The price index for each industry in each region, G_j^i, is

$$(G_j^i)^{1-\sigma} = \sum_{k=0,1,2} L_k^i (w_k^i)^{1-\beta\sigma} (G_k^i)^{-\alpha\sigma} (T_{kj}^i)^{1-\sigma}, \tag{18.14}$$

where α and $\beta = 1 - \alpha$ are the intermediate and labor shares respectively, and T_{kj}^i is the cost of shipping industry i output from location k to location j. We look just at cases where both industries have the same external trade costs T_0 and internal trade costs T.[6]

The wage equations take the form

$$(w_j^i)^{\beta\sigma} (G_j^i)^{\alpha\sigma} = \beta \sum_{k=0,1,2} (G_k^i)^{\sigma-1} E_k^i (T_{kj}^i)^{1-\sigma}, \tag{18.15}$$

and expenditure on industry i in location j is given by

$$E_j^i = \left[\frac{w_j^1 L_j^1 + w_j^2 L_j^2}{2} \right] + \frac{\alpha w_j^i L_j^i}{\beta}. \tag{18.16}$$

(These three equations are analogous to (16.3)–(16.8), but with the addition of the outside location and with $\gamma = 0$.)

As usual, this model has a symmetric equilibrium, and appendix 18.1 gives the values of endogenous variables at this equilibrium. The question is, what happens to the stability of this equilibrium as we change the external trade costs, T_0? Let us go straight to analytics. In appendix 18.1, we derive,

$$\frac{dw}{dL}\frac{L}{w} = \frac{Z}{\Delta}[(2\sigma - 1)\alpha - Z(\sigma(1 + \alpha^2) - 1)]$$

$$= \frac{Z}{\Delta}\left[\frac{\alpha(1 + \rho) - Z(\alpha^2 + \rho)}{1 - \rho}\right],$$

(18.17)

where L is the symmetric equilibrium value of L^i_j, $\Delta > 0$, and Z is defined by

$$Z \equiv L\left(\frac{G}{w}\right)^{\beta\sigma-1}(1 - T^{1-\sigma}).$$

(18.18)

The sign of dw/dL is positive for small Z and negative for Z close to unity (providing $\alpha < \rho$). Z is increasing in T and in T_0, the latter effect coming (as in section 18.2) via the dependence of G/w on T_0. This means that decreasing either internal or external trade barriers may switch $dw/d\lambda$ from negative to positive, taking the economy through the point of symmetry breaking. Figure 18.2 illustrates some possibilities. The BB lines give the break point values of T and T_0, drawn for three different values of L_0, $L_0 = 1, 2$, and 10. The symmetric equilibrium is stable above these lines and unstable below them. We see that the more open is the economy (the lower is T_0 or the larger is L_0) the more likely it is that the symmetric equilibrium is unstable. Of course, even if the economy is closed, there is always a value of T below which symmetry is broken, as in chapter 16.

When the symmetric equilibrium is unstable, there is a pair of stable equilibria in which each region specializes in a single industry, exactly as we saw in chapter 16.[7] From our current perspective, the point is then that external trade liberalization turns out to have effects similar to the reductions in internal trade costs that we studied in chapter 16. Firms and consumers become more outward oriented, but the dominant force is that consumers depend less on local firms. This causes symmetry to be broken and industrial clustering to occur.

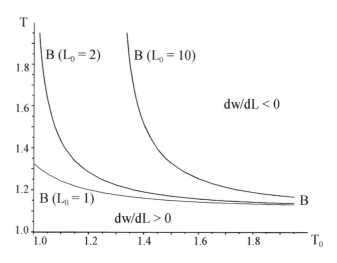

Figure 18.2
Break points

18.4 Industrial Structure and Urban Concentration

Let us now pull together the elements of preceding sections and consider what happens when labor is mobile between industries within each location, and also between locations. To do this, we need to specify the dynamics of labor mobility between industries within each domestic location, and also between locations. We do this by assuming that labor moves between industries within a location according to the difference between the industry wage and the average wage in the location. And it moves between locations according to the difference between the average wage in the location and the average wage in the economy as a whole.

Formally, we define θ_i as the share of location i employment which is in industry 1, so with λ denoting the share of total population in location 1, we have

$$L_1^1 = \lambda\theta_1, \qquad L_1^2 = \lambda(1 - \theta_1),$$
$$L_2^1 = (1 - \lambda)\theta_2, \quad L_2^2 = (1 - \lambda)(1 - \theta_2). \tag{18.19}$$

The interindustry (and intralocational) dynamics are then given by differential equations

$$\dot{\theta}_1 = \gamma_\theta(w_1^1 - \overline{w}_1)\theta_1,$$
$$\dot{\theta}_2 = \gamma_\theta(w_1^2 - \overline{w}_2)\theta_2, \tag{18.20}$$

where γ_θ is the adjustment speed and $\overline{w}_i$ is the average wage in region i,

$$\overline{w}_i \equiv \theta_i w_i^1 + (1 - \theta_i) w_i^2. \tag{18.21}$$

Interlocational labor mobility is given by

$$\dot{\lambda} = \gamma_\lambda (\omega_1 - \overline{\omega}) \lambda, \tag{18.22}$$

where γ_λ is the adjustment speed, ω_1 and ω_2 are average real wages in each region, and $\overline{\omega}$ is the average real wage in the economy,

$$\omega_1 \equiv \overline{w}_1 (G_1^1 G_1^2)^{-0.5} (1 - \lambda)^\delta,$$

$$\omega_2 \equiv \overline{w}_2 (G_2^1 G_2^2)^{-0.5} \lambda^\delta, \tag{18.23}$$

$$\overline{\omega} \equiv \lambda \omega_1 + (1 - \lambda) \omega_2.$$

The model is completely described by equations (18.14)–(18.16) and (18.19)–(18.23). If $\gamma_\lambda = 0$, this is the model of section 18.3, and if $\gamma_\theta = 0$ and $\alpha = 0$, it reduces to the model of section 18.1.[8]

We present no analytical results on this model, but instead use numerical techniques to illustrate how openness to international trade may change the structure of the economy. Figure 18.3 has the external transport cost on the horizontal axis and employment levels on the vertical, like figure 18.1. Unlike figure 18.1, it does not provide a full

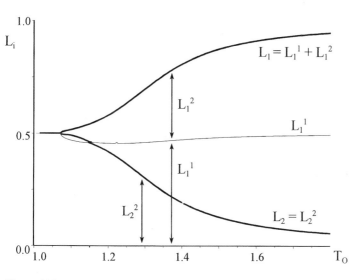

Figure 18.3
External trade and internal economic geography

description of all equilibria, but instead traces out a particular equilibrium path that the economy follows as external trade costs are reduced. The starting position is a high value of T_0, at which point one of the locations (call it location 1) has most of the population and most of both industries. L_1^1 is this location's employment in industry 1, and L_1^2 its employment in industry 2, these summing to L_1. The other location has a very much smaller total population, all of which is employed in one of the industries, so $L_2 = L_2^2 > 0$ and $L_2^1 = 0$. The situation is therefore one of concentration of total population and dispersion of industry, insofar as the larger location has employment in both industries.[9] This is reminiscent of the city hierarchy we saw in chapter 11, in which a location with a large population has both types of industrial activity and coexists with a smaller location specialized in a single industry.

Now consider the effects of reducing the external trade barrier. As we do so, two sorts of changes take place. First, the larger region loses total population to the smaller one ($L_1 = L_1^1 + L_1^2$ falls). As we saw in section 18.2, the backward linkages from consumer expenditure are less powerful as the economy becomes more open, and so the centrifugal forces created by the congestion costs disperse the population. Second, the larger region becomes more specialized, losing industry 2 to location 2 (L_1^2 falls, and L_2^2 rises), because external trade now plays the role of balancing supply and demand for each sector's products in each location, and this facilitates industrial specialization driven by intra-industry linkages. Reducing T_0 further eventually leads the economy to the point where the two locations have equal populations and are both fully specialized in one of the industries. External trade liberalization therefore brings dispersion of population but concentration of industry.

The outcomes illustrated in figure 18.3 are interesting both because they show how external trade liberalization can change internal economic geography, and also because they show how a quite complex internal geography can develop. Both industries and both internal locations are constructed to be symmetrical but, over a wide range of values of T_0, the economy has a regional hierarchy. One location has a large population and a presence in both industries, whereas the other location has a smaller population and specializes in a single industry.

18.5 Conclusions

We are accustomed to thinking of the gains from international trade as deriving from consumer gains and from producer gains that occur as industrial structure changes to exploit comparative advantage. To these, the trade and industrial organization literature added possible procompetitive gains from trade, as production within an industry reorganizes in response to trade. The analysis of this chapter suggests some further mechanisms through which international trade may change the welfare of the domestic economy. Trade may generate a reorganization of internal economic geography, bringing both a dispersion of manufacturing activity as a whole and the clustering of particular industries. We have derived no analytical results on the welfare effects of these changes, although intuition (supported by simulation analysis) suggests gains. Congestion costs are increasing and convex in population, so spreading population more evenly tends to raise welfare. And as we have already seen in chapter 16, there are real income gains from industrial clustering, deriving from the proximity of closely linked firms.

Appendix 18.1: Symmetry Breaking

The appendix is based on the general model of equations (18.14)–(18.16) and (18.19)–(18.23). The symmetric equilibrium values of employment are $L_0^1 = L_0^2 = L_0/2$ and $L_1^1 = L_1^2 = L_2^1 = L_2^2 = 1/4$. Symmetric equilibrium values of other variables follow the notational convention, for rest of the world, $G_0 \equiv G_0^1 = G_0^2$, and for internal variables $G \equiv G_1^1 = G_1^2 = G_2^1 = G_2^2$, etc. The symmetric equilibrium values are

$$G_0 = \left[\frac{1}{2} (L_0 G_0^{-\sigma\alpha} + w^{1-\sigma(1-\alpha)} G^{-\sigma\alpha} T_0^{1-\sigma}) \right]^{1/(1-\sigma)},$$

$$G = \left[\frac{1}{2} (L_0 G_0^{-\sigma\alpha} T_0^{1-\sigma} + w^{1-\sigma(1-\alpha)} G^{-\sigma\alpha} (1 + T^{1-\sigma})/2) \right]^{1/(1-\sigma)},$$

$$w^{1-\alpha} G^\alpha = \beta [E_0 G_0^{\sigma-1} T_0^{1-\sigma} + E G^{\sigma-1} (1 + T^{1-\sigma})]^{1/\sigma}, \tag{18A.1}$$

$$E = \frac{w}{4(1 - \alpha)}, \qquad E_0 = \frac{L_0}{2(1 - \alpha)}.$$

We want to find the effects of a small change in the allocation of labor between locations or sectors. Consider a change dL that alters the labor allocation according to

$$dL_1^1 = dL, \quad dL_1^2 = J dL, \quad dL_2^1 = -dL, \quad dL_2^2 = -J dL. \tag{18A.2}$$

If $J = 1$, then the change dL adds to both industries in location 1 and subtracts from both in location 2. We use this perturbation to test for stability of the locational migration model of section 18.2, to which the general model collapses when $\alpha = 0$. (When $\alpha = 0$, having two symmetrical industries in each location produces outcomes no different from having just one.)

If $J = -1$, then the change expands employment in location 1 industry 1 while holding total employment in each location and industry constant, and we use this perturbation to test for stability of the industrial clustering model (compare (18A.2) with (16.18)).

Totally differentiating the equilibrium conditions (18.14)–(18.16) and using Z defined in (18.18) gives

$$(1 - \sigma)\frac{dG}{G} = Z\left[\frac{dL}{L} - \alpha\sigma\frac{dG}{G} + (1 - \beta\sigma)\frac{dw}{w}\right], \tag{18A.3}$$

$$\beta\sigma\frac{dw}{w} + \alpha\sigma\frac{dG}{G} = Z\left[\frac{dE}{E} + (\sigma - 1)\frac{dG}{G}\right], \tag{18A.4}$$

$$\frac{dE}{E} = \left[\frac{\beta(1 + J)}{2} + \alpha\right]\left[\frac{dw}{w} + \frac{dL}{L}\right]. \tag{18A.5}$$

Eliminating dE/E from this we obtain

$$\begin{bmatrix} (\sigma(1 - \alpha) - 1)Z & 1 - \sigma + \alpha\sigma Z \\ (1 - \alpha)\sigma - ZB & \alpha\sigma + Z(1 - \sigma) \end{bmatrix}\begin{bmatrix} \dfrac{dw}{w} \\ \dfrac{dG}{G} \end{bmatrix} = \begin{bmatrix} Z\dfrac{dL}{L} \\ ZB\dfrac{dL}{L} \end{bmatrix}, \tag{18A.6}$$

where $B \equiv (1 + \alpha)/2 + J(1 - \alpha)/2$.

If $J = 1$ and $\alpha = 0$, then we derive

$$\frac{dG}{G}\frac{L}{dL} = -\frac{Z(1 - Z)\sigma}{\Delta}, \tag{18A.7}$$

$$\frac{dw}{w}\frac{L}{dL} = \frac{Z(1 - Z)(\sigma - 1)}{\Delta}, \tag{18A.8}$$

with the determinant, Δ, taking the form

$$\Delta = (1 - Z)[\sigma + Z(\sigma - 1)](\sigma - 1). \tag{18A.9}$$

The change in real wages is $d\omega/\omega = dw/w - dG/G - \delta dL/L$, from which we derive equation (18.11).

If $J = -1$, then

$$\frac{dw}{w}\frac{L}{dL} = \frac{Z}{\Delta}[(2\sigma - 1)\alpha - Z(\sigma(1 + \alpha^2) - 1)], \tag{18A.10}$$

$$\Delta = (\sigma - 1)\sigma(1 - \alpha) + Z\alpha(1 - 2\sigma)$$
$$+ Z^2[\sigma\alpha^2 + (\sigma - 1)(1 - \sigma(1 - \alpha))] > 0. \tag{18A.11}$$

Appendix 18.2: Simulation Parameters

Figure 18.1: $\sigma = 5$, $L_0 = 2$, $T = 1.25$, $\delta = 0.1$.

Figure 18.2: $\sigma = 5$, $L_0 = 1, 2, 10$, $\alpha = 0.05$.

Figure 18.3: $\sigma = 5$, $L_0 = 2$, $T = 1.25$, $\delta = 0.1$, $\alpha = 0.05$.

Notes

1. For example, Puga (1998) looks at a model with labor mobility and linkages within the industrial sector.

2. This specialization is at the two-digit, although not the four-digit, level (Hanson 1993).

3. Krugman and Livas 1996 treats land rent explicitly. For current purposes, however, all that matters is that there be some kind of centrifugal force, and we opt for the simplest version.

4. Location 1 congestion costs as a proportion of income are $1 - (1 - \lambda)^\delta$, so they are increasing and convex in population.

5. And depending on model specification, it also arises from immobile factor supply, as in section 16.5.

6. Formally, if $k = j$, $T^i_{kj} = 1$. If $k \neq j$, $T^i_{kj} = T_0$, if either k or $j = 0$, and $T^i_{kj} = T$ otherwise.

7. And the bifurcation is a tomahawk, just as was the case in chapter 16.

8. Unlike in section 18.1, there are two industries, but if they are symmetric and have no internal linkages (i.e., $\alpha = 0$) then the model's behavior is independent of the number of industries.

9. Only at much higher internal and external transport costs do we observe the smaller location having both industries.

19   The Way Forward

In this book we have pursued the consequences of two quite simple ideas. The first idea is that, in a world where increasing returns and transport costs are both important, forward and backward linkages can create a circular logic of agglomeration. That is, other things being the same, producers want to locate close to their suppliers and to their customers—which means that they want to locate close to each other. The second idea is that the immobility of some resources—land certainly, and in many cases labor—acts as a centrifugal force that opposes the centripetal force of agglomeration. And the tension between these centrifugal and centripetal forces shapes the evolution of the economy's spatial structure.

We have seen that these two ideas can give insights into a remarkable range of phenomena, from the broad division of national economies into manufacturing and farm belts, to the spontaneous emergence of highly structured urban hierarchies, to the dynamics of the product cycle in international trade. What is more, the models we construct to analyze many different issues turn out to have similar "deep structures": the same equations reappear, albeit with somewhat different interpretations of the parameters, and the qualitative behavior of the model economy usually turns on a couple of repeated expressions reflecting the tension between centripetal and centrifugal forces.

All in all, the flexibility of our basic approach and the underlying unity of its implications have proved gratifying. Yet as is always the case in economics, the modeling resolves some issues only to raise others. What are the next steps in this emergent field?

We would suggest four important directions for future work: enlarging the theoretical "menu"; buttressing the approach with empirical work; going from hypothetical calculations to real quantification; and addressing the welfare and policy implications of the whole approach.

19.1   The Theoretical Menu

One useful way to think about modeling choices in economic geography is in terms of a menu of possible options, as in the following table:

Centripetal forces	Centrifugal forces
Linkages	Immobile factors
Thick markets	Land rent/commuting
Knowledge spillovers and other pure external economies	Congestion and other pure diseconomies

On the left we show the Marshallian trinity of external economies, already described in chapter 1. On the right we show a somewhat comparable trinity of forces opposing agglomeration. There can be little doubt not only that all of these forces operate in the real world, but that all have at least some bearing on almost any real-world issue in economic geography one might discuss. Yet that is, of course, not the way we have approached the subject. In economic modeling it is natural and generally appropriate for the theorist to simplify matters, to focus on only some of the possibilities. So in our modeling we have generally allowed only for linkages as a force for concentration, factor immobility as a force against.

There are, of course, other possible choices. The traditional von Thünen analysis of land use may be interpreted as one in which pure external economies create an urban center, and land-rent gradients determine use around that center; the urban system literature of Henderson and followers in effect chooses to focus on pure external economies and diseconomies, generating an inverted-U relationship between population and utility. We ourselves have in some places departed from our normal modeling choices: The urban models of part III have a touch of von Thünen to them, and the trade-and-urbanization model of chapter 18 invokes pure external diseconomies as a source of centrifugal forces.

Still, we believe that it would be useful to carry out a more systematic exploration of the implications of our menu, to inquire into the behavior of models in which multiple centripetal and centrifugal forces are operating, to ask how the predictions of those models depend on the relative importance of those forces. Only by carrying out such an exploration will we be in a position to interpret the results of the obvious next step: empirical research.

19.2   Empirical Work

As a general rule, economic models with increasing returns and imperfect competition have proved difficult subjects for empirical work. Someone once remarked of textbooks in industrial organization that before the theoretical revolution of the 1970s, they contained many facts but little theory, and afterward they contained a lot of theory— period. One reason for this relative paucity of empirical work may be that models with imperfect competition and increasing returns are typically strongly nonlinear in their implications, posing a difficult challenge for traditional econometric methods. Another barrier to empirical work may be that to develop theoretically tractable models it is necessary to make simplifying assumptions that are difficult to relax, even though real-world data clearly demand that they be modified.

Still, empirical work that is at least informed by the new models has been an important part of the "new trade" and "new growth" revolutions, helping to provide at least a set of stylized facts and some constraints on plausible magnitudes. Some important work has already been conducted along similar lines in the new economic geography: cross-sectional studies of urban areas (e.g., Glaeser, Scheinkman, and Shleifer 1995), international comparisons (e.g., Ades and Glaeser 1997), and—recently—even some efforts to estimate structural equations, like the "market potential function," implied by new geography models (Hanson 1998). We clearly need much more such work, as closely tied to the theoretical models as possible, as a way of sorting through which of the intriguing possibilities suggested by the sorts of models developed in this book are truly relevant, as well as to indicate where further elaboration of the models is necessary.

19.3   Quantification

In certain fields of economics, notably public finance and international trade, quantified models play an important role as analytical tools. By a quantified model we do not exactly mean a model fitted to actual data; rather, we mean a theoretically consistent model whose parameters are based on some mix of data and assumptions, so that realistic simulation exercises can be carried out. The computable general equilibrium models often used for trade policy analysis are of this type; so are the calibrated models that have played an important role in the discussion of trade policy under imperfect competition.

(See, for example, the studies in Krugman and Smith 1993.) Although such models cannot be directly tested, they are often highly suggestive: For example, computable models of world trade have induced applied policy analysts to give much more weight to terms of trade impacts than is usual in the purely theoretical literature, and calibrated models in strategic trade did much to suggest that concerns over the international distribution of rents were of little practical importance.

We would clearly like to be able to carry out similar exercises for economic geography—to develop, if you like, "computable geographical equilibrium" models. In particular, we would like to have at least a first-pass estimate of the bifurcation diagrams for real situations: Under what conditions do economies really spontaneously evolve a core-periphery pattern? Is Europe really going to be able to maintain its polycentric industrial geography?

Such modeling is not easy. (We have made some preliminary efforts, and found enough technical difficulties to be unwilling to put them in this book!) Probably it will be necessary to introduce some new technical tricks to make the models consistent with the data (just as CGE models in trade generally depend on some version of the "Armington assumption"—an ad hoc assumption about tastes—to match the actual pattern of multilateral trade).

The payoff to such modeling would, however, be a major step toward making theoretical economic geography an actual predictive discipline, able to evaluate the impacts of hypothetical shocks—including policy changes—on the economy's spatial structure.

19.4 Welfare Implications

Some readers may have noticed a certain reticence on our part about welfare implications. In some cases the conclusions are clear: For example, in the models of international specialization developed in chapter 14, you would rather have your country become the industrialized, high-wage core than the low-wage periphery. But in general we have tended to stress the positive rather than normative economics of geography.

There are at least three reasons for that reticence. First, we feel that an economic approach ought to demonstrate its power to explain reality before it is used to prescribe it; to turn Marx on his head, the initial point ought to be to explain the world, not to change it.

Second is a more subtle point. The case for policy intervention typically rests on market failures, especially on externalities positive or negative: We think that the government should promote technological spillovers, discourage pollution. The spatial structure of an economy is, however, to an important extent the result of a tug-of-war between external economies and diseconomies, between the linkages and information spillovers that foster concentration, and between congestion and other diseconomies that discourage it. Which externalities matter more? For example, are big cities too big (just look at the traffic, the air pollution, the crime) or too small (think of the payoff to close-range interaction in a place like London or New York). The truth is that nobody knows, and nobody will know until there has been a lot of hard empirical work on the matter. More or less by definition, pure theoretical speculation cannot answer this question.

Finally, we have been engaged in a deliberate bit of intellectual strategizing. In the previous history of attempts to bring increasing returns into economics, most notably in the case of the new trade theory, there was something of a rush on the part of outsiders to hijack the new theories on behalf of interventionist policies. It later became apparent that this was premature: the policy implications of the new ideas were far more subtle in practice than the crude neomercantilism on whose behalf they were invoked. There will, surely, be important policy implications from the new economic geography, but we want the field on a solid theoretical and empirical footing before it begins speculating about potential interventions. That said, in the end one of the main points of economics is to provide policy guidance, and we would hope and expect the approach in this book eventually to give rise to a set of useful guidelines for actual regional, urban, and perhaps international trade policies.

19.5   Where We Stand

In the end, the main justification for studying the geography of economies is that it is so visible and important a part of the world. It is hard to see any reason—other than tradition, based on analytical intractability—why interregional and urban economics should receive any less attention than international trade, why the location of production should not be as central a concern of mainstream economics as capital theory or the distribution of income. In this book we have shown how one particular approach to the spatial economy works, and have shown, if nothing else, its ability to tell a wide range of interesting stories. There will be other approaches, and some of the stories will turn out to be more suggestive than convincing. But there is now no excuse for neglecting the spatial aspect of economic life. It has always been interesting and important; now it is possible to study it as rigorously as one likes.

One might say that the study of economic geography is a subject whose time has come. But we would prefer, for obvious reasons, to say that it is a subject which has finally found its proper place.

References

Ades, A. F., and E. L. Glaeser. (1997). "Trade and circuses: explaining urban giants." *Quarterly Journal of Economics* 110(1): 195–227.

Alonso, W. (1964). *Location and Land Use*. Cambridge: Harvard University Press.

Amiti, M. (1997). "Specialisation patterns in Europe." Discussion paper no. 363, Centre for Economic Performance, London School of Economics.

Anderson, S. P., A. de Palma, and J.-F. Thisse. (1992). *Discrete Choice Theory of Product Differentiation.*" Cambridge, MA: MIT Press.

Armington, P. S. (1969). "The geographic pattern of trade and the effects of price changes." *IMF Staff Papers* 17: 488–523.

Arthur, B. (1994). *Increasing Returns and Path Dependence in the Economy*. Ann Arbor: University of Michigan Press.

Bairoch, P. (1988). *Cities and Economic Development: From the Dawn of History to the Present*. Translated by C. Braider. Chicago: University of Chicago Press.

Baumol, W. J., and R. E. Gomory. (1987). "Inefficient and locally stable trade equilibria under scale economies: Comparative advantage revisited." *Kyklos* 49: 509–540.

Beckmann, M., and J.-F. Thisse. (1986). "The location of production activities." In P. Nijkamp, ed., *Handbook of Regional Economics*. Amsterdam: North-Holland, pp. 21–95.

Blaug, M. (1997). *Economic Theory in Retrospect*. Cambridge: Cambridge University Press.

Borchert, J. R. (1967). "American metropolitan evolution." *Geographical Review* 57: 301–332.

Brulhart, M., and J. Torstensson. (1996). "Regional integration, scale economies, and industry location in the European Union." Discussion paper no. 1435, Centre for Economic Policy Research, London.

Calmette, M.-F., and J. Le-Pottier. (1995). "Localisation des activites; un modele bisectoriel avec couts de transport." *Revue Economique* 46 (3): 901–909.

Carroll, G. (1982). "National city size distributions: What do we know after 67 years of research?" *Progress in Human Geography* 6: 1–43.

Chisholm, M. (1990). *Regions in Recession and Resurgence*. London: Hyman.

Christaller, W. (1933). *Central Places in Southern Germany*. Jena, Germany: Fischer (English translation by C. W. Baskin, London: Prentice Hall, 1966).

Cronon, W. (1991). *Nature's Metropolis: Chicago and the Great West*. New York: Norton.

Davis, D., and D. Weinstein. (1999). "Economic geography and regional production structure: An empirical investigation." *European Economic Review*, February.

Deaton, A., and J. Muellbauer. (1980). *Economics and Consumer Behaviour*. Cambridge: Cambridge University Press.

Dicken, P., and P. Lloyd. *Location in Space: Theoretical Perspectives in Economic Geography*. New York: Harper and Row.

Dixit, A. K., and J. E. Stiglitz. (1977), "Monopolistic competition and optimum product diversity." *American Economic Review* 67 (3): 297–308.

Dobkins, L. H., and Y. M. Ioannides. (1996). "Evolution of the U.S. city size distribution." Mimeograph, Tufts University, Medford, MA.

Ellison, G., and E. L. Glaeser. (1997). "Geographic concentration in U. S. manufacturing industries: A dartboard approach." *Journal of Political Economy* 105: 889–927.

Engel, C., and J. H. Rogers. (1996). "How wide is the border," *American Economic Review* 86(5): 1112–1125.

Ethier, W. J. (1982). "National and international returns to scale in the modern theory of international trade." *American Economic Review* 72: 389–405.

Fetter, F. A. (1924). "The economic law of market areas." *Quarterly Journal of Economics* 38: 520–529.

Fujita, M. (1988). "A monopolistic competition model of spatial agglomeration: Differentiated product approach." *Regional Science and Urban Economics* 18: 87–124.

Fujita, M. (1989). *Urban Economic Theory: Land Use and City Size*. Cambridge: Cambridge University Press.

Fujita, M., and P. Krugman. (1995). "When is the economy monocentric? von Thünen and Chamberlin unified," *Regional Science and Urban Economics* 25: 505–528.

Fujita, M., P. Krugman, and T. Mori. (1995). "On the evolution of hierarchical urban systems," Discussion paper no. 419, Institute of Economic Research, Kyoto University, Kyoto, Japan.

Fujita, M., and T. Mori. (1996). "The role of ports in the making of major cities: Self-agglomeration and hub-effect." *Journal of Development Economics* 49: 93–120.

Fujita, M., and T. Mori. (1997). "Structural stability and evolution of urban systems." *Regional Science and Urban Economics* 27: 399–442.

Fujita, M., and H. Ogawa. (1982). "Multiple equilibria and structural transition of non-monocentric urban configuration." *Regional Science and Urban Economics* 12: 161–196.

Gabaix, X. (1997). "Zipf's law for cities: An explanation," Mimeograph, Harvard University, Cambridge, MA.

Garreau, J. (1991). *Edge City: Life on the New Frontier*. New York: Doubleday.

Glaeser, E. L., J. Scheinkman, and A. Shleifer. (1995). "Economic growth in a cross-section of cities." *Journal of Monetary Economics* 36: 117–143.

Grandmont, J.-M. (1988). "Nonlinear difference equations, bifurcations and chaos: an introduction." Working paper no. 8811, Institute for Mathematical Studies in the Social Sciences, Stanford, CA.

Grossman, G., and E. Helpman. (1991). *Innovation and Growth in the World Economy*. Cambridge: MIT Press.

Hanson, G. (1996). "Increasing returns, trade, and the regional structure of wages." Mimeograph, University of Texas, Austin.

Hanson, G. (1998). "Market potential, increasing returns, and geographic concentration." Mimeograph, University of Texas, Austin.

Harris, C. (1954). "The market as a factor in the localization of industry in the United States." *Annals of the Association of American Geographers* 64: 315–348.

Helliwell, J. (1997). "National borders, trade, and migration." Working paper no. 6027, National Bureau of Economic Research, Cambridge, MA.

Helpman, E., and P. Krugman. (1985). *Market Structure and Foreign Trade*. Cambridge: MIT Press.

Henderson, J. V. (1974). "The sizes and types of cities." *American Economic Review* 64, 640–656.

Henderson, J. V. (1980). "Community development: The effects of growth and uncertainty." *American Economic Review* 70: 894–910.

Henderson, J. V. (1988). *Urban development: Theory, Fact, and Illusion*. Oxford: Oxford University Press.

Hirschman, A. (1958). *The Strategy of Economic Development*. New Haven, CT: Yale University Press.

Hoover, E. M. (1948). *The Location of Economic Activity*. New York: McGraw-Hill.

Hoover, E. M., and R. Vernon. (1959). *Anatomy of a Metropolis: The Changing Distribution of People and Jobs within the New York Metropolitan Region*. Cambridge: Harvard University Press.

Hotelling, H. (1929). "Stability in competition." *Economic Journal* 39: 41–57.

Ijiri, Y., and H. Simon. (1977). *Skew Distributions and the Sizes of Business Firms*. Amsterdam, North-Holland.

Isard, W. (1956). *Location and Space-Economy*. Cambridge: MIT Press.

Jones, R. (1971). "A three factor model in theory, trade and history." In J. Bhagwati, R. W. Jones, R. A. Mundell, and J. Vanek, eds., *Trade, Balance of Payments, and Growth*. Amsterdam: North-Holland, pp. 3–21.

Karaska, G., and D. Bramhall, eds. (1969). *Locational Analysis for Manufacturing*. Cambridge: MIT Press.

Kauffman, S. (1993). *The Origins of Order*. New York: Oxford University Press.

Keeble, D. E., P. L. Owens, and C. Thompson. (1982). "Regional accessibility and economic potential in the European Community." *Regional Studies* 16: 419–432.

Kenen, P. (1965). "Nature, capital, and trade." *Journal of Political Economy* 73: 437–460.

354 References

Kim, S. (1995). "Expansion of markets and the geographic distribution of economic activities: the trends in U. S. regional manufacturing structure, 1860–1987." *Quarterly Journal of Economics* 110(4): 881–908.

Krugman, P. R. (1980). "Scale economics, product differentiation, and the pattern of trade." *American Economic Review* 70: 950–959.

Krugman, P. R (1991a). "Increasing returns and economic geography." *Journal of Political Economy* 99: 483–499.

Krugman, P. R. (1991b). *Geography and Trade*. Cambridge: MIT Press.

Krugman, P. R. (1993a). "On the number and location of cities." *European Economic Review* 37: 293–298.

Krugman, P. R. (1993b). "First nature, second nature, and metropolitan location." *Journal of Regional Science* 33: 129–144.

Krugman, P. R. (1997). "Zipf's law and city size." Mimeograph, Massachusetts Institute of Technology.

Krugman, P. R., and R. E. Livas. (1996). "Trade policy and the third world metropolis." *Journal of Development Economics* 49(1): 137–150.

Krugman, P. R., and A. Smith, eds. (1993). *Empirical Studies of Strategic Trade Policy*. Chicago: University of Chicago Press.

Krugman, P. R., and A. J. Venables. (1995). "Globalization and the inequality of nations." *Quarterly Journal of Economics* 110(4): 857–880.

Krugman, P. R., and A. J. Venables. (1997). "Integration, specialization and adjustment." *European Economic Review* 40: 959–968.

Krugman, P. R., and A. J. Venables. (1997). "The seamless world: A spatial model of international specialization." Mimeograph, Massachusetts Institute of Technology, Cambridge: MA.

Launhardt, W. (1885). *Mathematische Begründung der Volkswirtschaftslehre*. Leipzig, Germany: B. G. Teubner.

Leamer, E., and J. Levinsohn. (1996). In "International trade theory: The evidence." G. Grossman and K. Rogoff, ed., *Handbook of International Economics*, 3, Elsevier, Amsterdam, pp. 1339–1394.

Lewin, R. (1992). *Complexity: Life at the Edge of Chaos*. New York: Macmillan.

Lorenz, E. (1994). *The Essence of Chaos*. Seattle: University of Washington Press.

Lösch, A. (1940). *The Economics of Location*. Jena, Germany: Fischer (English translation, New Haven, CT: Yale University Press, 1954).

Marshall, A. (1920). *Principles of Economics*. London: Macmillan (8th ed.).

Marshall, J. U. (1989). *The Structure of Urban Systems*. Toronto: University of Toronto Press.

McCallum, J. (1995). "National borders matter: Canada-U. S. regional trade patterns." *American Economic Review* 85: 615–623.

Mills, E. S. (1967). "An aggregative model of resource allocation in a metropolitan area." *American Economic Review* 57: 197–210.

Mori, T. (1997). "A modeling of megalopolis formation: the maturing of city systems." *Journal of Urban Economics* 42: 133–157.

Murphy, R., A. Shleifer, and R. Vishny. (1989). "Industrialization and the big push." *Journal of Political Economy* 97(5): 1003–1026.

Myrdal, G. (1957). *Economic Theory and Under-developed Regions*. London: Duckworth.

Nerlove, M. L., and E. Sadka. (1991). "The von Thünen model of the dual economy." *Journal of Economics* 54: 97–123.

Nicolis, G., and I. Prigogine. (1989). *Exploring Complexity*. New York: W. H. Freeman.

Ohlin, B. (1933). *Interregional and International Trade*. Cambridge: Harvard University Press.

Porter, M. E. (1990). *The Competitive Advantage of Nations*. New York: Macmillan.

Pred, A. (1966). *The Spatial Dynamics of U. S. Urban-Industrial Growth*. Cambridge: MIT Press.

Prigogine, I., and I. Stengers. (1984). *Order out of Chaos*. New York: Bantam Books.

Puga, D. (1998). "The rise and fall of regional inequalities." *European Economic Review*, forthcoming.

Puga, D., and A. J. Venables. (1996). "The spread of industry; spatial agglomeration and economic development." *Journal of the Japanese and International Economies* 10(4): 440–464.

Rauch, J. E. (1996). "Networks versus markets in international trade." Discussion paper no. 5617, National Bureau of Economic Research, Cambridge, MA.

Reilly, W. J. (1931). *The Law of Retail Gravitation*. New York: Knickerbocker Press.

Rosen, K. T., and M. Resnick. (1980). "The size distribution of cities: An examination of the Pareto law and primacy." *Journal of Urban Economics* 8(2): 165–186.

Samuelson, P. A. (1952). "The transfer problem and transport costs: The terms of trade when impediments are absent." *Economic Journal* 62: 278–304.

Samuelson, P. A. (1971). "On the trail of conventional beliefs about the transfer problem." In J. Bhagwati, R. W. Jones, R. A. Mondell, J. Vanek, eds., *Trade, Balance of Payments, and Growth*. Amsterdam: North-Holland.

Samuelson, P. A. (1983). "Thünen at two hundred." *Journal of Economic Literature* 21: 1468–1488.

Simon, H. (1955). "On a class of skew distribution functions." *Biometrika* 42: 425–440.

Smith, A., and A. J. Venables. (1988). "Completing the internal market in the European community: Some industry simulations." *European Economic Review* 32: 1501–1525.

Tobin, J. (1955). "A dynamic aggregative model." *Journal of Political Economy* 63:103–115.

Turing, A. (1952). "The chemical basis of morphogenesis." *Philosophical Transactions of the Royal Society of London* 237: 37–72.

Venables, A. J. (1996). "Equilibrium locations of vertically linked industries." *International Economic Review* 37: 341–359.

Venables, A. J. (1998). "Geography and specialisation: Industrial belts on a circular plain." In R. Baldwin, D. Cohen, A. Sapir, and A. J. Venables, eds., *Regional Integration*. Cambridge: Cambridge University Press, forthcoming.

von Thünen, J. H. (1826). *Der Isolierte Staat in Beziehung auf Landschaft und Nationalökonomie*. Hamburg (English translation by C. M. Wartenberg, *von Thünen's Isolated State*, Oxford: Pergamon Press, 1966).

Weber, A. (1909). *Urber den Standort der Industrien*. Tübingen, Germany: J. C. B. Mohr.

Weibull, J. W. (1995). *Evolutionary Game Theory*. Cambridge, MA: MIT Press.

Zipf, G. (1949). *Human Behavior and the Principle of Least Effort*. New York: Addison-Wesley.

Index